Contents at a Glance

Table of Contents

Introduction

Welcome to the fascinating world of British politics. Whether you're a student wanting to boost your chances of getting that A grade or just want the inside track on the big issues that face not just the UK but also the wider world, this is the book for you.

I wrote this book for newcomers and students alike so that you can have a one-stop shop to get to know everything you need to know without feeling overwhelmed or intimidated. I explain how Britain became the modern liberal democracy it is today. Thanks to this book, the next time you hear someone say at a dinner table, on the bus or down the pub that 'politics is all the same', you'll be able to tell them why they're wrong, and why politics and politicians make a fundamental difference to our lives.

About This Book

To make your reading experience a little easier, *British Politics For Dummies* follows certain rules. For example, every time I use a new term or important phrase, I *italicise* and explain it. The key word or term in a bulleted list is in **bold** so that it stands out. Occasionally, you see text in grey boxes. These sidebars are full of what I consider interesting information, but they're not essential to understanding the topic at hand, so you can read them or not as you choose. I explain everything very clearly and try to avoid political gobbledygook.

When reading a discussion of a particular aspect of politics in one chapter, I refer to another chapter when the information there ties into the issue I'm discussing. You can turn immediately to that chapter or just tuck the number away in your memory and decide to read it next.

Foolish Assumptions

Don't feel intimidated if you know nothing about politics. This book will bring you up to speed, fast. Politics can be complex, and even some seasoned commentators have difficulty grasping some aspects. But before long – after reading this book – you're going to be transformed into a nailed-on political expert.

Icons Used in This Book

To help you navigate through this book, keep an eye out for the icons – the little pictures that sit in the margin. They guide you to particular types of information. The icons in this book mean the following things:

This icon is unique to this book. Every so often I look in depth at a great politician or quirky character from past or present. Politics is full of interesting people!

Politics is chock-full of jargon. Fortunately, this book's mission is to bust it. Whenever you see this icon, you find an explanation of political terms that help you understand just what's going on in the game.

This icon is also unique to this book and you won't see it often. It draws your attention to some of the behind-the-scenes stuff that goes on in the cut and thrust of daily politics. Here's the info the media managers in the big political parties don't want you to know!

Paragraphs with this icon attached contain information that's especially useful to remember.

This icon indicates a technical discussion is underway. You can skip this stuff if you want to, because it isn't necessary for an understanding of the basics. If you read it, though, you can boost your political know-how.

Beyond the book

Your dummies reading experience doesn't stop here – between the covers of this book or when it flashes up 100 per cent on your digital e-reader. There is a whole extra layer of free online content to entertain and educate you, just a click of the mouse or a touch of a tablet away. Here is a brief description of this treasure trove of free digital content and crucially where it's hidden, just for you to discover.

- Cheat sheet This is bite size text which lets you know some of the key points contained in British Politics For Dummies but in an ultra-condensed form. Want to impress your friends in the run-up to an election with your political knowhow or simply want to grasp one or two key facts? This cheat sheet is there to give you the basics. All dummies books have a cheat sheet and they allow readers to quickly refer to a fact without having to carry the book around with you or power up the e-reader. Cheat Sheets are fast, fun and full of useful info and you can find them at `www.dummies.com/cheatsheet/britishpolitics`.

- Dummies.com online articles. There is information that I think it is really useful for you to have but is not contained in this book. I may be looking to expand on a particular point or explain something in ever more detail. Perhaps something has happened very recently in British politics and I want to let you know more. If you go to www.dummies.com/extras/british-politics) you will find several articles penned by me which I hope will add to your knowhow and enjoyment. For instance, you will find an extra Part of Tens just for you. In it I turn the ten great British Prime Minister theme on its head and name and shame those who I think are the ten worst British PMs in history – and believe me there were some real stinkers. In addition, there is a special article on the rise of the UK Independence party (UKIP) and what it means for the present and future of British politics. I have also reflected on the result of the momentous Scottish independence referendum and I let you know why I think the result went the way it did. Finally, I look at the Presidency of Barack Obama, who assumed office riding a tide of international goodwill. I ask whether or not the first US black president has been a success or failure? So there's plenty of bonus content to be getting along with – check it out!

Where to Go from Here

Don't be restricted by the order in which the contents of this book appear. This book is designed to be read in several ways. It's a reference book, so you don't have to read the chapters in chronological order, from front to back. Of course, if you want to, you can read it from cover to cover like a novel – and there are quite a few heroes and heroines in politics. Alternatively, you can pick a topic that you're doing at school or university or you just want to know much more about and read up on it. Or you can just flip through this book, and read whatever catches your interest.

But my favourite way of reading this book – and my editor has made sure I've read it a few times now – is to go to Part I outlining the basics of how politics works and then to the sections which interest you or are relevant to your studies. Whatever draws you to politics, *British Politics For Dummies* has something for you.

- What does all the jargon mean? What on earth is a spin doctor? (Chapter 7 explains.)
- Why is Britain a democracy and not a dictatorship? (Check out Chapter 5.)
- Who is Black Rod and what on earth does he do? (Turn to Chapter 13.)
- What does all the jargon mean? What on earth is a spin doctor? (Chapter 10 explains.)
- What's so important about the United Nations Security Council? (Head to Chapter 20.)

In short, it's up to you how you get to know the world of politics!

Part I

Getting Started with British Politics

getting started with British Politics

For Dummies can help you get started with lots of subjects. Visit www.dummies.com to learn more and do more with *For Dummies*.

In this part . . .

- Find out all the things you always wanted to know about British Politics.
- Discover what is so special about democracy and why politicians are considered to be so important.

Chapter 1

Taking in the Political Universe

In This Chapter

- Differentiating between local and national politics
- Building a very British democracy
- Legislating within the parliament
- Gauging the strength of the democracy
- Scrutinising politicians and the media
- Defining Britain's place in the world

> *Those who are too smart to engage in politics are punished by being governed by those who are dumber.*
>
> *– Plato, Greek philosopher*

Plato's quote highlights one – very cynical – way of looking at the wacky (and not so wacky) world of politics. But whatever your view of politics (or, for that matter, politicians), one thing's for sure: the laws made by politicians have a direct impact on your life.

In this chapter I take a speed-of-light trip around the political universe, through the town hall, the newspaper rooms, Buckingham Palace and the UK Houses of Parliament, to the outer reaches of big international bodies such as the European Union and United Nations.

Time to set out on a political journey of discovery!

Understanding the Difference between Local and National Politics

How many politicians do you think you can name? Five, ten, twenty? Well, there are literally thousands of politicians in the UK and many times that number around the globe. The fact that you and I may only be able to name a handful isn't because we're not very bright; it's because most of the politicians out there have a very low profile in the public eye. They may be big figures in their local community but they don't make any sort of splash on the national stage.

You can divide politicians into local and national ones. Local politicians get to decide what goes on in a particular village, town or city, whereas national politicians have a say in the laws that govern all our lives. Politicians who're elected to the House of Commons and the European Parliament are national ones because they make laws that apply to the whole country, not just to a particular village, town or city.

Here are some of the other key differences between local and national politicians:

- National politicians receive a salary from the state, whereas local politicians are volunteers with normal lives and everyday jobs.
- The national media, such as national newspapers and television/radio networks, covers the actions of national politicians, whereas local politicians gain coverage in local newspapers and on local radio and regional television news.
- The UK is a highly centralised state, which means that the national politicians have lots of power, including the main tax-raising powers, whereas local politicians have to do roughly what the central government says and have much smaller tax-raising powers.

The overwhelming majority of politicians in the UK are local councillors and parish councillors, often elected by a few hundred or thousand voters.

An election for membership of the House of Commons is called a *general election*, a European parliamentary election is called an *election to the European Parliament* and a local council election is called – guess what? – a *local election*.

Usually, voter turnout (the percentage of eligible voters actually going to the polls to vote) is much higher for general elections than for local or European elections. General elections tend to get much greater media coverage and voters are more interested in who wins. (Chapter 7 talks about the other factors influencing voter turnout.)

Splitting the Difference: The Devolved Parliament and Assemblies

The British are noted around the globe for a few things: producing great rock music, drinking too much (but let's not put that one on the tourist brochures!), writing great literature, creating great art and providing a world centre for financial services. But ask any foreigner to name a word that sums up Britain and the British, and 'tradition' would come fairly high up the list. Put simply, we're not supposed to do change.

But over the past decade we've gone in for political change in a big way. The Labour government of Tony Blair in 1999 set up the Scottish parliament and Welsh and Northern Ireland assemblies.

The big idea was to move some power away from the government in Westminster and hand it to the peoples – through an elected parliament or assembly – in Scotland, Wales and Northern Ireland. This process was called *devolution* and some say it's the biggest constitutional change in the UK for 100 years.

Why introduce devolution? Well, the Scottish, Welsh and Northern Irish have different identities and traditions, and many in these parts of the UK felt that these had been swamped over many hundreds of years by the more populous English.

Every four years the people of Scotland, Wales and Northern Ireland get to elect who they want to sit in their own parliament or assembly. These representatives then make the laws in the policy areas that have been devolved from the UK parliament; for example, health care, education or the environment. Plans are afoot to increase the number of powers devolved to the Scottish parliament and Welsh and Northern Ireland assemblies. (For a full rundown of which parliament or assembly does what, check out Chapter 17.)

Why do the Scottish have a parliament, while the Welsh and Northern Irish have an assembly? Well, this situation reflects the number of devolved powers that each institution has. A parliament is considered a more important and august body than an assembly. So the Scottish, who have more devolved powers than the Welsh and Northern Irish, thus have a parliament rather than an assembly.

In Wales and Scotland, nationalist movements want either greater autonomy from the UK or full-blown independence. This nationalism is most developed in Scotland. The Scottish National Party became the governing party and used that position to call a referendum on whether Scotland should be independent. The referendum was held in September 2014, with the Scottish people voting to stay within the UK. The result was very close, with 45% of votes cast in favour of full independence. In the final few days of the campaign the leaders of the UK's three main political parties – Conservative, Labour and Liberal Democrat – promised the Scottish people even greater devolution (in other words more power for the Scottish parliament) should they choose to remain in the UK. This promise won the day and now politicians in Westminster are looking at ways of delivering it. See Chapter 18 for full details on the great independence debate.

Evolving to Democracy: A Very British Story

Each democratic nation has trodden its very own path to the political system it has today. The US democracy was born when rebels beat the British in the American Revolution, and the French democracy can trace its roots back to the deposition and execution of Louis XVI in 1793 and the revolution that followed.

The UK too has had its fair share of strife – the odd bloody civil war – and has even chopped one king's head off (the singularly useless Charles I). But instead of one cataclysmic event, such as a war or revolution, leading to democracy, the UK has progressed more gradually to the modern liberal democratic society we have today. In fact, the UK is one of only a handful of countries to get rid of its monarch (between 1649 and 1660) and then decide to reinstate it.

Put simply, the British prefer political evolution to revolution, and the web of government is built up through a combination of laws, traditions and customs. For example, in legal terms the monarchy is hugely important in the British state; in fact, the government itself is there to serve the monarch. However, through custom and tradition the monarch actually plays a very minor role in the government of the country. Much of the power is vested in the hands of the prime minister (PM) and the cabinet.

The UK – unlike the US, for instance – doesn't have a written constitution. Instead, the government works through laws, traditions and customs. This situation is referred to as the UK's *unwritten constitution*, which I discuss in Chapter 5.

An unwritten constitution may sound weak and impracticable, but the UK system has stood the test of time. In fact, the UK was one of the few major European countries not to have seen its democracy suppressed by a dictatorship during the 20th century.

Assessing the Health of British Democracy

Some experts suggest that Britons are becoming less interested in politics and the following evidence does seem to bear that analysis out:

- **Falling voter turnout:** At election time fewer and fewer people are turning out to exercise their democratic right to vote.

- **Falling party membership:** The three nationwide major political parties – Labour, Conservative and Liberal Democrat (and by *major* I mean these parties always have Members of Parliament elected) – have seen their membership numbers plummet over the past decade. Politicians who stand as party candidates rely on help from party members but fewer members exist to offer help.

However, evidence suggests that people aren't bored with politics in itself; just with politicians and the main political parties. Some say that media training and the whips' control over what MPs say in public have made politicians increasingly bland. Smaller political parties like the Green Party and the UK Independence Party (UKIP) have done much better at election time in recent years, however, while pressure groups and trade unions continue to enjoy high levels of membership.

Glancing at the alternatives to democracy

Sitting in a strong democratic country like the UK, it's easy to think that democracy is a given around the globe. Surely, everyone must see how well it works and can't live without the freedom of speech and personal liberty, the two hallmarks of democracy.

But much of the population of the world doesn't live in a democratic state. In fact, a large number live under regimes where to be an opponent of the government is to risk liberty and even life and limb.

China, for example, is the world's most populous nation – roughly one in four people on the planet are Chinese – yet its people live in a one-party state. All the politicians are drawn from just one party, so people can only vote for the candidates representing it. Ostensibly, the party in government in China is communist, which means it's supposed to adhere to communist ideals such as common ownership of property and a society free of class or social divides. However, in reality the Chinese Communist Party promotes individual property ownership and individual wealth creation (two very Western and democratic ideals) as means to improve the national economy. In effect, China now practises communism-lite.

This situation hints at a fundamental truth of political systems around the globe: that nearly all of them, to a greater or lesser degree, have some measure of what we recognise as Western democratic ideals, such as free speech and the right to make and spend money without huge interference from the state.

A truly democratic society has to guarantee freedom of the press and the right to protest, as well as hold regular contested elections for government office. The UK, fortunately, ticks all of these boxes and so can be classed as a fully fledged democracy.

Many different forms of government operate around the globe, from communist regimes to Western democracies. Religious leaders even run the show in some countries, such as Iran – a system called *theocracy*. Check out Chapter 4 for more on different types of government.

The expenses scandal of 2009 was a key factor in undermining public confidence in politics and politicians. A host of MPs had claimed for expenses they shouldn't have and worked the system for all they could possibly get. An enormous public furore resulted, which led to scores of MPs deciding to stand down as candidates for the next general election. (Chapter 24 covers this major political scandal and others to boot.)

Some academics suggest that the way to reverse low voter turnout is to make it easier to vote. They probably have a point. At present, electors usually have to attend a polling station in person in order to cast their ballot, and elections are generally held on a work day. Allowing more postal or online ballots would make voting easier and hopefully encourage more people to do so. Making not voting illegal is another possible solution to low turnout. In Australia, for instance, people who don't vote are fined. (Chapter 7 has more on reversing falling voter turnout.)

Paying Homage to the 'Mother of Parliaments'

Standing at the very centre of British democracy is the Houses of Parliament in Westminster, London. This great gothic masterpiece, along with the many government ministries within a short walk, is the fulcrum of British political life. Many of the big government policy decisions and laws that affect all Britons' lives are made in Westminster by the politicians who work there.

The Houses of Parliament are divided into two distinct parts – the House of Commons and the House of Lords. Although they sit in chambers only a few hundred yards apart and have both been in existence for centuries, the houses are quite different in terms of who gets to sit in them and the powers and responsibilities of those who do so. Table 1-1 is a quick guide to some of the main differences between the two chambers.

The biggest party – in terms of number of seats – in the Commons forms the government, with that party's leader as prime minister.

Within the UK's unwritten constitution, the House of Commons is considered far more important than the House of Lords because most laws start their life there and the government is drawn from members of the biggest party in the Commons. What's more, under the Parliament Act of 1911, the House of Lords can only halt a law that has passed through the Commons for one year, whereas the Commons can kill laws that have passed through the Lords stone dead. Check out Chapter 13 for more on the House of Commons' supremacy in Britain's parliamentary democracy.

Table 1-1 Comparing the Houses of the UK Parliament

House of Commons	*House of Lords*
Members are elected by public vote, called a general election.	Members are either appointed by the monarch (on the advice of the prime minister) or have the right to sit as a result of an inherited title.
Laws are proposed, amended and voted down by a majority of members.	A majority of members can vote to amend or oppose legislation but ultimately they can't go against the wishes of the Commons.
Most of the members belong to a particular political party.	Members stay in place for life and tend to be more independent-minded.

When many people in the UK and around the world think of the Houses of Parliament they don't picture great debates and dramatic votes on whether or not a law should be passed. They probably think about some of the traditions of the place, such as splendid set-piece occasions like the monarch's official opening of parliament, the archaic language used by Members of the Lords and Commons when addressing one another, and even the tights-wearing and sword-carrying of some of the staff! Chapter 13 lifts the lid on some of the strange goings on and traditions followed in the UK parliament.

Both members of the House of Commons, called *MPs* (short for *Members of Parliament*), and members of the House of Lords (called *peers*) can introduce new legislation. However, without the support of MPs, peers have zero chance of seeing their legislative proposals become law. MPs have a better chance of getting their policy proposals made into law, but only if they belong to the biggest party in the Commons. (See Chapter 13 for more on how the UK's complex legislation process actually works.)

Politicians need civil servants to carry out their policies and the UK has one of the most extensive and highly trained civil services in the world. The civil service has a long history, with members following a well-defined code of ethics that's supposed to guarantee impartiality, integrity and honesty. Check out Chapter 15 for more on the inner workings of the civil service.

Westminster may be the beating heart of UK politics, but thanks to devolution and membership of the European Union (EU), it's no longer quite as important as it once was to the making of laws that actually affect your daily life.

Introducing the Players in the British Political System

Britain's long-standing democracy relies on the nation's politicians, judges and the monarch. Each of these key figures has jobs to do – big and small – in drawing up the laws of the land, running the government of the country, and preserving the freedoms of British citizens and the integrity of our democracy. The effective working of the British political system is based on co-operation between the politicians (elected by you and me), the judges and the monarch.

Here's a rundown of the big hitters in the British political system and what role they play in delivering effective democratic government to some 60 million Britons.

Gazing at the political summit: The central role of the prime minister

One of the major changes in the UK's political landscape over the past couple of centuries has been the concentration of a great deal of power in the hands of one person – the prime minister.

After a general election the monarch asks the leader of the political party with the most members elected to the House of Commons to form the government of the country. That party leader becomes prime minister, and it's up to him to ensure that the party governs the country and follows the policies his party told the electors they'd carry out during the general election campaign.

In the run-up to a general election every party publishes a *manifesto* – a collection of policy pledges that the leadership of the political party says it will carry out, if elected.

In order to be able to govern, the PM has at his disposal lots of powers, such as to

- Select politicians to be in charge of government departments. I cover these ministers and their powers in depth in Chapters 14 and 15.
- Draw up a list of potential people for appointment by the monarch to the House of Lords.
- Chair meetings of the *cabinet*, which comprises the heads of government departments. The cabinet has the say over which legislation is introduced into parliament with the aim of making it into law.
- Decide whether the country goes to war and, during wartime, tell commanders what to do.

The PM's power derives not only from the office but also from his role as the leader of the biggest party in the House of Commons. Party leaders have the power to throw badly behaving politicians out of the party and even to say who should or shouldn't stand for election as a party candidate.

The PM is far and away the most important politician in the country, which means that media attention centres on what he gets up to. Often the PM represents Britain at international conferences and gets to meet up with other world leaders. In fact, some say that the PM has transformed into a president in recent years and many see the PM as effectively the head of state rather than the monarch.

Declining importance of the MP

In politics, when one individual becomes more important it usually means that another has become less so. This state of affairs is certainly true when considering the relative importance of the PM and MPs. As more and more power is concentrated in the hands of the PM, the humble MP finds she has less and less influence over what's going on. This change in the balance of power has occurred for a number of reasons, including:

- **Whipping:** Although it sounds very rude, a *whip* is actually someone appointed by the party leader to ensure that the party's MPs vote the way the leader wants. Over the past few decades whips have become more important, keeping a tight grip on how individuals vote and even their public utterances.
- **Public apathy:** In the past, individual MP's speeches were widely reported and even backbench MPs were household names. This is no longer the case, with the press reporting far more of what the PM says or does than individual MPs.
- **Legislative squeeze:** The UK government is a big old institution and the PM and the cabinet take up the overwhelming majority of parliamentary time for debates and votes on new laws they want to see introduced. As a result, individual MPs are finding it harder than ever to get their own bills made into law.

An MP who isn't also a minister or a member of the opposition shadow cabinet team – in effect, opposition party leaders whose specific job is to confront an individual minister – is referred to as a *backbench MP*.

Some 650 MPs sit in the House of Commons. A vote held in an individual parliamentary constituency decides each MP. The first-past-the-post system decides who wins the seat, which simply means that the candidate who polls the most votes wins and takes her seat in parliament. (Chapter 6 has more on first-past-the-post and the myriad other voting methods used in elections across the UK.)

Some people call for electoral reform because they feel that the current system is unfair. Often those elected as MPs haven't actually polled a majority of votes cast – all they've done is attract the most votes. It's possible under first past the post to win a seat in the House of Commons by getting just one more vote than the candidate finishing second.

Checking the power of the politicians: The judiciary

The UK judiciary is independent. Judges are servants of the monarch and their job is to uphold and interpret the law of the land. The judiciary, through the new UK Supreme Court, provides an important check on the power of government, particularly in the area of civil liberties.

Parliament sets the laws of the land, but they don't cover every eventuality, and the judiciary has its powers in interpreting particular laws. The web of hundreds of years of judgements in different cases – called *legal precedent* – in effect sets out what's legal and what isn't. However, a new law passed by parliament can wash away legal precedent set by the courts.

Laws made by the UK parliament are called *statute law*, and form the premier law of the land. However, laws passed by the European Parliament have equal standing with statute law.

The UK doesn't have one or two legal systems; it actually has three. England and Wales share the same legal system, and Scotland and Northern Ireland each have their own. The patchwork of laws and courts in the UK is highly complex, but if you want the inside track, check out Chapter 16.

The UK's three legal systems all operate according to a hierarchical system. This system means that the decision reached by the highest court in the land – now the UK Supreme Court in most cases – is binding on all lower courts and also sets a future legal precedent.

The European Convention on Human Rights was adopted in UK law in the 1998 Human Rights Act. As a result, if someone feels their human rights have been violated they can go to a UK court and have it decide on the matter, rather than go to the European Court of Human Rights in Strasbourg. If that court decides that the individual's human rights have been violated, that violation has to stop!

Mixing in the monarch

The monarchy has been of crucial importance in British history. The first kings of England came to the throne over a thousand years ago, and although their descendants have found their powers reduced, modern monarchs still have their role to play in British life and politics. As head of state, the monarch isn't just a tourist attraction! In the UK's unwritten constitution, the monarch's powers include opening and dissolving parliament, appointing the prime minister, giving consent to bills passed by parliament (without this consent a bill can't become law) and appointing bishops and members of the House of Lords.

The monarch appears to have a lot of power, but in reality it's largely ceremonial. For example, the power to appoint the prime minister sounds great, but it's a constitutional convention that the monarch must appoint the leader of the biggest party in the House of Commons. Likewise, the power to appoint members of the House of Lords is curtailed by the fact that the monarch only does so in accordance with the advice of the prime minister.

Under a convention of the UK's unwritten constitution, the monarch must always take the advice of her ministers – that is, the elected government.

Most Britons, when asked, support the idea of the monarchy but a substantial minority (usually around a quarter) would prefer it to be abolished. They argue that the monarchy is outdated, elitist and costs too much. However, the UK shows no signs of becoming a republic (a state that doesn't have a monarch) anytime soon; all the main political parties – even the Scottish Nationalists – support the idea of a monarchy.

Coming under Greater Scrutiny: Politics in the Media

You wouldn't guess that widespread apathy towards politics existed in the UK if you turned on the TV, radio or opened up a newspaper. Politics is a major talking point on the airwaves and in the columns of most of the newspapers. In fact, as voter turnout has fallen, the actual coverage of politics has increased, thanks in particular to the advent of 24-hour TV news stations. With so much time to fill, the media pores over even the slightest piece of political gossip or smallest policy proposal. Likewise, the private lives of many politicians have been held up to the bright lights of media scrutiny and, as far as some of the general public are concerned, when it comes to politicians, familiarity breeds contempt. (See Chapter 10 for more on politics and the media.)

Despite the march of blogs and the Internet, the newspaper industry is still hugely important in the UK media. What's written in the papers can have quite an influence on the behaviour of politicians. For example, in October 2009 the UK's best-selling daily newspaper, *The Sun*, came out in support of the Conservative party and its leader David Cameron – abandoning in the process the Labour government and PM Gordon Brown – and caused quite a stir.

In the UK, each of the national newspapers supports one of the main political parties. For example, the *Daily Mail* and *Daily Telegraph* support the Conservative Party, and the *Daily Mirror* and *Guardian* support the Labour Party. Sometimes, a paper switches its allegiance; for example, prior to the 1997 general election the *Financial Times* declared its support for Labour but in 2005 it switched back to the Conservatives.

As with everything else in life, the Internet is playing a more important role in politics, particularly in the US but in the UK too. Politicians are increasingly using social networking sites, Twitter and blogs to get their message across to large numbers of eager readers. Political pundits and the average citizen can bypass the main media outlets and counteract what they see as biased reporting or just say what they want without journalistic scrutiny! (Chapter 11 talks about the burgeoning role of the Internet in politics.)

Sites like Twitter and Facebook and even messaging services like Blackberry have become increasingly important to individuals and groups looking to bring about political change through direct action such as street protest. In recent years several revolutions have taken place in the Middle East with protestors organising and spreading their message through social media and Blackberry messenger. See Chapter 11 for more on this very 21st-century political phenomena.

Britain: Making Its Way in the European Union

Few Britons probably understood just what they were getting into when the UK joined the European Economic Community (now called the European Union, or EU) in 1973.

The EU has metamorphosed from a group of west European nations trying to create a free trade area and improve economic co-operation into what many see as a super state of 28 countries and 500 million people. The EU has its own flag, anthem and parliament. What's more, the laws made by the EU apply in the UK and other member countries. This situation has changed the legal landscape in the UK and means that the government has to always consider whether or not its actions are in accord with European law.

But the EU has been changed by Britain's membership too. It was the British government that pushed for greater powers for the EU parliament within the constitution of the EU (see Chapter 21 for more on this) and for the entry of poorer countries from eastern Europe.

The EU has its own currency – the *euro*. In under a decade the euro has become the second most used currency in the world behind the US dollar. The recent global financial crisis led to fears among financial experts that the fledgling euro currency could collapse; fortunately, that hasn't happened yet!

Many say that EU membership has been a good thing for the UK. For example, the overwhelming majority of UK exports go to member states of the EU. Likewise, Britons are free to travel and work in any EU country of their choosing.

Looking Further Afield: The UK and the Wider World

The EU is crucial to the UK and its trade but it's not the only game in town. The UK has a major advantage in international commerce – the English language. Combined with strong historic ties with former colonies that now form the Commonwealth and the so-called 'special relationship' with the United States, the UK is a major economy and international power.

Looking east, the rise of China and India presents huge challenges and opportunities for British government policymakers and business.

On the international stage, the UK is a member of the United Nations and one of the five permanent members of the UN Security Council, along with China, France, Russia and the US. This membership gives the UK the right to veto UN resolutions, which are basically international laws. (Chapter 19 covers the work of the UN Security Council.) It's also a member of the G8 (the group of the eight most-developed economies) and the G20 (the G8 nations plus a dozen nations whose economies are developing fast), as well as countless other international organisations.

The UK isn't just a major economic power; it's also a key member of the North Atlantic Treaty Organisation (NATO), a military body that can deploy well-equipped armed forces nearly anywhere in the world. NATO was originally set up to defend western Europe against the threat of a Soviet invasion in the aftermath of the Second World War.

Chapter 2

Understanding Why Politics and Politicians are Important

In This Chapter

- Looking at what politicians do
- Examining some large issues politicians face
- Participating in politics as an activist

Most politicians aren't short on ego! They love the sound of their own voices, their names in the papers and their pictures on TV. But they do have, at least in part, good reason for their egos because, whatever you think about them, politicians are important. To name but a few of their jobs in a democracy such as Britain's: politicians make the laws, negotiate international treaties and even decide whether to go to war. They're also responsible for meeting the challenges of the major issues – from poverty in the developing world to fighting climate change – that affect not just the UK but the world. Yes, that's a lot of power!

As for politics itself – it's all around you, permeating your life. If you look out of your front window and see a road, that's because a politician took a political decision to build a road. Turn on your lights; they work because a politician (perhaps the same one) took a political decision to build a new power plant. And, of course, discussion of politics – political events and political controversies – pops up on your television, tablet or in your newspaper all the time.

In this chapter I look at the reasons why politics and politicians play such an important role in everybody's lives.

Looking at Different Types of Authority

I'm going to get all scientific on you for a moment. Don't worry, not test tubes and lab coats but the wacky world of the political scientist, whose job is to see patterns in the way politics plays out, from tribes in the darkest, deepest Amazon rainforest to the inner workings of the US president's White House.

One of the big names in political science and philosophy at the start of the 20th century was the German intellectual Max Weber. He looked at the world of politics and how politicians – and everyone in authority in the country – gained and held their power. He identified three types of authority:

- **Traditional authority:** People choose to obey authority figures because of national traditions and customs. The UK's unwritten constitution is largely based on traditions and customs. For example, the monarch in the UK has many legal powers, but tradition and custom mean that in practice the prime minister (PM) exercises much of this power.
- **Charismatic authority:** Leaders have big personalities and qualities that make them stand out. This charisma persuades others to follow what the leader says, which in turn gives power. The fascist leaders Hitler and Mussolini are recognised as having drawn much of their power from charisma, although they used it in a destructive way.
- **Legal authority:** People generally respect the law, and so a person who gains office through legal means automatically has authority. For instance, the US constitution, which is a legal document, outlines much of the authority of the country's government. Americans respect their nation's constitution and as a result respect those who hold political office by playing by its rules. Presidents, for example, have to win their party's nomination and then win the election to office. This process gives the president authority.

No country's political system fits perfectly into just one authority model. The power of the UK prime minister, for instance, can largely be said to rely on a mix of traditional and legal authority – and occasionally, in the case of Winston Churchill during the Second World War, for example – charismatic authority too.

Political scientists draw a distinction between the exercise of authority and coercion. Put simply, *coercion* is when people obey because they're afraid of the consequences of disobedience – dictatorships often rely on a heavy dose of coercion. *Authority* is when people obey because they regard who's telling them what to do as having some legitimacy – traditional, legal, charismatic or a combination. People even obey when they don't agree with what they're being asked to do. Generally, politicians and political systems relying on authority last a good deal longer than those using coercion.

Deciphering the Ultimate Purpose of Politics

'So, what's the point of politics?' is the sort of question you hear down the pub on a Friday night, normally followed by the statement 'Politicians are all the same!' In addition, falling voter turnout across much of the Western world highlights a general malaise around all things politics and politician. But understanding why politics exists is a serious question.

Political scientists have been busy coming up with reasons why politics matters:

- **Politics determines who exercises power:** In all societies someone, somewhere has to be in charge. Politics is the means by which the people decide which individual or collection of individuals should govern. In the UK, for instance, roughly 45 million people are registered to vote. These millions elect around 650 Members of Parliament and the party with the biggest grouping of these MPs goes on to form the government of the country. The daily cut and thrust of politics creates an impression in voters' minds regarding which candidate and party they'd like to cast their vote for at the next election.
- **Politics encourages compromise:** Put ten people in a room and you're unlikely to get any of them to agree about anything straight away; the only way they agree is through compromise. But how do you get people to compromise with one another? Politics is the best available answer to this question. People accept things happening that they don't agree with because they respect the political process – its traditions or its legality. You may not think that's the case when you see raucous scenes in the House of Commons, but politics encourages compromise.
- **Politics accommodates different interests:** It's an outlet for pressure groups, which as I discuss in Chapter 9 are professional bodies that have expertise and policy objectives skewed to one particular area of society. For example, the British Medical Association has a keen interest in how the National Health Service is run. Pressure groups are important in society and their views find expression through politics.

Gauging the Role of Politicians

Whether you love them, loathe them or are just indifferent (and most people seem to be in the latter two camps), politicians exist for good reason. But despite the opinions of some, they do much more than sip taxpayer-subsidised champagne and complete their expenses claims down to the last penny. They can have a huge impact on the lives of individuals and the future of great nations and can even decide whether countries go to war or live in peace.

Making the law

The key job of politicians the world over is to make the laws that govern society. These laws can be big and sweeping, encompassing fundamental changes to the way the economy and society are run, or they can be small and technical, tinkering with existing laws to make them, hopefully, better.

Changing the constitution

The UK constitution can change in a couple of different ways, as the following examples illustrate:

- **By custom:** In 1688 the unpopular monarch James II was overthrown. James had brought this situation on himself by ignoring the views of prominent politicians in parliament. After the Glorious Revolution, as James's ousting was called, the custom became that the monarch was able to act only on the advice of ministers – that is, monarchs had to do what the leading politicians of the country told them to do.
- **By law:** Just over two hundred years after James's reign ended, a constitutional crisis arose over a disagreement between the House of Lords and the House of Commons. The Parliament Act of 1911 solved this disagreement by changing the law (and thereby the constitution) so that the House of Lords could only delay rather than vote down laws passed by the House of Commons.

Politicians introduce draft laws to be voted upon and speak up for them, but more often than not civil servants undertake the actual writing of the laws. Civil servants (whom I talk more about in Chapter 15) are also responsible for seeing that government policy is implemented and that it stays within the law of the land.

Politicians making laws is all well and good, but they also need a functioning court system to carry those laws out. In addition, a competent and hopefully honest police force is necessary to catch people who break the laws.

Changing the constitution and the way government works

Politicians can alter who does what in the country's government by changing the constitution. The process of changing the UK's unwritten constitution is a fairly simple matter. All that's needed is for a majority of MPs to vote in favour of a new law changing what one part of government does, and for the House of Lords to approve that law and the monarch to sign off on it.

The UK's unwritten constitution relies on a combination of written laws and unwritten traditions and customs. Changing the way government works is possible by changing the law or through a tradition or custom altering over time (for more details, see the nearby sidebar 'Changing the constitution').

Ensuring a more stable state

In essence, the politician, particularly in a democracy, has to act as society's conciliator. A politician's job is to listen to the opinions of business, groups of professionals and individuals, and to design government policy that best reflects these views and brings these groups into agreement.

In addition, politicians oversee the civil service. Politicians have the power to hire and fire underperforming civil servants or those who fail to work for the public good. In some countries politicians also control the judiciary and even religious leaders.

You can think of politicians as the string holding the elements of much of government and society together. The leadership of politicians is what prevents different groups in society from coming into conflict.

Galvanising the country in times of crisis

Cometh the hour, cometh the politician. Politicians are often responsible for helping to bring the people of a country together in times of crisis. When an epidemic breaks out or a major climatic event occurs people look to the politicians for leadership and to ensure that the government is 100 per cent focused on providing the right response to help those in need.

Political reputations can be won and lost in times of crisis. In late 1940, with the UK facing defeat at the hands of Germany in the Second World War, the great speeches and leadership of prime minister Winston Churchill inspired the country. Churchill's reputation as a great leader was cemented forever. At the same time, in contrast, the French leadership crumbled in the face of military defeats at the hands of the Germans. The government disintegrated into factions and a disorganised rabble. This response destroyed the reputations of all the politicians involved. They failed the ultimate test of the politician – the crisis!

Listening to constituents

In the UK and many other democracies, politicians are elected by people living in a particular locality to represent that area. In the UK, even the prime minister is elected to parliament in this way. For example, David Cameron was elected to represent Whitney, Gordon Brown represented Dunfermline and before him Tony Blair was also the MP for Sedgefield as well as PM.

This close interaction between politicians and public is one of the strengths of the UK political system. MPs run a weekly surgery where constituents can come in to see them and discuss their problems. These surgeries are a good way of keeping politicians grounded in ordinary life and mean that the public feel that they have a hotline to those in power. One of the key jobs of politicians, in democracies, is to represent each and every person.

By convention in the UK, the prime minister must be an elected MP rather than an appointed member of the House of Lords. The last time a prime minister was also a lord was over 100 hundred years ago.

MPs aren't the only ones representing the interests of constituents; thousands of local councillors across the country also do so. These councillors are elected by a few thousand voters living in a *ward.* Their job is to listen to the views of these people and ensure that local services are delivered efficiently. Most of the contact that members of the public have with politicians is with local councillors rather than MPs or government ministers. Flip to Chapter 17 for more on local government in the UK.

Working for the good of the country

Politicians are meant to do what's best for the national interests of their country. At European Union (EU) summit meetings, for example, the British prime minister is meant to stand up for Britain's national interests first. If a new EU law is proposed that may damage Britain's economy or impair the civil liberties of its citizens, the public expects the prime minister and the government as a whole to oppose it.

In fact, along with ensuring the defence of the country, one of the absolute must-dos of government is always to represent the national interest.

Tackling the Big Issues: Current Challenges Facing Politicians

The world can be a dangerous, turbulent place and even countries with a long tradition of political and economic stability – such as the UK – still have to face up to major threats. In an increasingly globalised world, these threats seem more acute than ever; incidents thousands of miles away can suddenly snowball into massive global events.

Of course, lighting up the Bat signal or calling on Superman when problems happen would be great, but that's the world of comic books. In the real world, the humble (and not so humble) politicians are the best thing society has for solving crises and ensuring peace and prosperity for as many people as possible.

The job of politicians is to negotiate with one another and co-ordinate so that government can meet the challenges and defeat the dangers facing the world. As well as day-to-day issues – big and small – politicians have to address some pretty big themes too. No single politician is expected to come up with a complete answer to problems alone, but as a collective politicians have to face up to and deal with the big issues I highlight in this section.

All the issues I outline are of epoch-defining importance. Day to day, most politicians deal with far more mundane fare, such as National Health Service waiting list times or whether a weekly or fortnightly refuse collection service is more suitable. However, many of the issues in this section – such as the economy and protecting the environment – influence decisions taken on what may seem like less important matters.

Keeping up living standards – it's the economy, stupid!

When he was campaigning for the US presidency in 1992, Bill Clinton's campaign famously posted the slogan, 'It's the economy, stupid!' in campaign headquarters to keep everyone focused on that major talking point.

The economy is an issue in most elections, in most democracies, in most years. Electors like to see their *standard of living* – which is the money they earn and the goods and services available to them – increase year after year. Most of the time this scenario happens, but occasionally the economy goes into recession, jobs are lost and people get poorer.

Normally, governments up for election during a period of poor economic news are beaten by their opponents.

People see the job of politicians as being to ensure that the right conditions are in place for the economy to grow, but how do they do that? Well, although the government isn't omnipotent as far as the economy goes, it can have quite an influence through the following methods:

- **Setting tax policy:** The government takes a certain percentage of people's earnings and business profits through taxation. By adjusting the amount of money it takes in tax, the government can leave people and businesses with more or less to spend in the shops or invest. Generally, high taxes reduce economic growth while lower taxes increase it.
- **Targeting government spending:** Government spending is hugely important to the economy and accounts for around 40 per cent of the UK's total economic output. By adjusting this spending up or down, the government can have a major influence on the economy.

- **Deregulation:** Most businesses the world over complain of government *red tape*. The argument goes that if you cut this red tape and allow businesses to do what they're good at – doing business and making money – wider society benefits and everyone gets richer.

  The flip side to this argument is that business has to be regulated properly to ensure that the pursuit of wealth and profit doesn't damage wider society. For example, despite the expense involved, chemical manufacturers have to dispose of their toxic waste safely; simply dumping it can cause environmental damage.

The government doesn't try to create as much economic growth as it can, because doing so would have all sorts of consequences. For starters, high economic growth often leads to sharp rises in inflation, which can be especially harmful to poorer people. Likewise, a country focused purely on economic growth is likely to be polluted and to protect workers' rights poorly. The government's job – and thus that of politicians – is to balance the concerns of the few with the wider interests of society.

A country is deemed to be in recession when it suffers two consecutive quarters – six months in total – of *negative economic growth;* that is, the economy has shrunk in size rather than grown. The Office of National Statistics measures whether the economy shrinks or increases in size. Its job is to collect data on what's going on in the economy and wider UK society so that politicians can make better-informed decisions.

The current governor of the Bank of England is Mark Carney. Carney, a Canadian, is the UK's number one banker. As governor, his job is to head up the *monetary policy committee,* which comprises nine prominent economists and bankers and is responsible for setting the base interest rate. This rate is crucial because all the banks and building societies use it as a basis for setting their own interest rates on loans and savings. The governor, under instruction from the Chancellor of the Exchequer (a politician), also has to decide on how much new money to print and must increasingly oversee the activities of the banking sector as a whole. The Chancellor of the Exchequer appoints the governor who's re-appointed or replaced by the Chancellor every five years. In the City of London – so crucial to the health of the British economy – the governor is the biggest of the big cheeses!

Saving the planet

Superheroes are always being charged with saving the planet, but in reality the normally suited, booted and middle-aged politician is the one who takes on the job.

The overwhelming scientific consensus is that the industrialisation of the globe, the explosion in the number of cars and increased modern air travel have the potential to kill the planet. The Earth is warming, the polar ice caps are melting and sea levels are rising. Scientists warn that all this is just the start of a process, which could have untold consequences for humanity.

As you can imagine, the issue of the environment is one of the biggest if not *the* biggest facing politicians around the globe. However, dramatic environmental change doesn't occur in a short period of time – in 5, 10 or even 20 years. No, we're looking 50, 100 or even several centuries into the future before the environmental doomsday scenarios scientists outline are likely to come to pass. The problem with developing a long-term strategy to deal with this environmental crisis is that politicians come and go relatively quickly – the longest-serving British PM for the past 100 years was Margaret Thatcher, and she was in Downing Street for just 11 years – and they also have their eye on the next election. Politicians have difficulty making unpopular decisions in the short term in order to help ease a problem that's likely to start having a major impact only after they've long departed the political stage, or even after, to put it bluntly, they're dead.

In relation to the environment, politicians are often accused of short-term thinking and policy choices. But in recent years the issue of the environment has steadily moved up the list of subjects concerning electors.

The steps politicians can take to ease climate change include the following:

- **Make laws to limit carbon emissions:** Governments have the power to pass new laws that cap the amount of harmful CO_2 emissions released by airlines and petrochemical companies, for example. Although prosecutions can be used to back up laws if necessary, at present the UK prefers to use persuasion and financial incentives to try to encourage businesses to emit less CO_2.
- **Keep a lid on government emissions:** One of the biggest polluters is the government itself through the actions of its bureaucracy, military and health service workers. In fact, the government in the UK accounts for some 40 per cent of all economic output. Therefore, it has the ability to cut a heap of the nation's CO_2 emissions – and politicians make the policy for civil servants to follow to see that these emissions cuts happen.
- **Co-ordinate a global strategy:** Climate change is a global problem and therefore needs – you guessed it – a global solution. Governments get together every so often to discuss how each of them is facing up to the problem. The United Nations (UN) hosts annual global climate change conferences for politicians to meet, although these get-togethers have been criticised for being mere talking shops. But ultimately climate change is going to be eased only through politicians and governments around the globe coming to agreement, and crucially meeting the terms of those agreements.

UK politicians often say that, as a country, the UK can't itself do much about climate change, and they have a point. The UK is home to about 1 per cent of the world's population and is responsible for roughly 2.5 per cent of the emissions linked to climate change. However, the UK government has agreed to cut emissions and a key goal of British diplomats is to get other countries to do the same.

Blaming the newly industrialising Chinese or Indians for the recent expansion in harmful CO_2 emissions is easy. But the governments of these two economic super-powers make a simple point: all they're trying to do is enjoy the same standard of living as the West has enjoyed for years and that, even now, the Westerners – and particularly Americans – emit more harmful CO_2 per head.

Bringing an end to world poverty

Read any history book and you discover that poverty has always existed. But nowadays politicians around the globe are more aware of the inequities of global poverty. They question the fairness of a situation in which a couple of billion people live in relative luxury – with adequate food, clothing and heat – while another couple of billion struggle for survival crippled by disease and poverty. Just look at the ultimate indicator of poverty and wealth: in wealthy Japan the average woman can expect to live well into her 80s; in civil strife-torn Zimbabwe the average man can expect to die before he reaches 40. Enough said!

But poverty – like climate change – is one of those giant issues that's well beyond the scope of even the most dynamic of politicians or any single government. It requires a global solution, with many politicians coming together.

Only of late, however, through campaigns such as Make Poverty History, has the uncertain state of many countries and people in the developing world come to the fore. How poverty is best tackled is a matter of some debate, but in meetings of the G8 and G20 – the international bodies that bring together the world's biggest economies – politicians have identified the following ways to help the developing world avoid the poverty trap:

- **Cancel debts:** Incredibly, some extremely poor nations, particularly in sub-Saharan Africa, owe huge sums to international banks, foreign governments and the World Bank. In fact, until recently governments across Africa had to repay more in interest each year on loans than they gained through aid from richer countries. In effect, the developing world throughout the 1980s and 1990s was handing over more money than it was receiving from the wealthy – normally Western – nations. Doing away with these debts would significantly alleviate developing-world poverty.

- **Target aid:** At present, Western governments such as the UK contribute on average 0.5 to just over 1 per cent of their national income in aid projects for the benefit of the developing world. Now this figure may not seem enough, but when you combine all the monies flowing in from the G8 and G20 member nations it forms a tidy pile of cash. This money can then be given to the government of the country in need of aid and to UN agencies for spending on infrastructure investment in the developing world, such as clean water supplies, better hospitals, schools and transport links. Unfortunately, certain countries reneged to some extent on their aid promises and anti-poverty campaigners say that, long term, more money is needed.
- **Promote good governance:** One of the biggest problems facing the developing world is poor governance. Politicians and military leaders are often corrupt, incompetent or a combination of the two.

  Giving a developing world government lots of aid is pointless if it doesn't have the means – through honest civil servants and government officials – to spend the money on the right projects. Trying to ensure proper governance is absolutely key to seeing that a combination of aid and debt write-offs leads to practical improvements in living standards.

Fighting terrorism

If you'd asked a politician from the UK or US to rank the importance of Islamic terrorism on 10 September 2001, they probably wouldn't have put it very high on their list of must-tackle jobs. But on 11 September 2001, following the killing of thousands of civilians by Islamic extremist terrorists, suddenly terrorism became one of the most important issues facing politicians around the globe.

The 'War on Terror', as former US president George W Bush dubbed it, was a game-changing event. Subsequent US and UK foreign policy has been geared towards the elimination of the Islamic terrorist threat, with very mixed results. Invasions of Afghanistan and later Iraq proved unpopular and a source of disagreement between politicians.

Many years on from 9/11, politicians in the UK and elsewhere still face the massive problem of trying to stop international and domestic-bred Islamic terrorism while simultaneously preserving long-standing civil rights.

Reckoning with the decline of Western dominance

Western powers such as the US and UK have been the wealthiest, strongest militarily and most economically successful countries for the past few hundred years. In fact, just over 100 years ago even China looked set to be colonised by white Europeans and the British ruled India.

Oh, how times have changed! The economic powerhouses of the 21st century are likely to be China and India, and even America isn't as powerful as it used to be (I talk more about the US in Chapter 22). How to manage this relative change in the global pecking order peacefully is a key political issue for politicians around the world.

For example, what role should China – which has a very dodgy human rights record – play in big international bodies such as the G20, World Bank and other UN agencies? Likewise, what about preserving economic stability in a world where massive trade imbalances exist between East and West (in short, the East produces most of the manufactured goods that the West buys)?

Becoming Active in Politics

Open distrust and dislike of politics and politicians seems a very 21st-century phenomenon. In the US, for instance, barely half the population of voting age take part in presidential elections, and in the UK the situation isn't much better.

Lots of people do still care about politics, however, and because you're reading this book I assume that you're one of them. In fact, many people not only engage with politics and political discussion, but also want to get actively involved.

You can become politically active in numerous ways, from joining a party, forming a pressure group or social movement and demonstrating right through to redecorating the local school or tidying a nearby park. In a sense, all politics is social.

Playing your part

Placards and ballot papers at the ready; here's how you can become active in politics:

- **Run for office:** If you can't beat them join them is the idea here. If you want to change the law and the way people are governed, you're free to stand for elected office from tiny parish council to full-blown parliamentary constituency. To have a good chance of winning, however, you almost certainly need to belong to a particular political party.
- **Participate in public demonstrations:** In countries such as the UK, groups and individuals are free to protest through peaceful demonstrations, carrying banners and shouting slogans. Protestors aim to get their views across to politicians and other citizens.
- **Use the media:** Carrying out an action, granting an interview or otherwise attracting media coverage are effective ways to publicise your views to a large number of people. Activists that get lots of media coverage can often be successful.
- **Take part in direct action:** Direct action is normally associated with forms of protest that can be violent at times. The idea is to show the public and politicians that you feel so strongly about an issue that you're willing to take extreme measures. But a less confrontational type of direct action is aiming to assist directly the very people you're asking politicians to help. For example, a pressure group looking for better rights for asylum seekers may have volunteer lawyers available to help fight their cases in court.

You can rarely make much of a difference as an activist on your own. Instead, you need to form or join a pressure group of like-minded people, something I talk more about in Chapter 9.

In democratic countries, activists sometimes do see their policy proposals make it into law. But for this to happen, they need to convince the politicians that what they're calling for is the right thing to do and has the support of the wider general public. So, in reality, activists need politicians and often try to meet MPs and ministers to promote their causes.

Sometimes politics simply breaks down. Groups of people take to the streets with the aim of toppling the government, which is called a *revolution*. Although incredibly rare in Britain, violent street protests are far from unknown. Revolutions do occur, however, with surprising regularity across the globe. In 2011 for instance several Arab nations – most notably Libya, Tunisia and Egypt – erupted into violence and revolution with unpopular, oppressive governments being toppled in a matter of weeks, in an event that came to be called the Arab Spring.

From people having rants and arguments about politics on Twitter to demonstrators using Facebook and the like to co-ordinate protests during the Arab Spring, social media plays a huge part in political activism; turn to Chapter 11 for the low-down.

Taking up the paint brush: Political social action

In the UK and many other Western countries, traditional political parties are struggling to find new members. In fact less than 1 per cent of the UK population belongs to a political party. The parties try all sorts of wheezes to attract new members, from social events – lots of coffee mornings – to cheap membership deals. But their latest attempt to reach out deploys a new strand of activism called political social action.

Political social action involves showing how a political party can have a positive impact in the community. For example, if your local park is badly littered or a lot of graffiti needs cleaning up, you may see a group of volunteers from the local party turning up with brooms, brushes and refuse bags in hand and giving the place a thorough going over. The idea is not only to improve the environment, but also to show politics leading to real action – deeds not just words. Political social action may seem to be on a small scale – compared to huge topics such as the economy and fighting terrorism – but it can have a powerful, tangible effect on local communities and individual voters.

Chapter 3

Looking at Participatory Democracy

In This Chapter

- Qualifying what democracy means
- Examining different types of democracy
- Laying bare the rights that British citizenship brings
- Looking at the strengths and weaknesses of Britain's democracy
- Considering growing voter apathy

You take it as read that you live in a democracy and most of the people you know from overseas probably live in a democracy as well. But what does the word *democracy* mean and how do you as an individual benefit from living under this system, and use it to change the society you live in?

In this chapter I look at the ins and outs of Britain's unique democracy and how it affects your life.

Understanding What Qualifies as a Democracy

Democracy is a system of government where the people – either the general public, or their elected representatives – basically run the show. It's either the general public or their elected representatives who decide what the government of the country should do. The great 19th-century US president Abraham Lincoln talked in his famous Gettysburg address about 'government of the people, by the people, for the people', and that's about the best definition of democracy you can find.

Dozens of democratic countries exist across the globe; for example, the United States, India, France, Japan and, of course, dear old Blighty. But no two democracies are identical; each has its own twist on the democratic theme.

The US political system, for instance, is two-tiered. State and federal governments are elected in different ways and each part exercises very distinct power. Elections are held for all branches of government, from the president down to the local sheriff. In Britain, on the other hand, government was centralised until the advent of the Scottish parliament and Welsh and Northern Irish assemblies (see Chapter 18 for more on these). The UK parliament passes many of the laws of the land, and electors have the right to change the government in power usually only every four or five years.

Regardless of the approach to democracy a country takes, in order for a nation to be deemed democratic its elections must have some key traits:

- They must be held regularly for both local and national government positions.
- They must be free and fair so no one is pressured into voting a particular way and ballots are cast anonymously.
- The overwhelming majority of the population must be eligible to vote (some countries exclude groups like prisoners and the insane).

Holding elections doesn't automatically mean that a country is a democracy. Sometimes, countries that are very far from democracies call themselves democratic merely because they hold elections of some type. But elections to a talking shop (an unproductive, bureaucratic and self-serving organisation) or to a rubber-stamp institution for a dictator aren't true democratic elections. Here are some examples of countries that were clearly not democracies but held elections:

- During the Cold War (which ran from 1945–91, with the Soviet Union on one side and Western democracies on the other), East Germany called itself the German Democratic Republic (or GDR). It did so despite being a communist state and having a brutal secret police quelling all opposition to the government. However, the top brass of the GDR believed calling it a democracy was legitimate because the party that ran the country had a huge membership and party officials were elected by ballots of party members.
- Former Iraqi dictator Saddam Hussein regularly held elections in which he and his cronies were voted into power with an astonishing 99 per cent of the votes cast. Such results aren't the effect of free and fair elections; that the Iraqi people were frightened by years of murderous activity by Hussein's secret police and afraid to vote against his regime is much more likely.

In some fledgling democracies or countries holding their first ever elections, observers from the United Nations and European Union usually verify that the election is indeed free and fair.

Starting with Athenian direct democracy

The UK is often referred to as one of the world's oldest democracies, and it is. But long before anyone thought to create a parliament – in fact, about the same time as Britons were discovering that wheels are best if they're round – a flourishing democracy was up and running in the Mediterranean, in Athens to be precise.

The great Greek philosopher Aristotle defined the Athenian democracy of his day as 'rule by the many' or, alternatively, 'rule by the people'. Political scientists call it *Athenian direct democracy*. So what was Athenian direct democracy? Put simply, every Athenian citizen had the right to attend, speak and vote at meetings of the city's assembly to pass laws and decide on the level of taxation.

Ancient Athens is often held up as some sort of democratic Utopia. Some see it as a much purer form of democracy than exists in Britain today, because we only get to vote for candidates at election times, rather than vote on actual bills. Many things weren't quite right about ancient Athenian democracy, however. Citizens could vote but citizenship wasn't conferred on women or slaves, who made up the majority of the population of Athens at the time.

The Athenian democracy wasn't that durable either; it was eventually destroyed by invaders. In fact, once the Athenians were invaded, democracy in any form we'd recognise today virtually disappeared from the Western world right up until the 1700s and 1800s. But the Athenian model was crucial, because records that remained of how it worked informed many great political thinkers during the Enlightenment (a period roughly covering the 18th century, when scientific endeavour, the arts and political thinking flowered in Europe), who in turn had a key influence on those who formed some of the world's biggest modern democracies. These democracies grew up against a similar cultural and intellectual backdrop, and so influenced each other. Countries like Japan and Germany suffered cataclysmic events such as defeat in war and the overturning of rulers before they adopted democracy.

If anyone highlights how democratic ideas crossed borders over the past few hundred years, it's Thomas Paine. He lived in Britain until age 37, and his writings calling for greater democracy influenced many in his own country. He then emigrated to America, where he became a leading figure in the American Revolution and the formation of that nation's representative democracy. He wasn't finished there. He was in France during its revolution in the 1790s, and his ideas on democracy were hugely influential there too.

Referendums: Direct voting power

Probably the closest thing we have these days to Athenian direct democracy is a referendum. A *referendum* is a national vote involving all voters on just one key issue. Everyone who wants a say turns up on a specific day at a polling station and casts a vote: yes or no. After the votes are counted, the government then (usually) follows the course of action that the majority of those who cast their ballot in the referendum want to take.

On parts of the Continent and in the US – at a state rather than federal level – referendums are commonplace. But, controversially, in recent years some European governments have held referendums on whether to ratify European Union treaties, only to be told by voters that they don't want ratification to go ahead. The response? In all cases, the governments have waited a little while and then simply put the question to the people again.

Referendums are very rare in Britain. In fact, there have only been two national referendums held since the 1970s. The most recent was over a potential change to the voting system (from first past the post to the alternative vote system), and before that the Labour government of Harold Wilson, way back in the 1970s, asked whether people wanted Britain to remain a part of the European Economic Community (now called the European Union). Roughly two thirds of votes cast were for the UK to stay in the Community – so it did. More recent referendums have been held in Scotland and Wales, asking people there whether or not they wanted their own parliament or assembly, respectively. In September 2014 there was a referendum on whether Scotland should be independent from the UK, and the result was a victory for those who wanted to keep the status quo.

Getting into representative democracy

The Athenian model of direct democracy, with every eligible voter casting a vote himself (and, in Athens, all the voters were male), sort of worked, mainly because there were so few citizens to take part. But can you imagine asking the best part of 60 million Britons to turn up 40 or more times a year at the Houses of Parliament to decide on laws and taxes? For one thing, the catering would be a nightmare!

Modern democracies aren't direct like the Athenian model, but are representative instead. In a *representative democracy*, instead of voting directly on laws to be passed, people vote for candidates, and the winning candidates then vote on the laws.

In the UK, people vote for local councillors, Members of Parliament and Members of the European Parliament. In the United States, citizens vote for a president or members of Congress, and on a state level they vote for governors, members of the state legislature and local mayors, sheriffs and even the local refuse collector (the last is a joke, but lots of public offices aren't appointed in the US; they're elected). In fact, the Americans have lots of elections, full stop.

Claiming first place in the representative democracy race

Lots of different countries claim they're the first home of representative democracy. But probably the three main contenders are France, the US and Britain.

The French claim lies in what happened during its bloody revolution of 1789. Citizens overthrew a feudal society and monarchy – with lots of cutting off of heads – and replaced it with Estates, where the citizens were free to vote for their representatives. The French went from feudal to the most modern of democracies in the bat of an eye. Unfortunately, it ended in tears when within a few years Napoleon rose to become dictator and swept away meaningful democratic aspects of the political system.

The United States' claim to be the home of representative democracy holds more water. They had their own revolution – this time against the ruling British – and adopted a constitution guaranteeing citizens' rights and setting out a more fully fledged representative democracy (see Chapter 22 for more on the US political system). Like Athenian direct democracy, however, holes appear in this story too, with large numbers of citizens barred from voting in elections – slavery and segregation of the black minority until the 1960s mean that American democracy has only recently become truly representative of the people's views.

Britain has the oldest system of representative democracy, with elections to the UK parliament held for many centuries before the French and American revolutions. However, although Britain had a parliament that made the laws of the land, the overwhelming majority of people had no say in who sat in that parliament. Right up until the mid-19th century only male landowners could vote at election time. Some still question Britain's democratic credentials because a non-elected body, the House of Lords, has a key role in making laws for the country and most of its members are appointed by the monarch (who follows the advice of the prime minister), although there have been widespread calls to make members of the House of Lords stand for election.

Homing in on British Democracy

For most of Britain's history, the nation hasn't been, by modern ways of thinking at least, a democracy. In fact, in early Victorian Britain calling a politician a 'democrat' was often considered abusive. Earlier than that the upper echelons of society, such as the monarchy and landed classes of the realm, were horrified at the idea that common people – that's me and you – could ever be given the vote. We were illiterate and probably smelt; how could our small brains ever cope with the intricacies of political debate? You get the picture. But over time this attitude changed dramatically and nowadays even I – despite the fact that I occasionally still smell – have a vote to elect a representative to the UK and European parliaments and my local council.

You can find the full lowdown on Britain's path to democracy in Chapter 5 or, for even more detail, *British History For Dummies* (Wiley) is the best place to go. But the next sections talk about some key stages on the road to you and me getting the vote.

Putting the monarchy in its place

If you're reading this, Your Majesty, look away now because this section describes how your ancestors lost top billing. When the Normans invaded in 1066 they brought with them their own knights, lords and a monarch sitting at the top of the tree. The monarch was supposed to have absolute power, meaning anything – and I do mean anything – she said went. If the monarch said Wednesday was 'wear an onion on your head day', everyone would be sporting just that the following week.

This state of affairs continued for some six centuries, but all through that time lords, other powerful landowners and wealthy merchants wanted to have their say in the running of the country, from laws passed to taxes collected. After all, these men were paying taxes, and so expected something in return! Gradually, parliament became the forum through which powerful elites began to voice their grievances against the monarchy. Rather than act as a tool to be controlled by the king or queen of the day, in the 16th and 17th centuries it increasingly began to exert its own influence on affairs.

Over time, parliament gained increasing prestige and power. Eventually, after a bloody civil war and quite a bit of political machination, in 1688 – in what's known as the Glorious Revolution – parliament became in effect the supreme law-making body in the land. In future, all monarchs had to bend to the will of parliament and the election of its members became a very big deal.

Britain's transition from monarchy to representative democracy hasn't been without struggle or bloodshed. However, Britain has been more fortunate than a lot of other countries in that its march to democracy has been evolutionary rather than revolutionary. Contrast this situation with Russia, which now at least defines itself as a democracy. Russia has been through a bloody revolution and then 70 years of Communist Party control during which millions of people were put to death for having a different political ideology or simply on a twisted whim.

Expanding the franchise

Landowners and wealthy merchants had got one over on the monarch and parliament was now supreme. But parliament was one big club, and only landowners were able to vote members in or out. That situation suited the landowners and merchants very much but not the rest of the population – and they, after all, were in the overwhelming majority.

Fighting the good fight: Getting votes for women

Until 1918, the majority gender, women, weren't allowed to vote. If you suggested publicly that women should have the vote in Georgian or early Victorian Britain, there was every chance you could be locked up for being mad! Such was the ingrained prejudice in society and even among women themselves.

However, as more and more men got the vote and the country didn't collapse as opponents of expanding the franchise had feared, the idea of votes for women, or *women's suffrage* as it was called, started to take root. Groups of women called *suffragettes* and *suffragists* started to agitate for the vote. Following the crucial role that women played in winning the First World War, parliament granted the vote, at first only to women over 30 and then ultimately according to the same parameters as men.

As the population and the economy grew, the idea and practice of having so much power concentrated in the hands of so few became unworkable. So, during the 19th century, the *franchise* – the right to vote – expanded, slowly at first and then more quickly. First up, men who rented land were allowed a vote in 1832 (still, only one in seven men in 1832 were allowed to vote). In 1867 this was extended to all male householders but still upwards of 40 per cent of men didn't have a vote. This inequality was corrected through further acts in 1884 and 1918 when all men over age 21 were allowed to vote. The right to vote was extended to women over age 30 in 1918, after the First World War. Not until 1928 were women allowed to vote from age 21, the same as men.

At the start of the 19th century less than 10 per cent of the adult population could vote, but by 1900 this had shot up to around 30 per cent.

In the UK, all adults over 18 with some small exceptions – see Chapter 7 for more details – have the right to vote. However, some are calling for this age to be lowered further to 16 for general elections. They say that 16-year-olds have other legal rights and can pay income tax and national insurance in their own right, so why shouldn't they have a vote?

Throwing digital democracy into the mix

Grafting Athenian-style direct democracy (see 'Starting with Athenian direct democracy', earlier in this chapter) onto 19th- or 20th-century British society was obviously impossible. Too many people and too few resources made getting the citizens to make the laws of the land through a never-ending series of ballots unworkable. No one would get anything else done – and just think of the paperwork!

In the 21st century, however, we have the Internet and digital technology, which allow us to watch virtually whatever we want and communicate with whomever we want at the push of a button. It's possible, therefore, even in a country of 60 million, to actually run a direct electronic democracy, or *e-democracy*, with you, me and the postmaster all deciding what laws to introduce and approve – or not.

The Internet also allows everyone much greater access to information. Finding out whole reams of information, in fact enough to make informed choices on complex topics, is possible with a few mouse clicks.

Strong voices argue against e-democracy, making the following points:

- **Fraud danger:** Whoever controls the electronic method of gathering votes could have the opportunity to rig the ballot without anyone else knowing. This scenario may sound a bit Big Brother but is a concern for civil liberty groups.
- **Digital divide:** Not everyone is comfortable with or has access to new technology. In fact, for many people Twitter is something the birds do rather than the electronic communication of the minute. If you don't know that much about technology, you're less likely to take part in the e-democratic process.
- **Dumbing down of debate:** No matter how great the resources on the Internet for getting to know about a particular topic before voting on law changes, most people will still simply vote according to a combination of gut instinct, possible prejudice and what their favourite political party says is right. Who, after all, has the spare time to go through the minutiae of reports and data available on a particular topic to be voted on?

E-democracy is a long way off in Britain because the idea that the elected representatives make the decision on behalf of their constituents has a very strong pull.

The Scottish parliament has an element of direct democracy in that relatively small groups of voters get to vote on contentious issues. These votes don't impact the vote in the parliament directly, but the results of these polls are emailed to Members of the Scottish Parliament (MSPs). The idea is to let the MSPs know how their electors are thinking, but the members are free to ignore these snapshot polls. As for the UK as a whole, the cabinet office has run an e-petition initiative. Should an e-petition on the Cabinet office website get 100,000 signatures it automatically triggers a parliamentary debate.

Understanding the Rights that Come with British Citizenship

Cecil Rhodes, the Victorian colonialist, said that to be born British was to win first prize in the lottery of life. Now that's a fairly big claim that I'm sure people all over the world would have a few things to say about. Nevertheless, being a Brit brings with it certain fundamental rights enshrined in the law of the land. These key rights include:

- The right to a fair trial and not to be detained without due legal process.
- The right to vote if you're a citizen over age 18 and your name appears on the *electoral register* – the list of people that live in a constituency. All British citizens over age 18 must register as a legal requirement.
- The right to the protection of the Human Rights Act.

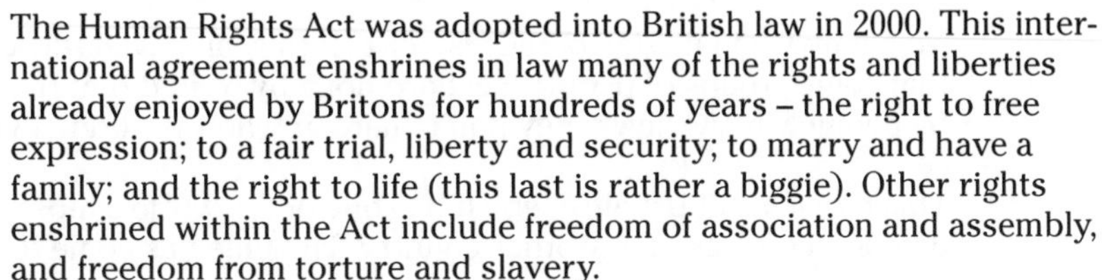

The Human Rights Act was adopted into British law in 2000. This international agreement enshrines in law many of the rights and liberties already enjoyed by Britons for hundreds of years – the right to free expression; to a fair trial, liberty and security; to marry and have a family; and the right to life (this last is rather a biggie). Other rights enshrined within the Act include freedom of association and assembly, and freedom from torture and slavery.

- The right to free speech as long as it doesn't libel others or incite violence.
- The right to state education and health care.

And these are just the big rights. Lots of little ones exist too, embedded in hundreds of years of laws passed by the UK parliament.

The UK doesn't have a written constitution, unlike the US, for example. Instead, the judicial system relies on a patchwork of new and old laws passed by parliament and overseen by the courts to protect civil liberties and to ensure fair play in society.

There aren't actually any British citizens; instead, we're all subjects of the Crown. However, these days the term *subject* is a bit out of date, a throwback to the days when the monarch was all-powerful, and so Britons refer to themselves as citizens.

Taking new-fangled citizenship tests

In the recent past, if you wanted to become a British citizen, all you had to do was either be born here, marry a Brit or live here long enough to qualify. Handing out citizenship to incomers was always a low-key affair, but that's no longer the case.

Tony Blair's Labour government introduced citizenship tests in 2005 to improve the knowledge of British culture and way of life among those who were seeking to become citizens. The tests aren't that hard and are multiple choice, but you have to pass or you don't get citizenship. (If you want to know more about these tests, check out *The British Citizenship Test For Dummies*, also written by your humble author and published by Wiley.)

As the icing on the cake, the government also decided to introduce citizenship ceremonies. These are simply gatherings where new citizens swear an oath of allegiance to their new home country and to the Crown.

Evaluating the Pros and Cons of UK Democracy

No country and no democracy is perfect; they all have little kinks that mean that some groups of people feel hard done by or find that they're governed by people whose views they don't share or who they don't even like!

This is as true of Britain – which has one of the world's most respected democracies – as of any other country. The time has come to look in the national mirror and see what's good and not so good about our system of government.

Looking at the strengths

Now you can puff out your chest with national pride because Britain is one of the most longstanding, stable and successful democracies in the world. In modern times, Britain hasn't succumbed to dictatorships, as has happened in Germany, Italy, Japan and Spain. The rights of the individual and the rule of law are held dear in Britain, as is freedom of speech and of the press.

In fact, only in wartime or when the country has been attacked by terrorists has the state acted to curb some civil liberties. These instances are always scrutinised and sometimes overturned by the courts.

It's a small world: Westminster Village

Political journalists often refer to something called the Westminster Village, which doesn't mean an actual village called Westminster with its own pub, post office or local shop (although Westminster does have plenty of all three). The term refers more to the community of politicians, civil servants, lobbyists and journalists located in (guess where?) Westminster.

Sometimes people use *the Westminster Village* as a condemnatory phrase to mean that the same politicians, civil servants, lobbyists and journalists get preoccupied with gossip or a political media story that doesn't really impact everyday Britons' lives.

Unlike the US, Britain doesn't have a written constitution with a clearly defined separation of powers that lets the executive branch, judicial system and legislature know precisely what they're allowed to do or not to do. Instead, the UK relies on laws built up over many hundreds of years to protect liberties and curb the powers of the executive. This system is a patchwork solution that holds the country together well.

These are some of the reasons people hold up British democracy as an exemplar:

- **Flexibility:** The British constitution, because it's unwritten, evolves naturally over time as laws or conventions change. Take, for example, the role of the monarch: she's head of state but it's generally agreed that she has little involvement in everyday politics.
- **Strong parties:** The UK's political parties are longstanding and have deep roots in communities and among large sections of society. Also, none of the main political parties – Labour, Conservative or Liberal Democrat – follow extreme right or left policies. (Chapter 8 has more on the party system.)
- **Judicial primacy:** Everyone is subject to the law in the UK and everyone is equal under the law. This very important principle means that no matter how politically powerful, rich, well-connected or famous any individual is, she has to obey the law. The same goes for organisations. The court system is what holds the invisible strands of Britain's constitution together; Chapter 16 delves into the role of the judiciary.

Recognising the weaknesses

Now, not all is good with Britain (the weather for starters), including its democracy. Here are some of the common complaints about Britain's democracy:

- **Behind the times:** Many say that Britain's approach of adhering to an unwritten constitution is very old-fashioned. In addition, we have a monarch when most nations got rid of theirs a long time ago. The system of electing MPs through the first-past-the-post poll is also longstanding and unique.

  MPs are elected through the first-past-the-post system. The candidate who polls the highest number of votes in an individual constituency takes the seat in the House of Commons. The winning candidate doesn't have to get a majority of the votes cast, just the biggest number. Under this system, MPs have the same power and legitimacy whether they win by 1 vote or by 30,000.

- **Not democratic enough:** Voters get to elect their local MP, councillor and Member of the European Parliament, but elections aren't that frequent (MPs stand every five years in general). Plus, some important positions, including membership of the House of Lords and the judiciary, aren't elected but appointed.

- **Too centred on Westminster:** Most of British government is located within a couple of miles of the Houses of Parliament in Westminster. The Department of Health, the Ministry of Defence and the prime minister's residence, 10 Downing Street, are all within a stone's throw of each other. Critics say that, as a result, politicians are out of touch with the rest of the country and that they don't give the concerns of people far away from Westminster due regard.

  Scottish and Welsh nationalists frequently use this argument as a justification for why they should have more power in their parts of the country and even complete independence from the British state.

Being a Citizen

Being a good citizen isn't limited to voting – although that basic obligation is one that many Brits are avoiding these days. Beyond voting, you can be as politically involved as you like.

Getting involved

Participation in politics is much more than simply turning up at a polling station on election day and casting a vote. For many people, politics is a day-in, day-out interest, something that helps them feel that they're contributing to wider society. Across the country, hundreds of thousands of people to a greater or lesser extent are involved in politics, from simply signing a petition to standing for elected office.

Some ways to be politically active include

- Joining a pressure group. (Chapter 9 has more on these.)
- Joining a political party and becoming an activist. (Turn to Chapter 8 for information on how the parties work.)
- Running for elected office.
- Becoming an eminent person in your field and advising civil servants or ministers.

Just about everyone is allowed to run for elected office in the UK. All you have to do is register as a candidate and pay a deposit of £500, which you get back if you win five per cent of the vote. See Chapter 17 for more on being a candidate at election time.

Gauging voter apathy

In recent British general, local and European elections, an odd thing has been happening: the number of people turning up to cast their vote has been falling, not by just a little but a lot.

After the Second World War around 80 per cent of those eligible to vote in general elections did so and, although this fell back a bit over time, in 1979 still around three quarters of eligible people participated. During the 1980s, however, voter turnout fell to just over 65 per cent. As the political tables turned and Tony Blair's Labour Party started to win elections comfortably, voter turnout again took a nosedive, this time to below 60 per cent at the 2001 general election. There was a minor recovery in voter turnout in 2005 and 2010, but still nearly four out of ten people registered to vote don't do so in a general election.

So why are fewer people voting? Well, for a number of reasons, including:

- **Disillusionment:** Many members of the public don't trust politicians to keep their constituents' interests at heart.
- **The result is known:** Many of the recent UK general elections have been almost a forgone conclusion, so many voters don't bother turning out.
- **Party similarity:** Many people see the policies of the UK's big political parties as substantially the same.

I explore voter apathy in greater detail in Chapter 7.

Voter turnout varies according to the type of election being held. Generally, elections to the UK parliament see the highest turnout, because people see them as the most important. They see European and local elections as less crucial, so voter turnout is lower; sometimes as few as one in three people eligible to vote do so.

Everyone aged 18 and over has to put their name on the electoral roll – that's the law. However, estimates suggest that as many as six million adults, as a result of chaotic life situations or wanting to keep a low profile, aren't on the electoral roll. The UK population is around 60 million, with around 46 million registered to vote (the lower number accounts for those not on the electoral roll, children and unregistered immigrants).

People have put forward lots of proposals for reversing low voter turnout, including compelling people to vote through legislation, making it easier to vote through online ballots and allowing more voters to use a postal vote rather than having to turn up at a polling station at a specific time on a specific day.

Chapter 4

Examining Political Ideologies

In This Chapter

- Getting to grips with ideologies
- Homing in on liberalism
- Scrutinising socialism
- Keeping the status quo: conservatism
- Looking at alternative ideologies
- Avoiding extremes in the UK

At its root politics is all about ideas and the British political system, with its parties, politicians and pressure groups, is no different. Behind the sound bites and the arguments that are the cut and thrust of British political debate lie some very big ideas indeed about how individuals should live their lives and how society is organised.

In this chapter I give you the lowdown on the big political ideologies that have shaped and continue to influence modern British politics and those of other countries around the globe.

Understanding What an Ideology Is

Put simply, an *ideology* is a single idea or collection of ideas relating to how to organise society, economics and politics. Ideologies are hugely important because they set out a roadmap for the policies pursued by politicians and they inspire political activists. In fact, politics is dominated by ideology; people enter politics inspired by these ideas and some will literally sacrifice everything for them, both for themselves and others.

Moderating ideologies: The British way

Sometimes people can use the pursuit of an ideology to justify downright cruelty, but fortunately in modern times in the UK this hasn't happened. The more revolutionary ideologies don't have many supporters in Britain.

Ideologies are hugely important in all countries and political systems. The major ideologies that hold sway in the UK include

- **Conservatism:** The support of national traditions and institutions in order to retain stability and continuity.
- **Liberalism:** Protecting the rights of the individual from interference from an overbearing state.
- **Socialism:** A way of organising the economy and society to benefit as many people as possible.

Conservatism, liberalism and socialism are represented through the UK's three main political parties. Working out which ideology goes with which isn't difficult. Socialism is the ideology of the Labour Party, conservatism of the Conservative Party and liberalism of the Liberal Democrats.

Although UK political parties are rooted in ideology, they're also what's termed a *broad church*, meaning they aren't slavish devotees to their ideologies and instead are practical, bending what they do to the prevailing mood of the public.

The ideologies of the main UK political parties are related to the class from which they draw their main support. For example, the Labour Party draws much of its support from the working class. Socialism is the predominant ideology among certain sections of the working class. As for the Conservatives, they draw much of their support from the upper and middle classes who have a vested interest in retaining the existing economic and political state of affairs. Liberalism is a bit different. Many of the key ideas underpinning liberalism – such as the importance of individual freedom – are supported by just about everyone in society, but many of the people who are most passionate about it are involved in the law or education.

Ideologies are all about 'isms', such as socialism, Marxism or conservatism. The mania for tacking on an 'ism' can sometimes apply to policies pursued by previous prime ministers (PMs) if they happen to have an ideological theme running through them. For example, Conservative PM Margaret Thatcher's policies were referred to as Thatcherism and Labour PM Tony Blair's as Blairism. In fact, if you're a politician and you have an 'ism' named after you, you know you're making a real impact on the political scene of the country.

Liberalising the world: The march of the Western democratic model

As recently as the 1940s the overwhelming majority of the world's population lived in undemocratic political systems. Since the end of the Second World War and the demise of communism in Russia and the Eastern bloc in the 1990s, the number of countries worldwide that you can class as democratic has increased many times over. What's called Western-style democracy, rooted in the ideologies of liberalism, has blossomed so much that for the first time in human history nearly the majority of the world's population now lives in a democracy. The reason democracy has taken off is that the ideology of liberalism that goes hand in glove with it resonates very strongly with people from all corners of the globe. For example, you can see a free press, the belief in government by consent, and equality under the law enshrined in the constitutions of many newly democratised states.

Focusing on Freedom with Liberalism

The British are among the most free people on the planet. You're free to say largely what you want, write what you like (as long as it's not *libellous*, in other words a false statement expressed as fact that harms an individual), travel as you see fit and choose who governs you. Add to this the fact that Britons enjoy the protection of a long-standing and deep-rooted legal system and you can easily see why people describe Britain, like America, as the land of the free.

Now these freedoms and individual rights didn't come about overnight; they were built up over centuries. Along with these freedoms grew the ideology of liberalism that runs through much of British politics today.

These are the main principles of liberalism:

- **Popular consent:** Effective government can only work if it operates with the consent of the majority of people in the country.
- **Equality:** People of every gender and race are equal, which means everyone has the same voting rights and access to justice through the law.
- **Individual liberty:** Citizens have certain basic rights such as freedom from imprisonment without criminal charges and the right to free speech. Ideally, these rights are enshrined in a written constitution but not always (in the UK, people's rights are guaranteed through a patchwork of laws and customs; see Chapter 12 for more).

- **Economic freedom:** People should be encouraged to set up businesses, and create and retain wealth. Liberals also like to see low taxes.
- **Small government:** If people are truly to be free, it follows that government should keep as much as possible out of their business and personal lives.

The roots of the liberal ideology date back a long time. Seventeenth-century English philosopher John Locke espoused the liberal principles of individual liberty and equality. Liberalism's view of economic freedom and belief in the free market is rooted in the writings of the great economist Adam Smith, who argued in the early 19th century for free markets and small government.

Exploring the origins of socialism

Historians and those wacky, laugh-a-minute political scientists often disagree about when socialism as an idea first sprang up in the UK. Some look for its roots way back in the Middle Ages among popular uprisings such as the Peasants' Revolt in 1381, when tens of thousands of ordinary Britons took up arms and marched on London, demanding better pay and an end to being bossed around by the rich landowners. Others look to the English Civil War of the mid-17th century, when a revolution led to the execution of Charles I and the propagation, through radicals using the printing presses, of all sorts of extraordinary ideas – for back then – such as communal ownership of land and even votes for men who didn't own land. One individual even suggested votes for women, but he was promptly locked up for being, according to the authorities, mad!

Whenever socialism was first espoused, it was definitely in the UK by Victorian times. During the late 18th and throughout the 19th century, Britain went through what's called the Industrial Revolution. In short, a small population that mostly worked on the land and lived in the countryside to produce food shifted to become a larger population, most of whom worked in industries such as cotton, coal and steel, and lived in large urban centres. This transition was far from easy and the living standards of most of the UK population actually got far worse during the Industrial Revolution while the factory owners got very rich indeed.

The average life expectancy fell for much of the period of the Industrial Revolution. For example, in 1839 in Liverpool, records show that the average man lived for only 19 years – that's 10 years less than in Ancient Egypt, 3,000 years earlier. Life in industrialising England was mostly harsh and short.

But workers didn't take this change in their circumstances lying down; they started to agitate for better pay and living conditions. They did this by forming trade unions and within this movement you can see the clearest signs of a socialist ideology developing. Large groups of workers started to talk not just about better pay and conditions but also about how they could change the way in which business was conducted and the country as a whole.

The ideology of liberalism is most strongly rooted in the Liberal Democrats, but it also influences the policies of the Labour and Conservative parties. For example, the liberal principles of economic freedom and small government are key components of modern Conservative Party ideology.

Liberalism is a very old ideology and the interpretation of it by politicians has changed over that time. In the 19th century, for instance, leading liberal politicians used to argue that only through a free, unfettered market could true liberalism be found. These days, adherents to liberalism tend to focus on the need to protect and extend civil liberties and promote greater democracy and equality in society, even if this actually means bigger government and curtailing the free market.

Many of the UK's most prominent pressure groups share the ideology of liberalism. Take Liberty, for instance (the clue is in the name, of course!), led by the prominent campaigner Shami Chakrabarti. The organisation speaks out very loudly when the government does things that it believes damage civil liberties.

Joining Together for the Greater Good: Socialism in the UK

Socialism arose from what was widely seen as massive inequalities brought about by the unbridled capitalism of the Industrial Revolution (see the nearby sidebar, 'Exploring the origins of socialism'). These ideas are the basis of socialism and they still have a very strong pull in British politics today.

Socialists strive for the following:

- An equal share of wealth so that land and industry is owned by the many rather than the few.
- An end to the exploitation of workers by bosses and the promotion of greater sexual equality in society as a whole.
- Making the job of government and communities to help those in most need.
- Raising educational and health standards across the whole population rather than just among a privileged few.
- The better organisation of society through rational government planning rather than reliance on capitalism and its market forces.

Socialism is a very big ideology, but what do I mean by big? Well, it has an all-encompassing vision that government should do no less than bring about a fair society and an economy built on the idea of sharing evenly, not on personal wealth and acquisition. Socialism is an alternative – to capitalism – way of organising society.

A fundamental trait of socialism is how it views competition between people. Capitalists see competition as desirable because it means that each individual strives to be the best at acquiring wealth, for example. Socialists, on the other hand, don't like competition because it suppresses the human desire to co-operate. They believe that people and society as a whole achieve more through collective actions rather than by acting alone, motivated by personal profit.

Focusing on the successes of socialism

Despite well over a century of socialism in the UK, looking around you today you notice that vast inequality still exists. However, socialists have scored some major successes and have done so by gaining political power through the election of Labour governments during the 20th century.

Some of the major victories for socialism in the UK include

- Recognising trade unions
- Setting up the National Health Service (NHS)
- Providing free education for all up to age 18
- Building large amounts of social housing and paying welfare benefits
- Improving pay and conditions for workers

Socialists believe in a *collective worker consciousness.* This term means that people from the same background, working more often than not in industry, believe in the same ideals and hold similar ambitions for how they'd like the economy and wider society to be run.

You don't need socialists to be in government in order to see socialism promoted through government policy. If enough people share socialist principles in a democracy, you find that politicians of whatever political party respond to this and design their policies so as to appeal to these voters. For example, after the Second World War right up until the election of Margaret Thatcher in 1979, all Conservative governments followed policies that may be considered to have socialist ideology behind them, such as closing grammar schools and forming comprehensive schools instead.

Rebranding socialism: New Labour

The ideology of socialism was key to the forming of the Labour Party. In fact, until recently most Labour Members of Parliament (MPs) would have proudly said that they were socialists and that they wanted British society to be organised along socialist lines.

But times have changed and the ideology of socialism is now less important in the Labour Party. In its efforts to appeal to as wide a group of Britons as possible in order to get into government and thereby gain power, Labour has come to accept some of what capitalism has to offer. This happened most noticeably under the leadership of Neil Kinnock and Tony Blair.

Blair, in particular, believed that the socialist message propounded by Labour didn't take account of how British society had changed in the 1980s and 1990s. The old working class, which had been the bedrock of socialism, had become fragmented and the old industries that had sustained this working class had died away. What replaced the working class was a society focused on more capitalist ideals of individual property ownership and wealth acquisition – particularly under Conservative prime minister Margaret Thatcher. (I talk more about the Iron Lady, as she was nicknamed, in the 'Changing conservatism: The Thatcher revolution' section, later in this chapter.)

As a result of this change in society, Tony Blair went about reforming the Labour Party and shifting many of its policies away from adherence to socialist ideals to instead accept capitalism and shave off its rough edges so as to create a more equal and fair society. Blairism, as this transformation of Labour Party ideology became known, proved very popular and Labour went on to win three general elections on the trot, in 1997, 2001 and 2005. Blair even rebranded the Labour Party, calling it New Labour instead. However, following election defeat in 2010, Labour moved back to the left of British politics under the leadership of Ed Miliband by calling for measures such as price controls on energy bills and renationalising the railways. At the time people saw this as a way for the Labour leadership to reconnect with their core support.

Blairism is also often referred to as *the third way*. Put simply, this term means neither strictly capitalist nor socialist. The idea is to create a society in which individuals can become rich through hard work if they want but that looks after those less fortunate at the same time. Many people who are avowed socialists don't see Blair's third way as a strand of socialist ideology at all.

When Tony Blair became leader in 1994, one of the first things he did was change the constitution of the Labour Party. He got rid of Clause IV of its constitution, which called for the 'common ownership of the means of production, distribution and exchange'. This phrase basically means the government should own the railways, hospitals, industries and even the banks and use them to bring about a society organised along socialist lines. Blair's ditching of Clause IV was a sure sign that Labour was moving away from its socialist roots. On being elected in 1997, Tony Blair famously said: 'We were elected as New Labour and we will govern as New Labour.'

The modern Labour Party follows a watered-down version of socialism, looking to create a more equal society but at the same time allow people the freedom to become wealthy and gain privileges such as private health care or education if they want.

Stirring things up: Revolutionary socialism

In the UK, socialists generally have tried to achieve their goals through largely peaceful and democratic means such as trade union action and mass support of the Labour Party. For a fair proportion of the last 60 years, in fact, the Labour Party has been the party of government, which means that the socialist ideology has had considerable influence.

However, some socialists believe that this reliance on democratic methods has been a bit of a waste of time, and that the vision offered by socialism has been watered down by Labour politicians looking to garner enough votes to get into government. These people would like to see a revolution overturning some of the UK's political institutions – such as the monarchy and Houses of Parliament – and replacing them with a government whose aim is to bring about a socialist society.

Revolutionary socialism has had some appeal in the UK; for example, in some parts of the trade unions, and what was called the Militant tendency of the Labour Party in the 1970s and early 1980s. In the main, however, revolutionary socialism hasn't gained much credence in the UK. But outside of the UK, in countries such as Cuba, China and most notably Russia, revolutions have occurred where a variant of socialist ideology called communism has come to the fore.

Looking far left: Marxism and communism

Globally, many people live in what are called Marxist or communist regimes. Marxism and communism are very similar ideologies and are simply an extreme variant of socialism.

Basically, Marxists and communists believe that capitalism is unjust and must be swept away – overthrown, if you like. Instead of capitalism, with its reliance on enterprise and business, they believe that the government should own everything – such as land and industry – on behalf of the people. In effect, they direct all individual effort towards producing better living standards for everyone rather than just for themselves.

Communism is a variant of Marxism and is defined as the community as a whole owning all property rather than individuals, with each person working for the common benefit according to his skill set. Communists in effect are the political embodiment of Marxist theory. Karl Marx and Friedrich Engels thought up the ideas, and the communists put them into practice in countries like Russia, China and Cuba.

By nature, Marxism and communism are revolutionary socialism, in that adherents believe in bringing about change by direct action and overturning the current political situation through revolution. Generally, Marxists and communists believe that the working class needs to be educated about the ways in which capitalists are exploiting them. Then, through this education, the workers will be radicalised and look to start a revolution through direct action.

Marxism gets its name from the great political thinker Karl Marx (1818–83). Marx was German but lived most of his life in England, observing at first hand the Industrial Revolution and the worsening living conditions of many British workers. These observations prompted Marx and his friend and fellow political thinker, Friedrich Engels, to write an analysis of capitalism and suggest that the workers needed to revolt, overturn their current society and build one based on principles of common ownership. Among the books published by Marx and Engels are *Das Kapital* and *The Communist Manifesto*.

Generally, British socialists believe in working within the political system to bring about their goals, but Marxists and communists argue that the whole system is corrupt and needs to be brought down and replaced. These days, very few people in Britain hold Marxist and communist views. In fact, membership of the British Communist Party is tiny.

Keeping with Tradition: Conservatism

A strong strand of conservatism is evident in the British psyche, and this is embodied in the Conservative Party – one of the big three UK political parties (which I talk about in depth in Chapter 8).

Conservatives believe in the following:

- Keeping Britain's political institutions intact
- Free market capitalism
- The right of everyone to own property
- Small government that doesn't interfere in people's lives

Whereas socialists and Marxists would like to see Britain's society radically reshaped or even overturned, Conservatives would like what they see as best about Britain to be retained.

Uniting under one nation conservatism

Conservative ideology may be about small government, free markets and the right to property ownership but it also states that all these 'freedoms' come with responsibilities. For example, people who do well and make money should have to pay a bit of tax so that those who are less fortunate can have welfare, health care and education.

Another tenet of what is called *one nation conservatism* is that, although small government should leave people largely alone to get on with their lives, the idea of the nation state should be a strong, unifying one. In addition, many Conservatives believe that government has less of a role to play in the economy but more instead in upholding order in society, so Conservatives often campaign for more police and harsher sentencing of criminals.

To a large extent one nation conservatism is quite close to Tony Blair's third way New Labour approach (I talk about this in 'Rebranding socialism: New Labour', earlier in this chapter). One nation Conservatives believe, like Blair, that the rougher edges of capitalism need to be smoothed down – wealth creation is good but with money comes responsibility to your fellow citizens.

Reforming with a small 'r'

Although a large part of Conservative ideology concerns the idea of retaining traditions and the prevailing political situation in a bid to promote harmony within society, this doesn't mean that Conservatives don't ever reform. Conservatives may be opposed to the idea of radicalism and revolution proposed by people following the Marxist or communist ideologies, but nevertheless they look to gradualist reforms that take account of Britain's past and its traditions.

Conservatives also say that they like to take a pragmatic approach to society's problems. For example, generally Conservative governments make fewer laws than Labour ones, preferring to let industries self-regulate rather than have regulation imposed by a central government. Take financial regulation in the UK, for instance. The Conservative governments in the 1980s and 1990s relied on banks and insurers to self-regulate how they dealt with customers; however Labour, from 1997 onwards, required banks and insurers to adhere to stricter regulations, although that didn't stop the credit crunch in 2007 and the global recession that followed. If Conservatives do reform, it tends to be with a small 'r'.

Changing conservatism: The Thatcher revolution

Having said that Conservatives reform with a small 'r' in the preceding section, the exception was the prime ministership of Margaret Thatcher between 1979 and 1990. Thatcher, who due to her tough stance on issues gained the nickname the 'Iron Lady', was elected when Britain was in economic and political turmoil. The country was nearly bankrupt and the trade unions had spent the winter striking. Against the odds, Thatcher set about sweeping away many of the policies that Conservative and Labour governments had pursued since the end of the Second World War. The main tenets of what became known as Thatcherism were the following:

- Reduce the power of the trade unions.
- Encourage individuals to start their own businesses.
- Lower taxes and reduce government interference in daily life.
- Restore national pride through having a strong foreign policy and defence.

Boiled down, many of the bullet points of Thatcherism look very close to core Conservative ideology, but Thatcher differed in the speed at which she tried to move the country in a conservative direction. For decades the country had been moving in a more socialist direction and in a few short years she shifted this around. No traditional conservative ideology of gradualism existed in Thatcher's approach. Instead, Thatcher was something of an oxymoron – a revolutionary conservative.

Margaret Thatcher was a highly divisive figure in the country. However she still managed to win three landslide election victories in the 1979, 1983 and 1987 general elections.

Modernising the Conservatives

After 13 years out of government the Conservatives finally regained power in 2010 as part of a coalition with the Liberal Democrats. This had a lot to do with the leader of the party, David Cameron, who'd looked to modernise the party since his election as party leader in 2006. The main thrust of his modernisation programme was to make the party more attuned to environmental challenges such as climate change and to try to ensure the party represented those people with jobs and aspirations, helping them to get on in life. Cameron's programme to modernise was a limited success, but he did become prime minister in 2010.

Examining Alternative Politics

Think of politics as a mighty river with lots of smaller streams of ideology running into it. Some of these ideologies rise and fall in popularity. They may not find their expression through a particular political party, as socialism has at times through the Labour party, but they're still important because they help form the opinions of millions of Britons as well as wider political debate.

Focusing on the far right: Fascism

Defining *fascism* isn't easy, but basically it concerns completely subordinating individual rights and freedoms to the power of the state. In effect, citizens in a fascist state are meant to be utterly patriotic and believe that their nation is top dog; they must be willing to sacrifice whatever is required – even their own lives – in the cause of advancing the power and prestige of that state. Pretty scary, eh? The fascist ideology goes further too. Fascists believe in a strong military and that conquest of other states can be a good thing.

Fascist ideology is in essence a racist one (its adherents believe in the superiority of their own nation and race; for example, the Nazis despising Jewish people and Mussolini arguing that his country should be able to invade Ethiopia because Italians were superior to Africans). What's more, fascists view democracy as weak and best got rid of, to be replaced by a strong leader able to lead the people.

Fascism is often seen as being at the other end of the political spectrum from Marxism and communism. But they actually share a common theme – that individuality isn't as important as advancement of the working class, in the case of Marxism/communism, or the unity of the state, in the case of fascism.

To be frank, if I was drawing up a dinner party guest list I think I'd leave both fascists and Marxists/communists off.

As with Marxism and communism, fascism hasn't gained much popularity in the UK, although the British National Party (BNP) is often dubbed as fascist by its critics due to its extolling of racist and nationalistic policies. (See Chapter 8 for the inside track on the BNP.) In fact, Britain doesn't do extreme politics well at all – which is a relief. A little like the nation's famous weather, British politics tends to be quite temperate and lacks extremes.

Fascism may sound very odd and frankly a bit far-fetched, but back in the 1930s and 1940s over half the population of western Europe lived in fascist states such as Germany, Italy and Spain. Eventually, Britain, America and Russia defeated fascist political regimes in the Second World War. But prior to this, fascism even had some supporters in Britain. The British Union of Fascists, led by the charismatic Oswald Mosley, used to organise marches attended by thousands of ordinary Britons.

Looking into the darkness: Totalitarian regimes

When an extremist leader – either from left or right – comes to power, it usually leads to the formation of a totalitarian regime. In short, this means that all power is concentrated in the hands of a leader or group of leaders and these leaders can't be removed by democratic means – an election. They have ultimate power and don't tolerate political opponents.

Totalitarian regimes are often propped up by a strong military and covert police force. Even the laws of the land are either altered or become subservient to the leader or leaders of a totalitarian regime.

Probably the best-known example of totalitarianism was Nazi Germany in the 1930s and 1940s. It was a regime with a fascist ideology and a supreme leader (the Führer, Adolf Hitler). At the same time, in Russia, Josef Stalin also headed a totalitarian regime, but this followed not a fascist but a communist ideology.

Although Britain doesn't do extremism very well, at times in British history the leadership can be seen as totalitarian. For example, many of the country's monarchs exercised huge power barely checked by legal niceties, and they ruled with a strong military and through fear. However, in the past few centuries, with the falling away of the power of the monarchy and the growth in parliamentary democracy, the British people have fortunately avoided falling prey to a totalitarian regime.

Looking to the heavens: Theocracy

Some would say that religion is the ultimate ideology because it maps out a way people should live their lives. Occasionally, religion becomes such a compelling force in society that leading adherents to the religion run the government according to religious principles. Those at the top of organised religious structures are also at the top of government and in effect run the show. This type of government is called a *theocracy*.

Probably the most famous modern example of a theocracy in action is the Iranian regime. Iran is effectively run by a group of leading Muslim clerics who dictate policy according to their take on religious texts.

If Britain were a theocracy, logically the leading bishops in the Church of England would be running the government. They don't run the government, however; elected politicians do.

Pulling everything apart: Anarchism

Anarchy in ancient Greek means 'no rule' and anarchists are people who are opposed to all forms of governmental authority. In effect, a true anarchist believes in absolutely nothing except that government should be torn down, which would then allow people to get on with their lives without interference.

Many anarchists are prepared to take what they'd call direct action, which means destroying property and even attacking elected politicians. In the past anarchist groups have carried out violent terrorist acts. Most recently they've staged mass street protests at meetings of the G8 and G20 groups of world leaders (this is a conference of the leaders of the world's largest nations by economic size; see Chapter 20 for more). These global shindigs have often taken place against a backdrop of street violence caused by anarchists. Other groups of protestors, including peaceful environmentalists, have complained bitterly that their protest message has been lost in the violence.

Anarchism has some major drawbacks in that it's by nature both incoherent and disorganised; therefore, the destruction of the governmental system that it wants is nigh on impossible to obtain. How, for instance, can a mob of people with all sorts of different backgrounds and personal agendas achieve anything substantial against an organised government, military and police force?

Releasing the bonds: Feminism

According to feminists, oppression of women by men runs throughout society – in the workplace, in politics and at home. Feminism itself is an ideology that can often have an influence on politics. It's based around the ambition to establish more rights and legal protection for women and to combat the subjugation of women.

Looking back through history it's not hard to see that feminists have a point. For example, women in the UK didn't get the vote on the same terms as men until 1928, and even today women earn nearly 30 per cent less on average than men.

Few can doubt that we still live in a sexist society, but nonetheless equality between the genders has made great strides. First up was the suffrage movement, which led the successful campaign for votes for women. Then, in the 1960s, second-wave feminism emerged, whereby the women's liberation movement agitated for equality at work and in wider society.

Political scientists have split feminists into three distinct groupings:

- **Liberal feminists** argue that women and men are equal, full stop, and the government must pass laws to ensure this equality happens in practice.
- **Socialist feminists** argue that the oppression of women is a by-product of capitalism. In order to change the lot of women it's necessary to change both the economy and society so that they're based on socialist principles. (I cover socialism in 'Joining Together for the Greater Good: Socialism in the UK', earlier in this chapter.)
- **Radical feminists** argue that women are in many ways better than men and that if women were in charge aggressive – male – pursuits such as war wouldn't happen.

Many people describe themselves as being feminists without also saying they agree with either liberal, socialist or radical feminism. Although feminism is an ideology, it's also an approach to everyday life, a general belief in equality of the sexes.

Saving the planet: Environmentalism

Very few people now doubt now that the planet's environment is under threat from the side-effects of human activities. Some people respond to this emerging threat by looking to cut down their impact on the environment;

for example, by taking fewer flights or driving a less polluting car. Others go further and adopt an environmental ideology. Put simply, *environmentalism* is about finding a way for people and the planet to co-exist. Environmentalists want an economic and social system based on a sustainable relationship with the planet.

Environmentalists

- View capitalism with distrust, because companies are responsible for much pollution and using up the planet's resources.
- Regard economic growth as less important than preserving the health of the planet. Being rich is pointless if sea levels are rising and life is endangered.
- Expect governments to actively try to change individual behaviour towards the environment, ensuring they minimise the damage they cause.

In recent years environmentalism has been on the rise as the true scale of climate change has come into sharper focus. Environmentalism as an ideology is currently gaining credence in the West, with more and more people becoming concerned about the planet's well-being.

In British politics, the party seen as representing the environmental ideology most closely is the Green Party, which I talk about in Chapter 8. However, all the big three UK political parties – Labour, Conservative and Liberal Democrats – have placed a greater emphasis on environmentally friendly policies in recent general elections.

Sitting at the top: Monarchy

Unusually for a major modern democracy, Britain is still a monarchy. The institution of monarchy was once based on an ideology called the divine right of kings. It was the dominant ideology in Britain right up until the English Civil War in the 1640s, when a parliamentary army took on the king and won. This ideology is much older than socialism or conservatism and, to be frank, is a little strange, so strap yourself in for this one.

As the name suggests, the divine right of kings means that the monarch draws authority to rule not from parliaments or elections but directly from God. The monarch is supposed to be, in effect, God's representative on earth and therefore everything he does is right and he must be obeyed at all times – yes, that is some sort of ego trip.

Nowadays, no-one believes in the divine right of kings, yet we still have a monarch. However, in a very British-style compromise, the monarch has few actual powers and the role is largely ceremonial. See Chapter 12 for more on the monarch and the British constitution.

Understanding Why the UK Doesn't Do Extremism

The British don't tend to do extreme ideologies like fascism or communism and plenty of good reasons exist for that. The UK

- **Is a long-established democracy:** The UK is one of the oldest and sturdiest democracies in the world, which makes the job of those who'd like to subvert it very hard indeed.
- **Has seen other countries go awry:** Britain fought a long bloody war against Nazi Germany between 1939 and 1945. The memory of that war and the crimes of the Nazi regime means most people in the UK discredit far-right ideology.
- **Is a rich, successful country:** History suggests radical ideologies tend to gather wide appeal following military defeats or economic turmoil. Although Britain is no longer as powerful as it was in the 1800s, it's very economically stable, which means it doesn't present fertile ground for revolution.
- **Has political parties that appeal to a wide range of citizens:** The UK's political parties are well organised with large memberships and have deep roots in local communities. This makes it difficult for smaller, more extreme parties to beat them at election time.
- **Has a unique electoral system:** The UK has a first-past-the-post electoral system, which means those candidates polling the highest number of votes win seats. This makes it harder for smaller parties to get seats in parliament.
- **Follows the rule of law:** In the UK, everyone is equal before the law and subject to it, which means that British society has an in-built system of redress that reduces the chances of totalitarianism and tyranny.

Britain is often referred to as a *liberal democracy*, which simply means the country is a democracy – where people get to vote to decide who governs the country – and it has strong traits associated with liberalism, such as primacy of the rule of law and acknowledgement of the importance of individual freedoms and liberties. Much of the world doesn't live in a liberal democracy but many peoples would like to.

Chapter 5

Forming the British Political State

In This Chapter

- Building up the power of monarchy
- Transferring power from the monarch to parliament
- Looking at the forming of political parties and the role of the prime minister
- Breaking with traditions: ending the power of the Lords, and giving votes to all

In this chapter I look at the big political events that have got us to where we are today – a democracy of some 60 million people with votes for the majority, a free press, an independent judiciary and civil liberties.

From monarchs to Machiavellian prime ministers, this is the chapter to look at for the lowdown on the key steps on the road to the British politics of today.

Getting to Grips with the Normans: From Conquest to Magna Carta

The date 1066 is etched into the history books of Britain – and throughout the world – because it's the year William, Duke of Normandy, in one of the great big gambles of history, successfully invaded England and defeated the Saxon King Harold at the Battle of Hastings. William became known simply as the Conqueror (he'd previously been known as 'the bastard', so this must have been a welcome change). He gave tidy portions of England to the hundreds of French knights who'd helped him, for them to rule on his behalf.

Make no bones about it, the Norman invasion was brutal. The Saxon upper classes suffered the indignity of losing much of their own lands and having to submit to their new Norman rulers, who even spoke a different language. As Saxons slid further down the social scale, they not only saw much of their native culture and customs eradicated but also had to pay substantial taxes and live under a multitude of oppressive laws. All in all, post-Norman conquest England wasn't a happy place. William and his descendants ruled over what was for much of the time a violent and totalitarian regime – no liberal democracy back then.

A succession of good, mediocre and downright rubbish kings led some of the descendants of the Norman knights and those Saxons who still had some land and money to question whether the king really should have total control over the country. In fact, in the reign of the particularly inept King John, in 1215, the great barons of the land rose up in mutiny and forced the king to sign an agreement called Magna Carta – meaning Great Charter – which limited (a little) the power of the king to go around killing or imprisoning those he didn't like without first having them tried in a court of law.

In effect, *Magna Carta* was a statement of basic rights, which in theory bound the king to act within the law of the land. In particular it set up the right of *habeas corpus*, which means the right to appeal against imprisonment.

Magna Carta is widely seen as the first major constitutional document in the Western world – coming a whole five and a half centuries before the American Declaration of Independence.

Although Magna Carta was very important, it didn't mean that everyone in England lived in peace without fear of being wrongly imprisoned or killed without due process. The monarch was still at the top of the tree and had enormous power for the next four and a half centuries and could do pretty much anything.

The legacy of Henry II

Henry II, the great-grandson of William the Conqueror, ruled England, parts of Wales and Scotland and even large chunks of western France in the second half of the 12th century. His reign was a long and successful one and he was one of the great state builders of British history. For starters, he set up the magistrates' courts, which still operate today, trying people accused of minor criminal offences. He moved to increase the power of the monarch over the Church and started a system of transparent tax collection. Henry's reforms helped form the basis of how the monarchy governed for the next five centuries.

Doing the Splits: Church and State Clash

For the five centuries after the Norman conquest the monarch wasn't the only powerbroker in the country. The Roman Catholic Church was also a big deal, with huge tracts of land, the right to raise taxes from the public and even its own system of courts to try people who'd broken its laws – called *canon law*. In effect, the Roman Catholic Church was a state within a state. For example, priests couldn't be tried by the king's courts but only by the Church courts.

Now for most of the time the monarch and the Church got on hunky dory. But when the pope refused to let Henry VIII divorce his wife, Catherine of Aragon, the monarch turned on the Church with a vengeance. He had Church lands seized, closed ancient monasteries, and melted the gold and silver they held for coins. What's more, Henry had himself installed as head of the Church, which meant he no longer obeyed the pope.

The battle between Church and monarch was a major turning point in Britain's history. It increased the power and wealth of the monarchy enormously, and because the Church land was sold to wealthy merchants, it also created a new group of landowners, who in time went into parliament and took part in government.

The break with the Roman Catholic Church and the construction of what's called the Church of England, with the monarch as head of the Church, is called the *Reformation*.

The legal framework for the Church of England was set up in the 1530s and 40s, and most of the Church land seizures took place then. It wasn't a straightforward transition; in fact, once Henry VIII died, his daughter Mary reversed the process and again England became a Catholic country. However she died soon after and younger sister (Elizabeth I) chose to break with the Roman Catholic Church once more.

The monarch is still head of the Church of England but nowadays the Church tends to play less of a role in public life, mainly due to a fall in religious observance by the UK population as a whole. At the start of the 20th century it was estimated that the majority of people attended a religious service at least once a week, whereas today fewer than one in ten do.

Gearing Up for Revolution: Parliament Takes on the King and Wins

The English parliament was set up by Henry II in the 12th century as a means by which to more effectively govern the country and raise taxes. Over the next few centuries the power of parliament gradually increased because the monarch needed the help of its members to raise more taxes to run the government.

Working hand in hand

Most of the time the monarch and parliament worked well together, pursuing policies that were widely agreed, particularly over the break with the Roman Catholic religion and its replacement with a Protestant one, with the monarch as head not just of the state but the Church too. Elections to the House of Commons – although not the Lords – were held regularly but only landowners got to vote (a very far cry from the liberal democracy of today). But apart from sporadic rebellions and the nasty Wars of the Roses in the late 15th century (between rival claimants for the English throne), the country was at peace and government worked well.

Chafing under Charles I and enduring Cromwell

Then along came the diminutive, lisping and rather useless Charles I. He hated ruling with the agreement of parliament and tried to go it alone; at the same time, he raised what were seen as punitive and potentially illegal taxes and even flirted with the Catholic faith, which didn't go down well with Protestants in parliament. The Members of Parliament, many of whom were also rich and powerful merchants and landowners, became increasingly fed up with Charles's style of kingship. Eventually, in 1642, civil war broke out. In 1649, Charles, having been defeated in the Civil War, was executed and the country became a *republic* (without a monarchy) for 11 years under the austere Oliver Cromwell.

Oliver Cromwell was a great general who'd risen through the ranks of the parliamentary army and ultimately swept to power as a military dictator. He fought wars on the Continent and in Scotland and Ireland. He was devoutly religious, even banning some Christmas festivities – bah humbug!

When old Scrooge Cromwell died he was replaced by Charles II, who was more politically astute than his father, Charles I. Charles II for a time restored the powers of the monarchy, but after he popped his clogs another short, useless rule, this time by James II, meant another civil war was in the offing. However, James was replaced in a relatively bloodless coup in 1688 by the Dutch King William of Orange.

Reaping the benefits of the Glorious Revolution

But the real result of the Glorious Revolution, as it became known, was that parliament was able to wrest control of the levers of state from the monarch. The Glorious Revolution came about after the unpopular Catholic king, James II, was overthrown in a coup led by leading landowners and parliamentarians. They offered William of Orange – a Dutch Protestant ruler – the English throne and he became King William III. The fact that a monarch had been deposed and a new one installed, in effect by parliament, was crucial, because it showed where the political power now lay. In future, although monarchs would at times have real power, they would govern the country only with the agreement of parliament. In effect, power shifted from a single monarch to the members of an elected parliament and the unelected House of Lords.

By the reign of Charles I (1625–49), England had swallowed up Wales and, although Scotland still had its own parliament, Charles was king of both England and Scotland, which was a big step towards the eventual union of the old enemies.

Scotland joined with England and Wales to form the United Kingdom in 1707. In the run-up to the signing of the Act of Union many people in Scotland were bankrupted by a failed attempt to establish a colony in North America. In return for the English government paying off the nation's debt, the Scottish parliament agreed to vote for the Act of Union, and itself out of existence. Scotland didn't have its own parliament again until 1999 (see Chapters 17 and 18 for more).

Throwing Political Parties into the Mix

From the Glorious Revolution to the forming of political parties wasn't a great leap. As power became concentrated in parliament, factions arose behind certain policies and certain individuals.

These early political parties weren't parties as you'd recognise them today. They were more a matter of powerful Members of Parliament and wealthy lords coming together, either to push through a piece of legislation or because they shared some common interests. Over time, these fluid factions started to form into what we'd call parties.

The first two great political parties were the Whigs and the Tories – the forerunners of today's Liberal Democrats and Conservatives. In the 18th and 19th centuries they became bitter rivals, but when one of the parties came to power they had to share out government jobs and privileged positions. Why were the Whigs and Tories at such loggerheads? Well, mainly it was because of big religious differences. The Tories were generally Catholic or Anglican and the Whigs were from a more Calvinist or radical Protestant tradition. Religion in the 18th and 19th centuries was a big deal and it was the root of the enmity between the two parties. (Turn to Chapter 8 for more on the formation and evolution of Britain's political parties.)

Ending the Power of the Lords

Back in 1908 Lloyd George – later a prime minister – was chancellor of the exchequer. He announced a radical budget that for the first time paid people an old-age pension and guaranteed some limited welfare payments for those less fortunate.

The bigwigs in the House of Lords hated this budget and blocked it. At the time, the House of Lords could in effect veto any laws drawn up by the House of Commons. But the Liberal government was having none of this and introduced the *Parliament Act* in 1911, which did away with the veto power the House of Lords enjoyed. As a result of the Parliament Act, the House of Lords has the right to scrutinise proposed laws drawn up in the Commons and to ask members of that house to think again three times. If the Lords rejects a law a third time, the House of Commons can say enough is enough and the proposed Act passes into law despite opposition from the Lords. The Parliament Act was a big deal because it finally established the primacy of the House of Commons over the House of Lords as the key legislative body. Any party holding a majority of seats in that house has huge power.

The retreat of the Lords has continued, and now it's little more than a debating chamber. Even its membership has changed: the Labour government of Tony Blair removed many of the hereditary lords – people whose right to sit in the Lords is passed down from parents and not through being appointed by the monarch. See Chapter 13 for how the House of Lords works and what role it plays in the day-to-day government of the UK.

A member of the House of Lords is often referred to as a *peer*, and no, it has nothing to do with your mates.

Expanding the Franchise: Democracy Arrives in Britain

In many people's eyes Britain didn't become a fully fledged democracy until after the second decade of the 20th century when the government finally granted half the population, women, the vote. Prior to this date only men were able to vote, and turning the clock back even further into the 19th century, only men who owned property in the form of a house or land. The overwhelming majority of the population didn't have a say in who governed them.

Before the expansion of the *franchise*, the right to vote, the number of people who actually had a vote in some parliamentary constituencies was relatively small. Whereas these days some seats have 60,000 to 70,000 electors, back in the 17th, 18th and early 19th centuries elections involving a few hundred people were commonplace because the population was much smaller and only property owners could vote. Having such a small electorate meant that the ballots were open to being rigged, with wealthy landowners bribing electors to vote for their candidates. This phenomenon became known as the *rotten boroughs*, and a lot of them existed.

Earning a stake

The reasoning behind limiting voting just to property owners went that only they had an interest, or stake, in the country – merely being born British and living in Britain didn't give you a stake.

Fighting the good fight: Emmeline Pankhurst

Emmeline Pankhurst was the leader of the British women's *suffrage* – right to vote – movement in the late 19th and early 20th century. She started out by hosting public debates to discuss votes for women and trying to persuade leading politicians of the time of the justness of their cause. But Pankhurst became convinced that she needed a more direct approach to shake up society so that votes for women would shoot to the top of the political agenda. To this end, activists inspired by Pankhurst – and her own daughters – took part in vocal protests, threw stones through windows, chained themselves to railings and even indulged in arson and assaults on police. Pankhurst and her activists were sentenced to repeated prison sentences but votes for women became a hot topic, and after the First World War – for the duration of which Pankhurst called off militant action – women eventually won the right to vote. In 1999, US magazine *Time* named Pankhurst as one of the most important people of the 20th century.

Overcoming this idea of only those with an interest being entitled to vote involved a long struggle. A host of political thinkers put forth the idea that all men – rarely back then did anyone say women as well – had the right to cast a vote.

As the population grew and the economy moved from being agricultural and rural to industrial and urban, what would be recognised as the working class formed. But despite their importance to the wider economy and their numerical superiority to the landowning class, they had no voting power and therefore no representation in parliament until 1884.

Mass movements of people, drawn largely from the working and to a lesser extent middle classes, in the middle of the 19th century called for more people to get the vote as well as a written bill of rights for each individual. Soon after, trade unionism started to take hold in the working classes and they too wanted votes for all. The politicians, worried about the potential for revolution, as had happened half a century earlier in France, started to make concessions to the working class, and slowly but surely the government extended the right to vote to all men, regardless of whether they were property owners or not. Simply being a male British citizen brought with it the right to vote.

Recognising the rights of women

Votes for women took longer, and many mid-Victorian politicians dismissed the idea as madness. But as the male franchise expanded and women's suffrage movements formed, a groundswell of support for votes for women took place too. However, it wasn't until after the First World War, during which women did difficult and dirty work on the home front while men were fighting in the trenches, that the majority of politicians came around to the idea of votes for women. And even then equality in the voting booth wasn't yet in place, because only women over 30 got the vote in 1918. Only in 1928 did the government grant women the vote on the same terms as men, from age 21.

Switching Parties: The Ebb and Flow of Party Influence

The government reflects the ideals of whichever party is in power at the time.

Both of the main UK political parties – Labour and Conservative – have what is called a *core vote* that turns out and votes for their chosen party election after election. The key to winning an election for either the Conservative or Labour parties is appealing outside this core vote to what's called *Middle Britain*

because their votes swing the poll, particularly bearing in mind the UK's first-past-the-post system (where candidates have only to win the largest number of votes, rather than a majority, to win the seat they're standing for).

Making a play for power: The Labour Party is born and thrives

Looking back from the early 21st century and gauging exactly how momentous and fast-changing the world of the Victorians was is difficult. In the 19th century the UK population nearly trebled and new industries rose and fell as millions migrated from the countryside to the towns and cities. Probably the closest parallel for Britain's industrialisation and modernisation is what's going on in China right now! But such massive changes inevitably bring about political change too.

In the same way that monarchs eventually found that they couldn't hold absolute power over thousands of landowners and rich merchants, those self-same landowners and rich merchants found that they couldn't hold the millions of new working class created in Victorian England in thrall.

The working classes started to become politically active, with shared ambitions and objectives such as increased pay, better working conditions, the vote, and health care and education. To help achieve some of these ambitions, workers formed unions, and from these unions came the Labour Party.

The Labour Party started to field candidates for seats in parliamentary and local government elections in the early 1900s. They didn't do well at first, but gradually more Labour MPs and councillors started to be elected, and once in office they could change things. By the 1920s the old Liberal Party was in decline and many voters had switched allegiance to Labour, so much so that in the 1928 election they won a majority of seats in the House of Commons and formed the government under their leader, Ramsay McDonald.

The first majority Labour government wasn't successful because it was soon hit with the economic cataclysm of the Great Depression of 1929–32 during which millions lost their jobs.

In fact, the Labour Party split for a while (the leadership disagreed over government spending cuts). Its leader, Ramsay McDonald, left to form a National Government made up of his supporters in the Labour Party and leading members of the Conservative Party. The big idea of the National Government was that in a time of crisis – such as the Depression and later the Second World War under Winston Churchill – politicians from all parties should come together for the greater good. However, the result was to split the Labour party in two for over a decade and make McDonald's name a byword among some in the Labour Party for treachery. But after the Second World War, with the sweet scent of military victory in the air, Labour won a landslide on the promise to provide more houses, schools, hospitals and jobs.

Playing musical chairs: Labour and the Tories swap power

As far as government power since the Second World War goes, the Labour and Conservative (Tory) parties have been playing their own version of the hokey cokey – one minute one party is in (power), the next they're out. In fact, during the 60 plus years since the end of the Second World War, the Labour and Conservative parties have spent relatively equal time in power.

In the mid-20th century the country switched from Conservative to Labour and back again every few years. More recently, from the 1980s on, Britain had first a long spell of Conservative government followed by a long spell of Labour. Some of the reasons for this slight slowing in the game of musical chairs include

- During the 1950s to the 1970s, the UK economy did badly, which always reflects on the government in power. So electors voted the current government out fairly regularly, which meant the parties traded being in power.
- After the Second World War, the Conservative and Labour parties seemed to represent very different ideologies, both of which had wide appeal and offered voters a real choice. Labour won the election in a massive landslide because it offered the voters a new vision for Britain based around the creation of a welfare state, and during the next six years the Labour prime minister Clement Attlee went about constructing the National Health Service and nationalising key industries.
- From the 1980s until the global recession of the late 2000s, the UK economy fared much better, which reflects positively on the government and encourages electors to stick with the party in power.

Over time, the Conservative and Labour parties have come together on many policies. Such consensus makes many voters wonder whether the parties differ at all and offer any real choice. When voters feel they don't really have a choice, they can become apathetic towards voting, an issue I explore in more depth in Chapter 7.

Leaving out the Lib Dems

You may have noticed that (until now) I've left out the Liberal Democrats (Lib Dems). That's because they haven't gained enough seats to form the government on their own since just after the First World War. In fact, for a large part of the post-war years they've had only a handful of MPs.

In recent elections the Lib Dems have fared better, but they're still very much the country's third biggest party and quite a long way behind the Conservative and Labour parties in terms of membership and influence. The UK electoral system doesn't favour whatever party is in third place in the polls. The Lib Dems regularly attain over 20 per cent of total votes in a general election but win under 10 per cent of the seats.

However, in 2010 the fortunes of the Lib Dems suddenly changed when neither the Conservative nor Labour party gained enough seats in the House of Commons to form a government. As a result, the Lib Dems negotiated with both the big two parties to see which one they'd like to form a coalition government with. Eventually, after five long days of tortuous negotiations, the Lib Dems chose to form a government with the Conservatives. This meant that the Lib Dems were in the big time! (See Chapter 6 for more on voting systems and why the Lib Dems lose out.)

The main advantage of a coalition government is that people from different backgrounds and representing a wide group of electors work together for the greater good. However, often coalition government can be short-lived and acrimonious. For example, the Lib–Lab pact of the mid-1970s lasted only a couple of years and senior figures from the two parties were often at loggerheads.

Concentrating Power in the Hands of the Prime Minister

The British, it seems, love having a head honcho, someone they can focus on when they think of government. In the six centuries after the Norman conquest the role was performed by the monarch. However, as parliament took over many of the powers of the monarch, prominent figures within the House of Commons or Lords became very important. Groupings that formed in parliament under these figures were the early incarnation of the Whig and Tory parties, and the leading figures in these groupings acquired jobs within government.

Although no one used the phrase *prime minister* (PM) officially until the 19th century, from the early 18th century onwards the person who led the biggest grouping of MPs or the leader of the party holding the most seats in the House of Commons was effectively the prime minister. Like most things in Britain's unwritten constitution, the role of prime minister evolved over a long period of time rather than being created on a specific day.

The prime minister forms a cabinet drawn from members of the party she represents to head up the government and divvy out jobs and titles. The post of PM has been at the top of the political tree for around 300 years. Over that time more and more power has centred on 10 Downing Street – the official home of the prime minister.

Within the cabinet the prime minister is supposed to be the 'first among equals', meaning that the PM is a member of the cabinet where each minister's views have equal weight. However, the PM is the leader of the group and in big matters the final decision rests with her.

It's hard to understate the power of the prime minister within the current political system. The incumbent gets to make appointments throughout government and largely forms government policy. That's not to say that the PM can be dictatorial or govern without consent. The PM relies on the support of cabinet members and MPs sitting in the House of Commons.

One of the biggest powers the prime minister has is to appoint members of the cabinet; in effect, the big decision-making jobs in government. Every so often the PM has a cabinet reshuffle, which involves the hiring and firing of ministers. See Chapter 14 for more on the cabinet and reshuffles.

Robert Walpole (1676–1745) is seen as Britain's first prime minister, although he wouldn't have recognised the phrase at the time. Walpole was the most prominent figure in the Whig party in the House of Commons and he was enormously powerful, acquiring jobs, titles and cash during his long career. At the height of his power he controlled the government, making appointments and handing out favours to friends and allies. He was the leader of the Whigs from 1721 to 1742, when he fell from power after a British military defeat.

Breaking Up the Union: Scotland and Wales to Go It Alone?

For much of its history the British Isles has been split into distinctive, separate and independent nations, namely, England, Scotland, Wales and Ireland. As one of these nations – England – became more powerful in terms of trade and military, the other countries, through a combination of imperialism and persuasion, joined in a political union. Four nations in effect became one. This is why Britain is also referred to as the United Kingdom.

As far as the English were concerned this union worked pretty well – although some people in the other nations may have disagreed. Great Britain, remarkably, became the most powerful nation on the globe in the 19th century, with an enormous empire. However, the Irish wanted out, and, after years of political and sometimes violent wrangling, in 1922 Ireland became independent but for the six counties in the north of Ireland, which remained within the union. Winding the clock forward about 90 years to now shows growing signs that the Scots and, to a lesser extent, the Welsh also want out of the union so as to become independent nations again.

Since 1999 the Scots and Welsh have had *devolution*, which means that they created a local parliament (Scotland) or assembly (Wales) in order to make laws that apply just to their countries.

Some say that devolution will help the union stay together, because the Scots and Welsh now have more control over their own lives and governance so they don't need complete independence. Others, though, believe that devolution is merely a prelude to independence, and that as people in Scotland and Wales get used to exercising their own power they and their elected politicians will want to go a stage further and try for full independence.

As an indicator that the latter may be true, at the 2007 Scottish general election the Scottish National Party (SNP), which wants independence, became the biggest party in the Scottish parliament and formed the Scottish government. Sure enough, in 2014 the Scots voted in a referendum over whether or not to go independent. A close-fought and often bitter campaign followed between those against and for independence. In the end Scotland voted to remain part of the United Kingdom. However, many observers believe that Scotland will be independent within a generation. See Chapter 18 for more on the great Scottish independence debate.

Alex Salmond became first minister of Scotland in April 2007 when the SNP won the highest number of seats in the Scottish general election. Salmond is considered a very capable communicator and has a large personal following, even among electors who wouldn't usually vote SNP. Salmond has been a long-time proponent of Scottish independence and is the prime mover towards that goal. In Wales the main nationalist party Plaid Cymru has also made great strides, but support among the Welsh for independence as yet is weaker than the Scots' desire to go their own way. See Chapter 8 for more on the Welsh and Scottish nationalist parties.

As for the English, growing signs exist that many people there are becoming disillusioned by the union and a system that they see as unfair, where more government spending per head goes to the Scots and Welsh than to the English.

Like the rest of the British constitution, the relationship between England and its smaller neighbours, Scotland and Wales, inevitably changes over time. Since the Norman conquest there have been periods when they've been closer together and others when they've been further apart; such ebb and flow is bound to mark all these countries' histories.

Encroaching on Britain's Turf: The European Union

Britain has been a member of the European Union since 1973. At that time the EU was called the European Economic Community and, yes, you guessed it, it was all about promoting economic growth in Europe. But since Britain joined the EEC it's increased its remit to include setting out a series of laws and rules that all members must abide by. Some senior European politicians have talked about EU member states joining together in some sort of federal European super-state. The EU itself has massively expanded its civil service and institutions and raises money from donations from its member states. Meanwhile, the EU has also become a big club, now covering 28 countries and over 400 million people from Ireland to the borders of Turkey. The EU is made up of a parliament, a commission and a council of ministers; it's a really complex setup, with hundreds of politicians and thousands of civil servants. (Chapter 21 gives you a full rundown on how the EU goes about its business.)

Gradually, the growing importance of the EU has caused major waves in British politics and is likely to do so for a long time to come. The EU is now virtually a super-state that has legal powers within the UK. In addition, some Britons looking for justice take their cases not only to UK courts but also to the European Court in Strasbourg. In short, for the first time since the Reformation and the break with the Roman Catholic Church, foreigners now have real sway over legal matters in the UK. Some welcome this move and think that many good laws come from the EU, which has helped bring about economic growth and enshrine more rights for citizens.

In 1985, the British parliament ratified the *Single European Act*. At the time this didn't cause much of a stir but it was hugely significant because the act gave laws drawn up by EU legislators equal power to those drawn up by the UK parliament.

Many within UK politics are opposed to the idea of a European super-state and want to see the UK either leave the EU or say clearly that it doesn't want to join any sort of political union. These people are *Eurosceptics*.

Britons get to vote for Members of the European Parliament in what are called European elections. Experts estimate that nearly two thirds of new laws affecting the lives of Britons result from legislation drawn up by the EU rather than the UK parliament in Westminster.

Part II

Elections and Britain's Parties

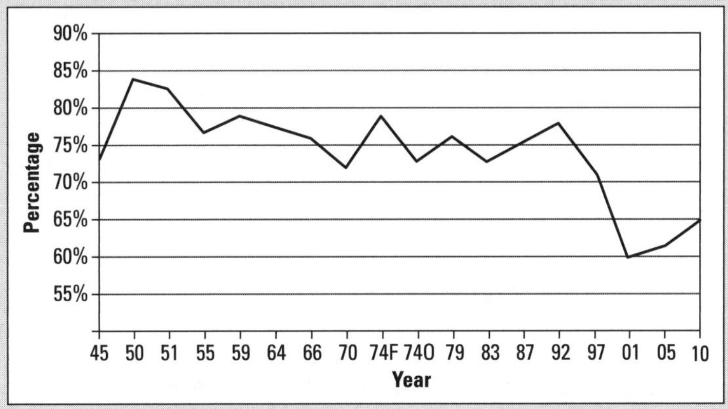

For some online extras about British Politics, head online and visit www.dummies.com/extras/britishpolitics.

In this part . . .

- Examine the process of parliamentary, local and European elections and find out more about the voting behaviour of the great British public.
- Take a good look at the political parties in Britain, from the big two (Conservative and Labour) to the minor and emerging parties.
- Find out how pressure groups exert their influence on politicians and who they are.
- Learn more about the relationship between politicians and the media.

Chapter 6

Counting the Votes: Differing Electoral Systems

In This Chapter

- Explaining first past the post
- Winning a majority of votes
- Looking at proportional representation

Elections are a big deal in the UK (and in all democratic countries around the globe for that matter). From deciding which party is to form the national government to who's going to be in charge of the local council, elections embody the democratic process in all its Technicolor glory.

Although election campaigns can go on for weeks and even months, the vote itself is squeezed into one day when electors are invited to attend a polling station and cast their votes. Election day is the people's chance to make a difference by saying who they want to represent them, as well as their opportunity to kick politicians out of office who they feel aren't doing a good job. For election day, read judgement day.

Get your calculator out now, because in this chapter I peer into the polling booths and explain exactly how people elect their politicians.

Listing the Big UK Elections

When you think about British elections your mind probably turns to a general election, with the high-profile national politicians going head to head and the airwaves crackling with all things political. However, the UK has lots of different elections in which you have a right to vote. Here's a quick guide to the UK's election scene:

- **General elections:** These elections are considered the biggies, with seats up for grabs in the UK parliament. Traditionally, these elections have the biggest turnouts and receive the most media coverage. Prime ministers (PMs) used to be able to call elections whenever they wanted, but under a new law introduced in 2010 general elections now occur once every five years, setting in stone five-year fixed-term parliaments.
- **Devolved elections:** The Scottish parliament and the Welsh and Northern Irish assemblies are big deals to the millions of people living in these parts of the UK. These bodies have lots of powers and in some ways are more important to people living within their compass than the UK parliament. Elections to these bodies take place once every four years and the system used is partly first past the post and partly proportional representation (check out the later sections 'Coming Up On the Rails: The First-Past-the-Post System' and 'Examining Proportional Representation', respectively).
- **Local government elections:** From county, parish and community councils to mayors, across the UK almost every year a new set of elections is held. These elections may not have the glamour of a general or devolved election but they're important, because local government is responsible for many of the nation's public services, as well as raising council taxes and business rates and approving or turning down planning applications. Chapter 17 has more on the inner workings of local government.
- **European parliamentary elections:** In some ways European elections shouldn't be last in this list of elections, because many of the laws governing the life of Britons come from the European Union (EU). Turnout tends to be low – usually only between 30 and 40 per cent of people registered to vote bother to do so – and they take place once every five years, under a complex system called the D'Hondt method (see 'Dividing in the D'Hondt method', later in this chapter). The last European election was in 2014, and so the next is scheduled for 2019.

In total, 766 Members of the European Parliament (MEPs) sit in the parliament building in Strasbourg, France. Of this number, 73 come from the UK, which slightly under-represents the UK's share of the total population of the EU. The UK has a population of just over 60 million, which works out to roughly one MEP for every 850,000 citizens, whereas Malta, for example, with its total population of just over 320,000, has six MEPs.

UK general elections are pure theatre. The monarch officially dissolves parliament – which makes the king or queen sound like some dastardly Doctor Who villain but in reality just involves signing a piece of paper. When parliament is dissolved all the MPs return to their constituencies to campaign for re-election. This period is called the *short election campaign* and lasts between three and six weeks. During this campaign, politics receives almost blanket coverage across the media, with politicians being quizzed by journalists and debating policy with each other.

Pick of the bunch: General elections

General elections are the stars of the electoral show. They can be a real watershed for British politics, with genuine policy changes of direction following soon after. The following list highlights some of the big turning-point general elections of relatively recent history:

- **1945: Goodbye Churchill, hello Attlee.** Prime minister Winston Churchill may have been instrumental in the UK winning the Second World War but electors still turfed him out at the 1945 general election. The Labour Party, under leader Clement Atlee, promised new schools and hospitals, as well as the construction of a more generous welfare state. These policies proved hugely popular with Britain's war-weary voters. Labour duly won and over the next six years the National Health Service (NHS) was set up, key industries nationalised and higher and more wide-ranging welfare benefit payments brought into being. British politics has never been the same since.
- **1979: The Iron Lady takes residence.** In the spring of 1979 Britain was ready for a change. Decades of economic underperformance, union militancy and a breakdown of the *post-war consensus* between the Conservative and Labour parties (meaning that they followed similar economic and social policies, on the premise that the government should manage the economy) led to the election of the radical reforming Conservative PM Margaret Thatcher. The Iron Lady, as she was nicknamed, went about reforming the unions, privatising former state industries and cutting taxes. As a result, the country boomed in the late 1980s but relapsed into economic difficulty in the early 1990s.
- **1997: Labour promises 'Things can only get better'.** After 18 years of Conservative rule, first under Thatcher and then John Major, the country was again ready for a change. The UK was wealthier than in 1979 and Labour said it wanted to use this newly created wealth to improve the lot of society's less fortunate. Under the leadership of the charismatic Tony Blair, Labour, which had done badly at the previous four general elections, won in a landslide. Blair acknowledged victory at a televised party to the accompaniment of the pop song 'Things can only get better'.
- **2010: Love-in at the Rose garden.** Unusually, no single party achieved an overall majority in the 2010 general election, and as a result the Conservatives and Liberal Democrats formed a coalition government. The two party leaders, David Cameron and Nick Clegg, were interviewed by the world's media in the Rose garden at number 10 Downing Street (the PM's residence). The obvious rapport the two leaders felt was dubbed the 'Love-in at the Rose garden' and the two leaders worked closely in government together. However, many of the MPs and party activists in the coalition have had a far less loving relationship as the two parties disagreed on policy.

Meanwhile, across the country thousands of party workers go *canvassing* – trying to drum up support for their party's candidate by knocking on constituents' doors, setting up stands in shopping centres, holding public meetings and so on. On election day itself, the polling stations are open from 7 a.m. to 10 p.m., allowing tens of millions of people to vote. The votes are then counted and usually by the following morning the party winning the largest number of seats is clear and it gets to form the next government.

Coming Up On the Rails: The First-Past-the-Post System

The UK parliament is an ancient institution and its members (MPs) are elected by a system that goes back a long, long way.

This long-used system is commonly known as *first past the post,* because it has all the characteristics of a race. Here's how the system works in general elections to the UK parliament and in local councils: voters cast their ballots on election day, putting an X by the name of the candidate they want to elect. All the votes are counted and the individual with the largest number is declared the winner.

The number of votes by which the winning candidate wins is irrelevant – just one suffices (as has happened on the odd occasion). More often than not, though, the winning candidate has a *majority* (the number of votes more than the next finisher) in the hundreds or thousands.

Table 6-1 shows the City of Chester candidates for its member of parliament and the vote totals from the 2010 general election.

Table 6-1 City of Chester Vote Totals in 2010

Candidate	*Party*	*Votes*	*Percentage of Vote*
Stephen Mosley	Conservative	18,995	40.6
Christine Russell	Labour	16,412	35.1
Lizzie Jukes	Liberal Democrats	8,930	19.1
Allan Weddell	United Kingdom Independence Party	1,225	2.6
Ed Abrams	English Democrats	594	1.3
Tom Barker	Green	535	1.1

The result is that Stephen Mosley (Conservative) won the seat with a majority of 2,583 votes (18,995 – 16,412).

Crucially, under first past the post, you don't need a mathematical majority of votes to win the election, just the largest number. For example, in the election for the City of Chester that I outline in Table 6-1, the Conservative candidate won despite getting only around 40 per cent of the vote. Look at that figure from another angle and nearly 60 per cent of voters in Chester voted for a different candidate than the person who won!

The race theme is also applicable to the forming of a government in parliament. If a party acquires more than 50 per cent of the seats in parliament, it holds a majority – which means that if all the party's MPs vote in the same way it can't lose the vote – and the monarch then asks it to form the government.

A constituency where the winning candidate enjoys a very large majority – over 10,000 votes – is referred to as a *safe seat.* On the flipside, a constituency where the winning candidate has a small majority is known as a *marginal.*

Looking at the advantages

First past the post has been around for a long time, which means that it must offer something that people like. Here's what's good – from some people's perspective – about first past the post:

- **Strong government:** A political party can win a majority of seats in the House of Commons without getting a majority of votes cast. For example, in the 2005 general election Labour enjoyed a 66-seat majority but only gained around 40 per cent of all votes cast. Holding a majority in parliament means that the governing party has a virtual free hand to carry out its legislative programme and often leads to a strong government.

  Under other systems, such as proportional representation – which I explain in 'Perusing Proportional Representation' later in this chapter – parties often have to work together and form coalitions to get legislation through their parliaments.

- **Community-centric:** Voting for an individual candidate to represent them in parliament allows voters to feel more ownership of their MPs. In fact, although MPs nearly always belong to a political party, they sometimes put the interests of their constituents over that of their party. For example, MPs may vote against their party over plans to close a hospital in the constituency. What's more, MPs meet regularly to hear constituents' concerns, regardless of whether the constituents voted for them or not. Under other election methods, such as the candidate list system – see the later section 'Varying PR: Candidate list system' – this connection between sitting MPs and their constituents is less strong.

A *coalition government* consists of more than one political party. Coalitions are rare in the UK because of first past the post, although one did occur in 2010. They're much more common in countries that employ proportional representation.

Taking in the disadvantages

Every argument has two sides, and that's certainly true when considering whether first past the post is right for the country. A lot of commentators simply don't like the system, because it:

- **Often ignores the majority of voters:** MPs are regularly elected with a minority of the votes cast. Therefore, a majority of voters end up with an MP that they've voted against. Many suggest that this outcome is undemocratic.
- **Aids the two major political parties and marginalises minor parties:** Apart from the coalition government of 2010 until 2015, and a brief period in 1974 when the Liberals and Labour also formed a short-lived coalition government, for the last 75 years only one of two parties has been in government – Conservative or Labour. The two-party nature of parliamentary election results is no doubt aided by the first-past-the-post system, which makes one party gaining a majority in parliament and thereby forming the government that much easier.

The prominent Labour turned Liberal Democrat politician Roy Jenkins (1920–2003) was a long-standing proponent of reforming the UK electoral system. After a long career in politics, Jenkins was asked by new PM Tony Blair in 1997 to produce a report on reforming parliamentary elections. Unsurprisingly, Jenkins recommended getting rid of first past the post and replacing it with proportional representation. Blair, equally predictably, ignored the recommendations of the report because he owed his majority in parliament to the first-past-the-post system. Even at its most popular, Blair's Labour Party never polled more than 43 per cent of all the votes cast in a general election.

The majority of votes in a general, local or European election are cast in person at the ballot box in the traditional way. However, in recent years the rules limiting postal voting have been relaxed to the point that anyone who wants to vote by post instead of through the ballot box on the day can do so. As a result, an increasing number of people are choosing to vote by post, which leaves the system open to the risk of fraud (see the nearby sidebar 'Hanging chads to rotten boroughs: Dubious election results', which also details other election shenanigans).

Hanging chads to rotten boroughs: Dubious election results

Whatever electoral system is deployed, no process is ever foolproof. Mistakes happen, controversy arises and sometimes even electoral fraud takes place. A quick delve into the electoral chamber of horrors brings the following problems to light:

- **Rotten boroughs:** Going back a couple of hundred years in the UK, lots of what were called rotten boroughs existed. *Rotten boroughs* were parliamentary constituencies containing very few voters – sometimes as few as a couple of hundred – who were often controlled by a local nobleman or landowner. The said nobleman or landowner could nominate who he wanted as a candidate and be assured that he (it was always a he in those days!) won hands down. Some rich and prominent noblemen and landowners had several of these rotten boroughs in their pockets, which provided – indirectly – quite an influence in parliament. After all, the MP who sits in the rotten borough seat is always going to act on the say-so of his benefactor. This abuse continued for years until the Reform Act of 1832 swept away many of the nation's rotten boroughs.
- **Gerrymandering:** An American term, *gerrymandering* involves the drawing of electoral boundaries to favour a particular political party at election time. The drawing of boundaries is often in the hands of the state governor or legislature, and so gerrymandering wasn't an uncommon practice in the past. In the UK, gerrymandering is a far less frequent occurrence because the boundary commissions are independent bodies. However, the 1960s and 1970s in Northern Ireland saw loud accusations that gerrymandering had taken place with the aim of reducing the impact of the Catholic vote in favour of the Protestant one. These accusations helped fuel Northern Ireland's civil rights movement and are believed to have inflamed the conflict between the Catholics and Protestants.
- **Hanging chads:** The US presidential election of 2000 was a very close-run race. At first count, the Republican candidate George W Bush had defeated his rival, the Democrat candidate Al Gore. However, in the aftermath of the count, reports of voting irregularities in the state of Florida – whose governor just happened to be Bush's brother – emerged, with accusations that many votes for the Democrats had been discarded unfairly. So began the *hanging chad controversy,* so named because up to 70,000 ballot papers were rejected by machine counters because a hanging fragment of paper (or *chad*) was where a clear punched hole should have been. A hanging chad on a ballot paper meant that it was discarded and the individual's vote went to waste. Eventually, after lots of legal to-ing and fro-ing and a Supreme Court decision, Al Gore conceded the election and George W Bush was declared the president of the United States.
- **Postal fraud:** The UK doesn't have hanging chads or counting machines but moves have been made towards more *postal voting* – allowing people to cast their votes through the post. Some people welcome this development, because it makes voting more convenient and improves turnout, but others point out that more postal voting has led to electoral fraud by some supporters

(continued)

(continued)

of the candidates standing for election. For example, postal votes have been tampered with and, in some cases, individuals have found that their votes have been stolen – they turn up at a polling station and are informed that they've already voted by post. Of course, they haven't – a fraudster has! In 2005 at an enquiry into voter fraud in Birmingham, Justice Richard Mawrey said that the UK's voting system was 'an open invitation to fraud'.

Securing Over 50 Per Cent of the Vote: Majority Electoral Systems

Nineteenth-century US president Abraham Lincoln summed up democracy in his famous 1863 Gettysburg Address by stating that it was 'Government of the people by the people for the people'. But can any government that attracts less than half the votes cast (which often happens under first past the post, as I describe in the earlier section 'Coming Up On the Rails: The First-Past-the-Post System') really live up to Old Abe's ideal? Many people think not, and therefore some electoral systems are geared towards ensuring that the winning candidate has the support of over half the voters. This section covers three such *majority electoral systems.*

A big advantage of these majority systems is that the wishes of those voters whose preferred candidate doesn't win are still taken into account. These voters may not get their preferred candidate but they may be able to avoid getting their least-preferred one.

Laying bare the two-ballot system

Basically, in a *two-ballot system,* instead of one vote to decide a winner, two votes are cast on separate occasions:

- **First ballot:** Voters cast ballots for their preferred candidates. If one candidate gets over 50 per cent of the votes cast that person wins and no more voting is necessary. But if no candidate gets 50 per cent of the votes, a second round of voting takes place.
- **Second round:** Only the two candidates with the highest number of votes can stand; candidates who finished third, fourth or lower are automatically eliminated.

The idea is that those who voted for the now eliminated candidates vote for one of the remaining two candidates in the second ballot. Even if they choose not to vote, it doesn't matter; with only two candidates standing in the second ballot, one of them is certain to achieve over 50 per cent of the votes and thereby win. French presidential elections use this system.

Playing the alternative vote system card

Strap yourself in for an explanation of the *alternative vote system* – it's a bit complicated! Under this system, voters get to rank all the candidates on the ballot paper from most preferred to least preferred. If a candidate receives more than 50 per cent of first-preference votes, that person wins the election and everyone can go home – job done! However, a candidate getting 50 per cent of first-preference votes is a fairly rare occurrence, which is where the complexity kicks in.

The candidate with the fewest number of first-preference votes is eliminated from the next round of voting. Ballot papers having that candidate marked as first preference are examined and the second-preference selections of those voters are then redistributed to the candidates remaining in the election. If these redistributed votes push one candidate over 50 per cent, that person wins and, again, job done. If still no candidate has over 50 per cent of the votes, again the candidate with the fewest number of votes is eliminated and the second preferences of that candidate redistributed.

The dampest of squibs: AV referendum

For David Cameron the price of forming the coalition with the Liberal Democrats in 2010 and therefore becoming PM was agreeing to a referendum to change the voting system in UK general elections from first past the post to the alternative vote system (AV). As the third largest party in UK politics, the Lib Dems stood to gain from AV because they'd probably get more seats in parliament.

But the referendum campaign was bitter, with those calling for the adoption of AV completely out-argued. The opponents of AV – and therefore those for the retention of first past the post – said that it would be expensive and people would lose their personal link with their MPs. The Lib Dems were unhappy with the tone and style of the no to AV campaign and even less happy with the result: the no campaign won, gathering a majority of votes. So for the foreseeable future the first-past-the-post system remains for UK general elections and AV stays firmly on the drawing board.

This process of elimination and counting second preferences – and, in some variants of the system, the third, fourth and even fifth preferences – goes on and on and, yes, on, until finally one of the candidates breaches the magic 50 per cent of votes cast.

The election for the mayor of London is carried out under the alternative vote system.

Throwing in the supplementary vote system

The *supplementary vote system* is a pared down version of the alternative vote system in the preceding section. Fortunately, it's a little less complex. Here goes: voters fill out first and second preferences. The votes are counted and if one of the candidates gets more than 50 per cent of the first-preference votes that candidate's the winner – time to open the champagne!

If no candidate gets 50 per cent, however, all but the two highest-polling candidates are eliminated. The second-preference votes are added to the first preferences of the two remaining candidates. This process leads to one of the candidates achieving the magic 50 per cent and is a good deal less long-winded than the alternative vote system.

Perusing Proportional Representation

The concept behind *proportional representation* (PR) is fairly clear-cut – which is a relief after the systems I cover in the earlier 'Securing Over 50 Per Cent of the Vote: Majority Electoral Systems' section. Under PR, parties are assigned seats according to the percentage of the votes they gather, as opposed to winning seats through a series of local election races where the candidate with the most votes wins outright.

For example, at the 2005 general election Labour, under first past the post, had a majority of 66 seats and yet only won 40.7 per cent of the votes cast. If the election had been run under the PR system, Labour would still have been the biggest party but wouldn't have come near to obtaining a majority of seats. As a result, in parliament Labour would have been forced to rely on the support of other political parties to see its bills made into law.

Proportional representation doesn't always result in a coalition government, but it happens more often than not. In order to have a majority of seats in parliament under the PR system, one party has to poll more than 50 per cent of all the votes cast in the country; looking at the history of UK general elections that's a very difficult task to achieve.

One of PR's main drawbacks is that, if adopted for elections to the UK parliament, it would break the bonds between MPs and their electors, because voters vote for the party rather than for individual candidates. Under PR, the politicians elected are drawn from candidate lists drawn up by the political parties. The more votes an individual party gets, the more candidates from its party list get elected.

Some people suggest that coalition governments are a good thing, arguing that they prevent one party from pursuing extremist policies. If no single political party has a majority, it has to rely on the support of another party or two to govern and the other parties in the coalition tend to rein in extreme policies.

Most European countries operate a system of PR and so coalitions are commonplace.

Refining PR: Single transferable vote

Strap yourself in again: this variation on PR is another complex electoral system.

Under the *single transferable vote system,* the country is divided into voting regions, for example the North West of England. The ballot papers contain the names of all the candidates running for election in that region. The voter ranks the candidates in order of preference. If one of the candidates wins enough first-preference votes to breach a preset quota – for argument's sake, say 40 per cent – that person's elected. But when more than one seat has to be filled for the same office – which is common because it's a whole region and there is a large population that needs to be represented and more than one person is needed to do the job – the second, third, fourth, fifth and so on preferences of those who voted for the highest-polling candidate are now redistributed to the other candidates.

If one of them now breaches the quota level, that candidate is elected. After the second candidate has been elected, that person's preferences are thrown into the mix, leading to other candidates breaching the quota level and being elected.

A slight variant on this process is that, after the second seat is filled, instead of the other preferences from the voters for that newly elected candidate being counted, the candidate who polled the fewest first preferences is eliminated and lower preferences on the ballots for that eliminated candidate are redistributed to the other candidates, all with the object of pushing another candidate over the quota to be elected.

This process continues until all the seats in the region are filled. This voting system is used in the Republic of Ireland – and it's clearly the one of choice for mathematicians everywhere!

Varying PR: Candidate list system

In the *candidate list system,* the country is divided into voting regions containing lots of seats. The political parties submit a list of candidates for election. The votes cast in the region as a whole are counted and seats given out to the parties in proportion to the percentage of votes each party gains.

For example, say ten seats are up for grabs in the whole of East Anglia. Labour and Conservative get 40 per cent of the vote each, while the Lib Dems and the United Kingdom Independence Party (UKIP) receive 10 per cent each. So, out of the ten seats Labour and Conservative get four each and Lib Dems and UKIP each get one.

What about those candidate lists? Well, Labour and Conservative see the first four candidates on their lists elected and the Lib Dems and UKIP only the name at the top of their list. Under this system, electors are voting for political parties rather than individuals.

Dividing in the D'Hondt method

Elections to the European parliament in the UK and the Northern Irish assembly are carried out under a variant of the candidate list system of the preceding section, called the *D'Hondt method.* In this system, the party with the highest number of votes wins one of the seats in the voting region. That party's number of votes is then halved and a new calculation made, with the party with the highest number of votes winning a seat and then seeing its vote tally halved. This process continues until all the seats are allocated.

Here's a simple example of a fictional region I call Mercia. Out of 935,000 votes cast, the political parties finish up with the following number of votes:

- Labour 400,000
- Conservative 300,000
- Liberal Democrat 110,000
- Green Party 75,000
- UKIP 50,000

Under the D'Hondt method, the region's five seats are distributed as follows:

- **Seat 1 goes to Labour:** It has the highest number of votes and the candidate at the top of its party list is a new MEP. Halving Labour's total vote tally results in the following numbers:
  - Conservative 300,000
  - Labour 200,000
  - Liberal Democrat 110,000
  - Green Party 75,000
  - UKIP 50,000
- **Seat 2 goes to the Conservatives:** Its vote tally is halved (again the candidate at the top of its party list is now an MEP), and for seat 3 the votes stand as follows:
  - Labour 200,000
  - Conservative 150,000
  - Liberal Democrat 110,000
  - Green Party 75,000
  - UKIP 50,000
- **Seat 3 goes to Labour:** The candidate second on Labour's party list is now an MEP. Its voting tally is halved again:
  - Conservative 150,000
  - Liberal Democrat 110,000
  - Labour 100,000
  - Green Party 75,000
  - UKIP 50,000
- **Seat 4 goes to the Conservatives:** The second candidate on the party's list is now an MEP. The Conservative's tally is again halved:
  - Liberal Democrat 110,000
  - Labour 100,000
  - Green Party 75,000
  - Conservative 75,000
  - UKIP 50,000
- **The final seat goes to the Lib Dems.**

If more than five seats were up for grabs, the process of distributing seats and filling them with candidates from the party lists goes on and on, with even the Greens and UKIP likely to get an MEP. Contrast this scenario with the first-past-the-post system (see the earlier 'Coming Up On the Rails: The First-Past-the-Post System' section) in which neither of these parties would win a seat despite the fact that, between them, they command around 15 per cent of the total votes cast in Mercia.

Looking North and West to the Additional Member System

The additional member system, used for elections to the Scottish parliament and the Welsh assembly, combines the basic fairness of PR with the representative benefits of first past the post. Voters, as a result, still feel a connection with the person they elect to represent them.

The *additional member system* works in Scotland as follows. Voters have two votes rather than one – lucky them! The first vote they cast is for an individual candidate to represent them as a constituency Member of the Scottish Parliament (MSP). This election is run according to the first-past-the-post system, with the candidate scooping the highest number of votes winning the seat. For the second vote, the voters simply have a choice of parties. The votes for the parties are tallied up across eight different regions of the country and seats distributed accordingly.

So if, for example, the Scottish National Party (SNP) gets 40 per cent of second votes cast across the country, it receives 40 per cent of what are called *additional members* (additional to the people elected through first past the post as constituency MSPs). As for who gets to sit as these additional members, names are drawn from lists of individual candidates submitted by the political parties.

Of 129 MSPs, 73 are elected via first past the post and 56 through the additional member system.

Those MSPs elected through the additional member system are referred to as *List MSPs*. If one of these List MSPs resigns the seat or dies, that person is automatically replaced by the next name on the party list. If, however, a constituency MSP resigns the seat or dies, a by-election is held in that constituency, with the new MSP decided by first past the post.

Scottish, Welsh and Northern Irish electors not only get to choose who sits in their own national parliaments and assemblies, but they also have an MP who they elect, through first past the post, to the UK parliament in Westminster.

The mix of proportional representation and first past the post in the Scottish parliament and the Welsh and Northern Irish assemblies means that coalition governments are more likely to form in these institutions than in the UK parliament, which elects via first past the post. However, this situation was turned on its head a little in 2010 and beyond when a coalition government came to power in Westminster while the SNP managed to form a majority in Scotland.

Expanding or shrinking according to the boundary commissions

Society doesn't stand still, and population patterns in towns and cities across the UK fluctuate over time. As a result, the parliamentary seat map has to change to reflect population moves. Locations with falling populations lose MPs while those with rising ones gain seats.

This ongoing reallocation of seats isn't done to suit a particular purpose or on the whim of a politician. Instead, every eight to ten years four boundary commissions – one each for England, Scotland, Wales and Northern Ireland – carry out a review of parliamentary seats. These commissions are politically independent and staffed by civil servants.

The commissions look at each constituency in turn to see whether its boundaries mean it still meets certain criteria. Voting patterns are never part of the boundary commissions' deliberations. The boundary commission looks at how many people now live in the constituency and its geographic span and decide whether or not it should remain as it is, be split up into two constituencies or merged with another constituency.

If the population of the constituency has declined since the last boundary commission review, a chance exists that it may be merged with a neighbouring one; if the population has increased, part of the constituency may be hived off to a neighbouring constituency or be split into two and a new seat created. Boundary changes were supposed to happen after the 2010 general election, but the coalition partners in government – the Conservatives and Lib Dems – were unable to agree over the size and scale of the boundary changes proposed by the boundary commission. As a result, no changes were made in constituency boundaries between 2010 and 2015, which means that the current constituency make-up doesn't reflect the latest distribution of UK population.

Following Scottish, Welsh and Northern Irish devolution, the job of the boundary commissions has expanded to include constituencies in the Scottish parliament and Welsh and Northern Irish assemblies.

Chapter 7

Voting Behaviour and Trends

In This Chapter

- Sorting out who votes, and why
- Paying attention to what motivates voters
- Persuading people to vote

Win or lose, we go shopping after the election.

—Imelda Marcos, former presidential First Lady of the Philippines

Shopaholic Imelda Marcos's husband was famously overthrown in the late 1980s; perhaps she should have paid more attention at election time!

In the UK and the other great democracies of the world, election time is a huge deal. Tens of millions of Britons each year take the time and trouble to vote. They elect the UK parliament, the European parliament in Strasbourg and the local council down the road. Elections in the UK are varied and colourful, with lots of different candidates and parties.

People often see an election as a major staging post in their lives – as with Margaret Thatcher's election in 1979, Tony Blair's in 1997 or the coming of the coalition in 2010. Elections are part of a country's shared experience, and yet also highly personal because each individual plays an essential part by voting.

In this chapter, I explore everything you need to know about what influences people to choose to vote (or not vote) and why they vote for the party they do. I also take in the tactics the political parties use to try to get you to put your X by their name at election time.

Looking at Who Can and Can't Vote

Just about everyone over the age of 18 has the right to vote at election time, whether in UK, European parliamentary or local council elections. In order to vote, you must register for the privilege on the electoral roll.

Registering to vote is easy. You can simply ring your local council and ask to register, do so online or wait until the local electoral registration office writes to your address and asks who at that address is eligible to vote. All in all, the overwhelming majority – above 90 per cent – of adults in the UK are registered to vote.

At election time you're sent a polling card that you take down to your local polling station to prove who you are, and then you get to cast your vote.

The UK is a democracy but plenty of people are still barred from having their say at the ballot box:

- Young people under age 18
- Foreign nationals
- Prisoners
- People convicted in the past five years of voting fraud
- Members of the House of Lords (on the premise that they don't need someone else to represent them in parliament)

Foreign nationals are barred from voting in UK general elections even when they've been granted residency. However, as a bit of a hangover from the days of empire, Irish nationals and people from Commonwealth countries living in the UK can vote in a UK general election. People who are granted UK citizenship are entitled to vote in all elections (see *The British Citizenship Test For Dummies* (Wiley) by yours truly for more details).

British monarchs are allowed to vote but never do. They're supposed to be neutral and above the cut and thrust of party politics.

Understanding Voter Turnout

Not every eligible voter casts a vote; the proportion of voters that do is called the *voter turnout.* Voter turnout varies according to the type of election being held. Generally, elections to the UK parliament – called *general elections* – see the highest turnout because voters view them as the most important.

Meanwhile, people see elections to the European parliament and local councils as being less crucial, and so voter turnout is lower – sometimes only half the level seen at a UK parliamentary general election.

All people of voting age must be registered as a legal requirement. But many people slip off the radar – they may not have a permanent address or simply decide that they don't want to appear on the electoral roll. A study suggests that anything up to six million people living in the UK who should be on the electoral roll are not, and are therefore technically breaking the law. Many commentators dispute this figure, suggesting it is less, but frankly no one knows the true scale of the problem.

Counting declining voter turnout

Voter turnout has been declining over the past 50 years, gradually at first but more recently at a considerable pace. Turning back the clock to the 1950s, around 85 per cent of all the Britons registered to vote did vote in a general election. In the 1970s this turnout had slipped to around 75 per cent. By the 2001 and 2005 general elections only around 60 per cent of voters turned up at the polls, as Figure 7-1 shows. The figures picked up a bit in 2010, however, when 65 per cent of those eligible to vote cast their ballots.

Apparently, the closer the election is likely to be, the more people choose to vote. For instance, the 2001 and 2005 general elections were considered foregone conclusions – a Labour victory – and in such situations many voters stay at home because they don't think that they're going to make a difference to the final result. In contrast, 2010 was closely fought. The general election in 2015 is also likely to be a close-run thing and so voter turnout may well be above 60 per cent. Over the long term, however, voter turnout has been trailing away, much to the chagrin of politicians.

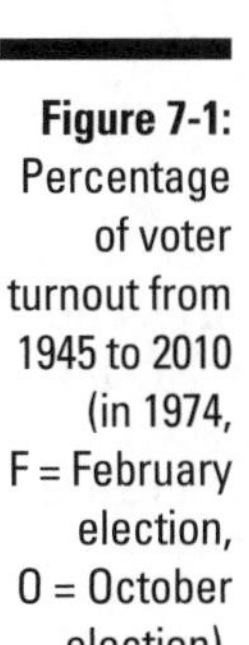

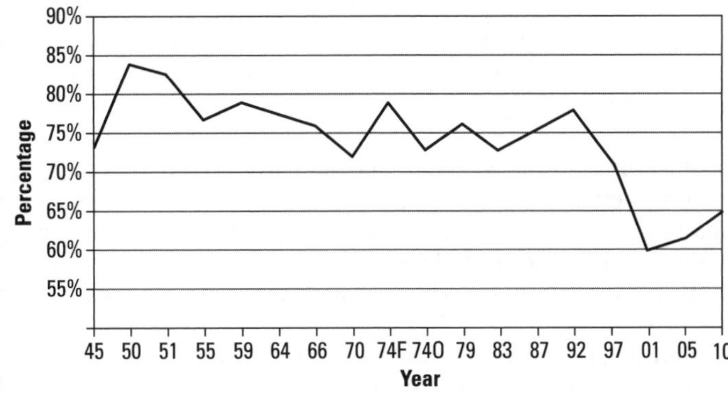

Figure 7-1: Percentage of voter turnout from 1945 to 2010 (in 1974, F = February election, O = October election).

Politicians don't like low voter turnout for a couple of reasons:

- **Low voter turnout damages a government's legitimacy.** When the government receives only a fraction of people voting for it, some people argue that it doesn't have a proper mandate to implement its policies.
- **Low voter turnout highlights political failure.** Generally, low turnout is an indication that politicians are failing to connect with the public. In short, the public is turned off by the policies, message and even personalities of the political parties.

In some parliamentary constituencies voter turnout at a general election is much lower than the national average. At the 2010 general election, for example, some turnouts were as low as 45 per cent.

Political commentators blame falling turnout at UK general elections on:

- Declining trust in politicians
- People leading ever busier lives and a general feeling that politics is increasingly irrelevant to daily life
- The policies of the UK's big political parties being widely seen as very similar

Falling turnouts aren't confined to the UK. In the United States, for instance, the presidential elections regularly see voter turnouts of only 50 to 60 per cent.

Observing the reduction in local democracy

All people on the electoral register have the right to vote in UK local elections. In areas with several tiers of local government – perhaps county, district and parish – voters cast several ballots. Council seats are usually contested once every four years and at first glance local democracy seems to be in rude health.

Turnout at local elections is on average only around half that at general elections and sometimes even lower (30–40 per cent as against 60–65 per cent). Usually only a minority of those eligible to vote at local elections do so; this is seen as an indication of the general decline of local democracy across the UK. Here are some of the reasons given for widespread voter apathy to local elections:

- **Council work is unimportant:** A lot of the work of local councils is viewed as mundane and as a result people rarely get excited about which group of councillors is doing what.

- **The parties are no different from each other:** Across British politics a view persists that all politicians are the same and that the political parties don't have distinctive enough characters or policies.
- **Councillors aren't representative of ordinary people:** The average age of a councillor in England for example is nearly 60, which can make some younger people feel that they don't have much in common with their elected representative.
- **Councils are powerless to effect real change:** Although councils provide many key services and set Council Tax rates they get most of their money from central government. Therefore many electors associate their daily engagement with government with the party in power in Westminster (or Holyrood in the case of the Scottish parliament) instead of their local council offices.
- **Councillors are unknowns:** Councillors tend to have a much lower profile than national politicians.

Reversing the decline in voter turnout

After each recent general election, politicians and pundits asked what happened to all the voters. Politicians agree that they need to do more to 'engage' with voters. In other words, they need to do a better job of communicating why people need to get out and vote. But more radical solutions to declining voter turnout have also been suggested:

- **Offering more ways to vote, including via the post and the Internet:** The idea is to make voting easier to encourage those who want to vote but can't find the time. Instead of taking a polling card down to the polling station, people should be able to send their votes through the post or even go to a website and tick a box online in a few seconds. See the nearby sidebar 'When postal ballots go wrong' for a real-life look at some problems associated with this alternative voting method.
- **Compulsory voting:** Registering to vote is already a legal requirement, so why not take things a stage further and pass a law so that everyone casts a vote or faces a fine? Compulsory voting has been introduced in Australia and is one way to ensure far bigger voter turnout. But in the same way that voting is a democratic right, choosing not to vote, according to some people, is also just that.

Traditionally, polling stations are open from early in the morning until 10 p.m. to allow voters the maximum amount of time to cast their vote.

Sometimes people turn up to vote but instead of putting a cross next to the name of a candidate they choose to write a message or put multiple crosses on the ballot paper. Doing so is called *spoiling a ballot paper* and the vote is counted but not assigned to any candidate.

When postal ballots go wrong

After the 2001 general election, grave concerns were expressed regarding low voter turnout. In response, the government decided to make using a postal ballot easier for voters. Previously, applicants for a postal ballot had to give a good reason for why they weren't able to turn up in person to vote at a polling station. But making the right to a postal ballot easier had unforeseen consequences.

Instances of voting fraud occurred in the 2005 and to a lesser extent 2010 general elections and in several local government elections, with postal votes going missing or people turning up at polling stations only to find that they'd apparently already voted by post. An investigation into voting fraud in the Birmingham area led to the examining magistrate describing the situation as more akin to the practices of a 'banana republic' (a politically unstable and corrupt country).

As a result of these controversies, the further loosening of rules governing the availability of postal votes has been put on hold.

Considering What Sways Voters

Voters put a cross beside a particular candidate or party usually for a combination of reasons, including:

- The attitude of the party or its candidate to a particular issue.
- The personality of the candidate or of the leader of the party.
- The social background of the voter.

I explore each of these issues in this section.

Often people describe themselves as *traditional* Labour, Conservative or Lib Dem voters. The traditional status normally means that their parents or grandparents usually voted for the same political party all their lives. Pressure from family members and peers on voting patterns is difficult to measure but is no doubt a factor.

Taking in the big issues

Every so often pollsters ask members of the public what they see as the big problems or challenges facing the country. Some issues come and go but generally the public thinks that the following specific policy areas are the most important, and they look favourably on the party that seems to offer the best plan for each:

- **State of the economy:** If the economy is doing well and people feel prosperous, it's good news for the government in power. If not, the public probably want a change – bad news for the current government.

Former US president Bill Clinton won the 1992 election on the issue of the economy. At the time, the US economy wasn't doing well and unemployment was rising fast. The incumbent president George Bush Senior made foreign policy the centre of his campaign, while the Clinton campaign kept the now-famous phrase 'It's the economy, stupid!' as his motto. Clinton communicated to the electorate that he knew what the real problems facing the US were and painted his opponent as being out of touch. Clinton won a landslide election victory.

- **Public services:** Normally, *public services* means health and education services. People like to see that hospitals and schools are well funded yet efficient. Under some circumstances many voters would agree to pay higher taxes for these services, but they don't want to feel their hard-earned cash is being wasted.
- **Military conflict:** Wars can change the political landscape in no time at all, particularly when they go badly or well. If the public feels a war is justified and, crucially, won, it can reflect well on the government in power. The opposite, though, is also true.

In 1982 Conservative PM Margaret Thatcher was very unpopular at home. Then the Argentinians invaded the Falkland Islands, which were inhabited by over 2,000 British citizens. Britain fought and won a war to liberate the Falklands. At the general election the following year Thatcher won a massive victory. On the flip side, Tony Blair's decision to support the US invasion of Iraq in 2003 was hugely unpopular and a key reason why he resigned as prime minister in 2007.

Digging into the growing importance of green issues

The damage being done to the environment and the effects of climate change are becoming increasingly important issues. People like the idea that the environment should be protected. However, many also want to see economic growth and lower domestic fuel bills at the same time. Balancing the need to produce economic growth and using fossil fuels with protecting the environment has joined health and foreign policy as an issue at election time.

Understanding the power of local issues

Not everyone is preoccupied with the economy, public services or foreign policy. Instead some voters make their decision based on single issues, such as the need for a better rail network or opposition to nuclear power.

'All politics is local', Thomas 'Tip' O'Neill, a long-time Speaker of the US Congress, rightly declared, knowing that people can be swayed to vote for a particular party or candidate because of something happening in their locality. For example, the closure of a local hospital can garner support for candidates who are opposed. Voting decisions aren't all based on big national issues – particularly not at local election times.

Throwing personality into the mix: The leadership wild card

The leaders of the main political parties are central figures in British politics, because they're the ones vying for the job of prime minister.

Many voters don't agree with the individual policies of the parties, and instead judge who to vote for based on their take of the capability or otherwise of the individual party leaders. They know that the biggest job in British politics is that of prime minister, and so they want someone in the hot seat who they think is up to the job and someone to whom they personally relate. A leader with charisma who can communicate well on television is a huge bonus to the party – and the converse is equally true.

In short, if a party wants to be successful at the polls, it needs a leader who appeals not only to party members, but also to the general public as a whole. In recent years the personality of the leader has become crucial to election results, probably as a result of the main political parties moving their policies to the centre in order to appeal more to Middle Britain electors (in essence, people not wedded to the political left or right, though check out the later section 'Broadening party appeal' for a more detailed description).

Former Labour leader Neil Kinnock was favourite to lead his party to election triumph in the 1992 general election. The Conservative government at the time was unpopular and the economy was in deep recession. But Kinnock was famous for being verbose and often didn't come across well on television and through the media. In a tightly fought election, Labour lost and many blamed Kinnock for not connecting sufficiently well with the voters.

On the other hand, having a great, popular leader doesn't guarantee success at the polls. Back in 1945 the Conservatives had Sir Winston Churchill, a proven brilliant wartime leader, and yet Labour won a landslide victory, despite being led by Clement Attlee, who some observers suggested unkindly had had a charisma bypass. Labour's stunning victory was the result of its policies homing in on Britons' hopes at the end of the war, such as building a free health care system, which became the National Health Service (NHS).

Personality can also play a part in local and individual parliamentary seat elections. Usually an incumbent who has a good profile in the local community can expect to do well against any opponents, because that person has a track record and is known by at least some of the voters.

Looking at the voters themselves

Demographic factors – where you live, how much money you make, your ethnic background, your age and gender – also affect how you vote.

No single element determines how people vote. Sometimes class, gender or where the voter lives has more of an impact than age or religion – sometimes it's the other way around. Normally, a combination of factors influences how you vote.

Voting and class

The class system has always been a big part of British society and experts generally reckon that for most of the post-war period from 1945 to the 1970s people voted in line with their class. Therefore, people who worked in manufacturing and other industries that were heavily unionised voted for Labour, while most non-unionised people voted Conservative and to a much lesser extent Liberal – the forerunner of the Lib Dems.

But in the 1970s this old class–party alignment started to fragment, particularly after Margaret Thatcher's victory in 1979. Despite the fact that she was a Conservative, much of her support came from the working class, partly because of widespread disenchantment with union militancy. In addition, the number of people considered 'working class' has fallen in recent years as heavy industry and manufacturing have declined.

But class is far from dead as an influence on how people cast their votes. Labour, for instance, can still count on big support from those who consider themselves working class or those who don't have a job.

Even at the start of the 21st century, the class system still plays a big part in British society and in how people vote. Although something of a stereotype, the higher up the class system you are, the more likely you are to vote Conservative. Generally, you have more to gain by maintaining the current state of affairs. (Chapter 8 has more on the natural supporters of the political parties.)

Voting and women

Up until the 1920s British politicians didn't have to think about appealing to women because that half of the population didn't have the right to vote. However, after a short matter of several centuries of having elections, women were finally allowed to take part. For the almost exclusively male – often moustached – politicians, it took a while to work out what they needed to do to appeal to women in order to get elected.

Now political analysts consider women to be the key constituency to swing an election one way or the other. The large parties spend a lot of time and money trying to make their policies and presentation attractive to women. Generally, policies relating to public services, such as health and education, and traditional family values play well with female voters.

Pundits often talk about a Worcester woman whose vote is paramount in an election. They're not referring to an actual woman, but to a type of voter to whom they want to appeal. The *Worcester woman* represents females with families in small-town England. These women are often seen as *swing voters* which means that they're open to persuasion instead of having a specific and long-standing preference for a single political party. Having policies that attract Worcester woman can be key to winning a general election in the UK.

The Conservatives used to do well among women voters, mainly because of their emphasis on the importance of family values. But in recent elections this situation changed, because Labour has actively courted female voters.

The Labour Party has had women-only candidate shortlists for several elections, with the aim of getting more female candidates standing in winnable seats at election time. This tactic has resulted in an increase in the number of female Labour MPs. But, interestingly, male MPs are still comfortably in the majority. Many attribute this paucity of female MPs to women being put off entering politics because of negative public perceptions of politicians and the difficulty of balancing a political career with bringing up a family – a job still assigned in most minds exclusively to women.

Former Labour PM Tony Blair did very well with female voters. Most agree this success was because he often talked about issues that resonated with the female electorate, such as improving schools and hospitals. Blair was also noted as an excellent communicator on television, and his clean-cut family man image no doubt helped too.

Voting and age

Ex-British PM Sir Winston Churchill wasn't just a great wartime leader and a lookalike for a large baby later in life, he was also a dab hand at producing clever quotes. One attributed to him is: 'If you're not a liberal when you're 20, you have no heart. If you're not a conservative when you're 40, you have no brain.'

Churchill meant that younger people naturally gravitate towards left-wing parties, because their message of greater equality and looking after those less fortunate appeals to the emotions of youth. But as people get older and wealthier and see more of how the world works, they tend to become more conservative or right-wing in outlook, and want to preserve the country's institutions and retain low taxes.

The figures bear Churchill out and generally the Labour Party does better among teenagers, students and those in their early 20s, while the Conservatives traditionally do well among the over-65s.

At the 2010 general election, 31 per cent of people aged 18–24 voted Labour while 30 per cent voted Conservative. By the time electors reach age 65 and above, this situation is very different, with 44 per cent choosing the Conservatives and just 31 per cent Labour. The Lib Dems also tend to do better among the young. In 2010, nearly one in three voters in the 18 to 24 age bracket chose the Lib Dems but only one in five over the age of 65 made the same choice. However, following the 2010 election and the Lib Dems entry into coalition government with the Conservatives, the Lib Dems reneged on a promise to abolish University tuition fees. At a stroke many younger voters felt alienated from the Lib Dems and it will be interesting to see if this is reflected in a declining share of the vote amongst younger people at the 2015 general election.

Voting and where you live

All the main political parties have what are called *heartlands* – areas of the country where they do best. Political scientists say that these voting patterns are due to *socioeconomic* factors. Put simply, the type of industry that dominates the area, the level of unionisation and local traditions all play a role in making people in a particular part of the country more likely to vote for a particular party.

The following list gives you the low-down on what parts of the country are more likely to vote Conservative, Labour or Lib Dem and why:

- **North of England, Wales and Scotland:** The Labour Party tends to do better, because traditionally these parts of the country are dominated by manufacturing and industry, with a strong working-class culture and union movement.
- **South-east of England:** The Conservatives do better here, because people have higher incomes and a lot invested in maintaining things as they are. They also like the party's expressed commitment to low taxes and free-market economics. Crucially, union membership is lower in this part of the UK.
- **South-west of England:** Here, the Lib Dems tend to do well. This area of the UK is rural but also poor, and so it doesn't have the same interest in preserving the current state of affairs as do Conservatives living in the south-east; but it's also not a working-class area and union membership is low. In short, much of what makes the Conservatives and Labour appeal to the rest of the UK doesn't strike a chord in the south-west, and so the Lib Dems step into the breach and have long-standing support and strong local community ties.

Saying that because someone lives in the north they vote Labour or in the south-east Conservative is obviously too simplistic. In fact, at times the Conservatives garner major support in the north or Labour does well in the south-east.

Breaking the north–south divide

For many years in British politics a large dividing line existed, and the Conservatives did well in the populous and prosperous south of the UK while Labour held sway in the less well-off north.

Today, though, the old certainties of party heartlands have become a little less, well, certain. The UK economy has changed dramatically over the past 40 years, moving from manufacturing to services. With substantial immigration, the make-up of the population has also changed. Communities are no longer as uniform as they used to be; instead, people of different backgrounds and outlooks live cheek by jowl across the country.

A fragmentation of the class system also occurred as a result of the economic changes. Compartmentalising millions of Britons as Labour, Conservative or Lib Dem voters is no longer possible; they're more likely to switch allegiances, which in turn is breaking up the old certainties such as the north–south divide.

Having said that, the south of England is densely populated, which gives the party that does well there a very good chance of winning enough seats in parliament to form the government.

The rise of the United Kingdom Independence Party (UKIP) with its strong anti-European and anti-immigration stance has cut across some of these old political certainties, taking votes from all the political parties in much of England. Likewise in Scotland the success of the Scottish National Party (SNP) has also shaken up the political landscape. Despite UKIP having no MPs, in a sense England is currently a four-party system: Conservative, Labour, Lib Dem and UKIP. In Scotland though, UKIP is almost non-existent and the Conservatives and Lib Dems of marginal importance, which leaves a straight race for power between Labour and the SNP (see Chapter 8 for more on the current state of the parties).

Voting and ethnicity

The Labour Party tends to do well among Britain's expanding ethnic groups. A number of factors explain this appeal:

- Labour is seen as an anti-racist party and, particularly through the promotion of an inclusive policy at local government level, as being pro-immigration (or at least not anti-immigration).

- Labour is seen as the party most likely to look after the underdog, which can be important to those struggling to establish roots in the UK.
- Labour is traditionally strong in the north of the country where much mass immigration has occurred.

Within ethnic minorities, differences in voting patterns still exist. For example, British Asians are much less likely to vote for a left-wing party than, say, British Afro-Caribbeans. Economically, British Asians have tended to do better and as a result the Conservative's message of lower taxes and maintaining the current economic and political situation resonates.

Voting and religion

In countries such as the US, people's religion is a huge deal at election time and can have a substantial impact on whether they vote Republican or Democrat. In the UK, however, religious observance is much lower and as a result faith doesn't tend to have as major an impact on voting intentions. Another factor is that the big political parties have very similar policies on issues such as abortion or stem-cell research, which are big bones of contention in the US.

It was said of former Labour PM Tony Blair that he 'doesn't do god', despite that the fact that he was deeply religious and converted to Roman Catholicism on leaving office. However, Conservative PM David Cameron, who has expressed a degree of agnosticism over his faith and pushed gay marriage laws into being – angering many religious groups in the process – has openly talked about the importance of faith to the country and that Britain should be proud to be a 'Christian country'. Perhaps religion and politics do mix, at least a little, in Britain after all.

The recent rise of religion in UK politics – particularly over controversial gay marriage laws – perhaps reflects politicians scrabbling around for some way of remaining relevant. Religion is after all a rock on which many people base their lives and it has deep-seated appeal, something politicians would also like to have.

Enticing Voters to Vote: Party Strategies

To win elections, political parties and their leaders have to get their loyal supporters excited enough to get out and vote. But simply appealing to this so-called core vote is never enough – they have to attract enough other voters to beat the competing parties at the polls (in political jargon called going 'over the top'). This section talks about these strategies.

Appealing to the core vote

Generally, the large political parties, even when their fortunes are low in the polls, can rely on a proportion of the population to vote for them. This *core vote* comprises party members and those who've always traditionally voted for that party. My great-grandmother, for instance, turned up at her local polling station right into her 90s sporting a rosette in the colour of the party that she'd supported since she was a young woman.

Despite being able to rely on a core vote, the parties still have to keep in with these people and not take them for granted, or they may choose to abstain from voting (although they're unlikely to vote for an opposition party).

The parties appeal to this core vote through the following methods:

- Party policy tries to keep close to the outlook of these core voters, representing their hopes and ambitions.
- Local party members identify core voters and then try to encourage them to attend and vote on polling day. I know one party worker who ferries elderly and infirm people to the polling station to ensure that they vote.

Getting the core vote is crucial. Without it, no political party can hope to do well at an election.

Broadening party appeal

To win elections, political parties have to gather broad support beyond their core vote, among people who voted for other parties in the past or don't usually vote at all.

When political scientists talk about *Middle England* or *Middle Britain,* they're not referring to a geographical location or even the middle class, but to a group of people who don't naturally support the political extremes of left or right. These people may have once considered themselves working class but now have access (or want to have access) to some of what used to be seen as the trappings of middle-class life, such as home-ownership and private schooling for their children. People defined as being part of Middle Britain don't tend to have deep-rooted allegiance to a particular political party; instead they tend to vote for the party that best matches their ambitions for their families and for the country as a whole.

Appealing to Middle Britain is often seen as the electoral Holy Grail – it can be the difference between success and failure.

Here are some of the dos and don'ts of wooing Middle Britain:

- **Don't suggest policies seen as too extreme.** In the 1980s Labour did badly partly because it wanted nuclear disarmament; in the 1990s the Conservatives were seen as adopting extreme policies on immigration and the European Union.
- **Don't tax too highly.** Middle Britain wants to keep its cash and if it does have to pay taxes it wants the money spent wisely.
- **Do provide good public services.** For its money, Middle Britain wants good schools and hospitals provided – if not for themselves, then for their friends and relations.
- **Do promote a better society.** Middle Britain likes stability and the idea that they and their loved ones are safe. As a result, policies to tackle crime and ensure a fairer society tend to go down well.

People who shift their allegiances between political parties are called *swing voters.* Much of Middle Britain consists of swing voters.

Voting to thwart: Tactical voting

Tactical voting is when people choose to vote for a party that isn't their preferred choice in order to prevent their least-favourite party from winning a seat. Tactical voting is unique to the British first-past-the-post system, where MPs and local councillors are elected if they poll the highest number of votes in a particular constituency.

Picture a fictional constituency in which Labour holds the seat with a narrow majority over the Lib Dems, and the Conservatives trail way back in third place. These Conservative voters are a bit fed up because they have little chance of ever electing their own candidate and they really don't like the Labour Party. In fact, they dislike Labour more than they dislike the Lib Dems. Therefore, some of these disgruntled Conservatives choose to vote tactically at the next election. Instead of voting for their own candidate they put a cross beside the Lib Dem candidate's name in an effort to remove the Labour Party candidate. When the votes are counted, the Conservative vote shrinks, Labour holds the same, but the Lib Dems do best and win the seat: just enough Conservative voters switched to vote Lib Dem to ensure that Labour loses.

At the 2005 and 2010 general elections, tactical voting played a major part in the outcome. In these two elections, generally, a strong anti-Conservative vote was evident, with some Lib Dems voting for Labour in constituencies where Labour had a better chance to beat the Conservative candidate and the other way around.

Gazing at Election Campaigning

Most people don't live and breathe politics; they have important stuff to get on with, such as marriages, bringing up families and forging careers. But every five years the party in government calls a general election, which is the voters' big chance to change the party of power or, if they like what's going on, keep the government in the box seat. Suddenly, public interest in politics rises, and the parties, their members and leading politicians start to campaign. Many electors make up their minds as to which party they're going to vote for during the campaign. Some studies even suggest that up to 12 per cent of electors decide on the polling day which party to support.

Typically, during a general election the parties use certain tactics including the following to encourage people to vote for their candidates:

- Party political broadcasts on TV
- Adverts in the press, online or on street billboards
- Party members knocking on electors' doors and telephoning them at home
- Politicians giving lots of interviews to the media, taking part in debates and answering questions from the public
- Party leaders touring the country, holding rallies with the aim of getting extra media coverage for their campaign
- Parties using texts, emails and blogs to contact electors

General election campaigns usually last around three weeks. The newspapers and airwaves are dominated during this time with political discussion.

Modern politics is as much about doing down the opposition as telling the public how good you are. At recent general elections, in the US in particular, politicians have been accused of employing *negative campaigning,* which is focusing the communication effort on exposing what they see as the shortcomings of their opponents.

Glancing at the Effects of Media Bias

Particularly when they're beaten at the polls, politicians are keen on pointing out that a lot of the UK media is biased against them. This assertion isn't sour grapes because certain parts of the media – in particular the national newspapers – are definitely biased. They have allegiances to a particular political party and often attack its opponents. The newspapers say they're merely reflecting the views and preoccupations of their readers.

The BBC (British Broadcasting Corporation) is a public service broadcaster and, according to the rule of its charter, is supposed to be independent. Journalists at the BBC have to work within strict guidelines to ensure that they're balanced and fair in what they say, and that they devote equal air time to opposing politicians. Nevertheless, the BBC is regularly accused of bias, often by those on the right of the political spectrum.

In the close-run 1992 general election, Labour leader Neil Kinnock said that the negative attitude of many national newspapers, and in particular *The Sun,* damaged Labour's chances at the poll. On polling day itself, *The Sun*'s front page featured a picture of Neil Kinnock's head superimposed on a light bulb next to the headline 'will the last person to leave Britain please turn out the lights'. Labour lost the election and Neil Kinnock resigned as leader straight after. The next day *The Sun* headline read: 'It's *The Sun* wot won it'.

Newspapers' attitudes towards a particular political party are important but not the be-all and end-all. Newspaper circulations are falling, for example, and people get their news from so many different sources these days that one newspaper's bias is easily counterbalanced. (Chapter 10 covers the media and British politics.)

Lord Beaverbrook is widely considered the greatest press magnate of 20th-century Britain. Not only did he own the *London Evening Standard* and the *Daily Express,* he was also given two key jobs – Minister of Aircraft Production and Minister of Supply – in Winston Churchill's wartime government. His newspapers were staunchly loyal to the government during the difficult, bloody and protracted conflict that was the Second World War.

Chapter 8

Homing in on Political Parties

In This Chapter

- Seeing how political parties work
- Looking at the major parties
- Taking a peak at minor and nationalist parties

If from this chapter's title you're expecting to read about shindigs and knees-ups, sorry to disappoint: no festivities here, except for the winning party candidates on election night, of course, when silly hats and champers are the order of the day.

What I do tell you about in this chapter is everything you need to know about Britain's political parties, large and small, mainstream and extreme. I describe their different organisations and the ways in which they function, including how they maintain discipline with stern words and whips (now that's a party!). I also show how their various fates have waxed and waned.

Understanding Political Parties and How They Operate

Put simply, a *political party* is a group of people who come together with the aim of winning government power. These people don't just meet randomly in the street, look each other up and down, and decide that they want political power; they need to have something in common, some sort of shared interest or view of how the country should be governed.

Sometimes a shared interest extends to just one issue. In recent years, parties formed in some parliamentary constituencies with the aim of saving a local hospital or because the local Member of Parliament (MP) has been accused of corruption and people want to see a reputable candidate brought in. These single-issue parties don't tend to last long, because members generally become more preoccupied with other policy concerns and find that they don't have much in common with their fellow members.

By George, Bell's elected!

Two of the most high-profile independent MPs of recent times are Martin Bell and George Galloway. In the 1997 general election, former BBC News war reporter Bell stood against Conservative MP Neil Hamilton, who'd been accused of shady dealings, and won. He said he'd clean up politics and wore a white suit about the place to emphasise how clean-cut he was. However, in 2001 normal service was resumed and he lost his seat.

George Galloway was more controversial. He was drummed out of the Labour Party and formed his own (Respect) party on an anti-Iraq-war ticket in 2005 – and he won. In 2010 he lost his seat but made a remarkable recovery by winning a by-election in Bradford West in 2012.

Recognising the role of the major UK parties

Britain's big political parties – Labour, Conservative (the Tories) and Liberal Democrat (the Lib Dems) – have been around in one form or another for generations. A reason for their longevity is that each has a philosophy with which a substantial number of people throughout the country identify.

All the political parties have *natural supporters* – people whose social and economic background makes them naturally more attuned to a particular political party, and its philosophy and policies.

The big parties are totems in British life, with hundreds of thousands, if not millions, of people gathering around them in one form or another. Party supporters do everything from joining up to voting for their party, or even promoting the party's views in the pub – if you encounter the latter, best drink elsewhere unless you want earache!

The two biggest parties – Labour and Conservative – have their natural supporters that they can usually rely on. However, the key to electoral success lies in appealing beyond this base to the wider electorate. For example, Labour can't win a general election if it doesn't gain some seats in the Conservative stronghold of the south-east of England. The Tories, on the other hand, have to win some seats in the north of England to win a majority.

The most long-lasting model for a political party is one in which a shared philosophy guides positions on many issues and lies behind the policies the party proposes to carry out if it gets into government. The more people who share this philosophy, the more support the party has and the better its chances of being elected and obtaining power.

Some people feel so strongly about the philosophy and policies of a party that they join it and become an activist or even stand for election under the banner of that party.

Even people who aren't party members often identify themselves as being a Tory, Labour or Lib Dem supporter or voter, because it allows other people to gauge the sort of things they believe in.

Forming party policy: The approach of the Conservatives, Labour and the Lib Dems

A political party's policy is crucial because it forms the basis for a *manifesto* – a public declaration of principles and intentions – at election time. As one of the major factors influencing how people vote, this manifesto is a big deal. If the public likes the manifesto, so the thinking goes, the party gets more votes and has a better chance of forming the government.

The three main political parties have different approaches to how party policy is formed; here's a rundown:

- **Conservative:** The leadership forms the policies, but if one is against the wishes of a substantial proportion of party members or senior figures, public disagreements are likely. In effect, this ability to disagree provides a check and balance on the leadership and its policies. Crucially, the leader doesn't form policy on a whim, but has policy advisers who're normally senior figures in the party.
- **Labour:** *Policy forums* – comprising people the party leader appoints – put together potential policies for consideration by the party's National Executive Committee, which is elected by a ballot of all party members. The forum participants draw up policies to put before the party's annual conference, where they're voted upon. The leadership does have the power, however, to ignore conference voting outcomes if it wants.
- **Lib Dem:** As with the way they elect their leader (see the next section), the Lib Dems have a convoluted way of deciding policy – a local and federal system. Policies that affect particular localities, such as Scotland and Wales, are decided and voted upon at small party conferences held in that locality. Policies affecting the country as a whole are debated and voted upon at the national party conference. The leader has a say over the forming of party policy by appointing the members of the Federal Policy Committee, which draws up policy proposals for the national conference and also pens the party's election manifesto.

Lib Dem leaders don't have quite the same sway over party policy as the Labour and Tory leaders.

Choosing and following the leader – and other senior party figures

Much of the power in a political party lies with the leader, who's usually elected through a poll of members, although the party's MPs or groups affiliated to the party may have a say as well (for example, the trade unions also influence who gets to be Labour leader).

The three major parties in the UK use three different methods to choose their leaders:

- **Conservative:** Tory leaders are elected through a combination of ballots among the party's MPs and members. If three or more candidates stand for leadership, MPs are balloted and the top two in this poll go through to a final ballot, on which the entire membership of the party votes.
- **Labour:** The leader and deputy leader are elected through an *electoral college system,* which is divided into three parts. Labour MPs and Members of the European Parliament (MEPs) vote in one section, ordinary party members in another and individual members of trade unions affiliated to the Labour Party in the third. The percentage of the vote each candidate receives in each college is totted-up and this forms their final vote figure. In 2010, Ed Miliband became Labour leader with a shade over 50% of the vote but much of this was made up with votes from the affiliated members college; his brother David Miliband actually gained more votes in the Labour MPs & MEPs college as well as the ballot of party members. However, it was the total percentage of votes which counted across all three colleges, so Ed Miliband won – just!
- **Lib Dem:** The leader is selected by the highly complex *single transferable vote system.* In short, party members vote for not only their favourite candidate (called a *first preference*), but also their second-favourite (called *second preference*). After the votes are counted, the candidate recording the fewest number of first preferences is eliminated and the second preferences of the people who voted for that candidate are then added to the totals of the remaining candidates – I told you this system was complex! The process goes on as the candidates are whittled down to just two. The ultimate winner is the one who polls the highest number of first- and second-preference votes.

Although certainly the party's head honcho, the leader can be challenged. If eligible voters are unhappy with a leader's performance, they can elect someone else to the role.

The leader appoints the senior posts within the party, including spokespeople on particular policy areas such as health or the economy, and when the party is in government decides who gets to be a minister. The leader also appoints people to help with the day-to-day running of the party, making sure, for instance, that enough funds are raised to fight elections and that party membership remains high. Political parties are big institutions with lots of volunteers as well as full-time employees.

Key party bigwigs include the following:

- **Party chairperson:** Ensures that the party's operations are up to speed. The chairperson is a crucial bridge between the high echelons of the party and the grassroots members. A good chairperson can galvanise the grassroots while simultaneously letting the leader know what members are thinking.
- **Party treasurer:** In charge of fundraising for the party, wooing big donors and ensuring that the party has enough cash to communicate its message and fund the fighting of elections.
- **Head of communications:** Responsible for the party's advertising and media strategy, and ensuring that the party is seen in as positive a light as possible in the media and hopefully therefore the country. The communications head may not even be a party member – often, a prominent journalist is employed in this role.
- **Head of candidates:** Makes sure that the best possible candidates represent the party at election time. Each party has a different approach to how this process is done.

The big political parties have different hierarchies. For example, the Labour Party doesn't have a party chairperson; instead, it has a deputy leader who's elected in the same way as the leader.

The Labour party has often been criticised for being too close to the unions – for instance, much of its campaign cash comes from this source. As a result, the Labour leader Ed Miliband decided to reform the relationship with the unions so that money from individual trade union members' subscriptions doesn't go automatically to the Labour Party. Instead individual members have to opt in to having their cash given to the party. This decision is seen as reducing the power of the unions in the Labour party, but the question remains of what happens to the Labour Party's finances as a result.

Whipping up discipline: Keeping party members on the same page

The key phrase for successful political parties is 'united we stand, divided we fall', and parties that endure for generations rather than a few years heed this message. In other words, the party philosophy comes first. If a political party isn't disciplined, it eventually falls apart as the individuals who comprise it go off pursuing their own policy hobby horses and disagreeing in public.

No single politician – even if that person has wide appeal among the electorate – is ever as big as the party as a whole. Parties are professionally organised – a little like a business – with chains of command and internal disciplinary procedures. At the top of UK political parties sits the leader who's above senior party members – such as the deputy leader in the Labour party, party chairperson in the Conservatives or president in the Lib Dems. The leader appoints senior politicians as ministers (if the party is in government) or shadow ministers (if it's in opposition).

This group of politicians is collectively called *the party leadership* and its responsibility is to oversee the making of party policy and be the most visible representatives of the party in the media. But in order to be successful (get elected, in other words) the party leadership has to seem united and they expect the adherence of other party members. Even among people who share the same political philosophy, disagreements can occur over what policy the party should be pursuing. Public disagreements, along with personal scandals, can tarnish the image of the party as a whole.

In modern politics, image – if not quite everything – is crucial, and retaining good party discipline is key to putting across a good image to the voters!

Leading figures in the party who hold an official role, such as chairperson or minister, are expected to adhere to collective responsibility, which is as serious and solemn as it sounds. *Collective responsibility* means that, after the party makes a decision, all the ministers and members in official positions are expected to support that position in public – even if they disagree with it behind closed doors. People breaking with collective responsibility can expect to be sacked from their posts or asked to resign.

Parties whose leading figures disagree in public often do badly at elections. Generally, the electorate doesn't like divided parties, feeling that they won't get things done in government because they'll be bickering among themselves – and the people have a point!

The party's leadership and *whips* (senior party figures who try to ensure that MPs vote in line with the leadership's desires; flip to the next section for more details) can punish an MP for 'crimes' such as speaking out against the leadership (criticising the leader is a big no-no) or a key party policy, as well as personal transgressions such as having an affair or being involved in corruption. Basically, politicians are expected to behave in a morally upstanding manner.

Key ways in which parties keep discipline to present a united front to the electorate include the following:

- **Whipping MPs:** Yes, you read it right. Fortunately, whipping in this context doesn't refer to some dodgy after-hours practice. Whipping's all about getting MPs to vote in favour of their party's policy or a measure proposed by the party leadership.

The *whip* refers to membership of the party in the UK parliament.

MPs who don't comply with the party bosses can have the whip withdrawn, becoming outcasts from the party and having no help from party workers at election time. See Chapter 13 for more on the inner workings of what's called 'the mother of all parliaments' – and, oh yes, more whipping!

- **Giving and withholding promotion:** Senior figures in the party often get to decide who moves up the party or governmental ranks. For example, the prime minister (PM) makes ministerial appointments. Party members who don't toe the line may not get promoted or can lose their position within the party.

  The ultimate arbitrator of this big appointments merry-go-round is the party leader, who's also the PM when the party is in government.

Often, when senior politicians resign following a scandal, they say that it's 'for the good of the party'. Such resignations emphasise the key mantra at the heart of successful political parties: no one is bigger than the party.

Looking at the role of the whips

Whipping is crucial to the UK law-making process. All the major parties have a whip who usually also has a couple of deputies. The whip's role is to get the party's MPs to vote the way the leadership of the party wants them to. Whips are key to parties in government: they strive to ensure a majority so that it can push its bills into law.

Witnessing party breakdowns

In times of great crisis – such as during war or an economic depression – the political party system can appear to break down, because the established parties no longer seem to have the answers to the problems of the day. The main parties often fragment – lose support and membership – and new ones form, or smaller, single-issue parties see a surge in support.

Sometimes this scenario can be healthy, but other times less so. In pre-war Germany, for instance, economic collapse caused a dramatic haemorrhaging of support from the main established political parties as people sought new answers to their economic woes. One party to benefit was the National Socialists (Nazis) under Adolf Hitler. He took power and a few years later plunged the world into the bloodiest war in history. The rise of Hitler was, at the start at least, facilitated by the breaking down of the established political parties.

Whips are powerful and often Machiavellian in their behaviour. Their job is to persuade their fellow MPs to support the party leadership. They've been known to threaten recalcitrant MPs with all sorts of sanctions, from denying them government posts in the future (when a whip tells the PM a particular MP is a troublemaker, the chances of that MP becoming a minister in the future are slim) to de-selection as a party candidate at the next election.

MPs receive weekly instructions from their whips, telling them when they're expected to turn up to the House of Commons and how they're expected to vote (I know it all sounds very controlling, and believe me it is!).

The leadership is more bothered about some votes than others. For example, the whips don't usually instruct all a party's MPs to vote down a Private Members' Bill (which I discuss in Chapter 13), because just a few votes against normally suffice.

The whips have a code to indicate to their MPs how seriously they should take an instruction to turn up and vote a particular way:

- **Three line whip:** Attendance is absolutely essential and MPs are expected to vote with their party leadership. Failure to follow a three line whip can lead to serious consequences for the individual MP.
- **Two line whip:** Attendance is expected but MPs can *pair off,* which isn't some sort of speed-dating game but an arrangement in which an MP finds a member from an opposition party and they agree not to turn up. In practice they negate each other's vote and so the voting mathematics remains the same.
- **One line whip:** A request from the whips for MPs to attend. The world doesn't end if this is ignored, but the whips still aren't happy.

Some areas of legislation are considered *matters of conscience,* which means that the leadership stays neutral and whips don't issue voting instructions: examples include the re-introduction of the death penalty and changing the legal limit on abortion. On such occasions MPs are given a *free vote.*

Sometimes an individual MP annoys the whip so much that the whip *withdraws the whip.* You may think that's happy days for the MP – no more threats and orders from the whip. Not a bit of it though. Withdrawing the whip is in effect suspension from the party. No MP who has the whip withdrawn can stand as a party candidate at election. Often withdrawal of the whip is a temporary measure, but if the MP doesn't want the constituency party to de-select him as a candidate, he has to get back into the good books of the whip and have the whip restored.

Ineffective whipping leads to government bills not passing. The media and the electorate at large see a government that loses lots of votes in the House of Commons as weak – hardly vote-winning qualities!

Breaking the mould: Famous party schisms and rebellions

Despite being around for many years, the main UK political parties have had rebellions and splits within them that caused disastrous consequences at the polls. Two big rebellions include:

- **The Gang of Four:** Following defeat at the 1979 general election, the Labour Party adopted more radical left-wing policies, such as unilateral nuclear disarmament, which led to four of its most prominent MPs – Roy Jenkins, David Owen, Shirley Williams and Bill Rodgers – leaving in 1981 and forming their own new party, the Social Democrats (SDP). After some initial success at the polls and a further disastrous defeat for Labour in the 1983 general election, the SDP started to fragment and eventually was swallowed up by the Liberal Party, which then changed its name to the Liberal Democrats. Ultimately, the SDP took a large chunk of Labour's natural support base and inadvertently helped Margaret Thatcher's Tories win a majority at a couple of general elections.
- **Maggie kicked out:** Margaret Thatcher polarised opinion across the country in the late 1980s, because the UK was in recession and she pursued unpopular policies such as the poll tax. Eventually, in late 1990, she was forced to resign as PM following a rebellion among her own MPs and a leadership challenge from rival Michael Heseltine. The party elected John Major and went on to a surprise win at the 1992 general election. However, supporters of Thatcher never forgave those who deposed her and the Major government was disastrously split, which contributed to a heavy defeat at the 1997 general election.

The House of Lords also has whips, but they tend to operate more gently – after all, they're dealing with the nobility. What's more, the Lords don't need party support because they don't stand for election.

Living it up at party conferences

Everyone loves a knees-up, and that's particularly true of the UK's main political parties' annual conferences. These big bashes are often held in seaside towns and offer party members the chance to rub shoulders with leading politicians. They normally take place in the early autumn in what's known as the party conference season. Lively debates and fringe meetings are followed by a fair amount of drinking and socialising.

Party conferences aren't just about having fun, though; they serve the following purposes too:

- Debating, though these days rarely changing, party policies.
- Encouraging new ideas at fringe meetings, which may ultimately be incorporated into party policy.
- Attracting massive media coverage, making conferences a good platform for the party to let the wider population know its policies.
- Raising huge funds from party members and party donors, which helps the party fight elections.

In the not too distant past, party conferences were dramatic occasions, with huge rows erupting between leading politicians. In the 1970s and 1980s the Labour Party's annual conferences, for instance, were scenes of heated arguments about policy and leadership. At the time, party policy was decided by votes taken at conference, and so the decisions taken really mattered. Although party policy is still discussed at conference, however, the leaderships of the main parties no longer have to follow what the conference decides.

Today's party conferences are stage-managed, choreographed occasions, with leading politicians making carefully prepared speeches that members on the conference floor often greet with delirious applause. The aim is to project the party's message and the personality of the leader to the whole country.

This lack of substantive decision-making at conferences doesn't mean a lack of drama, though – far from it! These days, the drama's to be found in the fringe meetings, where policies and sometimes the future of the leader are debated openly by members. These fringe meetings still retain a little of the old fireworks previously seen on the conference floor.

Forgoing party to form a national government

In the normal course of events political parties are at loggerheads, trying to make their opponents look ponderous and frankly a bit daft and themselves bright and full of answers to the nation's problems. This scenario is particularly the case at the big once-weekly set-piece event when the leaders of the opposition and backbench MPs (which the Speaker of the House of Commons selects to speak) from all parties quiz the PM on what the government is up to. Prime minister's question time is all very entertaining and part of the rough and tumble of party politics.

Sometimes, however, the country's in such a big mess that politicians realise that being at loggerheads is inappropriate: the public won't stand for rowing politicians – they want united action. Such a situation can lead opposition parties to fall into line behind the government and support its policies. In extremely serious national emergencies, the government can even invite leading members of the opposition into government. Called a *national government,* the intention is to unite the major political parties to meet the emergency.

National governments are very rare in the UK because the country tends to be highly stable. When such arrangements have been made in the past, they've been in response to the following national emergencies:

- The country is at war and has suffered some serious military reverses.
- The country is in the grip of an economic crisis.

National governments have been formed twice in the last 100 years. The first was in response to the Great Depression in the early 1930s and the second was during the Second World War, after allied forces were defeated first in France and then Norway.

Winston Churchill was prime minister during most of the Second World War. He came to power as the head of a government containing members of the Conservative, Labour and Liberal parties when the UK was facing the very real possibility of being invaded by Nazi Germany. (Chapter 23 lists ten of Britain's great PMs.)

A national government results in the following benefits:

- The country's most talented politicians from all parties come together.
- It has an automatic majority in the House of Commons and so can press ahead with new laws.

National governments are meant to be a temporary response to a particular crisis. In the past, as soon as the crisis has been addressed, the old parties reform and start competing again.

Looking at the Benefits of the Party System

Love them or loathe them, Britain's political parties are crucial to the running of the country, bringing solidity and permanence to the political system. The people who run the government are usually drawn from the most popular political party in an election.

Climbing the ranks to power

Previous PMs John Major and Margaret Thatcher prove that someone can start off as a virtual unknown to the general public. Both PMs came from relatively humble backgrounds – Thatcher's father ran a corner shop and Major's was brought up in Brixton and spent his early life in the circus! But neither Thatcher nor Major fancied the life of a retailer or juggler and so chose a career in politics instead. They first went canvassing on behalf of their chosen party's (Conservative) candidates and then stood for election. After many years of climbing up the ranks of the party, they were elected leader, and finally, when their party was in government, became prime minister.

Some of the plus points of the party system include:

- **Parties bring stability in government.** Party members share the same outlook and philosophy, and so (in theory) they can work well together.
- **Parties help formulate government policy.** Party members decide what policies they want their party to pursue if they get into government.
- **Parties provide opportunities for advancement.** Anyone can become PM but only by rising through the ranks of a political party to be leader – look for the nearby sidebar, 'Climbing the ranks to power'.
- **Parties mobilise the wider electorate.** Parties help highlight crucial issues for the electorate and individual members can motivate friends and neighbours to vote. Without strong political parties, voter turnout would most likely be even lower than it is (see Chapter 7).
- **Parties provide scrutiny of government.** When not in power, parties can highlight the failings of government and propose alternative solutions to the country's ills. Sometimes the government agrees with what they're saying and adopts policies recommended by their political opponents – although they rarely admit they're doing so.

When in power, political parties ensure that the actions and philosophy of the government are closely aligned to at least a substantial minority of the population, even if not always the majority.

Exploring the Tories

The Tories – the nickname for the Conservative Party – have been around in one form or another for a couple of hundred years, which shows that they're getting something right in terms of public appeal.

The term *Tory* goes back to the 17th century and is short for *Toraidhe,* an Irish word for outlaw. Originally, it was a term of abuse for English Catholics and those who supported the monarch over the mostly Protestant parliament.

The Tories tend to be seen as being on the right of British politics, which means that they support:

- Promoting free trade and enterprise over a big welfare state
- Retaining important constitutional and cultural institutions
- Keeping Britain independent from a European 'super state'
- Maintaining a strong military and Britain's senior position in the world

Generally, the party's policies reflect in some shape or form these key philosophies, particularly its adherence to free-market economics.

The Conservative Party is often referred to as being a little old-fashioned; out of the three main political parties in the UK, its members are the oldest. However, ageism alone doesn't make people brand the Tories old-fashioned; the party's desire to defend the nation's institutions, such as the monarchy and a shared British national identity even when campaigning in Scotland and Wales, also creates this image.

Whigs and Tories square off and give birth to the Lib Dems

For about 150 years, until around the end of the 19th century and the reign of Queen Victoria, the UK had only two main political parties: the Whigs and the Tories. Put simply, the Whigs believed that parliament should run the country and that the Protestant religion should be the only type of Christianity allowed. The Tories, on the other hand, tended to believe that the monarch should have plenty of power in the constitution – even perhaps more than parliament – and that the Catholics weren't to be persecuted.

For most of this time the Whigs headed (geddit?) the government because their anti-Catholicism and desire for a parliamentary system was more in tune with rich merchants, the growing band of industrialists and the wider population in general. The Whig party started to slowly fragment in the 19th century, however, over key issues such as free trade and constitutional reform. This fragmentation left the Tories suddenly centre stage, and to counteract this situation the remaining Whigs formed a new party called the Liberals – the forerunner of today's Liberal Democrats.

Occasionally, Conservative Party candidates for election to the UK parliament refer to themselves as belonging to the Conservative and Unionist Party. They're still Conservatives, but adding 'Unionist' emphasises to voters that they believe wholeheartedly in the union between England, Scotland, Wales and Northern Ireland. 'Dipping into Northern Irish Politics' later in this chapter has more on what Unionist means in Northern Irish politics.

Re-inventing the Tories: Cameron's conservatism

When David Cameron was elected Conservative leader in 2005, the party had just suffered its third consecutive crushing electoral defeat. It was at a low ebb and the new youthful leader's response was to give the old party a modern makeover. Cameron went about trying to change the party's image from being old and fuddy-duddy to bright, new and representing the whole country, with limited success.

Out went the blue-torch logo, replaced by a green-leafed English oak. Continuing the green theme, Cameron changed the party's policies to make them more environmentally friendly. A former public relations man, he also overhauled the process of choosing MPs and MEPs (the latter sit in the European parliament). Prior to the 2010 general election, he set about upping the number of women and ethnic-minority candidates to make the party more representative of the UK population.

At the 2010 general election the Conservatives polled the most votes and won the most seats, but not enough to form the government alone. As a result, it formed a coalition government with the Lib Dems. A success of sorts, but still some way short of what pollsters had predicted.

Tapping natural Tory supporters

Most Conservatives believe in a mix of creating a conducive environment for businesses and individuals to create wealth while maintaining the status quo (not ensuring that the band continues to tour – you can't credit or blame the Tories for that! – but that things stay as they are). In short, they support making money while keeping what they think is right about Britain.

These principles have a pretty broad appeal and the party has been in government many times, polling between 40 and 45 per cent of the vote at its best and around 30 per cent at its worst.

The Tories tend to do better:

- Among older people
- With people living in the countryside
- In the south-east of England – London and the counties surrounding it

They do better than any other party in southern England because these people have higher average incomes and a lot invested in maintaining the status quo. They also like the party's expressed commitment to free-market economics and low taxes. The south of England is densely populated, which gives whatever party is doing well there a good chance of winning enough seats in parliament to be able to form the government.

Looking at the Labour Party

The Labour Party had a difficult beginning but grew with speed into one of the two parties, along with the Tories, that usually forms the UK government. Labour is usually referred to as being on the left or centre-left of British politics, because most of the party's supporters believe in the following:

- A more extensive and generous welfare system
- Limits on the excesses of the free market
- Quality public services funded by taxes

At general elections, when the Labour Party is popular it tends to poll around 40 to 45 per cent of the electorate, enough to form a government. On the other hand, when the party and its policies aren't popular it can poll around 25 to 30 per cent of votes.

Forming the Labour Party

The Labour Party's difficult birth arose from its origins in the British trade union movement of the 19th century. This movement struggled desperately for recognition, with many activists imprisoned and even deported for trying to get themselves and fellow workers a fairer deal. But despite the problems, in time the unions gained recognition and grew into a powerful force.

As the 19th century became the 20th, the union (or labour) movement wanted a party to represent the aspirations and concerns of its millions of members. In short, union chiefs felt that the big parties of the time – the

Tories and Liberals – had precious little in common with their mainly urban, working-class membership. The Labour Party was formed to give a voice to millions of Britain's workers.

Keir Hardie is often seen as the founding father of the Labour Party, although in reality he was only the most prominent of a whole batch of people who brought the party into being. He's considered so important because he was the first avowed Socialist to be elected to the UK parliament, in 1892. He lost his seat again in 1895 but didn't give up. A renowned public speaker, Hardie stayed close to his roots as a coal miner and union organiser. In 1900 the Labour Party was formed and he became one of its first two MPs and its leader, a position he resigned in 1908 to concentrate on campaigning for votes for women and an end to racial segregation policies in South Africa.

Gauging Labour's followers

The Labour Party tends to do better among voters with the following characteristics and those living in the following areas of the country:

- People in the north of England, Wales and Scotland
- Trade union members and public sector workers
- Lower income voters and social housing tenants, often living in urban areas

This bedrock support among the working class and union members means that it does better in areas once dominated by manufacturing and industry.

Breaking with the unions: Hard to do

The previously strong relationship between the Labour Party and the trade unions has become strained in recent years, with even suggestions that they ought to split. But the unions remain crucial to Labour for these reasons:

- Some unions levy a duty on their members, which is paid to the Labour Party
- Union members provide many of the activists and canvassers for Labour Party candidates
- Many Labour candidates for election to local government, the UK and European parliaments come from the ranks of the unions

Trade unionists have a key role in the election of Labour's leader and deputy leader. In fact, Labour leader Ed Miliband owes his own election to the backing of the unions.

Borrowing the other side's clothes: Blairism

Labour suffered a series of electoral defeats in the 1980s and 1990s during what's known as its 'lurch to the left' (referring to its strong left-wing politics at this time): the party was seen as behind the times and didn't have a wide enough appeal among the electorate. The party's links with the trade unions – who'd been comprehensively beaten in a series of industrial disputes by the government of Tory PM Margaret Thatcher – didn't help with this image problem.

Then along came the charismatic Tony Blair. A great TV performer and communicator, he set about modernising the Labour Party, changing policies to represent more of the concerns of the general population rather than the private concerns of the party membership and trade unions. Blair moved the party into the centre of British politics, accepting many of the changes that the then Tory government brought about. In effect, his pitch was simple: to accept the reforms of Thatcher but in the future promote a fairer society (through policies such as introducing a national minimum wage). Labour's new stance was alluring to the electorate and in 1997 it was elected to government in a landslide victory.

With the general election loss of 2010 and the election of Ed Miliband as leader, however, Labour is perhaps again moving to the left. He proposed a price cap on energy bills and capping property rents, two policies that Tony Blair during his tenure wouldn't have touched.

Taking in the Lib Dems

The Lib Dems – or Liberal Democrats in full – have been around for a long time, with the party tracing its roots to the Whigs in the 18th and 19th centuries. But the party has had a chequered history, sometimes claiming the top prize of government but also almost disappearing altogether in the 20th century (for several decades, the Lib Dems had only a handful of MPs).

The simple truth is that, of the UK's three main political parties, the Lib Dems almost always poll the fewest votes. The party is often seen as the Cinderella of British politics, never quite garnering enough support at UK parliamentary elections to form the government of the country. But don't feel too sorry for the Cinderella party; it still plays a big role in UK politics:

- It traditionally does well in council elections. In fact, large parts of UK local government are either run by the party on its own or as part of a ruling coalition with the Tories or Labour.
- It can hold the balance of power when the two main parties run each other close at a general election – a concept I explore in the next section.
- It tends to be seen as the progressive party of British politics, its policy ideas often derided by Labour and the Tories but then quietly adopted.
- It's often said to be at the centre or centre-left of British politics.

Understanding the balance of power

The Lib Dems often talk about holding the balance of power. Sometimes neither the Tories nor Labour get enough MPs to form the government on its own, as happened in the 2010 general election. Therefore, one or the other needs the support of another party or two with sufficient MPs to join together to form a *coalition government.*

In such situations, the Lib Dems come into their own. They can lend their support to a larger party, but usually extract a price – some senior politicians made into ministers and some policies adopted by the government. This is exactly what happened in 2010, with the Lib Dem leader Nick Clegg negotiating with Labour and the Conservatives on these two points.

Coalition governments like the one formed after the 2010 general election are few and far between in the UK and, what's more, the Lib Dems aren't the only game in town. Labour or the Tories can form governments with the help of minor parties – such as the Scottish and Welsh nationalists or the Ulster Unionist party, which I describe later in this chapter in 'Taking a Look at the Nationalists: SNP and Plaid Cymru' and 'Dipping into Northern Irish Politics', respectively. Generally, coalitions are more likely at local government (council) than UK parliamentary level.

Supporting proportional representation

Local government and UK parliamentary elections are run on a first-past-the-post system, where, put simply, the party candidate polling the highest number of votes wins the seat. This winner-takes-all scenario doesn't help the Lib Dems (or any smaller party) and they often struggle to get enough votes to win a constituency outright, but they do manage regularly to run a close second to the Tories or Labour.

The Lib Dems would prefer a system of *proportional representation* (PR), whereby seats are awarded according to the proportion of total votes cast. At the 2010 UK general election, the Lib Dems attracted around 23 per cent of the votes cast; under PR, this result would've given them roughly 140 seats in parliament, whereas they managed only 57 seats under the current system.

The first-past-the-post system isn't changed because neither the Tories nor Labour wants to amend a system that gives it a good chance of forming the government outright. Refer to Chapter 6 for the merits or otherwise of different voting systems, including first past the post and PR.

Following the 2010 general election no one party had a majority. During five days of intense negotiations the leaderships of the Conservatives and Lib Dems hammered out an agreement that allowed them to form a coalition government. As part of this agreement, they agreed to hold a referendum on changing the UK parliamentary voting system to a type of PR called the alternative vote (AV) system (refer to Chapter 6 for more). Much to the chagrin of the Lib Dems, however, the referendum result was a resounding no to AV.

Looking at Lib Dem supporters

Defining the natural supporters of the Lib Dems is harder than for Labour and the Tories. Some cynics say that Lib Dems are people who don't naturally gravitate towards the Tory or Labour parties. But this view is a little simplistic. The Lib Dems do have natural supporters and parts of the country where they do better than others:

- People in the south-west of England
- People very concerned about the state of the environment
- People who want to see the UK play a fuller part in the European Union

When the Lib Dems are popular in the country they can attract around 25 per cent of the UK electorate; when they're doing less well they can gather only 10–12 per cent.

Tearing up the Establishment: The Rise of UKIP

Many commentators suggest that the UK currently has four rather than three main political parties, with the steady rise of the United Kingdom Independence Party (UKIP). Formed in 1993 by a small group of people opposed to the increasing influence of the European Union over the lives of Britons and the nation's laws, the party gathered substantial support in recent years – even polling as high as 27 per cent at certain times.

UKIP has expanded its appeal from an anti-EU party to one that talks about controlling immigration more tightly, lowering taxes and protecting personal freedoms. Initially, UKIP gathered much of its support from disaffected Tory voters (its policies are to the right of the political spectrum), but it now seems to be drawing from a deeper well of ex-Labour, ex-Lib Dem voters and even those who'd given up on politics and not voted for several elections.

Wherever UKIP's support is coming from, it looks to be a well-organised, more professional party with a growing membership. UKIP is here to stay and the big three parties had better get used to it!

Much of the success of UKIP is undoubtedly down to its charismatic leader Nigel Farage, seen by supporters as a man of the people not worried by political spin and able therefore to speak his mind. In an age of polished, media-trained politicians Farage's more colourful approach appeals to many voters fed up with the old three-party status quo, though that's not to say that he isn't a canny politician who knows exactly what he's doing.

Although UKIP has done well in the polls, much of its support lies in more rural parts of England and its pro-British message has gone down poorly in Wales and Scotland.

Focusing on the Minor Parties

Under the UK's first-past-the-post electoral system, minor parties rarely gather enough votes in one constituency to have an MP elected. But this doesn't stop the minor parties combined taking a substantial proportion of the popular vote – sometimes as much as 20 per cent.

The UK's major minor parties – if you get what I mean – include:

- **British National Party:** The BNP has been around for many years and has its roots in the British Union of Fascists, which supported the rise of Hitler in the 1930s. The BNP would like to see all non-white Britons repatriated to the country that they or their ancestors hailed from. Opponents accuse the BNP of being simply a racist party and almost universal disquiet is felt about the party's showing at the polls. At the 2009 European election, for instance, the BNP managed to attract enough votes to get two MEPs elected. But more recently, support has fallen dramatically away as its undeniably racist policies and leadership have come under ever greater public scrutiny.
- **Green Party:** The Greens focus on promoting more environmentally friendly government with the aim of reducing carbon emissions and saving the planet. It's a big ask, but the Green Party has had some major successes in European and, to a lesser extent, local elections. Its best showing saw the party attract 5–10 per cent of the votes cast.

  The Green Party in the UK is somewhat the poor relation of its counterparts on the European mainland. In Germany, for instance, the Green Party played a part in a past coalition government.

  Although the UK Green party is relatively minor, it did manage to get an MP elected in the 2010 general election: Caroline Lucas to the Brighton Pavilion seat. The Greens also have substantial representation on several local councils around the country.

In many other EU countries minor parties can play a substantial role in government due to the use of PR, where if a minor party gets 5 per cent of the vote it gets 5 per cent of the seats in parliament. As a result, large parties often have to work with smaller ones to gain a working majority in parliament and govern the country. The Greens in Germany and the Communists in Italy, for example, have been part of coalition governments.

The UK's first-past-the-post voting system makes a party polling 5 per cent of the vote unlikely to get any seats – apart from the Scottish and Welsh nationalist parties (see the following two sections). Minor parties are thus not as important in the UK.

Often votes for the minor parties are referred to as *protest votes,* which means that people are protesting the policies of the big political parties – Labour, Tory and Lib Dem – by giving their support to a minor party.

Minor parties tend to do best at European and local elections, because turnout is lower and people see the election as being less important than a general election. Registering a protest vote at a European or local election is thus seen as safer than doing so at a general election.

Embracing strange small parties

The British love eccentrics, and election time brings them out in spades. In fact, one of the most colourful aspects of British political life is all the strange minor parties and weird individuals who stand for election to the UK parliament. Some of the minor parties that fielded candidates for election in the past and may do so again include the following:

- **Monster Raving Loony Party:** Offering policies such as a bottle of gin for everyone, the Loonies are a comic addition to any election campaign.
- **Natural Law Party:** This now defunct party believed that crime and economic problems can be solved through a type of meditation called Yogic Flying – and, yes, you read that right!
- **Mums' Army:** Started by *Take a Break* magazine as a campaign against yobbish behaviour, this small party has fielded candidates in many parts of the UK.
- **Fancy Dress Party:** This party's an offshoot of the Monster Raving Loony Party and the candidates insist on wearing – guess what?

Beyond the minor parties, nearly all individuals are allowed to stand for parliament provided they pay a deposit. This easy path to standing for election can lead to some real eccentrics getting onto the ballot paper. My favourite is a man who stood in the Dover constituency in 1979 and canvassed door to door dressed as a circus impresario, leading a friend (presumably) dressed as a mouse on a chain!

Taking a Look at the Nationalists: SNP and Plaid Cymru

Although the Scots and Welsh nationalists – called the Scottish National Party (SNP) and Plaid Cymru, respectively – can be classed as minor parties because they attract only a small percentage of the total UK electorate, in their own parts of the country they're very big deals indeed.

In fact, the SNP has been the biggest party in Scotland for the past few years and is currently in government in the Scottish parliament. (I cover the Scottish parliament and Welsh Assembly in Chapter 18.) At the most recent elections the SNP attracted more than 35 per cent of votes cast in Scotland.

Plaid Cymru in Wales has also made significant strides in recent years, taking many votes from the Labour Party, traditionally the biggest and most popular party in Wales. But Wales isn't likely to become independent from England anytime soon, though many within Plaid Cymru would like that to happen. Wales is generally poorer than Scotland and has a smaller population; many people worry that it's unable to stand on its own without help from its much larger neighbour, England. At present, they're probably right!

Both the SNP and Plaid Cymru tend to be on the left of British politics, believing in tight regulation of the free market and strong, well-funded public services paid for, if necessary, through higher taxation.

Not only the Scots and Welsh have nationalist parties; the English do too. For example, in the south-west of England, the Cornish National Party often fields candidates, as does the English National Party elsewhere in England. But neither of these parties is anywhere near as popular in its part of the UK as the Scots and Welsh nationalists are in theirs.

Dipping into Northern Irish Politics

To someone from mainland Britain, the way in which Northern Ireland's society and politics are divided can be difficult to fathom. Parties aren't split along the same lines as in the rest of the UK but according to sectarian affiliation. Electors vote for parties that represent their own religious ideal.

Put simply, *sectarianism* is a division based on religion – in Northern Ireland, the adherence to the Protestant strand of Christianity or the Catholic.

Yet religion isn't the only factor at play; it's intertwined with British and Irish nationalism. Here are some of the realities of Northern Irish politics:

- People from the Protestant community are often *Unionists* (also called Loyalists) who believe in being joined with Britain, which is ostensibly a Protestant country.
- People from the Catholic community are often *Nationalists* (or Republicans) who want Northern Ireland to leave the UK and join with the Irish Republic, which is ostensibly a Catholic country.

Now this division probably wouldn't matter quite so much if it wasn't for the fact that the population is roughly evenly split between Catholics and Protestants and that, for much of the last 40 years, certain people within both communities have resorted to violence to advance their causes.

Until relatively recently, many in the Catholic community felt that their views weren't listened to, because many of the top governmental jobs and businesses in Northern Ireland were in the hands of prominent figures from the Protestant community. In the early 1970s, this situation sparked a civil rights movement and the discontent that grew from this perceived inequality led to many young men and women joining terrorist organisations.

To complicate matters further, not all Catholics are Republicans and not all Protestants are Unionists.

These issues make Northern Ireland's party politics very different to the rest of the UK, with Labour, Tory and Lib Dem having little impact. Instead, parties rooted in the Catholic and Protestant communities hold sway and even these communities have different strands, each sparking its own party.

Here are the main Protestant parties and what they stand for:

- **Democratic Unionist Party:** The DUP is currently the biggest party in Northern Irish politics. In the past, it's been staunchly opposed to any closer ties to the government of the Irish Republic in Dublin. However, British and Irish MPs brokered a deal in 2007 that saw the DUP enter into a power-sharing agreement with the ultra-Irish nationalist Sinn Féin party.

  For many years, the firebrand Reverend Ian Paisley led the DUP, standing up for what he perceived as the rights of his community. Like his party, though, he too came round to the idea of power-sharing.
- **Ulster Unionist Party:** Throughout the 1970s, 1980s and 1990s, the UUP was the largest party representing the interests of the Protestant community in Northern Ireland. It held several seats in the UK House of Commons and was often called upon to support Labour and Tory governments when they were struggling to reach a majority. Generally, the UUP was considered to be more moderate in its outlook than the DUP, and its former leader, David Trimble, was key in the early stages of the peace process in Northern Ireland.

On the Catholic side of the community, the major parties are as follows:

- **Social Democratic and Labour Party:** Traditionally, the SDLP was the biggest party representing the Catholic community in Northern Ireland, but, like the UUP, it's been supplanted at the top of the polls by a rival party hailing from the same community (Sinn Féin). The SDLP was for years seen as a moderate voice in Northern Irish politics, looking for union with the Irish Republic through peaceful, democratic means.
- **Sinn Féin:** This party is the most controversial in Northern Irish politics as a result of its close links with the Provisional Irish Republican Army (IRA). For many years the British government ignored Sinn Féin and its leaders' voices were even banned from being broadcast. Some of its leading members are widely presumed at one time or another to have been involved with the IRA and therefore violence. However, the party was key in arranging an IRA ceasefire and then getting it to renounce violence. As part of a wide-ranging peace agreement, Sinn Féin was invited into government in Northern Ireland and is now the largest party in the Catholic community. Currently, it shares government with the DUP and former IRA members occupy high posts in government.

A few parties have pitched themselves as being 'cross community' – including the Alliance Party of Northern Ireland – but generally they've attracted only minor support.

Northern Ireland has an assembly and a government, which at present is a coalition between Republicans and Unionists comprising leading figures from very different parties such as Sinn Féin and the DUP.

The Northern Ireland Assembly sits in Stormont Castle and has 108 elected members. Its powers are limited, though. For example, the assembly can decide health, education and environmental policy, but the UK government in Westminster has control over criminal justice and matters of international trade and diplomacy. Interestingly, all bills passed by the assembly must have *royal assent* – be agreed to by the UK head of state – to become law.

Chapter 9

Piling on the Pressure Groups

In This Chapter

- Introducing pressure groups
- Dividing groups between 'insiders' and 'outsiders'
- Understanding how pressure groups exert pressure

British politics isn't just about political parties, big-name politicians and close-run elections. Below the theatre of national politics and the everyday workings of local government are organised pressure groups looking to influence government policy and public opinion. These pressure groups aren't to be confused with political parties – they don't seek government office; instead, they have particular objectives in mind to which they dedicate all their energies.

Whatever the sizes or resources of the pressure groups, they're a key part of the UK's democracy.

In this chapter I explore the world of the pressure group, from the small local organisations – perhaps little more than a single person leafleting and lobbying – to huge well-staffed bodies that are experts at public relations.

Taking in the Universe of Pressure Groups

A *pressure group* is a body or organisation that tries to influence government policy and wider public opinion; but, unlike a political party, a pressure group doesn't seek elected office. Pressure groups, particularly in the US, are also referred to in the media as *special interest groups*.

Literally thousands of pressure groups exist in the UK. Some are concerned with a single issue – keeping a local hospital open, for example – whereas others concentrate on a range of issues with one overarching theme. For example, the NSPCC (National Society for the Prevention of Cruelty to Children) focuses on improving the welfare of children across the country. Some groups represent a particular section of society, such as nurses, lawyers or musicians.

Detailing all the pressure groups in the UK would require a book in itself. They come from all parts of the political and social spectrums. For example, pressure groups exist *lobbying* (finding ways to influence decision makers in government) for the legalisation of cannabis (the Legalise Cannabis Alliance), representing doctors (the British Medical Association, BMA) and even looking out for the police (the Association of Chief Police Officers). To make things easier, I divide pressure groups into two main types:

- **Sectional pressure groups:** Promote the interests of a group of people and are normally related to a profession or occupation.
- **Cause-related pressure groups:** Concerned with a particular social or ethical issue, such as protecting the environment or promoting civil liberties.

Generally, the bigger and more geographically spread the issue or the group represented, the larger the pressure group. Some of these large pressure groups are sizeable enterprises, employing hundreds of people and needing to raise lots of money to pay wages and to aid the group's lobbying of politicians and the public. Smaller, less well-funded pressure groups have to rely on volunteers to do the administration and fundraising. The bigger bodies, though still using some volunteers, are organised more along the lines of a business, employing lots of staff with skills to help the group better raise funds and get its message across to the public and politicians alike.

Like political parties, some pressure groups have long histories dating back 50 and even 100 years. Why do they have such staying power? Well, the cause they're working for or section of society they represent has widespread support so that the pressure group is adequately resourced and able to exert influence on politicians and the public.

Sorting out sectional pressure groups

These pressure groups look to promote the interests of a particular section of society, normally relating to an occupation. By far the best-known sectional pressure groups are the trade unions, each representing the interests of thousands or hundreds of thousands of workers according to their occupation.

Usually, membership of these pressure groups is restricted. For example, a plumber can't join a teaching trade union or become a member of the doctors' body, the BMA. What's more, these sectional groups can often claim a high proportion of people working in a particular occupation or industry as members. Sometimes, in fact, membership of the group is a requirement of being able to practise. For example, dentists have to belong to the British Dental Association, which not only polices good practice in the industry and can stop wrongdoers from practising, but also represents and promotes the interests of its members.

Not all sectional pressure groups, however, are professional bodies or unions. Groups exist representing business owners, for example, such as the Confederation of British Industry (CBI) and the British Chambers of Commerce.

Sectional pressure groups can have a big say in government policy. For example, no government would dream about reforming the National Health Service (NHS) without at least discussing its plans with the BMA, which represents doctors, who in turn would have to implement any government-inspired reforms.

A sectional pressure group usually sticks to trying to influence policy in a single area of daily life. For example, the Law Society looks to influence how the UK court system operates but doesn't touch the workings of the NHS.

Seeing to cause-related groups

As the name suggests, these pressure groups look to promote a particular cause. Members of cause-related groups are people from all walks of life coalescing around a particular social or ethical issue. For example, Greenpeace wants to see greater protection of the environment, and in the 1970s and 1980s hundreds of thousands of Britons from all walks of life were members of the Campaign for Nuclear Disarmament (CND).

Crucially, unlike sectional groups, membership of cause-related groups is open to anyone. However, members may be asked to make a regular financial donation to the group so that it can better fund its operations.

Most serious, long-term, cause-related pressure groups achieve some level of success as they continue to lobby and pressure government and persuade the public of the justness of their causes. They tend to make slow progress rather than no progress.

Lobbying failure: The case of CND

In the 1970s and 1980s, CND had a huge membership and attracted widespread media coverage for its campaign for the UK to get rid of its nuclear weapons. It even had a strong influence on the Labour Party, which went into the 1983 general election saying that it would scrap the bomb.

However, Labour lost the 1983 election by a landslide and the Conservative government under Margaret Thatcher retained Britain's nuclear weapons capability. The government argued that CND was too extreme and didn't have enough public support to justify it changing its policy.

Over time, the Labour Party also abandoned its plans to decommission nuclear weapons and CND drifted from being a high-profile pressure group into relative obscurity.

In some cases, the government of the day consults cause-related groups about its policies. For example, the Labour government of Tony Blair in the late 1990s consulted Age Concern, which represents the interests of elderly people, before introducing key reforms to the benefits it paid to this socio-demographic group. It wanted to get Age Concern 'on side' so that when the policy was presented to the media and the wider electorate the government appeared to have the support of a key pressure group. Sometimes this consultation may be a matter of mere courtesy. However, if a pressure group comes out and decries government policy it can persuade some of the electorate who feel strongly about the issue at hand to move their support from the government to the opposition parties.

Generally, cause-related groups find persuading politicians to do what they want them to do harder than sectional groups. Sectional groups tend to be well-organised and can in some cases withdraw their labour if they're angered by a particular government policy – for example, in the past teachers have gone on strike in reaction to the introduction of new working practices. Cause-related groups don't have the option of withdrawing their labour, because they come from such diverse backgrounds.

Going Inside, Outside, Up and Down with Pressure Groups

As well as dividing up pressure groups into sectional and cause-related (as I do in the preceding section), you can also categorise them by which groups have the ear of government on a regular basis – are on the *inside,* so to speak – and those that don't – the ones on the outside. As you can imagine, a pressure group generally prefers to be an insider rather than an outsider.

Differentiating between inside and outside

Table 9-1 shows the main ways to tell whether a pressure group is inside or outside.

Table 9-1 Traits of Insider and Outsider Pressure Groups

Insiders	*Outsiders*
Ministers think that the group's objectives are reasonable and desirable.	Ministers think that the group's objectives aren't reasonable and that their implementation is undesirable.
The government needs the group's support to better carry out its policy – for example, reform of the NHS requires the support of doctors' and nursing groups.	The group is unable to block the course of government policy; instead it can only look on from the sidelines.
The group has wide public support or extensive appeal among a particular section of society.	The group appeals only to a very limited group of people.
The group employs peaceful methods to achieve its ends and always acts within the law.	Members of the group employ civil disobedience and may break the law.
People working for the group have skills and expertise that ministers find useful when they're looking to consult about the group's issue area.	Leading members of the group aren't considered to have useful expertise or are seen as too biased to give objective assessments to ministers.

The phrase 'united we stand, divided we fall' applies well to pressure groups. If members of a group are united, with a strong leadership talking with one voice and expressing coherent themes, the group has a better chance of influencing government policy and wider public opinion than a group with lots of different factions all claiming to represent the members' interests. A group without a coherent stance, whose members are divided over key issues, is likely to have outsider status rather than insider access.

The bigger, better organised and more popular the pressure group, the more likely it is to be on the inside rather than the outside. After all, politicians rely on electors and if a pressure group has wide support, the amount of attention the government – or opposition parties – pay to it can influence voter behaviour.

A tale of two pressure groups: One inside, one outside

The Royal Society for the Prevention of Cruelty to Animals (RSPCA) is one of the UK's biggest, richest charities and also a strong pressure group for better animal welfare. The RSPCA enjoys widespread public support, garners lots of media coverage and often advises the government – regardless of which party forms it – on aspects of its policy relating to animal welfare. The RSPCA is very much an insider pressure group.

The Animal Liberation Front (ALF), in contrast, employs direct action as its method of combating what it sees as the systematic mistreatment of animals. In fact, sometimes the actions of the ALF are illegal and, although it does enjoy some support – often among students and those involved in what may be termed Britain's counterculture – it has no real influence on government policies on animal welfare. The ALF is very much an outsider group.

Sometimes different pressure groups come together to fight a particular cause. They may intrinsically have very different outlooks, but they put these differences aside to work together towards a common cause. One major example is the opposition to the High Speed Rail link between London and Birmingham. This controversial project has led to environmental bodies and some pro-hunting country-sports groups to work together. In the normal scheme of things they'd probably not have much in common and may well be on opposite sides of debates.

Watching the political ups and downs of pressure groups

Which pressure groups are inside or outside changes over time. For example, trade unions often have significant influence when the Labour Party is in power, because the latter draws much of its funding and parliamentary candidates from the trade union movement. This situation gives unions unique access to Labour government ministers and, although their influence has dwindled over time, they're very much on the 'inside' when Labour is in power. Check out Chapter 8 for more details on this evolving relationship.

In the 1970s, for example, the leaders of Britain's big trade unions were regularly at 10 Downing Street talking over the minutiae of government policy with the prime minister. These get-togethers were famously dubbed the 'beer and sandwiches' meetings. The unions had huge power and influence.

When the Conservatives came to power in 1979, they believed that the unions were too powerful and brought the 'beer and sandwiches' meetings to an abrupt halt. Under Conservative prime ministers Margaret Thatcher and John Major, members of business pressure groups such as the CBI and the British Chambers of Commerce had the ear of ministers. So, groups that were insiders became outsiders to some extent, and vice versa.

Looking at How Pressure Groups Exert Influence

The goal of all pressure groups is to get the government of the day and the general public to support their goals and to act accordingly. To achieve this aim, pressure groups employ a range of methods and pull many political and public relations levers.

Nearly every pressure group uses the following two tactics:

- **Having members contact politicians:** Individual members of pressure groups often write to their MPs expressing their views on an aspect of government policy. This approach can have quite an influence, because MPs have to stand for re-election every four or five years, and if they anger their constituents they may not get voted back into parliament.
- **Employing a professional lobbyist:** This more sophisticated method of influencing MPs instructs the lobbyist to make contact with MPs and put the pressure group's case before them. Professional lobbying has grown apace in the UK in recent years and is now a multi-million pound industry.

  The better a lobbyist's contacts, the more it can charge the pressure group for its services. However, some pressure groups employ people from within their own organisation – as head of public relations, say – to do the lobbying.

Sometimes pressure groups strongly disagree with government policy and challenge its legality in the courts. Lawyers for the pressure group may argue that ministers have exceeded their legal powers or that a policy is discriminatory against a particular group or breaks European human rights legislation. However, legal action can be ruinously expensive, and so in many cases it's usually a last resort for the pressure group or not deployed at all.

I sort out some of the main paths to influence in the following sections.

Understanding that size is important

Usually the more members a particular pressure group has, the more it can influence the formation of government policy and public opinion. This influence results from the following:

- **Electoral impact:** Each member of a pressure group has a vote, and the government is more likely to attract the votes of those members if it listens to or supports the group's objectives. The more members, the more votes and in theory the more likely the government is to want to tailor its policies to reflect the concerns of the pressure group.
- **Funding muscle:** The more members, the greater the level of donations and subscriptions, which can help a pressure group pay for professional staff and advertising campaigns to convey its message effectively.
- **Campaign resources:** More members means a wider pool of volunteers to call upon when the pressure group undertakes marches and demonstrations.

Saying that big equals powerful in the world of pressure groups is a bit too simplistic. Some groups don't have large numbers but do have considerable wealth and therefore influence. For example, the Confederation of British Industry (CBI) is made up of business owners. Now the CBI doesn't ask its members to take part in demonstrations or vote for a particular party, but what it says has a great deal of influence in government because its members control much of the wealth of the country and employ millions of people. In short, governments are happy to listen to the CBI because they can see that doing what it says is usually good for the UK economy and ultimately its own chances of getting re-elected. After all, at election time the health of the economy is usually a deciding factor in terms of whether the government wins or loses.

Getting the ear of ministers and civil servants

Government policy is implemented by ministries. At the top of these ministries are a handful of politicians (called *ministers*) aided by senior civil servants. (I talk more about ministers and ministries in Chapters 13 and 14.) Any pressure group that can put its views to these politicians and civil servants has a real chance of influencing what the government does.

When a pressure group is able to grab the ear of a minister or senior civil servant (not literally, of course, that would be called 'lobey-ing' not lobbying – groan!), it can be said to be an insider in the workings of government (refer to 'Differentiating between inside and outside' earlier in the chapter).

The relationship between ministers/civil servants and pressure groups is a two-way street: the pressure group gets access and its views listened to; and the minister and civil servant can call on the group's specialist knowledge, gain co-operation for the implementation of government policy and (they hope) garner the group's support in public, which can help at election time.

Focusing on backbench MPs

Only a limited number of pressure groups have direct access to ministers and senior civil servants. For one thing, only so many hours are available in the day for ministers and civil servants to listen to the views of pressure groups.

Those pressure groups finding themselves left out in the cold don't just give up; instead, they look to influence the views of backbench MPs. After all, the MPs may one day be ministers themselves. In addition, MPs have the power to introduce legislation for debate in parliament (though backbench MPs have great difficulty seeing this into law without the support of ministers – see Chapter 13 for more on this process). MPs also get to sit on parliamentary select committees, whose job is to scrutinise proposed government legislation to see whether it will work.

So, although individual backbench MPs have limited power, a pressure group that can get enough of them on side and believing in what it has to say can have an influence on the formation of government policy.

Courting public opinion

Pressure groups – even those with access to ministers – also seek to appeal to the public directly. The idea is that the government also then listens, because it fears that, if it doesn't, the public will vote for its political opponents at election time. Unlike meeting ministers or lobbying MPs, appealing to the public is an indirect method of trying to change government policy.

Pressure groups look to court public opinion through getting stories in the media that present their ideas in a positive light. To this end, some groups organise media stunts to get their name and their cause coverage in the press – such as Fathers for Justice staging a protest on the roof of prominent Labour politician Harriet Harman's house to push for greater account to be taken of father's rights after a family breakdown. Most attempts to get media coverage are a lot more subtle, though, and involve pressure groups employing professional public relations agencies that have access to prominent journalists.

Sometimes, pressure groups don't try to appeal to the whole public, instead focusing on just the middle class. Many politicians, journalists and opinion formers are drawn from the middle class (*opinion formers* are people with high public profiles who are seen as possessing expertise). What they say often attracts media coverage. The idea is still to influence ministers and other senior politicians – just by using a roundabout way.

The rise and rise of social media has made the job of pressure groups simpler in recent times. The likes of Twitter and Facebook make reaching a wide number of people and gathering support much easier – while bypassing the traditional media. The accessibility and relative simplicity of social media allows campaigns to be set up and dismantled in the blink of an eye. As a result, causes can more quickly rise out of nowhere, enter the public consciousness and influence political decisions. After the financial crash, the Occupy movement was born with the aim of highlighting economic and social injustice in the rich capitalist West. The Occupy campaign, which involved street protest and also the occupation of prominent locations – such as Wall Street and outside St Paul's Cathedral in London – was fuelled by stories posted and contacts made via social media. Although many of the Occupy demonstrations were broken up, the issues of greedy bankers and ongoing economic and social injustice were highlighted.

Joining the throng at party conferences

Many of the UK's biggest and most influential pressure groups try to appeal not only to government ministers, leading opposition MPs (who may one day be in government) and the general public, but also to the rank and file of the big political parties. They do so by setting up stalls at and sending members of their group to the annual party conferences of the big political parties.

As I discuss in Chapter 8, party conferences are big shindigs where party members meet up with leading politicians and ideas are exchanged, policies formed, speeches made and plenty of drinks downed.

Pressure groups show up at conference time to exert indirect influence on the leading members of the party, who may be government ministers or have the potential to be so in the future. This tactic is subtle but it can help move opinions among leading politicians and over time influence political debate.

Taking it to the streets: Direct action

Direct action means demonstrations, marches and rallies. The idea is to bring members of the pressure group together in one place to show the politicians, the public at large and the media that the group is organised and has strong feelings about a particular issue. People have a legal right to gather together and express their views and direct action makes the most of this right.

Thousands of peaceful demonstrations take place across the UK each year. These gatherings represent pressure group politics at its most raw, and they can have a real effect on government policy if the views of the pressure group strike a chord with the public, the media and the politicians.

Direct action can go further than simple demonstrations. Trade unions, for example, have organised sit-ins and strikes. In the 1980s CND held large-scale protests outside the American nuclear weapons base at Greenham Common. For a discussion about more extreme direct action, check out the nearby sidebar 'Taking in the dark side of direct action'.

The increasing use of social media has proved key to direct action. During the Arab Spring of 2011, for instance, much of the street protests that helped topple several regimes in the Middle East were organised via social media. See Chapter 11 for more on social media and politics.

Appealing over the heads of politicians

Many pressure groups don't target politicians directly, and instead try to mould public opinion to their way of thinking. Usually, this approach simply involves trying to get the press to cover the issues they're concerned about or paying for advertising campaigns to generate support and perhaps attract extra members.

Members of pressure groups have also on occasion decided to influence things by standing for election themselves, perhaps feeling that to beat the politicians they have to join them. In 2001, for instance, retired doctor Richard Taylor stood for parliament. As the Kidderminster Hospital and Health Concern candidate, he was part of a local group worried about the closure of a local hospital. Mr Taylor overturned a substantial Labour majority in the Wyre Forest seat to win by a landslide.

Taking in the dark side of direct action

Direct action is usually legal and peaceful but at times it crosses into violent protest. For instance, on May Day 2000 a host of pressure groups gathered in London to protest what they saw as the inequality brought about through economic globalisation.

Many of those involved acted peacefully and merely marched and rallied; a minority, though – most involved in anarchist groups – rioted, causing millions of pounds worth of damage in the process.

Likewise some extreme animal rights groups are notorious for violent protest. Staff working at the Huntingdon Life Sciences animal research centre have been subject to harassment and intimidation from animal rights campaigners. Nevertheless, the work of the laboratory continued. What's more, the Animal Liberation Front has in the past broken into labs and released animals used in research. Although many members of the public share the concerns of the anti-globalisation and animal rights activists, the use of violent or illegal protests has lost these groups considerable support among the general public and also ensures that they don't have access to ministers and senior civil servants. In short, in the UK violent or illegal direct action rarely results in a change in government policy.

Placing Pressure Groups in the System

Political lobbying involves large sums of money and much of the conversation between pressure group lobbyists and politicians goes on behind closed doors. Now that seems like a recipe for potential corruption! However, MPs have to declare in the Register of Members' Interests – a public document – any gifts given to them. Whether the reporting requirement is a factor or not, Britain's politicians generally are considered to be honest and corruption in public life is a rarity – unlike in the case of politicians in many other countries.

When multi-million pound contracts are at stake, however, a little bit of what you and I call corruption to oil the wheels may be very tempting – and politicians do enjoy a fair few freebies from friendly lobbyists. For the lobbyist, the idea is to get access to the politician, which in turn helps the client.

Unfortunately, instances exist in the EU of politicians allegedly (yes, I'm being careful for the lawyers!) accepting gifts or freebies from lobbyists in return for the politicians looking favourably on the arguments of the pressure group.

Looking at the downsides of pressure groups

Not everyone thinks that pressure groups are all good. In fact, some people believe that pressure groups can have a detrimental impact on the country's democracy, aside from the potential for corruption among politicians through the well-funded lobbying system.

Here are some of the main criticisms of pressure groups:

- **They're too powerful.** Pressure groups try to exert influence on politicians with a variety of means. When they're very successful they themselves become powerful and their voices may drown out those of other groups or the wider general public.
- **They're too limiting.** Some pressure groups have lots of power through the scale of their membership and the specialist skills of those members. For example, the British Medical Association represents doctors; if the government wants to reform health care and see its plans carried through, it has to consult with the BMA, which makes that group very powerful indeed.
- **They're too disruptive.** Some pressure groups stop at little to see their objectives met – even committing violent and illegal acts. Their behaviour can have an unsettling effect on wider society.

In the US, pressure groups and the lobbyists they employ are believed to exert huge influence on politicians. According to some reports, lobbyists representing oil companies and motor manufacturers had a strong influence on the Bush administration's (2000–2008) take on environmental policy: for much of his presidency, George W. Bush denied the existence of climate change. Similarly, President Obama's administration (from 2008) faced dogged opposition to its reforms to provide more free health care from lobbyists working for private health companies, who feared a loss of revenue.

Taking in the plus points of pressure groups

Every argument has its flip side and this is particularly true of whether pressure groups are good for society or bad. The main arguments for the existence of pressure groups include the following:

- **They keep politicians grounded.** Pressure groups can keep politicians informed about the opinions of the wider public or a section of society.
- **They help debate.** Pressure groups can inform political debate within groups of politicians or in the country as a whole, often through the media.
- **They protect minorities.** By their nature, many groups represent a section of society. They allow the voice of this part of society to be heard more effectively and stop it from being drowned out completely.
- **They provide expertise.** Pressure groups have access to committed and knowledgeable individuals as well as useful information about their area of expertise. This bank of knowledge can be very important when the government wants to consult over the formation of policy.

Identifying the UK's Big Pressure Groups

Thousands of pressure groups operate in the UK. However, not all pressure groups are equal in terms of public appeal or political influence. Although a golden league of pressure groups doesn't exactly dictate government policy, they definitely have influence in the corridors of power in Whitehall (the civil service) and among the electorate as a whole.

The following sections provide an overview of some of the pressure groups that politicians ignore at their peril.

Bossing for business

The most prominent business pressure group is the Confederation of British Industry (CBI), but other bodies represent the interests of those who own businesses in the UK as well, including the British Chambers of Commerce and, in the agricultural sector, the influential National Farmers' Union.

Members of these bodies employ millions of people and the wealth they create pays the taxes to fund schools and hospitals. As a result, they have access to leading politicians and what the group leaders say garners substantial media coverage.

Powerful multinational companies employ professional lobbyists to make contact with leading politicians in order to try to influence government policy as it relates to their particular firm. For example, an oil or gas company may want ministers to ignore objections from environmentalists and local residents over a proposed drill site in a beauty spot; they argue that the greater good dictates that the work should go ahead.

Charting the influence of charities

A staggering 16,000 charities are registered in the UK. Most of these are tiny – some quite literally consist of one person stuffing envelopes and producing newsletters at home. But whether the charity is big (and some multi-million pound charities exist) or small, they all dream of persuading the public and politicians to adopt their cause.

Some of these charities are well-resourced and help the government carry out its policies or perform a wider social service – for example, the National Childbirth Trust runs antenatal clinics and the Royal Society for the Prevention of Cruelty to Animals runs animal shelters. These bodies often have direct access to ministers and civil servants.

Another way of exerting influence is through possessing expertise in a particular field and receiving lots of media coverage.

Other notable charity pressure groups include the National Society for the Prevention of Cruelty to Children (NSPCC), Which?, the Wellcome Trust (which carries out biomedical research), Cancer Research UK and Mencap (representing people with learning disabilities and their families).

Advocating human rights

Since the terror attacks on America in 2001 and the anti-terrorism legislation that followed in the US, UK and other European countries, civil liberties have gradually risen up the political agenda. Human rights groups have been lobbying for the repeal of anti-terror laws and the continuation of what once seemed guaranteed liberties such as the right not to be imprisoned without due legal process.

The pressure group Liberty campaigns for greater civil liberties and has come to the fore in recent years as the government has sought to impose anti-terrorism laws in the face of Islamic extremism. Although it has a relatively small membership, Liberty attracted widespread publicity as it fought the government over anti-terrorism laws in the courts.

Amnesty International is another prominent human rights pressure group. However, it focuses most of its energies on helping to draw attention to the human rights abuses of foreign governments. Amnesty has a particularly strong pull for students and other young people.

Pulling for the planet

Climate change is now a widely recognised reality, and the influence of the environmental lobby has grown apace with increasing knowledge.

Groups such as Greenpeace and Friends of the Earth have many thousands of members in the UK and abroad. The reports they issue and policy statements they make can attract considerable media coverage, and more politicians than ever are now adopting green policies. As well as lobbying and using the media, environmental groups also often deploy direct action – refer to the section 'Taking it to the streets: Direct action' earlier in the chapter.

Promoting professions

One of the key types of pressure group is that which represents a section of society. The UK has a long history of professions forming their own pressure groups to protect their own interests and those of their clients. These groups are normally associated with the public services, such as education or health care. Groups exist for every type of profession but some of the most influential include the Law Society, the British Medical Association (BMA), the Royal College of Nursing and the National Union of Teachers.

If the government wants to enact policy in, say, the NHS or the courts, it usually consults the relevant professional body, because it represents the people who have to enforce new government initiatives.

Working for the workers

Around six million people belong to a trade union in the UK. These members pay subscriptions, making unions wealthy. A trade union's main job is protecting the pay and working conditions of its members, but it also gets involved in general aspects of promoting greater social justice.

Most trade unions actively support the Labour Party, and this overt party political alignment means that they tend to exert more influence when Labour rather than the Conservatives are in power. In recent years, though, Labour and the trade unions have drifted apart – particularly during the prime ministership of Tony Blair from 1997 to 2007. Nevertheless, the Labour Party still draws a lot of its financing from the unions (flip to Chapter 8 for more on the key role that the unions played in the development of the Labour Party).

Labour is reforming its financial links with the unions, with leader Ed Miliband trying to move away from union members being compelled to pay a levy to the Labour Party. Again, Chapter 8 has more on these potentially historic reforms.

Working on a Bigger Stage: Pressure Groups and the EU

Much of the law affecting the lives of Britons is passed by the parliament of the European Union (EU) rather than the UK parliament based in Westminster. From labour relations to weights and measures, the EU passes hundreds of laws each year. Therefore, if big British pressure groups want to get their messages across and see their ambitions reflected in new laws, they need to have influence not just at Westminster but also at the European parliament in Strasbourg and among the European Council of Ministers in Brussels.

Ever since the passing of the Single European Act in 1986, EU laws have exactly the same weight in UK law as those made by the UK parliament.

UK-based pressure groups are unlikely to have large numbers of members across the whole EU, and organising demonstrations, marches or other direct action overseas is thus difficult. What's more, no significant European-wide media exists; instead, each country has its own unique media culture (though some overarching international newsgathering organisations such as the BBC and CNN have an international presence). Therefore, putting pressure on EU politicians through a media-savvy campaign isn't easy.

What tends to happen as a result of these difficulties is that pressure groups employ professional lobbyists to get their views across to members of the European parliament and politicians sitting on the European Council of Ministers.

Pressure groups looking to gain influence in the EU often need to gain good contacts with groups of politicians from across the EU, particularly those who sit in the European parliament, because they can amend proposed legislation. The key is that member states of the EU agree to abide by the laws that its legislative bodies draw up. Any groups wanting to see a change in the law have two avenues: their own country's parliament, and the EU legislative bodies. In effect, pressure groups get two bites at the cherry of influencing lawmakers: national politicians, and those such as Members of the European Parliament (MEPs) who make laws for all 28 member states of the EU.

Many UK pressure groups have an office in Brussels or Strasbourg or are part of a bigger European-wide pressure group that shares resources and costs. For example, the UK Law Society is a member of the EU's International Bar Association and the UK's Federation of Small Businesses is part of the European Small Business Alliance.

Some of the bigger, more well-resourced pressure groups operate a *mixed approach* to lobbying, which means that they lobby both UK-based politicians and media as well as politicians from the EU. These groups hope to maximise their chances of success by putting their message across to as many politicians as possible. Sometimes a pressure group can see itself ignored in relation to a particular issue in the UK but its feelings reflected in EU law, and the converse is also true.

Pushing the Intellectual Envelope: Think Tanks

A *think tank* is an organisation that carries out research and formulates policy ideas that may be adopted by the government. In effect, as the name suggests, think tanks are all about idea generation.

Think tanks have been around for a long time. The left-leaning Fabian Society, for instance, was formed way back in 1884. Generally, most think tanks are seen as being either left leaning – supporting the idea of greater social justice and equality – or right leaning – wanting to see more free market solutions adopted to meet the challenges of government.

Putting a finger on how powerful a particular think tank is isn't easy because it often depends on which political party is in power. For example, think tanks that are perceived as left leaning may not have that much influence when a Conservative government is in power. Conversely, think tanks that are seen as more right leaning may not have the ear of government ministers when the Labour Party is in office.

Think tanks generally take a long-term view. What they propose right now may not carry much weight in government but a few years down the line, perhaps after a change of government or in different economic and social circumstances, suddenly the policy change proposals or insights made by the think tank can be in vogue.

The UK has hundreds of think tanks. Some are big operations with dozens of staff, who produce lots of policies and studies for politicians, the media and the wider general public to mull over. Others have only a handful of people working for them, aren't so well resourced and produce papers of variable quality. In practice, some of these smaller think tanks are barely disguised pressure groups or even have strong links to a particular political party, and what they say can be seen as a bit biased.

Here's my rundown of some of the major UK think tanks:

- **Adam Smith Institute (`www.adamsmith.org`):** This think tank is named after the great Scottish economist Adam Smith, who believed in the free market over state intervention. Unsurprisingly, the Adam Smith Institute suggests free-market solutions to society's and the economy's problems. According to its president, Madsen Pirie, 'We propose things which people regard as being on the edge of lunacy. The next thing you know, they're on the edge of policy.'
- **Centre for Policy Studies (`www.cps.org.uk`):** This right-leaning group proposes how public services can be reformed while reducing the size and expenses of the UK government. The CPS approaches some of the big issues of the day from the perspective that the country needs less not more government interference in people's lives.
- **Institute for Fiscal Studies (`www.ifs.org.uk`):** This impartial think tank looks at how well government finances are being run, personal debts and the prospects for the UK and international economy.
- **Institute of Public Policy Research (`www.ippr.org`):** The IPPR is often referred to as Labour's favourite think tank. It has a big staff and its papers on all matters of British life, from financial inclusion to welfare reform – even to the spread of the Internet – often hit the headlines and draw the attention of politicians.

- **National Institute of Economic and Social Research (`www.niesr.ac.uk`):** This think tank receives government financing and is charged with looking at the prospects for the UK economy, as well as tracking important social trends.
- **The King's Fund (`www.kingsfund.org.uk`):** This group looks at the provision of health care in the UK, monitors efficiency within the NHS and proposes changes to it to bring about improvements.

This list is just a small sample of the UK's think tanks. At least one dedicated think tank, and sometimes more, inform and review nearly every aspect of public policy, from transport to crime. Some think tanks, including the IPPR and the Adam Smith Institute, conduct research and make proposals in a huge variety of different areas of UK life.

Think tanks don't just advise on policy or carry out research on British matters. Some, such as the International Institute of Strategic Studies, also look at foreign relations and Britain's place in the world.

The lighter side of chocolate

One of the most influential think tanks in the area of how best to alleviate poverty is the Joseph Rowntree Foundation (JRF). Named after the great social researcher Joseph Rowntree, a member of the York-based confectionery-producing family, the JRF has been operating for over a century. At the beginning of the 20th century, Joseph Rowntree used some of his considerable resources to examine the conditions of Britain's poor in cities such as York. These early studies of poverty are considered pioneering works and highlighted for the middle class, perhaps for the first time, the plight of the poor.

Chapter 10

Scrutinising Politics and the Media

In This Chapter

- Exploring the relationship between politics and the media
- Looking at national newspapers' coverage
- Breaking the mould with 24-hour TV news

Britain is a country of over 60 million people, with the seventh-largest economy in the world, but it's a small place compared to China, the US, Russia and even France. You can fly from one end of the country to another in an hour. Although the UK is a diverse society with large numbers of immigrants, as well as strong independent Celtic cultures in Scotland, Ireland and Wales, in terms of media it's remarkably concentrated, with the BBC and the national newspapers able to command large numbers of viewers and readers across the length and breadth of the country.

The UK has probably the strongest cross-section of national newspapers in the world, still read by millions each day – though their power and reach are waning. In addition, the popular national broadcaster – the BBC – is a great news-gathering operation, employing thousands of journalists.

The strong national coverage that the BBC and newspapers offer means that when they report political events and interview politicians, millions of electors get to hear or read about what's going on in the corridors of power. In this chapter I look behind the headlines and unravel the complex, contrasting relationship between politicians and the media.

Exposing an Uneasy Relationship: Politics and the Media

Politicians and journalists have the archetypal love–hate relationship. Politicians know that they need the media to get their message across, and yet they don't like the awkward questions they get asked or their personal foibles being splashed over the newspapers and the airwaves from time to time.

Members of the media know that they need politicians because they're the lawmakers, the people in power and a great source of stories and, of course, juicy gossip – the very lifeblood of journalism. Simultaneously, however, many journalists distrust what politicians say and do.

All in all, the attitude is one of 'can't live with them, can't live without them' on both sides.

Most of the time politicians and journalists get along fine, with politicians being given an opportunity to put their views across and journalists allowed to ask searching questions.

The can't-live-without-politics aspect of media coverage is exemplified by the *silly season,* which is when parliament isn't sitting and MPs are on their summer holidays. Newspapers and TV stations sometimes have difficulty finding material, and often relatively minor stories hit the headlines – cue breeding panda stories or the latest viral video craze as newspapers try to fill their pages and TV stations their airtime.

Wheeling out the sound bite

As the media became bigger and more sophisticated, so did the way politicians dealt with it. For decades after the Second World War – to the late 1970s – the newspapers, television and radio treated politicians with deference. But society and the approach of the media to politicians has changed: today, journalists' questioning is fairly aggressive and pointed.

Journalists are always on the lookout for the story, which can often entail searching for differences of opinion between politicians from the same political party and exposing the failings of individual politicians and their policies. Any slip-ups in speeches or interviews by politicians are broadcast over the airwaves in a matter of minutes and journalists love to talk up the idea of politics and politicians being in crisis.

Partly in response to how members of the media talk to them, in recent years politicians have changed the way they talk to the media.

Modern politicians try to master the art of the *sound bite* – a carefully prepared statement summing up their view, which is brief and succinct enough to have a good chance of getting into newspaper articles and onto television news bulletins and the radio.

A good sound bite serves politicians, who get their message out unchanged by individual journalists, and journalists, who get a pithy take on an issue that can serve as a launching point for other facts and opinions.

This careful thought before speaking can mean that you never hear a simple yes or no answer from politicians; instead, they turn questions around to make a positive point about their policies or to attack those of their opponents.

Opinion is divided on how beneficial or detrimental effective modern media manipulation by politicians is for democracy. Some people suggest that the overuse of sound bites and the media training that many politicians undergo turns off quite a few voters, who feel that they're being spun a line rather than given the simple, straight and honest views of politicians.

Being media savvy: Special advisers

Nowadays politicians need a media presence in order to communicate with the electors. Virtually all politicians pay experts to train them in how to deal with questions from journalists and how to best craft their public utterances so that they get their message across effectively.

Many top politicians employ special advisers to advise them on how to deal with the media and also act as gatekeepers, ensuring that they speak only to journalists and media outlets that may be sympathetic to what they have to say.

Someone who advises politicians on how to deal with the media is called a *spin doctor.* The phrase was coined in the US in the 1990s but is widely used in the UK. Often these special advisers come from journalism or public relations, which gives them a unique insight into how the media works.

Probably the most prominent special media adviser in recent decades was Alastair Campbell, confidant and close political adviser to the Labour prime minister Tony Blair. Campbell was extremely loyal to Blair and highly combative. He reportedly tore strips off journalists if he believed that they didn't treat Blair or his government's views fairly. He was also known to give senior ministers a dressing-down if they veered in their public uttering from the agreed party or prime ministerial line on a particular issue.

Getting revenge: The media witch hunt

Occasionally, the relationship between politicians and journalists breaks down spectacularly. A particular political scandal or action by a politician can lead to some elements of the media openly attacking individual politicians. Referred to as a *media witch hunt*, it doesn't involve a ducking stool, pitchforks and an angry mob – although the politician under fire can feel like that.

Often a witch hunt involves the media and political opponents (and even colleagues) scrutinising the private life of the politician, perhaps calling on the person at the centre of the controversy to resign. The middle of a witch hunt isn't a comfortable place to be.

Probably the biggest witch hunt of recent years occurred in 2009, when the scandal over MPs' expenses came to light. Many MPs were discovered to be claiming huge expenses, sometimes for quite unnecessary things such as a moat-cleaning service or the construction of a duck house on a private pond. The media – reflecting the public mood – became incensed by some of the items claimed for, and newspapers, TV and radio outlets joined together to pour scorn on MPs in general. This massive story dominated the summer of 2009 and caused several MPs to announce that they wouldn't stand for parliament at the next general election.

Many of the MPs at the centre of the witch hunt felt that the media had treated them unfairly. Most in the media felt that they were only doing their job by exposing a scandal, and according to opinion polls the public agreed.

Campbell often said that he wanted Blair's MPs and ministers to be *on message* – meaning that they needed to stick to the same line on an argument or issue as the one the prime minister held.

Many commentators say that special advisers have become too numerous and too big for their boots – after all, they're not elected by the public. Special advisers can exercise huge power, because they're so close to senior politicians and the media goes through them to gain access to their political employers. (Chapter 14 has more about these influential creatures.)

Reading the UK's Newspapers

The UK boasts lots of national newspapers, which appear seven days a week, 364 days a year (no papers on Christmas Day). They come in three types:

- **Qualities:** Tend to take a serious approach to the news, covering political stories in detail and often avoiding celebrity gossip. They draw most of their readers from the management and professional groups.

- **Mid-markets:** Have more of a mix of politics, social affairs and the inevitable celebrity stories. They also take some readers from the management and professional groups as well as from the public sector and middle management.
- **Red-top tabloids:** Widely read titles that feed off a diet of sex scandals and celebrity gossip. They cover politics but not in great detail and draw most of their readers from the working class.

Most of the UK's newspapers naturally support Conservative or Labour; no paper overtly supports the UK's third-biggest party, the Liberal Democrats.

The political views of the person who owns the newspaper can have a major impact on editorial content. Politicians often court these *press barons* because they're believed to have direct or indirect influence on the political leanings of the newspapers they own.

Detecting a waning influence – or not?

The great American writer and humourist Mark Twain wrote, after seeing his own obituary printed in a newspaper, 'The report of my death was an exaggeration.' The same may now be said about the great British newspaper trade. According to some commentators – particularly in the blogosphere – newspapers, whether national or local, are over and done with. They've been supplanted by free access to online content.

Although publishers are struggling, readership is shrinking and advertising revenues are falling, national newspapers still play a huge part in the life of the country. Politicians still want to sweet-talk newspaper editors and tip off prominent political reporters with stories and gossip. A big political story still gets to people in the streets, and fuels conversation in homes and offices.

Even newspapers' detractors use them as sources, following up on exclusive stories first reported in print. Evidence that what newspapers write can still make huge waves was supplied in 2009. The *Daily Telegraph* – one of the UK's influential national newspapers – obtained the expenses claims of MPs. Many of the claims were shown to be fatuous and even corrupt in some cases, with some MPs and Members of the House of Lords being sent to jail. As a result of the *Daily Telegraph* story, a host of MPs resigned or were *deselected* (sacked by their party). The MPs' expenses scandal was one of the biggest UK political stories in decades – see Chapter 24 for the low-down on what happened – but it also re-confirmed the power of the press in the UK.

Taking in the qualities

The Times, Daily Telegraph, Guardian, Financial Times and *Independent* are often referred to as the *quality newspapers,* because they take a serious approach to the news, reporting stories that wouldn't find space in the mid-markets and the red-top tabloids. The qualities tend to produce more pages than other papers and to be less reliant on gossip.

To describe the quality newspapers simply, just replace the word *quality* with *serious,* although some would say plain old *boring* is more apt.

The varied coverage of the qualities mixes politics and business with the arts and, of course, sport. They often do in-depth investigations of political and social matters. The qualities break many of the biggest political stories in the country and carry out lengthy interviews with politicians. Despite claiming strong traditions of journalistic excellence, to a greater or lesser extent all the qualities have their own political axes to grind. In other words, they like to support particular issues or political parties and generally present themselves, and are perceived, as being left- or right-wing:

- *Left-wing* means to support the idea of a bigger state, acting to tax more highly and distribute this cash to help the most needy and to work toward equality across society.
- *Right-wing* means supporting the institutions of the country, wanting low taxes and promoting free trade.

Chapter 8 has more on what distinguishes right- from left-wing politics.

Unlike the BBC, UK newspapers don't have to appear independent as regards their political stance. In fact, each one has its own slant and position:

- ***Daily Telegraph:*** The biggest-selling quality newspaper supports the Conservative Party and often stands up in its editorials for what are seen as traditional British values and preserving things as they are. It's a firm supporter of institutions such as the monarchy.
- ***The Times:*** Owned by billionaire and media mogul Rupert Murdoch, *The Times* usually supports the Conservatives but has on occasions switched to Labour. Generally, it's seen as being right of centre in its politics.
- ***Guardian:*** Seen as the newspaper most read by people working in the public sector and among urban-based intellectuals, the *Guardian* supports the Labour Party, generally, and often features stories exposing society's inequalities. The *Guardian* is unashamedly on the left of British politics. The *Guardian*'s Sunday edition is called the *Observer.*

- ***Independent:*** This paper is supposed to be, well, independent in terms of party politics. However, it's an avowed supporter of preserving the environment and promoting a more liberal society and is thus often grouped with the *Guardian* on the left of British politics.
- ***Financial Times:*** The 'Pink 'un', because it's printed on pink paper, is the voice of top UK management and City staff. Its predominant focus is business matters, but it also covers politics extensively. The *FT* tends to be on the right of British politics, supporting free trade and lower government taxes. In the past the *FT* has supported Labour and Conservatives at general elections but more generally the latter.

On general election day each national newspaper editor writes an editorial setting out which party the newspaper supports and putting the case for its readers voting that way. Opinions differ as to the impact of these editorials. In a close election – like the one in 1992 – some suggest that newspaper editorials do make a difference to the result. Back then, the *Sun* – the UK's biggest-selling newspaper – urged its readers to vote Conservative rather than Labour. The Conservative leader John Major won a narrow, surprise victory and the paper trumpeted its role in the victory on its front page.

Meeting the mid-markets

The mid-market UK national newspapers are so-called because in terms of content and outlook they occupy the space between the qualities' fairly serious approach and the red-top tabloids' focus on sex and celebrity. Where the qualities tend to have quite serious, lengthy articles, the mid-markets are a bit – well – lighter in their outlook. They cover politics but also throw in a little more gossip – celebrity and otherwise. The mid-markets don't go as far as the red-tops, though, which live off a diet of celebrity and scandal.

New kid on the block – the *i* newspaper

This paper has a red tabloid-like 'i' and is tabloid size, but it draws its content from the *Independent* newspaper, which is considered a quality newspaper. The content is cut down in length and re-sized and lots of bright graphical elements are added to help it appeal to younger readers.

So is the *i* a quality paper? Perhaps it's best described as a hybrid newspaper between quality a and tabloid. One thing is certain: since its launch in 2012 it has been a surprise success, selling nearly 300,000 copies a day (helped by a low cover price), at a time when many people laughed at the idea of launching a new national newspaper.

The combined sales of the two main mid-market newspapers are as great as all the quality newspapers combined:

- ***Daily Mail:*** This mass-circulation newspaper sells around two million copies a day. In terms of making money the *Daily Mail* is the most successful newspaper in the UK (due to revenues gathered from the MailOnline website, which is the most-read news website in the world). Interestingly, the paper enjoys a high female following, mainly because it runs more lifestyle features. Generally, major politicians try to court the *Daily Mail* and are keen to appear within its pages, because they know it holds significant influence. When the *Daily Mail* campaigns on a topic, politicians often support that cause. This paper is seen as right-wing and a natural supporter of the Conservative Party.
- ***Daily Express:*** Back in the 1950s the *Daily Express* was the UK's bestselling newspaper but those glory days are long gone. The paper still has a large following, though, and tends to tread a similar path to the *Daily Mail,* supporting the establishment and the Conservative Party.

Prime ministers, such as Tony Blair and John Major, often briefed the editors of major national newspapers, particularly the *Daily Mail*, the *Sun* and *The Times*, before announcing major policies publicly to gauge press reaction to new laws and fresh party policy. Politicians are always sensitive to shifts in public opinion – because ultimately they rely on votes to stay in office – and the support of the press is seen as crucial to convincing the public to support a particular new law or policy.

Checking out the red-tops

The red-top tabloids are often seen as embodying all that's good and bad about British journalism. (They're called red-tops because the *Sun*, *Mirror* and *Star* all have a bright red backdrop to their names on the masthead.) The tabloids tend to be irreverent, full of humour, simple and straight to the point in ways many politicians – and their constituents – can only dream of, and they have large-scale followings. On the downside, tabloids thrive on scandal, can indulge in tactics many consider unethical to find stories and oversimplify political debate by presenting complex arguments and important matters in glaring black and white.

The tabloids love gossip and celebrity stories and, of course, sex scandals. When politics gets covered it tends to be in only the barest terms, but the papers' huge readerships can be influenced by what line their chosen red-top tabloid takes. The red-top market is bigger than the mid-markets and qualities combined – millions of copies of these papers are sold day in, day out.

Here's an outline of the main tabloid players and their political leanings:

- ***Sun:*** One of the biggest newspapers in the English speaking world, selling nearly three million copies a day. It was a strong supporter of Margaret Thatcher and her Conservative government, but in 1997, courted by Tony Blair, it switched to Labour. With Blair's departure, the *Sun* moved back to the Tories and is once again a staunchly Conservative paper. The Sunday edition, imaginatively called the *Sun on Sunday,* has a similar outlook in terms of its politics.
- ***Mirror:*** Sells over a million copies a day. Whereas its deadly rival the *Sun* is seen as a Tory paper, the *Mirror* has always supported Labour. It has its fair share of celebrity and scandal but gives space to leading politicians to write editorials, particularly from the Labour Party. The *Mirror* is often viewed as the newspaper of the UK trade union movement, which itself is very strongly linked to the Labour Party (I talk about this connection in Chapter 8).
- ***Star:*** The smallest-selling red-top carries the least political coverage. Instead it tends to obsess about reality TV stars. Its political allegiances aren't as easy to gauge as those of the *Sun* and *Mirror,* but at the last election it supported the Conservatives.

Stepping over the line: The great hacking scandal

MPs had their expenses scandal and in 2012 newspaper journalists – particularly on the tabloids – met their hacking Waterloo. Rumours had circulated for years that unscrupulous journalists were hacking into the mobile phones of politicians and celebrities in order to listen to voicemail messages to gather gossip on which to base a story.

Then investigators claimed that the mobile phone of missing teenager Milly Dowler had allegedly been hacked. This caused heartache for the parents – who'd known that messages had been listened to and had seen that as a sign of hope that their beloved daughter was still alive. However, this wasn't the case and a national outcry followed. Journalists, of all people, found themselves at the centre of a media storm, several were arrested by police (phone hacking is a crime), and the extent of hacking was exposed for the world to see. The outcry led to the government setting up a public enquiry under Lord Leveson who controversially recommended curtailing some press freedoms and allowing people wronged by the press greater redress.

Most newspapers opposed the enquiry's conclusions and instead compiled their own suggestions for press reform. At the time of writing, none of Leveson's recommendations have been put into effect.

Digging into the grass roots: Regional newspapers

Although the national newspapers have the readers, and to a certain extent the glamour, hundreds of local newspapers also devote column inches to politics and local political debates. At election time, their political coverage can be crucial in swinging votes in the constituency. At several recent *by-elections* (those held between general elections to fill a vacancy), local newspaper coverage was seen as key to the final result.

Generally, local newspapers don't tend to be overtly biased towards one party or another. Instead they look at the individual candidates and explore the major local campaign issues, exposing what they see as any flaws in the arguments of the party candidates.

Scotland has its own national newspapers: the *Scotsman*, *Herald*, *Daily Record* and *Scottish Sun*. Although their circulations are small compared to the UK national newspapers – which sell across the country, including in Scotland – they have considerable influence in the Scottish political scene. Politicians from all the parties seek the support of a particular newspaper, particularly now that Scotland has its own parliament. In September 2014 Scotland held a national referendum on whether or not to go independent. It was a very close call but ultimately Scotland remained in the UK. The role of the newspapers was key in the campaign as all but one backed Scotland remaining in the UK. See Chapter 18 for more on the Scottish situation.

Balancing Politics at the BBC

The British Broadcasting Corporation (BBC) is probably the most influential public service broadcaster in the world – it's certainly the largest. Generally, the BBC covers politics in great depth, with politicians regularly appearing on its TV and radio stations to be closely questioned by journalists. Politicians like to appear on the BBC because they know that it has huge reach and other media outlets report its interviews. For example the *Today* programme on Radio 4 attracts an audience of millions and its interviews are widely reported in newspapers and even on rival radio and TV networks.

The job of a BBC political correspondent (journalist) is considered to be the pinnacle of British journalism. Politicians often give the stories or explain their opinions to these correspondents because the stories they put out get wide coverage within the BBC and outside.

Some politicians accuse the BBC of bias against them. Whereas most of the UK's national newspapers do favour one of the two main political parties, as a public service broadcaster the BBC is supposed to be completely impartial.

A very large part of the BBC's funding comes from the TV licence fee paid by everyone who owns a television – something like 99 per cent of UK households. The TV Licence currently costs £145.50 for a colour set and funds the BBC's offerings on television, radio and online.

Not only does the BBC offer TV and radio programmes and online material for the whole of the UK, but also it provides TV programmes, radio stations and websites specifically targeted at the regions. The BBC's main political programmes include the following:

- **Radio:** Radio 5 Live provides 24-hour news and sport coverage; Radio 4 has the *Today* programme, which attracts nearly six million listeners a day, as well as *The World at One, PM* and *Today in Parliament.*
- **Television:** BBC television has a dedicated digital channel screening debates in parliament, catchily called 'BBC Parliament'. The BBC broadcasts news programmes throughout the day and shows *Daily Politics* every weekday lunchtime, *Newsnight* every weekday evening, *This Week* on Thursday evenings and the *Politics Show* on Sunday, not to mention regional political debates. Its flagship political debating programme, *Question Time,* airs on Thursday evening.
- **Online:** The widely read BBC News website (`www.bbc.co.uk/news`) carries a 'Politics' section and each of the main political programmes on TV and radio has its own dedicated Internet pages.

This list provides just a sample of the BBC's political coverage broadcast. It also has a 24-hour news channel, which I cover in the next section.

Offering News around the Clock

Broadcast and online media sources have exploded in recent years. Whereas in the 1970s and 1980s the UK had only a handful of TV stations, now it has literally hundreds. In addition, there are two 24-hour news stations – Sky News and BBC News 24. Add to that the proliferation of political websites, blogs and other modern media, and you have access to news and politics limited only by the speed and availability of your Internet connection.

Political parties are now using new mobile and Internet technology to get their message across. This approach has expanded, with parties regularly emailing potential voters with newsletters from their leaders or criticism of their opponents' plans.

When Sky launched the UK's first national 24-hour TV news channel in 1989, no-one knew what its impact would be on the reporting of politics. 24-hour TV news was a bit of a novelty and many people wondered how programme makers would fill all those hours. By the time the BBC launched its rival channel, News 24, nearly a decade later, the cut and thrust of party political debate was making up much of the 24-hour news channels' time.

Politicians are forever making appearances on 24-hour news, talking about policy, the latest political scandal or simply blasting their rivals. Often, debates in parliament are shown live on 24-hour news. The idea is to keep the public informed as to what legislators are doing, and it's working. The advent of 24-hour news channels has helped increase public awareness of politics and politicians enormously. Viewing figures for 24-hour news stations are often small, but they shoot up when big political stories break or crises occur. Put simply, 24-hour news has become a key way for many people to get to know their politicians and what they stand for.

Looking at the Media in an Election Campaign

Media interest in politics and politicians becomes more frenzied during an election campaign. Suddenly, newspapers are full of political comment and the airwaves buzz with politicians being interviewed and debating with one another. The leaders of the big political parties run daily press conferences during the three weeks or so of an election campaign, during which they make statements and face questioning from journalists. At a local level, party workers go door to door in their constituency and try to persuade people to vote for their party's candidate.

In addition, each party publishes a *manifesto* – a document setting out the policies it would pursue if elected. The media is keenly interested in the launch of the big parties' manifestos and closely scrutinises what's in them.

The BBC must abide by strict rules stipulating that it remains politically impartial and doesn't favour one party over another. During the period of an election campaign these rules are adhered to even more closely, with all the major parties canvassed for their comments.

Opinion is divided over how much impact election campaigns have on the result of a general election. At the last four general elections, for instance, the party that was leading at the start of the election campaign was still leading at the end. In fact, most people vote for the same party election after election and are therefore barely influenced by what goes on in campaigns.

Party election broadcasts

In each national election campaign, whether it's a general election for seats in the UK parliament, European elections or when lots of local council elections are held at once, each of the main political parties are entitled to party political broadcasts – the Lib Dems, Labour and the Conservatives and, depending on the proportion of votes at the previous election, the Greens, UKIP and even the British National Party. The BBC and ITV screen these broadcasts during the campaigning period, which normally lasts around three weeks.

These broadcasts are free and last between five and ten minutes. The parties get a chance to explain their policies and tell the public what they'd like to do if they were in power. Increasingly, parties use much of the allotted time to attack their opponents without giving a huge amount of detail as to what they'll do themselves. Newspaper, billboard and, increasingly, Internet advertising often supplement party election broadcasts as part of the campaign.

Crucially, party political broadcasts are scrutiny-free zones; no journalists are present to ask awkward questions and the party is free to say what it wants. However, journalists watch the broadcasts and if the party makes false claims then it's most likely reported in the media.

Broadcasts are also a good way for a party to convey the merits of its leader. In fact, leaders feature a good deal in broadcasts, because they're the individuals bidding to be the next prime minister. The personal appeal of the party leader is a big determinant in how electors vote.

The 2010 general election was the first to include live TV debates between the leaders of the three main party leaders. After the first live TV debate during the run-up to polling day, Nick Clegg, leader of the Liberal Democrats, received a huge boost in support with people even coining the phrase, 'I agree with Nick.' He didn't perform quite so well in the next two TV debates, however, and his party ended the election campaign back where it started – in terms of its share of the vote. In the end, too few people agreed with Nick!

Political parties spend a lot of money at election time. The Conservative and Labour parties have budgets for advertising and other costs of £5–10 million. The Lib Dems spend less. This money is raised through party membership subscriptions, from rich donors and, in Labour's case, the trade unions.

Testing the Temperature: Opinion Polling

Politicians and the media want to know voters' views about the big political issues and which party they'd vote for if a general election were called. Conducting an opinion poll is the best way to discover voters' intentions.

Opinion polling methods range from quick phone calls to a cross-section of voters around the country to researchers carrying out in-depth interviews in people's homes. Increasingly, email is used to canvass people's opinions. Polls tend to involve a minimum of 1,000 voters – sometimes several thousand. The six main organisations conducting opinion polls in the UK are Mori, Gallup, YouGov, NOP, ICM and Populus. But the rise of the Internet makes putting together an opinion poll easier, cheaper and quicker than ever, and so private companies and wealthy individuals also sponsor polls, which may have a political angle in order to secure a headline and a bit of publicity.

Polls are carried out frequently during general election campaigns. Sometimes several newspapers and TV stations conduct a poll each day so that they can run a story highlighting the party that's likely to do well. But polls aren't confined to an election campaign period. In fact, nearly every week the public is asked who they'd vote for and what events or policies are likely to influence their decision.

Here's why polls are considered useful and important:

- **Story generation:** The media loves polls because they give the perfect excuse to run a story about which party or politician is up and which one is down.
- **Political barometer:** Polls allow politicians the chance to see how popular their policies are and what they may need to change to attract more votes at election time.
- **Signal of next government:** An opinion poll showing one party streaking ahead of the others can be a strong indicator of which party will win the next election and form the government. This information can be useful for businesses making plans in relation to which party they'll have to deal with down the track.

Politicians whose parties are doing badly in opinion polls often say that they take no notice of their results and that the only poll that matters is the one at election time. The idea is to appear calm and collected and undeterred from pursuing their policies. This stance is utter rubbish: politicians are avid readers of the polls and often make crucial decisions on the back of them.

Opinion polls tend to be highly accurate at estimating support for individual parties. They're generally correct to within two or three percentage points – called the *margin of error.*

As well as polls conducted for media outlets, the big political parties carry out their own private polling, often with small groups of voters called *focus groups,* to see in detail what voters feel about the policies they're pursuing or their views on particular political subjects.

Chapter 11

Taking Politics to the Masses: Social Media

In This Chapter

- Grasping the importance of social media
- Breaking the mould through political blogging
- Taking to the streets with Twitter

Newspapers, magazines and even political TV programmes are just so last century (like brick-sized mobile phones and Britpop). Nowadays, individual politicians, political parties and pressure groups have to get their messages across through social media as well as through traditional or mainstream routes.

A picture on Instagram, a tweet retweeted 10,000 times or a Facebook post shared among the masses is the new political Eldorado. Many politicians may not understand the ins and outs of social media, but they do know that it can help them communicate their messages to a brand new audience or re-engage people who've become disillusioned with all things political.

To discover just how social media is changing the political landscape in the UK and across the globe, read on, as I discuss the benefits and dangers for politicians. This chapter is for you whether you post, tweet, blog or trat (okay, I may have made the last one up).

Understanding that Politics Is Now Mobile

The UK contains more mobile phones than people – surely some mistake? Not at all: many people have not only one but two or even three handsets for conducting their busy social and work lives. What's more, you can also read your emails and so on with tablets galore, laptops and smart TVs; today's world is awash with mobile communication and information.

This situation happened in a relatively short period of time and politicians have been racing to catch up. Mobile technology in all its guises gives them a tremendous opportunity to connect with individual voters in a way that the humble leaflet through the letterbox or knock at the door never quite managed.

Climbing aboard the social media express

Politicians, political parties and pressure groups want to jump aboard the social media bandwagon for the following reasons:

- **Cost:** Put simply, it's cheaper. Sending a tweet or post on Facebook is free, but leafleting a home or canvassing in person costs money. Social media interaction is also far less time consuming than direct face-to-face politics: for instance, some MPs send out 1,000 tweets a year but only leaflet a home a couple of times in the same period.
- **Simplicity:** A tweet takes only a few seconds and is sent without the mainstream media looking to qualify the comment or asking political opponents to put across their points of view. Social media allows politicians and other political groups to have a direct interaction with the electorate.
- **Less constrained:** On TV and in the mainstream media, politicians and those involved in the world of politics are usually asked to comment on a particular narrow topic (say the latest political controversy). But in the online world they can say virtually anything (for good or ill), which gives them more chance to engage with people who're normally turned off by politics.

No surprise, therefore, that all high-profile politicians worth their campaigning salt employ at least one individual in their back office who specialises in social media messaging. In fact, savvy politicians realise that having a strong social media presence is key to their own political advancement and not just a straight tool to gain votes.

MPs such as Zac Goldsmith for the Conservatives and Stella Creasy for Labour have gathered huge followings on social media, which helps their political careers and influence. They both ran high-profile successful campaigns using social media as a key tool: Goldsmith fought Heathrow airport expansion and Creasy secured reform of the payday lending sector.

Social media is hugely important to politicians, political parties and pressure groups, but it's not the be-all and end-all. It's best deployed as part of an overarching media campaign also involving the newspapers, TV and radio. Campaigns that combine all these elements tend to have the best chance of success.

Reaching out: How politicians can bypass mainstream media

Politicians, political parties and pressure groups can use several tools to bypass traditional media and go direct to the wider public with their messages:

- **Email newsletters:** Just about all MPs send out a regular email newsletter to their contacts in the constituency. The distribution lists can be in the tens of thousands of people and email allows direct communication with the wider public. In addition, hundreds of thousands of people across the country subscribe to the main political parties' email newsletters, normally sent by the leaders or on their behalves.
- **Facebook:** Now the granddaddy of all social media, though in recent times its declining growth and relevance is subject to much discussion. However, in the UK in 2014 an individual voter is about eight times more likely to have a Facebook account than a Twitter one. Facebook is far more widely used than Twitter, therefore politicians, political parties and pressure groups tend to put far more emphasis on Facebook than on any other social media. They regularly post pictures and statements to accounts and viewers are invited to share them with their Facebook friends.
- **Twitter:** Twitter allows people to post thoughts and comments and share links to pictures and video with other users, so long as the comments aren't more than 140 characters long. Millions of Britons regularly tweet and check out tweets from others: I'm on it and so's my mum!

  Politicians and political groups of all sorts invariably have their own Twitter accounts where they send out short messages, keeping people informed of what they're doing, pointing their followers towards interesting stories in the media or even getting into debates over issues. Individual politicians may even simply tweet what they've watched on TV or the result of a football match: doing so makes them seem more grounded, which in turn may make some electors more likely to vote for them.

  Leading politicians such as Barack Obama, David Cameron and Ed Miliband use Twitter. Always bear in mind, however, that many tweets and blogs said to be the work of politicians are actually authored by professional publicists.
- **Viral messaging:** Better than leaflets or even TV party political broadcasts (check out Chapter 10) is getting the public to share messages, pictures or videos among themselves through social media. The mere act of sharing shows these individuals engaging with the message and saying to their friends, family or anyone they interact with on social media: 'here's something worth seeing; here's someone worth listening to'.

Despite the explosion in social media in the UK and the rest of the world, the traditional methods of voting – casting a physical vote at a ballot box or returning a postal vote form – are still used. Although some discussion has taken place of the need to allow online voting, many observers are worried that such a method would be difficult to monitor and therefore potentially open to manipulation by, say, hacking. Chapter 6 has more info on voting methods.

Treading carefully: the political gaffe

No doubt you've suffered a seriously bad case of foot-in-mouth disease in your private life . . . most people have: that awful moment when you say something and as you hear the words coming out of your mouth you think, 'What on Earth am I saying?' Now, foot-in-mouth is an embarrassing condition, but it's only temporary and probably doesn't have long-term consequences – unless you're a politician.

Combine foot-in-mouth with the world of social media and a politician's career status can switch from rising star to crashed and burned within moments. Social media is a fantastic tool for politicians, parties and pressure groups but it's a double-edged sword: say something wrong or get photographed in the wrong pose and it can be hugely damaging. After something is tweeted, posted on Facebook or emailed, anyone can capture it: if embarrassing, it can be political career cyanide.

Before every election – general or local – dozens of stories seem to circulate in the days before polling of one candidate or another having to resign because of an insulting, racist, sexist or generally unpleasant comment they posted on social media – usually Twitter or Facebook. Journalists and political opponents are wise to this possibility and regularly trawl the social media profiles of politicians in order to find such unguarded comments.

What a Weiner!

Probably the most spectacular fall from grace of a major political figure because of something done online happened in the US in 2011. Anthony Weiner was running for re-election (yes, that's right, *re*-election) to the House of Representatives when it emerged that he'd sent explicit photos of himself and messages to women inviting them to . . . ahem . . . meet and discuss the hot political issues of the day with him.

At first, he denied all knowledge of the messages and photos but eventually had to fess up and make a humiliating admission that he had indeed been 'sexting' women while in office. The married Weiner resigned in farcical scenes, with journalists and observers jeering at him as he made an ever so painful apology. What made the whole episode even more appealing to America's army of TV and Internet satirists is that 'weiner' is slang for a man's private parts in the US.

Putting Your Thoughts in Writing: Political Blogging

Growing numbers of people are becoming informed about political goings-on online through political blogs and commentaries.

A *blog* is a diary or ongoing commentary posted online about any subject the author wants to write about.

Blogs tend to be highly opinionated, and some go further and spread untruths and gossip online. Generally, journalistic standards aren't as high in what's called the *blogosphere* as in traditional media outlets such as TV and newspapers. In several instances, bloggers have found themselves falling foul of libel laws and had damages awarded against them for lying about an individual or organisation.

Such cases are relatively rare though, and the blogosphere has a touch of the wild west about it; crackpot conspiracy theories jostle for virtual space with respected (and sane) commentators.

The anonymity of the web allows political bloggers to be a little more daring in what they say. But just because something's online rather than printed in a newspaper doesn't mean that it's exempt from the UK laws of libel.

In the UK, the world of political blogging and online commentary is catching up fast with the US. Some of the big beasts of the online political blogging and commentary jungle include the following:

- **Nick Robinson's blog:** The BBC's political editor writes a regular and lively blog published on the widely read BBC News website (`www.bbc.co.uk/blogs/nickrobinson`).
- **Order-order:** 'Guido Fawkes' authors this blog, which spreads political gossip and rumour (`www.order-order.com`).
- **The Green Benches:** This blog tries to lift the veil on some of the workings of government, which many in the political class would no doubt prefer to keep private. So, for example, the processes of awarding government contracts are often explored in depth (`www.greenbenchesuk.com`).
- **Political betting:** Authored by polling expert Mike Smithson, this blog examines the thousands of polls issued in the UK each year and tries to make sense of what they reveal. Smithson is non-party political in his approach, but he doesn't shrink from 'telling it as he sees it', which can be uncomfortable reading for many politicians (`www.politicalbetting.com`).

President Iguana's teeth fall out!

The Internet is probably the greatest mine of information in history, but it's also full of its fair share of crackpot political theories.

A recent online poll in the US for instance found that 4 per cent of people (or more precisely respondents) believe that the governments of the world are run by lizards disguised as humans. Plus, 9 per cent think that putting fluoride in the tap water is being done as a means of mind control instead of simply trying to improve dental health.

Just imagine: many of these people are eligible to vote – though probably too paranoid to do so.

- **Party blogs:** Members of the Conservative Party run `www.conservativehome.blogs.com`, Labour members run their own website (`www.labourhome.org`) and the Liberal Democrats have `www.libdemvoice.org`.
- **Commentary blogs:** Although often closely aligned to a political party – as you can see from the titles – these tend to think a little more 'outside the box' than standard party blogs, giving activists and major figures in a party the chance to theorise and debate on the current political landscape: you may even read criticism of the party leadership. Examples include `www.leftfootforward.com`, `www.labour-uncut.co.uk` and `www.liberalconspiracy.org`.

Political blogging is a big deal in the US. The 2008 presidential election cycle saw an explosion in the number of new blogs. Millions of Americans were energised by the election of the first black president, Barack Obama. And not only supporters of Obama blogged and commented; those who wanted to see his opponent, the Republican candidate John McCain, win also filled the Internet. Most blogs only got a few hits but some caught the public imagination and attracted millions of readers.

Talking 'bout a Revolution: Twitter and Street Protest

Almost all major street protests in recent years have been organised with the use of Twitter and other social media. The likes of Twitter allow people looking to organise protests a quick, virtually free means of connecting with hundreds, thousands and even millions of people.

Probably the most notable recent example was the protests around the Arab Spring in 2011. Oppressive regimes in the region had been used to quashing protests almost before they'd started through a network of informants and strong-arm tactics. But a few tweets, pictures and Facebook messages enabled those who were fed up with their governments to arrange to gather and protest.

Before the authorities grasped what was going on, they suddenly saw mass rallies and protests. What's more, other potential protestors could see what was happening through mobile phone footage uploaded onto the Internet. These governments may well have controlled TV, radio and newspapers, but they had no control over what was being posted and viewed online.

In a few short months, regimes in places such as Egypt and Libya that had denied their people democracy for decades were thrown out of office and governments in Saudi Arabia, Iran and Syria faced major challenges to their authority. The coming of social media really did give birth to the Arab Spring.

Not just Twitter is being used as a means of organising street protest or civil unrest; Blackberry Messenger (BBM) is hugely popular and was widely used during the London riots of 2011. BBM is harder for the authorities to monitor because it allows people to message one another's mobile phones directly and instantaneously due to operating on its own network outside the Internet.

Part III

The Ins and Outs of Parliament

Five limits to parliamentary sovereignty

Parliament may have huge power within the UK constitution but it's subject to limits. Here are the main ones:

- **Devolution:** Since the late 1990s the decisions of the UK parliament have been playing less of a role in the lives of people living in Scotland, Wales and Northern Ireland. Some areas of law-making in these nations, such as education and health care, have been devolved from the UK parliament to the Scottish parliament and the Welsh and Northern Irish assemblies. I cover this power transfer in detail in Chapters 12 and 13, but I just want to note here that the move to devolution is now a major check on the sovereignty of the UK parliament in Westminster.
- **Elections:** Parliamentary elections are held every few years. If the laws the governing political party has passed are unpopular, it may be voted out of office.
- **EU membership:** As a part of its membership of the European Union (EU), Britain has to agree to its laws. In fact, EU law has precedence even over statute law passed by parliament – see the nearby sidebar, 'Witnessing the growing role of European law'. Some commentators say that this situation undermines parliamentary sovereignty, but the UK parliament has the option to withdraw from the EU, thereby repealing the right of EU law to precedence over statute law.
- **Media scrutiny:** The press and TV examine parliamentary laws closely. Efforts to change the constitution get reported, as do the views of opponents. The electorate pays attention to such issues.
- **Party system:** Even PMs are accountable, because they rely on the support of Members of Parliament (MPs), who in turn rely on the support of members of their party. Politicians who use parliamentary sovereignty to push through laws unpopular with the people and with their own party struggle to get re-elected.

Find out more about British Politics at `www.dummies.com/extras/britishpolitics`.

In this part . . .

- Get to the heart of the matter as you explore Britain's ancient democracy.
- Examine Britain's unwritten constitution and the strengths and weaknesses of the British way of practicing politics.
- Discover more about devolution and the Scottish Referendum.
- Take a peek behind the door of 10 Downing Street and see exactly what the prime minister and the cabinet do.
- Find out how Westminster makes laws that affect all our lives.

Chapter 12

Examining Britain's Constitution

In This Chapter

- Looking at the variety of constitutions
- Cheering on Britain's successful constitution
- Weighing up monarchy versus republicanism

The Constitution is the sole source and guaranty of national freedom.

—Former US president Calvin Coolidge

Although you often hear people talk about a country's constitution, most famously the written one of the United States, you hear less discussion about the UK's constitution. Don't think, however, that its lack of a written constitution means that the UK doesn't have one. Something doesn't need to be written down to exist – for example, no document decrees that the England football team has to fail, but it happens nonetheless!

In this chapter I examine who calls the shots in the British political system. I take an in-depth look at what characterises a constitution and give you the low-down on how Britain's constitution works, including the reasons for its success and the roles of politicians, the courts and the monarchy.

Focusing on Why Countries Need a Constitution

In simple terms a *constitution* is a set of rules outlining how a nation is to be governed. Crucially, a constitution looks to constrain the powers of politicians by giving them a set of rules to work within.

Most countries around the globe have a constitution and many of them share the following characteristics:

- **It curtails the power of those at the top.** In every society, certain people or groups of people (usually the leaders of political parties) exercise *executive power* – simply put, being able to make the final decision on lots of important areas of government (for example, how tax money is distributed to different departments or, more dramatically, whether a country goes to war). Setting limits on what they can do is where a constitution comes in.
- **It provides a key role for the courts.** Constitutions need to be interpreted to suit everyday situations, which is a responsibility given to the courts. Law courts decide what is and isn't constitutional and politicians exercising executive power are required to obey the decisions of the court.
- **It sets out who does what in government.** Most governments have several different branches – the UK has a cabinet, a parliament and a monarch. A constitution sets out clearly the powers of each governmental branch. The courts can interpret the constitution and make a ruling when one branch of government is believed to have exceeded its constitutional powers.
- **It lists the rights of individual citizens.** Constitutions guarantee certain freedoms for the individual – the rights to free speech, to vote at elections and, even more fundamentally, not to be arrested without due legal process, a right called *habeas corpus* in the UK. Again, the courts decide whether these rights are being breached.

Much of a nation's constitution concerns outlining the rights of the individual and the power of the executive to impinge or not on those individual rights. The courts exist to apply constitutional protections to everyday situations. Their decisions result in *legal precedents* – outcomes establishing a principle or rule that a court or other judicial body uses when deciding subsequent cases involving similar issues or facts.

Academics can trace human society back some 10,000 years, and against that timescale constitutions are a relatively modern invention. The world's first fully fledged constitution was written in the newly formed United States of America in 1787. The US was a brand new country starting from scratch and the founders felt that a written constitution was needed to limit the powers of government and guarantee the rights of the individual.

Constitutions often come about as a way of preventing tyranny. For example, in the midst of the French Revolution (1789–99) a constitution was drawn up – called the 'Declaration of the Rights of Man and of the Citizen' – that was intended to guarantee the fundamental rights of the individual while simultaneously curtailing the power of the monarch. This constitution aimed to prevent tyrannical rule by any future French monarchs. The French revolutionaries did have a plan B, though – namely executing King Louis XVI, which they did in 1793.

Exploring Differing Types of Constitution

Political scientists tend to categorise the different constitutions of individual countries as follows:

- **Written or unwritten:** This one's pretty clear – a constitution is either recorded on a piece of paper, parchment or bark, or it isn't. The UK constitution is unwritten.
- **Unitary or federal:** In the case of a *unitary* constitution, ultimate power resides in a central government. A *federal* constitution provides for shared power and bars the central government from overruling the actions of regional governments.
- **Rigid or flexible:** As the names imply, a rigid constitution allows for no changes and a flexible one can be amended.

These categorisations can be a little confusing, but basically a constitution can belong to three of the six categories at the same time; a constitution can have one attribute from each pair. So, for example, the US constitution is written, federal and flexible, whereas the UK constitution is unwritten, unitary (although becoming more federal, as I discuss in 'Taking in unitary and federal constitutions' later in this chapter) and flexible.

Just to confuse matters even more, a country can be unitary and yet have a degree of federalism (if you really want to know, this set-up's called *quasi-federalism,* which would be worth a big score if you could use it at Scrabble) and differing degrees of flexibility. Although the US constitution is often defined as flexible, amending it is very difficult, and so any statement that the US constitution is flexible has to be qualified in some way.

Classifying constitutions as unitary/federal or rigid/inflexible can be useful, but each nation's constitution is unique and is categorised according to which definition it fits most closely. I think I need a lie down now!

Each nation develops in its own unique way and at its own pace. For example, the US created a constitution in 1787 after it rebelled against British rule. Some countries in Eastern Europe adopted a constitution in the 1990s after throwing off rule by the Soviet Union.

Recording the differences between written and unwritten constitutions

Setting out the differences between written and unwritten constitutions is relatively easy: Table 12-1 provides a quick guide to tell one from the other.

Table 12-1 Comparing Written and Unwritten Constitutions

Written	*Unwritten*
A written constitution is one that's enshrined in the law of the land.	An unwritten constitution comes about through many years of tradition, legal argument and custom.
Written constitutions are created – for example, top politicians and political thinkers of the late 1700s wrote the US one.	Unwritten constitutions arise organically over many years, reflecting the history of the country.

Sadly, I'm going to confuse matters again. No constitution is completely written or unwritten. The UK is often said to have an unwritten constitution that arose organically over many years, and yet many of the key components of a constitution put limits on the executive branch of government. Guaranteed rights for the individual have come about through laws passed by the UK parliament, and these laws, of course, are written down. So, although not having a single document called the constitution that everyone can refer to and argue over, the UK does have a patchwork of laws that do much the same thing – limiting the power of the government and protecting the rights of the individual.

Most democratic countries have a written constitution – a single document to which lawyers, judges, citizens and politicians can refer. In fact, out of western democratic nations, only the UK, New Zealand and Israel can be said to have unwritten constitutions. Strangely enough, however, a constitution doesn't need to be written down to secure the rights of the individual. Britain has an unwritten constitution and yet is seen as one of the most stable and free countries in the world.

Taking in unitary and federal constitutions

The key points relating to federal and unitary constitutions are as follows:

- **Unitary:** The constitution provides that central government wields supreme power over any locally based government or parliament.

- **Federal:** The constitution stipulates that power is in effect shared between a central government and regional-based governments or parliaments. In short, the central government can't encroach on the powers held by regionally based governments.

Until 1999, the UK essentially had a unitary constitution: power was vested in the central government through the UK parliament. However, the establishment of the Scottish parliament and the Welsh Assembly means that those parts of the UK now get to make their own laws to govern themselves, with some limitations. (Chapters 17 and 18 explain the situations in detail.) The UK is still technically defined as having a unitary constitution but with the qualification that some elements of federalism apply. What's more, over time the Welsh Assembly and Scottish parliament have gradually seen the areas over which they have direct power increase. Who knows, perhaps soon the UK may well be described as a federal country.

Germany offers a good example of a federal constitution at work. After the Second World War a written constitution was established that shared out power between the central government and the parliaments and governments in the regions of the country. Regional governments in Germany have substantial powers and central government can't ride roughshod over them.

Changing the rules: Rigid and flexible constitutions

Some constitutions are easier to change than others. Political scientists use the ease with which this process can take place as the measure to decide how flexible (or not) a country's constitution is.

In a country with a written one, as well as dividing powers and enshrining the rights of the individual, the constitution usually establishes a process to change it in the future. A *flexible* constitution anticipates that future generations will reform it and so provides the means of doing so. The idea is to allow the constitution to adapt over time so that outdated laws and institutions can be jettisoned and more up-to-date and relevant ones adopted.

A *rigid constitution* is one that's hard to change. This rigidity may be a deliberate decision, because the people who drew it up didn't want the contents to be altered at a later date, perhaps to protect the individual rights outlined in the constitution forever.

Getting the process right from the beginning of how a constitution can be changed in the future is crucial. Specifying an impossibly high threshold for change – say, everyone in parliament has to agree to any change – risks the constitution becoming less relevant over time and ultimately being ignored as a method to improve the country. On the flip side, making change too easy means that chaos is likely, as politicians try to do so to suit their short-term political objectives. In a worst case scenario, an easily changeable constitution is a weak one and a dictatorship may result.

Unwritten constitutions are generally seen as more flexible than written ones. However, this flexibility doesn't make them weak. The patchwork of different laws, traditions and customs that together create an unwritten constitution are incredibly difficult to unravel by someone wanting, for example, to form a dictatorship. Take the UK: it has an unwritten constitution and yet has been a healthy democracy, with renowned civil liberties, for many years.

The UK's constitution is one of the most evolutionary in the world. Often key changes take place in response to particular events. For example, after the 2010 general election the Conservatives and Lib Dems formed a coalition government. The leadership of the parties felt that the economic crisis meant that the UK people and the nation's international lenders needed reassurance that the coalition would offer stable long-term government. As a result, the coalition introduced fixed-term parliaments – of five years – at a stroke, ending hundreds of years of the right of prime ministers (PMs) to call elections when they saw fit. The coalition achieved this major constitutional change in a matter of weeks through a series of votes in parliament, showing that the UK constitution is very flexible indeed.

Celebrating Britain's Constitution

If you're British, time to puff out your chest with pride. The UK constitution is just a bit, well, special and highly successful. It developed over many hundreds of years from the Magna Carta (which means 'great charter'), where the rights of landowners and some civil liberties were set out in writing in the 13th century, to the forming of the civil courts and parliament between the 12th and 16th centuries. Development continued with the curtailment of the power of the monarchy in the 17th and 18th centuries and the extension of voting rights and rights for women in the 19th and early 20th centuries – and that's just a few of the milestones.

A few wars and disagreements occurred along the way but for much of this time Britons have been among the freest people in the world, able to express themselves without fear that some unhinged dictator or over-powerful government is going to come along and do them harm.

Think of the UK constitution as being like a spider's web, with lots of different strands leading in all sorts of different directions and yet remarkably strong at any point you choose to touch.

No such thing as a single British constitution document exists; instead, the following support the whole edifice of laws, traditions and customs:

- **Parliament:** The UK Houses of Parliament are responsible for making *statute law*. Enacting statute law is the single most important support for the UK constitution, because statute law made by parliament outranks all the other laws, traditions and customs. Sometimes statute laws merely enshrine other less important laws, traditions and customs. (See the upcoming 'Granting parliamentary sovereignty' section for more on the central role of parliament in the constitution.)

  Changes to UK statute law are made through an Act of Parliament. Basically, a bill is put before the House of Commons; it's then voted upon several times and members are free to *table* amendments, which means that they want to make a change to the wording of a bill. After the bill passes, the monarch signs it and it becomes law (for more details on the monarchy's role, check out the later section 'Crowning the Constitution: The Monarchy').

- **Common law:** A patchwork of laws based on customs and traditions, common laws often arise through *legal precedent* – a judge's decision in one case becomes binding on all subsequent cases based on the same principle. For example, in recent cases individuals have argued that euthanasia (being allowed to die) should be legalised. The ruling in these cases sets a precedent for similar cases in the future.

  If the government of the day doesn't like the court's ruling, however, it can seek to alter future interpretations by introducing new statute law through parliament.

- **Constitutional conventions:** Defining a convention can be tricky, but in essence *constitutional conventions* are unwritten rules followed through force of habit and tradition if for no other reason. For example, one constitutional convention is that the government of the day calls an immediate general election if it loses a vote of confidence in the House of Commons. No law decrees this outcome: politicians and the public just accept that certain actions must follow from a particular event. Constitutional conventions are the most baffling part of the UK constitution for most observers, but they act as a real check on the authority of those in a position of power.

  In the UK the monarch is theoretically allowed to make laws – termed the *royal prerogative* – on a whim. However, monarchs never exercise this right because they're bound by the 17th-century convention that parliament is the place for drawing up laws. The monarchy not taking advantage of its royal prerogative is an example of how conventions influence the UK constitution.

The UK constitution is quite flexible, because incremental changes happen through changes to common law or conventions while bigger changes can be brought about through new statute laws. Changing the UK constitution doesn't take long – in fact, statute laws can be rushed through parliament in a matter of weeks if needed.

No one person has the power to change radically the UK constitution – not even the PM. Instead, for changes to statute law, politicians must secure a majority in parliament, whereas alterations to common law only occur following a court case in which judges decide the outcome.

Granting parliamentary sovereignty

Parliament makes the law for the UK. The laws passed by parliament have precedent over all the other parts of the constitution. In addition, parliament has the right to repeal or change laws passed by previous parliaments and British courts have to enforce the laws passed by parliament. Parliament is thus pre-eminent in the UK constitution.

This situation means that the UK government is centralised, with much of the power in the country concentrated in the hands of the people at the top of the biggest political parties sitting in the House of Commons. The PM and the cabinet therefore have a huge say in the actions of the government and any constitutional changes that take place.

But what the bigwigs have to say doesn't necessarily go – I talk about the several checks and balances in place in the next section.

Parliament became of central importance over a few hundred years. Originally, it was set up to allow the monarch to better collect taxes but over time, and after the Civil War in the 1640s, parliament supplanted the monarch as the main source of power in the country.

Limiting parliamentary sovereignty

Parliament may have huge power within the UK constitution but it's subject to limits. Here are the main ones:

- **Devolution:** Since the late 1990s the decisions of the UK parliament have been playing less of a role in the lives of people living in Scotland, Wales and Northern Ireland. Some areas of law-making in these nations, such as education and health care, have been devolved from the UK parliament to the Scottish parliament and the Welsh and Northern Irish assemblies. I cover this power transfer in detail in Chapters 17 and 18, but I just want to note here that the move to devolution is now a major check on the sovereignty of the UK parliament in Westminster.

- **Elections:** Parliamentary elections are held every few years. If the laws the governing political party has passed are unpopular, it may be voted out of office.
- **EU membership:** As a part of its membership of the European Union (EU), Britain has to agree to its laws. In fact, EU law has precedence even over statute law passed by parliament – see the nearby sidebar, 'Witnessing the growing role of European law'. Some commentators say that this situation undermines parliamentary sovereignty, but the UK parliament has the option to withdraw from the EU, thereby repealing the right of EU law to precedence over statute law.
- **Media scrutiny:** The press and TV examine parliamentary laws closely. Efforts to change the constitution get reported, as do the views of opponents. The electorate pays attention to such issues. (See Chapter 10 for the relationship between politics and the media.)
- **Party system:** Even PMs are accountable, because they rely on the support of Members of Parliament (MPs), who in turn rely on the support of members of their party. Politicians who use parliamentary sovereignty to push through laws unpopular with the people and with their own party struggle to get re-elected.

Some people argue that the courts are a check on parliamentary sovereignty, but even the High Court doesn't have the right to alter statute law passed by parliament. The courts do have the right, however, to review allegations that ministers or officials in government have acted illegally. So, governments aren't above the law despite the fact that they create much of it!

Witnessing the growing role of European law

As a member of the EU, the UK agrees to adopt its laws and treaties. In recent years, this situation has had a profound effect on the UK constitution. European laws apply to Britain, as do the judgements of European courts such as the European Court of Human Rights. Whereas in the past individuals wanting to right what they saw as a wrong would go solely to a UK court to argue their case, these days they have the right to take their case to European courts too.

Many people see this move as undermining the British constitution and national sovereignty. The UK independence party (UKIP) has made great play of the fact that much of the law affecting UK citizens is now made in Brussels where the UK is only one voice among many. However, others see the increasing encroachment of EU laws as adding to the freedoms and rights of the individual and further limiting the power of the UK government. Working out precisely how many of the UK's laws the EU now makes is difficult, because after the EU passes a law, a member state often adopts and adds to it. In effect, the UK parliament often uses new EU law as a base on which to add new laws and amendments. This process is often called *gold plating* of EU law and the UK is quite good at it.

Quantifying the success of the UK's constitution

Although the UK constitution has lost some of its gleam in recent decades, it's been admired – though rarely copied – around the globe. Some of the reasons for the constitution's status include the following:

- **The UK is a stable democracy.** Many European countries, such as Spain, Germany and Italy, have succumbed to dictatorships within the past century, but not Britain. Many people say that this stability results from its constitution and that its mix of laws, traditions and customs provides an in-built mechanism for preventing dictatorship and retaining a democracy.
- **The UK's government is efficient.** The UK constitution concentrates a lot of power in the central government based in Westminster. As a result, the government can more easily execute the policies it was elected to carry out without the fear that, for example, the judiciary is going to stand in its way. All in all, UK governments can take decisive action when required.
- **The UK constitution is rooted in history.** The UK constitution has grown organically over a long period of time. According to some, Britons feel protective of, value and respect their constitution much more because it's part of their collective history.

As recently as the financial crises in Greece and Italy, normal constitutional government has been postponed because politicians were unable to agree on the size and scale of spending cuts to get their national deficits under control. As a result, *technocrats* – civil servants and leading financial figures, usually bankers – took charge of both countries for well over a year to ensure that spending cuts were made and financial stability restored.

Moving towards a written constitution

Some people argue that the UK's constitution, resting as it does on a combination of parliamentary statute law, the courts and convention, is past its sell-by date. Political analysts state that the country needs a written constitution so that people know where they stand. This argument isn't new; calls have been made for Britain to have a written constitution ever since the American and French revolutions of the late 18th century.

Critics of the UK's constitution make the following points:

- **The centralised government holds too much power.** The PM and the majority party in parliament can change statute law as they like, which leaves the constitution at the mercy of the majority party.

The UK Supreme Court

The UK's Supreme Court came into being in 2009. Put simply, this court swept up the judicial powers of the House of Lords and the privy council (which formerly acted as the highest court of appeal for the UK and even some former colonies). The Supreme Court hears appeals against rulings in all the other courts in England, Wales and Northern Ireland (it doesn't have power over Scottish criminal courts though).

The Supreme Court makes legal decisions that set precedents. In turn, these precedents form part of the nation's unwritten constitution. The Supreme Court can't, however, overturn statute law passed by the UK parliament in Westminster.

- **The centralised government can ignore civil liberties.** UK central government is so strong that it can sometimes ride roughshod over civil liberties. For example, in 2007 the government proposed detaining terrorist suspects for 120 days without charge – a move that alarmed civil liberties campaigners. Note, however, that the government was defeated in parliament and the detention limit is currently 28 days.
- **The current constitution lacks definition.** Knowing what parts of the constitution stand for can be tricky. Many constitutional conventions change over time. For example, in the past a constitutional convention held that government ministers would resign if their senior advisers told a public untruth or acted in an incompetent manner. These days many ministers simply sack the adviser and carry on in their jobs!

The UK is gradually having more elements of its constitution enshrined in law. Unwritten parts of the constitution, such as conventions, have been put in writing. For example, freedom of speech – long seen as a part of the UK constitution but not preserved in law – now forms a key part of the Human Rights Act.

Crowning the Constitution: The Monarchy

For much of Britain's history the monarch – not parliament – ruled the roost. For more than six centuries successive kings and the odd (by which I mean occasional, not peculiar) queen were at the pinnacle of the political system and at the centre of what today people recognise as the constitution. Monarchs controlled the army, made political appointments, called and dissolved the House of Commons whenever they liked and had all the high offices of state in their gift. From the 1540s onwards, they even controlled the Church, appointing bishops and acquiring huge tracts of land that formerly belonged to the Roman Catholic Church. In short, the monarch was number one.

During the 17th century, however, the Civil War resulted in parliament seizing some significant powers from the monarch. As a result, many of the powers to appoint government officials started to fall into the hands of politicians instead of the sovereign.

But unlike many other Western countries, Britain didn't get rid of its monarchy. Instead, the institution transformed into a *constitutional monarchy.* This term means that, instead of exercising absolute political power, modern-day monarchs exercise their authority within the confines of the UK's constitution. In short, the monarch acts within certain limits set by accepted conventions of behaviour.

In practice, monarchs perform several roles, but their power is largely ceremonial, such as:

- Opening and dissolving parliament
- Appointing the prime minister
- Consenting to all bills passed by parliament (without this consent they can't become law)
- Appointing bishops and members of the House of Lords

These powers may seem pretty similar to the ones monarchs exercised way back in the 17th century before parliament took over, but a crucial caveat applies today: they must always act with the *advice of ministers.* In effect, monarchs do as the leaders of the government tell them.

Even the power to appoint a PM is illusory because, by constitutional convention, the monarch has to ask the leader of the party holding a majority in parliament. Personal feelings or desires don't come into it. The monarch's job is to rubber-stamp what goes on in parliament.

Take the relationship between Queen Elizabeth II and ex-Conservative prime minister Margaret Thatcher, for instance. Rumours abounded that the Queen didn't like Margaret Thatcher or the policies of her radical, reforming government. But Her Majesty had to appoint Thatcher as PM three times because she kept winning elections.

So what would happen if a monarch decided to disobey ministers – the elected government – and appoint someone to be prime minister or refused to give consent to bills passed by parliament? Well, the majority of MPs in parliament would likely vote to ask the monarch to abdicate or even abolish the institution of monarchy altogether.

The monarch has a team of advisers called *privy councillors* who sit – yes, you guessed it – on the privy council, which has been around for hundreds of years and used to be a powerful body. These days being a privy councillor is little more than a ceremonial role and its members are drawn from the House of Commons and the House of Lords – yes, politicians! The monarch appoints privy councillors and they get to sit for life.

Causing mischief among the chiefs

A mischievous monarch could certainly cause plenty of agonising among politicians.

Imagine the political dilemmas if the monarch refused to appoint an elected right-wing prime minister. Left-wing anti-monarchists would have to decide whether to support the monarch, despite objecting to the institution, and pro-monarchy Conservatives would have to consider challenging the monarchy, which their party has staunchly supported since its inception hundreds of years ago. Such fun!

Hundreds of privy councillors exist, but the council meets in full on only two occasions: when the monarch dies and the council proclaims the accession of the heir; and when a monarch intends to marry. The council's judicial wing still does act as a court of last appeal for some Commonwealth countries, sometimes when defendants face the death penalty.

Stirring Things Up: Republicanism

Britain has had a monarchy for nearly a thousand years, but for the last four centuries some thinkers and politicians have called for its abolition to make the country a republic. England was a republic (it didn't have a monarch) between 1649 and 1660, following the Civil War and the execution of Charles I by parliament.

Most Britons, when asked, support retaining the monarchy but a substantial minority (usually around a quarter) would prefer to see it abolished. Table 12-2 sets out the main arguments for and against.

Table 12-2 Arguments For and Against Retaining the Monarchy

Arguments For	*Arguments Against*
It still enjoys widespread support because the monarch symbolises national unity.	It's an elitist institution with no real practical purpose – in other words, the institution's powerless, so why keep it?
It's above petty party politics and is a welcome check on the power of the prime minister (although if the monarchy exercised its power independently it would risk being abolished).	Monarchs ascend the throne through the hereditary principle, which many believe is unfair and anachronistic in what's supposed to be a meritocratic society.

(continued)

Table 12-2 *(continued)*

Arguments For	*Arguments Against*
As an institution, it provides welcome continuity in a fast-changing, globalising world.	The monarchy is no longer as popular as it used to be and incidents such as the treatment of Princess Diana have lessened respect for the institution.
It attracts lots of tourism. Just think of the thousands of foreigners who flock to Buckingham Palace each year, and they all spend, spend, spend.	It costs too much to keep it; the monarch receives money (called the Sovereign Grant), which is a proportion of the revenue flowing from rents and profits made from Crown estate – land given by a former monarch George III to the state. Without a monarchy, the government could pocket this money.

Although the monarchy has suffered periods of declining popularity, don't expect it to be abolished anytime soon. All the major UK political parties have pledged to keep it.

Queen Elizabeth II has been widely acknowledged – even by some republicans – as a successful constitutional monarch. She has reigned for over 60 years during a time of political upheaval and fundamental change to society. Nevertheless, she's always carried out her ceremonial duties to the letter and assiduously avoided getting involved in party politics. She may not exercise political power but opinion polls show that the overwhelming majority of Britons have always respected her.

Many of the difficulties affecting the UK monarchy in the past few decades can be blamed on the behaviour of some members of the royal family. Divorce, infidelity and conspicuous expenditure of public money have undoubtedly led some to question the institution as a whole.

But the monarchy has shown a real panache for bouncing back in recent years. To start with, Queen Elizabeth II agreed to the abolition of the civil list – where members of the royal family received an annual payment from taxpayers – and then the country experienced Kate and Wills mania. The Queen's grandson Prince William Duke of Cambridge and his wife the Duchess of Cambridge proved real hits with the public at home and abroad. These events helped make the monarchy seem more modern and cemented its place in the affections of much of the public.

Chapter 13

Britain's Parliamentary Democracy

In This Chapter

- Exploring parliament – the Houses of Commons and Lords
- Looking at the jobs of MPs and peers
- Following the passage of government and private members' bills
- Putting Commons committees under scrutiny
- Ascending to the top of government

In this chapter I explore the inner workings of Britain's parliamentary democracy, peeking behind the oak-panelled doors of the Palace of Westminster to see where the real power lies in the UK.

Honouring the Mother of Parliaments

The UK parliament is often referred to as the 'mother of parliaments' as a result of its long history and because people around the globe have copied and admired its traditions and approach to the execution of democracy.

Even the building that the UK parliament sits in shouts out history, power and tradition. The Palace of Westminster is recognised as a gothic masterpiece, with its stained glass, medieval timbers and, of course, iconic Big Ben – read more about this building in the nearby sidebar, 'Visiting the Palace of Westminster'.

But the Palace of Westminster isn't just a great building; it's also a workplace, with 1,100 offices, 100 staircases and the small matter of 5 kilometres of corridors – all of which help the hundreds of Members of Parliament (MPs) and peers in the House of Lords do their job. And what a job it is – making the laws that govern the lives of around 60 million Britons. They draw up, scrutinise, debate and vote upon these laws in two legislative chambers:

- **The House of Commons**, made up of MPs elected by the public in individual constituencies
- **The House of Lords**, made up of appointees suggested by the monarch (who in turn takes the advice of the prime minister, or PM for short) as well as some lords who've inherited their title and right to sit in the Lords

People often refer to the House of Commons as the *lower house* and the House of Lords as the *upper house*. These terms date back to before the 20th century when society was very different and the House of Lords was more important than it is today. Back then people considered members of the House of Lords to be of high birth, and members of the Commons as, well, common and of low birth. In short, these terms are anachronistic and rooted in Britain's ever-so-complex and long-standing class system.

Visiting the Palace of Westminster

So much of Britain's history has been made in the Palace of Westminster. Here, important laws have been passed, major debates have taken place and even a king was tried as a criminal (following the Civil War, Charles I was tried and executed for treason in 1649).

The oldest part of the Palace of Westminster – Westminster Hall – was built in the reign of William II, son of William the Conqueror, in the late 11th century. Originally, Westminster Hall was the home of successive English kings and queens, right up until the reign of Henry VIII in the 16th century.

It also housed the first English parliaments, whose main jobs were voting on tax-raising measures for the monarch and making the laws of the land, usually on the instruction of the monarch. Despite the fact that monarchs moved out of the building in 1512, it was still called a palace and its main role became that of home for the House of Commons and House of Lords. After the Civil War (1641–51) broke the power of the monarchy, the Palace of Westminster became the centre of power in England and eventually the whole of the UK.

But not all was plain sailing. In 1605 Guy Fawkes and other plotters tried to blow up the Palace of Westminster and kill the country's leading politicians and the monarch. They failed. However, in October 1834 fire gutted much of the building. It was rebuilt in the gothic style of the day according to the plans of architect Charles Barry. One of the most notable innovations from this time was the building of a clock tower at the north-eastern end of the palace, the bell of which became known as Big Ben. The building was controversial at the time and criticised by some but is now viewed as a masterpiece, attracting hundreds of thousands of visitors a year.

Westminster Palace isn't a museum, though – it's a hive of activity, with office space for each MP and hundreds of staff providing administration, security and even catering. You even find restaurants – very good ones too – and bars in the palace. Yet despite its huge size, the palace can't house all of government. Many MPs work from nearby Portcullis House and the Norman Shaw Building. Also nearby are individual ministerial buildings housing thousands of civil servants putting into practice the laws drawn up in the Palace of Westminster. Nevertheless, the palace is one of the most iconic images of Britain.

Within parliament, many committees made up of MPs and members of the House of Lords pore over the small details of new laws and monitor old laws to see how they're working. All this activity stems from one grand building in Westminster, which is at the very centre of Britain's democracy.

The UK parliament is still of crucial importance, but some of its powers have been *devolved* – in effect, given away – to the Scottish parliament and the Welsh and Northern Irish assemblies. Flick to Chapter 17 for more about devolution.

Taking It to the Top: The House of Commons

More so than probably any other institution in the country, what happens in the House of Commons impacts on you in some way or another. The House of Commons is the major law-making body and the laws it makes affect your life for good or ill. For example, consider your car: laws made in the House of Commons dictate that you need to pay road tax and have car insurance, and a budget voted upon by its members decides how much tax you pay on the petrol in the tank. The job of the Commons is also to scrutinise the activities of the government of the day (run by politicians from the biggest political party in the Commons) as well as protect the liberties of Britons. Even in this modern media age, what happens on the ancient floor of the House of Commons chamber and in its committees does count because it's at the very heart of our democracy.

Laws made by parliament are called *statute law* or *acts of parliament*. They're the most important laws in Britain because no court is allowed to overturn statute law – only another act of parliament can do the job.

Aiming for a seat in parliament

At the 2010 general election, a grand total of 650 people were elected to the House of Commons – each MP representing a constituency. On election, these people become known as Members of Parliament, or MPs for short.

All three main national political parties in the UK have their own methods of selecting a candidate to stand for election to parliament or the devolved national assemblies (see Chapter 17 for more on devolution).

The following list offers a basic guide to hurdles to jump for candidates in each of the three main national parties:

- **Conservative:** Party members have to make it onto the approved candidate list. Selection for the list is via an application form, interviews and a half-day assessment programme. If you're successful and make it onto the list, you're free to apply to individual constituency Conservative Party associations. The members of these party associations choose who'll stand as candidate in the election.
- **Labour:** The Labour Party has a tradition of devolved selection of candidates, but in recent years the party bigwigs working at Central Office have had more of a say in who should be a candidate for parliament. The Labour Party operates a central list of approved candidates that local parties can select from. The party's National Executive Committee chooses who should be on the approved list; however, members of the local Labour Party can choose candidates not on the approved list but nominated by a trade union or individual council ward. Final selection of the candidate is down to a vote of party members in the individual constituency.

  The Labour Party's National Executive Committee (NEC) is made up of its MPs/MEPs, prominent local councillors and trade unionists and other affiliated organisations. Its job is to help form party policy and impose discipline on party members. Drawing up the list of approved party candidates is another of its key roles.

- **Liberal Democrat:** A candidate has to make it onto a centrally approved list. Just like going for an ordinary job, the candidate fills in application forms and goes to interviews. When the candidate has made it onto the list of candidates, she can start applying to individual constituency Lib Dem associations, which conduct interviews with potential candidates and make the selection via a secret ballot of local party members.

From the time when a party selects an individual to stand for an election to the UK parliament until the calling of the general election, she's referred to as a *prospective parliamentary candidate*.

Generally, the more winnable a constituency is for a particular party, the greater the number of people looking to become a candidate. For example, the Conservative Party often wins the constituencies in the south-east of England. When one of these candidacies becomes available, therefore, competition among people on the party's approved list of candidates tends to be very fierce indeed. On the flip side, the Conservatives do less well in the north-east of England and Scotland and so competition to become a candidate for those seats is less heated. (See Chapter 8 for more on the inner workings of all the main political parties.)

Looking at the job of MPs

Being an MP is a very important job. Here are some of the key responsibilities and powers that come with being an MP:

- Vote on proposed changes to the law.
- Help amend existing laws.
- Propose changes to the law through private members' bills (which I explain in the upcoming section, 'Introducing private members' bills').
- Sit on committees that scrutinise proposed law changes and the effectiveness of existing laws, as well as the actions taken by government ministers and their departments.
- Table written questions of government ministers and even the prime minister over their actions. Ministers and even the PM are expected to answer these questions fully and truthfully.
- Take part in debates over new laws and matters of public policy concern.
- Meet with constituents to hear their concerns over local matters or wider public policy.

Above and beyond their official duties, MPs do lots of different things:

- Host receptions in the Palace of Westminster for pressure groups or noteworthy constituents.
- Meet press journalists and give them stories or do TV interviews.
- Visit other countries so that they can see how policy initiatives and law changes work in practice.

If you ask a group of MPs how long their hours are, they'll probably give you a host of different answers. Some are real workaholics, others less so. Some MPs focus on one or two aspects of the job, such as meeting with their constituents and listening to their concerns, while others love the limelight of the TV studio or like to propose myriad changes to the law. I've even met one MP who took pride in the fact that he routinely killed off law changes proposed by colleagues by talking and talking so that the bill ran out of legislative time. He saw keeping as many laws as possible off the statute books and thereby freeing Britons' lives from red tape as his duty. I suppose someone's got to do it!

Recognising that the House of Commons holds the power

The House of Lords used to be equally and at times actually more powerful than the House of Commons, but this is no longer the case. Although the House of Lords can vote against legislation sent to it from the House of Commons, it can't kill it. All the Lords can do is propose amendments and ask the House of Commons to think again about legislation. In the final analysis, the House of Lords has an advisory role to the Commons and little real power.

In 1909 Chancellor of the Exchequer Lloyd George proposed a radical budget introducing the first old-age pensions. Many in the House of Lords voted against this budget, threatening to kill it off and send government finances into chaos. The Liberal government wasn't having unelected peers telling it what to do over such a crucial issue and so it passed the 1911 Parliament Act. In effect, this act removed the right of the House of Lords to vote down legislation sent to it by the House of Commons.

Britain has an unwritten constitution based on tradition, custom and convention. This situation is best highlighted by the fact that the Parliament Act is used very rarely indeed. In effect, if members of the House of Lords don't like legislation sent to them by the House of Commons, they vote against it and ask the Commons to reconsider. On the third and final reading, however, even if their concerns haven't been reflected in amendments to the legislation, they'll vote it through anyway. Why? Well, many peers in the House of Lords recognise that the House of Commons, as the elected body, has the greater rights and that opposing its bills isn't their job.

Lording It Up: The Job of Peers

Members of the House of Lords aren't elected by you and me. Instead, they get to sit in that chamber because they're peers of the realm – which sounds very grand, and it is. Their official title is 'lords'.

Before taking up their seats in the House of Lords, peers have first to attend a ceremony to swear an oath of allegiance to the monarch. For this occasion, they dress up in ermine-trimmed ceremonial robes.

In the past, being a lord brought all sorts of extra legal rights and powers – in effect, they were considered extra-special; some lived in castles and kept their own armed forces. Nowadays, being a lord is less about castles – although some still live in them – and more about ceremony. Modern lords either inherit their title or are appointed by the PM to sit in the House of Lords. As well as attending the State Opening of Parliament, when the monarch reads out the government's legislative programme for the parliamentary session ahead, the lords have other key jobs to play in Britain's parliamentary democracy, including

- Voting on whether to accept or reject legislation drawn up by the House of Commons
- Proposing amendments to legislation drawn up by the House of Commons
- Debating legislation drawn up by the House of Commons
- Introducing new laws to be debated in parliament

The House of Lords does draw up legislation but all the really important laws tend to start their journey through the legislative process in the House of Commons.

Party loyalty tends to play a less important role in the House of Lords than in the Commons. Peers are often older than MPs because they've had notable careers in industry, the church, the sciences, the military or the House of Commons itself before joining the House of Lords. Lords have been there, done that and got the T-shirt – although lined with ermine, of course!

Some members of the Lords don't belong to a particular party grouping. These peers are referred to as *crossbenchers* and they sit on benches opposite the throne in the House of Lords rather than on the side of the government or its opponents.

Inherited power: Hereditary peers

Until 1999, up to 700 peers who'd inherited their titles – called, catchily enough, *hereditary peers* – were allowed to sit in the House of Lords and take part in votes. However, successive Labour governments deemed this state of affairs undemocratic and most of the hereditary peers were turfed out by the Labour government of the day under PM Tony Blair. As a compromise, the Labour government allowed a small group of hereditary peers – just 92 – to keep their seats in the Lords. Nowadays membership of the Lords is by appointment and not through birth (apart from the remaining hereditary peers).

Many commentators suggest that the House of Lords is anachronistic and point in particular to the continued presence of hereditary peers to prove their point. And it's true that hereditary peers aren't representative of modern Britain; for example, only 2 of the 92 hereditary peers are women. For this reason, the Liberal Democrats, as part of the coalition government that came to power in 2010, wanted to reform the Lords and end hereditary peerages. However, the Lib Dems' coalition partners, the Conservatives, disagreed and as a result a reform of the House of Lords, at least in the parliament that ran from 2010, didn't get off the ground.

Nominating peers for life

The prime minister has the job of nominating peers to sit in the House of Lords – for life. Thus, they're called *life peers*. After they die, their title lapses.

On the face of it, nominating peers seems a huge constitutional power in the hands of the PM and the PM alone. However, usually the PM asks the leaders of the two other main parties to submit names for inclusion. So, in practice, in 2014 David Cameron as PM asked Labour's Ed Miliband and Liberal Democrat leader and Deputy Prime Minister Nick Clegg for a list of men and women to include in the list of new life peers.

Usually, PMs – of whatever party – try to draw up a final list of peers that ensures that their party has a majority of supporters in the House of Lords but also gives the other parties a substantial number of sympathetic peers.

The PM sends the list of life peers to the monarch for approval, but this is just a technicality. The monarch always approves the peers that the PM wants because of a constitutional convention that the monarch must always take the advice of the PM. (Chapter 12 explains the inner workings of the British constitution.)

When individuals become lords, they're *ennobled*, which means that they're now members of the nobility.

Introducing Bills

In the UK, laws only come about when the House of Commons, House of Lords and the monarch all agree. These days the agreement of the monarch is a given because, according to Britain's unwritten constitution, she has to agree to new laws made by parliament (refer to Chapter 12 for more on this). What's more, the House of Lords can only suggest changes to legislation drawn up by the Commons. So, in a power battle between the House of Commons, House of Lords and the monarch, there'll be only one winner – the Commons.

Laws can emanate from both the House of Commons and the Lords. A proposed new law debated by parliament is called a *bill*. The two types of bill are

- **Public or government bills:** These are sponsored by the government, with wording carefully drawn up by civil servants and introduced by the minister responsible for that area of government. So, for example, a bill proposing extending compulsory education to age 18 would be introduced by the minister for children, schools and families.

Government bills nearly always become law because the ministers who introduce them can rely on a majority of MPs to support them.

- **Private members' bills:** These are sponsored by individual backbench MPs in the House of Commons. Private members' bills have only a marginal chance of success – about one in ten bills become law – because the government gives them little debating time, and if it opposes such bills, they don't have a chance of getting a majority.

Explaining government bills

The government introduces bills for a number of reasons, including the following:

- **To fulfil manifesto pledges:** During elections, each party states in its manifesto what it will do if it gets elected. The party that gets into power is then expected to carry these pledges through by introducing new laws.
- **To maintain the regular workings of government:** Each parliamentary session the government introduces a budget, or finance bill, that sets up the legal framework for the collection of taxes. Without this bill the government can't raise the cash to fund day-to-day operations.
- **To deal with an emergency:** Sometimes a major event, such as a war or outbreak of disease, means that the country needs new laws fast. In this scenario, other bills go on the backburner and parliamentary time is freed up to allow the government to introduce its new law.

Often, the government consults pressure groups and interested parties prior to introducing new legislation. (Chapter 9 has more on the role of pressure groups in forming government policy.)

Circulating new ideas: Government Green Papers

Often, before introducing a new bill to parliament, the government checks out what interested parties think by publishing a *Green Paper.* In this document the government sets out its ideas and presents what it thinks are the policy options. Interested parties can then comment on the contents of the paper and the government can take their views into account when it finally publishes its White Paper, which I explain in the next section.

Green Papers are only appropriate when the government has time to spend on introducing the new law. In the case of an emergency, the government won't bother with a Green Paper, but move straight to introducing the bill to parliament.

Moving the law along: The White Paper stage

A *White Paper* is the final stage before a minister introduces an actual bill to parliament. The minister whose area of responsibility the bill falls into uses the reaction to the Green Paper and the policy proposals contained within it to inform the contents of the White Paper. Some proposals in the Green Paper fall by the wayside and others make it into the White Paper.

The minister who'll be introducing the bill to parliament shows the White Paper to her colleagues in cabinet and to the PM, and they debate its contents. The Cabinet may make changes, particularly when the Bill could affect many different departments. Usually, following White Paper stage, a bill is drawn up by civil servants and the minister then introduces this bill to the House of Commons or in some cases the Lords first.

In recent years, the Green Paper has fallen out of fashion. Nowadays the government often looks to undertake what is catchily called *pre-legislative scrutiny* before introducing a White Paper. This scrutiny often involves select committees considering draft legislation and asking interested individuals to give evidence before them.

Introducing private members' bills

Although private members' bills have only a slim chance of actually passing into law, individuals still try. Bills brought to parliament by backbench MPs can be devoted to big issues of the day or to addressing very small local concerns.

Time is short, with only 13 Fridays in each parliamentary session set aside for MPs to debate and vote upon private members' bills. What's more, debates often involve only a handful of MPs because many members return to their constituency homes on Thursday evenings. Passing a bill requires at least 100 MPs to vote, out of which a majority has to be in favour. So an MP wanting to introduce a bill not only has to get a majority in the chamber but also has to persuade 100-plus MPs to stay in Westminster on a Friday in order to cast a vote in the debate – no easy task!

Here are the four methods MPs use to introduce their private members' bills:

- **A bills ballot:** Because parliament allocates very limited time to hearing private members' bills, a pre-selection process is in place. MPs put their private members' bills on a list and a ballot decides the 20 most popular. The MPs of those 20 present the bills to the Commons on allotted Fridays. The higher up the list, the more likely the Commons is to debate the bill.
- **Ten-minute bill:** I said debate time was short, but ten minutes? Individual MPs get ten minutes of parliamentary time to present the case for a new piece of legislation. However, these bills very, very rarely make it into law.

Generally, the MP introducing a ten-minute bill is doing so as a chance to bring greater publicity to a particular area of concern or to a policy hobby-horse.

- **Bills from the House of Lords:** Peers can introduce their own bills in the House of Lords and they can team up with an MP who'll introduce their bills in the House of Commons as well.
- **Standing Order No. 57:** I know it sounds like a perfume but this order is actually a parliamentary procedure allowing individual MPs to introduce this type of bill on a Friday (the time set aside for this procedure) without making a supporting speech – which saves on precious time. The MPs get to read the bill (if they want) and can vote to debate it if it tickles their fancy. Usually, though, Standing Order No. 57 bills don't make it to debating stage.

A private members' bill has the best chance of making it into law if a widely respected and senior MP introduces it in a ballot. Success in the ballot brings debating time and means that a bedrock of support among MPs is already in place. However, the overwhelming majority of ballot bills don't make it into law either.

Getting Bills Passed: The Process

Parliament operates to a strict calendar. Each year around November, or just after a general election, a new parliamentary session begins, with the monarch visiting parliament and making a speech outlining what bills the government hopes to introduce into parliament in the coming session. During this session, debates take place and MPs vote on laws.

During Christmas, Easter and over the summer parliament is in *recess*, which means it doesn't convene. The amount of time parliament has in recess varies. A general election can alter things. But parliament is often in recess. In the 2014–15 parliamentary session, for example, the programme is as follows:

- Summer recess: 22 July to 1 September
- Recess to allow MPs to attend their respective party conferences: 12 September to 13 October
- Autumn recess: 11 to 17 November
- Christmas recess: 18 December to 5 January

In normal years MPs could also expect a nice long break at Easter, but a general election in May 2015 coincides. However, it's clear that MPs get a lot more time off from their day job than ordinary folk. In fact, they even do better than school holidays!

Long, hot, stinking summer

Parliament enjoys a long summer holiday – a bit like schoolchildren – as a result of tradition. Until the 20th century, the River Thames gave off an awful stink in the summer months and being close to its banks when the weather was warm was considered very unhealthy. Therefore, it was decided that parliament shouldn't sit during the hot summer months. This tradition has continued, which some cynics say is very convenient indeed for the MPs and peers.

Detailing the passage of bills

Bills have to jump over lots of hurdles and undergo oodles of scrutiny before they can become law. But government bills often have a majority of supporters; therefore, these bills usually get through even when opposition parties and pressure groups outside the UK parliament don't support them.

A bill must pass through these stages:

1. **First reading in the Commons:** MPs vote on whether the bill will pass to the next stage of the process.
2. **Second reading in the Commons:** MPs vote on whether the bill will now be sent to a parliamentary committee for closer scrutiny.
3. **Committee stage:** The relevant Commons standing committee examines the bill. For example, a pensions bill is examined by a committee of MPs put together specifically to examine it (I explain the types of committees in 'Poring Over the Detail: Parliamentary Committees' later in the chapter). Individual MPs can *table* – put forward – amendments to the bill, and the committee debates these. The committee then sends the bill back to the Commons with some amendments attached.
4. **Report stage:** The House of Commons considers the amendments proposed by the committee and may attach new amendments.
5. **Third reading in the Commons:** MPs vote on the bill and its amendments again. Usually, the Commons accepts the amendments only if the minister who introduced the bill agrees to them.

   The government tells its MPs to vote for or against amendments.
6. **Readings in the House of Lords:** After the bill passes third reading, it goes to the House of Lords, where it again goes through a process of first, second and third readings.

The House of Lords has the power to table its own amendments to the bill. The bill then goes back to the House of Commons and MPs debate and vote on the amendments. The House of Commons does, however, have the ultimate say over whether or not amendments from the Lords see the light of day.

Though rarely used, the House of Lords has the right to vote down a bill. Doing so doesn't kill the bill off, however; it merely delays it for a year. Parliament presents the bill to the monarch for royal assent; however, the legislation doesn't come into force for one year. The exception is the government budget: if the Lords vote against this, the Commons can send it to the monarch for royal assent and it becomes law straight away.

By taking a vote the House of Commons can choose to bypass the committee stage of a bill. It thus passes straight from second to third reading. Cutting this stage speeds up the process of law-making and is useful in emergency situations.

If the bill falls at any one of the above hurdles, it won't become law.

When little debating time is available in the House of Commons, the government may choose to introduce its bill to the House of Lords for debate first. The bill still has to jump the same number of hurdles – first, second and third reading – but it may do so in a slightly different order. MPs and members of the House of Lords may team up to introduce a bill and they can choose to go through the Commons or Lords route.

Sitting by tradition

On the floors of both the House of Commons and the House of Lords even the seating is dictated by tradition and parliamentary custom. In both houses the governing party occupies the seats to the right of the Speaker's chair – from the viewpoint of the Speaker – and government ministers sit on the very front bench. Opposite them sit the MPs from the opposition parties. The biggest opposition party occupies the benches closest to the Speaker's chair, while the third-biggest party and any representatives from minor parties sit in the bottom left of the chamber as the Speaker sees it.

The chambers of both Houses are quite small (though they look much bigger on television), and when all the MPs and lords are in attendance not everyone can sit down and many members have to stand in the gangways. The actual distance between the benches occupied by the government and the opposition parties is also very small. In fact, two red lines roughly two sword lengths apart are marked on the floor of the House of Commons chamber and members from either party aren't allowed to cross them.

The seating arrangement in the Commons and Lords pits opposition parties physically against each other across a small distance and aids what's seen as a very adversarial approach to politics.

Talking it over: Debating

When an MP refers to a fellow member in the House of Commons she always prefaces the comment with either 'my honourable friend' or 'the honourable member'. The word *friend* indicates that the MP is on the same side as the MP speaking, and *member* refers to an MP from an opposition political party.

The leader of the House is an MP and cabinet minister who decides how much time parliament spends on a particular bill – with the assistance of her party whips – but the leader doesn't have a completely free hand. The main opposition party, usually either Conservative or Labour, has the right to a set number of opposition days each session, when the Commons has to set aside other business and the opposition gets to debate an aspect of government policy. Generally, the opposition chooses opposition days so as to cause maximum embarrassment to the government.

After a debate begins, the speaker presides and she calls individual MPs to speak in the debate. After the time set for the debate has elapsed (and this is set out on a case-by-case basis, from an hour or two to several days), it's up to the speaker to bring the debate to an end. If the debate is over a piece of legislation, the speaker calls on MPs to cast their vote to decide whether it moves on to the next stage of the legislative process. The Speaker announces the result of the vote on the floor of the House of Commons.

Members of the House of Commons and House of Lords enjoy *parliamentary privilege*. This privilege means they can say what they want in the debating chambers of these two houses without fear of facing action for libel or slander. However, members must be polite. The nearby sidebar, 'Minding your language in parliament', explains what MPs can and can't say. What's more, members are free from arrest on civil matters within the Palace of Westminster. However, this isn't the case if they commit a criminal offence.

Icing the legislative cake: Receiving royal assent

Even after a bill has been through the exhaustive process of numerous votes and debates in the House of Commons and House of Lords, it still isn't actually law. No bill from parliament can become law without the monarch's signature – grandly termed *being given royal assent*. Parliament presents the monarch with the act of parliament to sign.

Getting the monarch's signature is partly a constitutional convention but it's also meant to be a final check on the law-making of parliament. However, the monarch must always follow the advice of ministers, which in this instance means she must sign or risk sparking a constitutional crisis.

Minding your language in parliament

The UK parliament is an ancient institution with all sorts of solemn, confusing and downright silly traditions. Minding your language is one of them. The government considers certain words and phrases inappropriate to use on the floor of either house.

If an MP or lord breaks the rules and conventions of the house, the speaker (see 'Keeping Order: The Role of the Speaker' later in this chapter) will take action. Such action can involve public censure, asking the MP or lord to withdraw the comment or even, in some cases, suspending that person from sitting in the house – the equivalent of being told to stand outside the classroom at school.

Some of the things you're not allowed to say include

- **Rude words or swearing:** Parliament is supposed to be a serious place and language that is deemed offensive and insulting is way out of line.
- **Accusations of lying:** MPs and lords may think an opposition member is telling porkies but they're not allowed to accuse that member of lying. In fact, the speaker rules any suggestion that a member is being dishonest out of order. The speaker asks any member who accuses another of lying to withdraw the comment.
- **Direct insults:** Personal insults directed at a fellow member aren't allowed. Over time, the speaker of the Commons has ruled the following words as being out of order: coward, hooligan, git (yes, git!), traitor, stoolpigeon (delightfully 1930s' gangster movie language), sod, slime, warty and, wait for it . . . guttersnipe. Referring to a member as being drunk or under the influence of illegal narcotics is also out of order. The only person allowed to drink alcohol in the chamber is the chancellor, when delivering the budget speech.

A few weeks usually take place between the bill passing through parliament and it receiving royal assent and becoming law. In emergencies, though, the monarch can usually sign in double-quick time.

Without the signature of the monarch the bill doesn't actually become law. After it becomes law, the bill changes into an act of parliament, which sounds very grand and official, and is!

Poring Over the Detail: Parliamentary Committees

Committees of MPs and, to a lesser extent, committees of lords carry out much of the work of parliament. Two main types of committee exist:

- **Public Bill Committees:** A temporary committee formed to examine a particular bill.

- **Select committee:** A permanent committee whose job it is to scrutinise the effects of legislation already on the statute book or examine the decisions taken by ministers.

These committees can shadow a particular department or they may look across the activities of a host of different departments. In short, though, parliamentary committees are a big deal, and they can call experts from different walks of life to give evidence.

Looking at standing committees

The House of Commons sets up *standing committees* temporarily to examine a particular bill put before parliament. The job of a standing committee is to debate and consider amendments to the bill they're examining.

The phrase *standing committee* is very confusing – as with many terms used in parliament. Because the committee is only in existence temporarily, sometimes its work is done and it's disbanded within a few weeks – so it doesn't stand for very long at all.

The Commons Committee of Selection decides membership of the committee according to the number of MPs each party has in parliament as a whole. In a committee with 30 places to fill, the majority of members come from the government party (reflecting the fact that it has a majority of MPs), a large minority from the biggest opposition party and a smaller minority from the third-biggest party, and so on until all 30 places are filled. The key is that the committee is meant to be a microcosm of parliament and reflect the relative size of the parties (in terms of seats won) as closely as possible. So if one party has two thirds of the seats in parliament, its members make up two thirds of the members of each standing committee.

A government with a significant majority of seats in the House of Commons can usually expect to see its legislation go through committee stage without too many unwelcome amendments. MPs may tack on amendments that don't undermine the basic thrust of the legislation and instead look to improve it, and the government may look at these amendments and agree that they're a good idea.

Standing committees tend to have quite large memberships – anything from 14 to 50 members. Interestingly, members of standing committees sit with members of their own party, opposite the opposition parties. Therefore, Conservative members of a standing committee sit opposite Labour members. This seating arrangement can make committee meetings quite adversarial in character.

The individual party whips decide which of their party members get to sit on the standing committees. This is in contrast to select committees (discussed in the next section) where MPs get to choose which of their colleagues will be the chairperson, for example.

Examining select committees

Much of the work of standing committees doesn't gain public attention, whereas select committees – permanent committees that meet regularly – are sometimes televised and have produced set pieces of political theatre.

Typing select committees

Two types of select committee exist:

- **Departmental:** These examine the actions of a particular government department or the effects of laws in that area.
- **Non-departmental:** As the name suggests, these committees aren't related to a particular government department. Instead, they focus on the general operation of government as a whole, the internal running of parliament and even UK relations with the European Union (EU).

Of around 20 departmental select committees, the major ones include

- **Treasury:** Looks at how well the Treasury is performing – is it, for example, collecting taxes and paying benefits as efficiently as it ought? It also examines areas of wider public life relating to finance.
- **Foreign Affairs:** Looks at how effective UK foreign policy is.
- **Defence:** Looks at how the ministry of defence spends its money and equips the UK's armed forces.
- **Health:** Examines how the government manages the National Health Service as well as aspects of public health.
- **Home Affairs:** Examines the workings of the criminal justice system and the police.
- **Education:** Examines the state education and university system.

The relative importance of the select committee reflects the importance of the department whose work it's shadowing. A whole host of committees don't follow a particular department but still examine an aspect of UK government or the running of parliament itself. Lots of these committees exist but here are some of the most important:

- **Public Accounts:** The most prominent non-departmental committee, well known for examining how government spends its money and bringing waste to light.
- **Public Administration Committee:** Examines the work of the parliamentary ombudsman, a position I explain in 'Tying Up the Loose Ends: The Other Parliamentary Players' later in this chapter.
- **Standards and Privileges:** Dedicated to monitoring the behaviour of MPs.
- **European Scrutiny Committee:** Looks at laws being passed by the EU.

Like standing committees, the Commons allots places on select committees according to party size in the House of Commons. Therefore the government has a majority on all the select committees. However, one of the MPs has to chair the committee and she's elected to this post through a ballot of MPs (in the case of Commons committees) or peers (in the case of Lords committees).

Working out what select committees do

Committees meet about once a week while parliament is in session. They question ministers and civil servants, and call witnesses from the general public with special skills or knowledge.

Although committees can question ministers and ask for information from ministries, the minister or their civil servants aren't automatically obliged to tell the committee what they know or give them access to private departmental documents. Ministers and civil servants who want to keep their dealings secret can always cite national security for not 'fessing up and telling the committee everything they know. For example, during the exhaustive Foreign Affairs Select Committee's examination of the reasons for war in Iraq in 2003, the committee often met with the argument that to disclose certain information would put national security or the work of the intelligence services at risk.

The House of Lords has its own committees but these don't tend to play a major role in legislative procedure and often their public meetings and investigations get little or no media coverage.

Keeping Order: The Role of the Speaker

One of the most notable figures in parliament is the speaker of the House of Commons. She sits on a chair between the government and opposition benches. The speaker is an ancient role, dating back to 1376.

Introducing two notable speakers

The speaker is a major figure, not only in parliament but also in British politics. The speaker may not have the power of the PM or a leading cabinet member but she embodies the grand old institution of parliament, is the protector of its traditions and privileges, and is often a larger-than-life and colourful character. Here are two recent takers of this particular hot seat:

- **Betty Boothroyd** was the first female speaker of the House of Commons. She acted in the role from 1992 to 2000 and was widely regarded as a highly competent speaker. Ms Boothroyd often displayed a sense of humour while at the same time maintaining strict discipline. Ms Boothroyd was used to life in the limelight; as a young woman in the 1940s she'd been a member of the Tiller Girls, a famous dance troupe of the day.
- **Michael Martin** became the first speaker in four centuries to have to resign the post. Martin was deemed by many to be partly responsible for lax monitoring of MPs' expenses. The MPs' expenses scandal of 2009 – see Chapter 24 for more on this – caused widespread discontent among the public and the media. What many viewed as Martin's mishandling of the expenses regime and the ensuing crisis led to many MPs calling for him to resign. He duly did so in May 2009.

The speaker's main jobs are:

- Ensuring that an MP follows the procedures of the House of Commons to the letter.
- Deciding which MPs can speak in debates.
- Ensuring that MPs behave themselves and don't use un-parliamentary language (see the 'Minding your language in parliament' sidebar, earlier in the chapter, for more on this).
- Disciplining MPs who don't behave themselves. Sanctions include naming them publicly to suspending their privileges as an MP.

A ballot of all MPs elects the speaker of the House of Commons. This is a free vote, which means the party whips don't try to influence how MPs vote (check out Chapter 8 for more on the role of the whips). MPs have a list of candidates – any MP can put her name on this list – from which they pick. When elected, the speaker sits for the duration of the parliament.

The speaker is supposed to be independent and, although a sitting MP and belonging to a particular party, she only votes when a tie occurs, which is very rare indeed.

Tying Up the Loose Ends: The Other Parliamentary Players

As well as the speaker (see the preceding section), several other significant figures play an important role in the UK parliament:

- **Leader of the house:** This is a government minister whose job it is to set out what debates and bills parliament will focus on in the forthcoming session. The leader's role is crucial because the amount of time she gives to a debate often dictates whether or not a bill will make it through first-, second- and third-reading stages. The leader generally gives preference to government bills.
- **Parliamentary ombudsman:** The basic job of the parliamentary ombudsman is to investigate maladministration by the government that may have harmed the public. The ombudsman generally sticks to big subjects and spends a long time hearing evidence, writing reports and making recommendations about how the government can right its wrongs. As government gets bigger and stretches into different walks of life, the workload of the parliamentary ombudsman steadily increases.
- **Black Rod:** The role of gentleman usher of the Black Rod, to give this person's full title, dates back to 1350. Black Rod accompanies the monarch when she attends the state opening of a new session of parliament.
- **Serjeant at arms:** The serjeant's job is to escort out of the chamber MPs who've been asked to leave by the speaker. The post dates way back to 1415 and traditionally the people who become serjeant at arms – and Black Rod – are former members of the UK police force or military.

Black Rod and the serjeant at arms are now just ceremonial roles. The nitty-gritty of day-to-day security in the House of Lords and Commons is taken care of by a professional security co-ordinator who has a background in counter-terrorism.

Climbing the Greasy Pole to the Top Jobs in Government

People refer to the climb in government as the 'greasy pole' for good reason – slipping back down is very easy.

Most MPs have ambitions above simply being a good constituency MP. They want to make a real difference by becoming a minister who gets to pilot government legislation through the Houses of Parliament and has a real say on government policy potentially affecting the lives of millions of Britons.

However, only a small number of MPs become ministers or rise further up the ranks to the highest jobs in government, such as the home secretary, foreign secretary, chancellor of the exchequer and, of course, the top slot, prime minister.

In fact, if you're an MP representing an opposition party rather than the party of government, you have no chance of becoming a minister until and unless your party secures a majority of seats in the House of Commons and therefore forms the government. But even for those MPs on the government benches in the Commons, making it into ministerial office can still be very hard. Many get close to the summit but don't quite make it.

The following list outlines the path to ministerial power. Usually, MPs ascend each step in turn and reaching the top can take many years:

1. **Parliamentary under-secretary:** This minister's job is to support the departmental minister of state – usually a more senior MP. An under-secretary basically does the work that the more senior minister doesn't have time for.
2. **Parliamentary private secretary:** This job is the first rung on the ladder to the top ministerial posts. The PPS acts as the go-between for ministers and parliament. She helps keep track of backbench MPs' opinions as they relate to the minister and the legislation they're trying to introduce in parliament.
3. **Minister of state:** Below the cabinet minister are two, three or even four other ministers whose job it is to look after a particular part of the ministry's work. For example, the Ministry of Defence has a minister for defence procurement, whose job it is to oversee expenditure on weapons and equipment, as well as ministers for the armed forces and international security co-operation.
4. **Cabinet minister:** This politician heads a government department. The minister's job is to defend the department to cabinet colleagues and the PM and to argue the case for more money for the department's coffers from the chancellor of the exchequer. People often refer to cabinet ministers as secretaries of state.

The prime minister appoints ministers. Ambitious MPs courting ministerial office need to keep the PM sweet, and they do so by remaining loyal and voting the way they're told to by the whips. (Chapter 14 talks more about the role of ministers in government.)

Chapter 14

Gazing at the Summit: The PM and Cabinet

In This Chapter

- Taking in the prime minister
- Looking at cabinet responsibilities
- Meeting the bigwig cabinet members
- Moving things around in the cabinet

This is the chapter to read if you want to know about the real bigwigs in British politics – the ministers and the prime minister – whose decisions affect your daily life, propel the economy into boom or bust, and even send soldiers to war.

The prime minister and cabinet are at the very pinnacle of British politics and in this chapter I explain why they're so powerful and how they run the government day in, day out.

Going Straight to the Top: The Prime Minister

Whoever is prime minister (PM) is the most important person in British politics: the big cheese, the head honcho, the main man or woman – you get the idea!

The PM wields so much power for a whole host of reasons, including that the PM

- Leads the biggest political party in the House of Commons, the main law-making body in the country
- Gets to appoint ministers who perch at the top of all the main branches of government, called ministries, which I talk more about in 'Concentrating on the Cabinet', later in this chapter

- Gets to decide which ministers sit in the *cabinet*, the key decision-making body of government
- Appoints junior ministers and has a say in senior civil service appointments
- Usually takes the lead in forming government policy, and when disagreements occur among ministers or MPs, makes the final call
- Oversees how government is organised, and can actually set up or abolish whole government departments
- Chairs meetings of the cabinet, where the government takes key policy decisions and sets the legislative programme for parliament
- May not be the head of state – that's the monarch's role – but represents the country when visiting other states and is very much the nation's leader

Much of the PM's power derives from the fact that he also leads the biggest political party in the House of Commons. The role of party leader is also very powerful (check out Chapter 8 for more on the inner workings of political parties).

As you can probably imagine, just one of the many jobs a PM has to do would be more than enough for most individuals to cope with. The PM often has to work long hours and is always in the public eye, with his slightest move causing comment. In some ways, being the PM resembles being a major celebrity but without the option of selling your wedding photos. Seriously, though, the job of PM is exhausting and deeply taxing and a few of the people who reach this pinnacle aren't always up to the task.

Facing Prime Minister's Questions

Prime Minister's Questions (PMQs) is one of the great set-piece events in British political life. Each Wednesday when parliament is in session the PM goes to the House of Commons and answers questions from MPs about the governance of the country for around 30 minutes. Most of the time, though, is taken up with questions from the leader of the main opposition party. PMQs gives backbench MPs a chance – albeit a very limited one – to put their own questions to the most important politician in the country.

The idea of PMQs is for the head honcho to explain what government is doing and for its actions to come under scrutiny. In recent years questioning during PMQs has often had more than one eye on creating a sound bite for the television news bulletins. However, PMQs is still dramatic and gaffes made by the PM or opposition leaders can become big news stories.

The PM lives and works in 10 Downing Street. From the outside, Number 10 seems little more than a grand Georgian terrace house – which it is – but behind its famous black door exists an inordinate amount of office space. In fact, the PM's residence resembles Doctor Who's TARDIS – small on the outside, cavernous on the inside. The PM doesn't live and work at 10 Downing Street full time. As a perk of the job, he gets the use of a country estate called Chequers, at which to entertain visiting world leaders.

Getting to be the PM

Only one person can be PM at any one time and the job doesn't change hands that often. In fact, since 1979 we've had only five prime ministers. With the thousands of politicians around the UK, the odds of becoming PM are very long indeed. For well over a century all the PMs have followed this path:

1. **Get elected as an MP.** All PMs for the past century have been members of parliament.
2. **Get elected party leader.** It's a constitutional convention that only a party leader can be the prime minister.
3. **Get a House of Commons majority.** The monarch asks the leader of the party with the majority of seats in the House of Commons to form the government and be prime minister. No majority, no keys to number 10!

The monarch appoints the prime minister, but in reality the monarch has little choice. By a convention of Britain's unwritten constitution, the monarch must appoint a PM capable of rallying a majority of MPs in the House of Commons. As such, the leader of the largest political party in the House of Commons usually gets the job.

By constitutional convention, PMs must also be Members of Parliament (MPs) because they're supposed to have a majority in the House of Commons. The last time a member of the House of Lords was also PM was way back in 1895, when Lord Salisbury was appointed to the role.

Usually, the PM leads the political party that has the majority of MPs in the House of Commons. However, in 2010 no party achieved an overall majority. As a result, the leaders of the two biggest parties, by the number of seats gained at the election, negotiated with the leadership of the third biggest party – the Lib Dems – for support in forming an effective government. After five days of tense negotiation, the Lib Dems said that they would support the Conservatives, led by David Cameron. This support meant that Cameron could secure a majority in the Commons and the queen then asked him to form the coalition government.

Gauging whether the PM is really 'first among equals'

The PM is supposed to be *primus inter pares*, which means 'first among equals'. The PM is first because he heads up the government and is the face that the electorate knows best, but equal because he chairs the cabinet rather than telling it what to do.

In theory, each member of the cabinet has an equal say in what policy the government pursues. But theories don't always work out in reality, and despite the pretty Latin phrases and the idea of equality, the power that the PM wields – particularly to hire and fire government ministers – means that he's far more than an equal. In fact, usually what the PM says goes, and any minister wishing to oppose him had better have his arguments well stacked up.

Limiting the power of the PM

Some PMs take a dictatorial approach to the job but even they know that they're not untouchable. The power of the PM is built on powerful pillars, but through political misjudgements or bad luck these pillars can crumble away over time and the power base of a PM can erode. In fact, even the most successful PMs last little more than a decade in modern times and many have to high-tail it out of 10 Downing Street much sooner. Someone once said that all great political careers end in failure and that's especially true for the PM.

Some of the ways the PM can have their power constrained or simply find themselves out of a job include

- **Losing an election:** The PM is always the head of a political party, and if that party does badly at an election then it loses its majority in the House of Commons, which means that the monarch asks whoever leads the new majority party to form the government. In other words, the PM is turfed out along with the government.
- **Losing party support:** Much of the PM's power comes from being the head of a political party. However, when it comes to leaders and political parties, power is a two-way street. If the PM doesn't follow policies popular with the rank and file of the party, or is seen as ineffective or a bad leader, then he loses support. Ultimately, a party can even replace the leader in an internal ballot. If this happens, the PM loses his job automatically.
- **Losing cabinet confidence:** The PM may be the head honcho in cabinet and have the job of hiring and firing ministers but these ministers have their own following in the party, media and wider general public. In short,

certain ministers are harder for the PM to sack or ignore than others. If enough of these minsters gang up on the PM then the person being turfed out of office may well be the PM. Although they're super-powerful, PMs have to govern with the consent of their cabinet colleagues and, more generally, the MPs and members of the party they head up.

All the main political parties have a mechanism for getting rid of their leader. Doing so often involves a substantial minority of MPs proposing that someone else should be leader. If this candidate has enough support, a leadership election takes place. Very few party leaders survive a serious leadership challenge.

Sometimes MPs want to give their leader a warning to let him know that they're unhappy with his behaviour. In the past, this warning has led to a leadership election and a stalking-horse candidate running for the top job. A *stalking horse* isn't a very serious contender because he doesn't have enough support and experience. Instead, the role is to galvanise opponents of the party leader into taking action.

Observing the changing nature of the PM's relationship with the cabinet

It used to be that PMs used meetings of the cabinet as a way to thrash out ideas and genuinely debate policy initiatives. The diaries of former Labour minister Tony Benn revealed that in the 1960s and 1970s, under PM Harold Wilson, cabinet meetings were a real hotbed of discussion. Some meetings would go on for hours, often involving heated disagreements.

But in the 1980s, under Margaret Thatcher, cabinet meetings changed in character, and the thoughts of the PM took centre stage. Members of the cabinet could argue with the fearsome Mrs T but they needed to come well prepared and accept that sometimes – particularly in her final few years as PM – she wouldn't listen.

In the 1990s and 2000s, under Tony Blair, cabinet culture changed again. Government policy was being formed elsewhere – in cabinet committees or by the PM with his close advisers. Cabinet meetings became less about debate and more about ministers simply reporting their progress in pushing policy through. Instead of lasting many hours, cabinet meetings would be over in an hour or under.

The birth of coalition government in 2010 changed the realities of cabinet government once again. Small groups of cabinet ministers from the two parties inside the coalition make many of the key decisions of government, meeting outside of cabinet and thrashing out a course of action.

Many argue that, as a result of these changes, the cabinet is no longer as powerful a body in the constitution as it once was. Any idea, therefore, that the PM is first among equals must probably be consigned to the dustbin of history.

Concentrating on the Cabinet

The cabinet is a group of the top politicians from the ruling political party and its members are called *government ministers*. The PM can bring anyone he wants into the cabinet but generally he selects ministers from the ranks of MPs of the governing party in the House of Commons. The odd lord finds his way into the cabinet but these days convention dictates that it's best if elected politicians rather than peers take the top jobs in government.

The job of the cabinet is to decide what policies the government will pursue, and after it decides on a policy it's up to whichever minister is overseeing the pursuit of the policy to report back to the cabinet on progress. The PM chairs the cabinet and, with the help of the cabinet secretary and senior civil servants, he decides what the cabinet discusses at its weekly meetings. The number of politicians sitting in the cabinet tends to vary. Not all ministers sit in the cabinet, but certain officials, such as chancellor of the exchequer or health secretary, automatically sit in the cabinet by constitutional convention. Ultimately, though, the PM decides which ministers sit in on cabinet meetings.

Occasionally, a PM wants to give an individual a seat in cabinet – presumably because the PM values that person's advice or acumen – but all the ministries already have a minister in place. Well, that's not a problem! The PM is free to appoint who he likes to the cabinet and can simply bestow the title of *minister without portfolio*, which basically means a minister without a government department.

The cabinet has its own secretary. Now this person's job isn't taking notes, booking meeting rooms and ensuring all the ministers have sufficient tea or coffee. Cabinet secretary is one of the most senior civil service jobs in the country. The cabinet secretary runs the Cabinet Secretariat, which provides vital administrative support services for cabinet committees, ensures decisions are consistent across government, monitors how well ministries are following through on government policy, and circulates minutes from meetings of cabinet and cabinet committees.

Governing the UK is a massive undertaking, with literally thousands of civil servants based in Whitehall alone. In order to ensure that ministries don't go stepping on each other's toes and contradicting one another, the Cabinet Office exists. The role of the Cabinet Office is to co-ordinate government action across ministries. In the day-to-day running of the UK government, the Cabinet Office is very important.

Taking in the great offices of state

The PM isn't the only big mover and shaker in cabinet; several other posts within government carry with them enormous power. Some ministerial jobs carry more clout and power than others.

At the top of the tree is the PM, of course, but just below this office are other ministers whose jobs are equally historical and whose positions are important. Here's a rundown – PM aside – of the great offices of state:

- **Chancellor of the exchequer:** The chancellor is second in importance in the UK government only to the PM. This job involves setting government economic policy and ensuring that public finances work. The chancellor presents a Budget (spring) and Pre-Budget report (autumn) to MPs in parliament that change tax rates and set government spending. The chancellor also runs the Treasury, which sets the spending budgets for all the other departments of state. And, in politics as in daily life, power often rests with whoever controls the purse strings.
- **Foreign secretary:** This person oversees foreign policy. The job involves lots of international travel and diplomacy and is often seen as the glamour gig in the UK government. The foreign secretary often acquires a high public profile and he has control over a big budget and gets to meet world leaders face to face.
- **Home secretary:** This minister is responsible for policing, national security, internal affairs, immigration and citizenship. In recent years the job of home secretary has been something of a poisoned chalice, with successive ministers being sacked or resigning. In fact, the performance of the Home Office as a whole has come under such close scrutiny that in 2008 the PM decided to remove some of its powers – such as control of the prison service – and give it a newly formed justice ministry. Nevertheless, people still see home secretary as a top government job.
- **Deputy prime minister:** A relatively recent advent, dating back to only the 1990s. The DPM fills in for the prime minister when he's out of the country or on holiday, chairing cabinets and even attending parliament and answering Prime Minister's Questions. Although important, the post wasn't as crucial to the running of government as the others in this list until 2010, when the coalition was formed. Then the leader of the Lib Dems, Nick Clegg, took on the DPM role, which gave the post added impetus and importance. The role of DPM is here to stay and whoever occupies the role sits near the top of the cabinet tree.

Observing the big beasts of the cabinet jungle

Even the PM has to tread carefully around certain cabinet members. These figures carry *political weight* – what they say and do normally attracts considerable attention in the media and among commentators, who refer to them, not entirely flatteringly, as the *big beasts*. A minister's big beast status depends on whether he

- Occupies one of the great offices of state such as chancellor of the exchequer or foreign secretary (I cover the great offices of state in the preceding section)
- Is popular in the party, with a personal following among MPs and party members
- Has wide appeal among the public and is well liked or seen as good at his job

A minister can hold high office but not be a big beast because he doesn't have a high public profile or wide popularity in the party – and the converse is also true. Have a high office, a strong public profile and a following in the party, however, and you're definitely a big beast.

Sensible PMs try to keep big beasts on board by involving them in decision-making and consulting them. Collective cabinet responsibility, which I describe in the upcoming section 'Explaining collective cabinet responsibility', helps keep big beasts reined in as well.

The biggest beast in Tony Blair's cabinet was undoubtedly his chancellor, Gordon Brown. Brown had a lot of support among party members and was seen widely as being a capable chancellor, so Blair let him have an enormous say in party policy, particularly over domestic matters, while Blair kept tight control of foreign affairs and diplomacy. Brown's power was so great that it was even likened to having two PMs. However, the two men didn't see eye to eye, and their advisers often bickered and briefed against the other side. In fact, in the Labour Party of the late 1990s and 2000s MPs and advisers were often referred to as either being 'Blairites' or 'Brownites'. Brown eventually replaced Blair as PM in 2007.

Looking down the political food chain to other ministerial posts

Outside of the great offices of state around another 30 ministers attend cabinet meetings, which are held once a week on a Thursday. Some of these ministers are called cabinet ministers because they're expected to attend every meeting. These include

- Health secretary
- Education secretary
- Defence secretary
- Leader of the House of Commons
- Leader of the House of Lords
- Work and pensions secretary

- Justice secretary
- International development secretary
- Transport secretary
- Secretary for business, innovation and skills
- Secretary for culture, media and equalities
- Secretary for environment, food and rural affairs
- Secretary for communities and local government
- Chief secretary to the Treasury
- Secretary of state for Wales
- Secretary of state for Northern Ireland
- Secretary of state for Scotland
- Secretary for the Cabinet Office
- Secretary for energy and climate change

In addition, several cabinet posts exist that may not mean that much – chancellor of the Duchy of Lancaster and parliamentary secretary to the Treasury come to mind. PMs often give these positions to the people who act as chief whips for the party in the Commons or House of Lords.

Other ministers attend cabinet meetings when those present are likely to discuss their particular area of concern, either directly or indirectly. The cabinet secretary lets the individual minister know when he's expected to attend cabinet meetings. For example, the housing minister isn't actually a cabinet minister, but whenever a matter likely to touch on housing is on the cabinet's agenda, along comes the housing minister.

Apart from the housing minister, the following ministers get to attend cabinet meetings occasionally:

- Minister for universities and science
- Minister for women
- Attorney general

Assuming Cabinet Responsibilities

A seat in cabinet comes with certain responsibilities – work that the minister is expected to perform for the government. The PM decides who will and won't be a member of the cabinet, and if the minister fails to live up to the responsibilities, the PM's likely to sack or demote him at cabinet reshuffle time.

Explaining collective cabinet responsibility

Ministers are supposed to act according to the catchily named *ministerial code*, which states that 'decisions reached by the cabinet are binding on all members of the government'. In short, this means that ministers can disagree with each other as much as they want behind closed doors – and they often do – but after the collective voice of the cabinet has spoken (if the cabinet's taken a vote or reached a majority agreement), it's time to get into line.

This concept of public unity is called *collective cabinet responsibility* and is meant to ensure the government seems united in the eyes of the electorate and speaks with one voice. It supposedly makes government action more effective as well.

Publicly stating disagreement with a decision reached by cabinet colleagues is a ministerial cardinal sin. A minister who states that he doesn't like a policy or new bill usually resigns from the cabinet or, in some cases, is sacked by the PM.

Collective cabinet responsibility is close to the heart of PMs because it means that the government can be seen as acting in unison and the electorate likes to think it's governed by people who have a clear purpose. However, often collective responsibility, while not fully breaking down, does become a little frayed. Ministers don't publicly disagree with cabinet policies, but they get friends and advisers to talk to journalists to let them know what their real feelings are. The media then reposts this dissent but attributes it to an anonymous source. (This is called *briefing* and is an everyday occurrence at Westminster.)

Taking in individual responsibility

As well as a responsibility to their colleagues, cabinet ministers are also responsible for their own ministry. A minister is thus expected to do the following:

- Explain before parliament the actions of the ministry. A minister may do so in debates in the chamber of the House of Commons or in front of a select committee – refer to Chapter 13 for more on debates and committee meetings.
- Take responsibility when senior civil servants within their own ministry make mistakes. Ultimately, a minister may resign his job because of the mistake of an adviser or civil servant.

In recent times the convention that ministers are responsible for the actions of their civil servants and that, ultimately, they should resign if these mistakes come to light has gone a little by the wayside. Under PMs Tony Blair and Gordon Brown ministers have no longer resigned under such circumstances, although Conservative leader David Cameron has argued that they should.

Ministers can't know everything that's going on in their department. In fact, they leave even some major decisions to senior civil servants.

Civil servants are supposed to be both independent and permanent employees – therefore surviving changes of government.

Working Behind the Scenes: Cabinet Committees

Many of the big government policy decisions are no longer taken by full meetings of the cabinet. Instead, the PM selects a few ministers – often no more than four or five – to sit on small committees whose job it is to form government policy and then present their work to the PM and the cabinet. Obviously, these cabinet committees are hugely important.

The PM forms committees because they work more quickly than the full cabinet, mainly as a result of involving far fewer members, and they're quick to set up and abolish, making them very flexible. At any one time generally between 8 and 15 cabinet committees are operating to review important policy areas.

Some ministers sit on several committees at once. Over some topics, the PM has face-to-face meetings with a minister to thrash out policy in his area. This approach was a popular method of government for Labour PM Gordon Brown.

Conservative PM Margaret Thatcher was known for her – how shall I put it? – combative leadership style (put simply, she liked a tear-up). She regularly met with ministers face to face to discuss policy and was noted for holding and espousing strong views at cabinet meetings. Thatcher had a very black-and-white view of politics, and she famously used to ask even her own cabinet colleagues, 'Are you one of us?', meaning did they hold similar convictions to her. Eventually, fed up with her dictatorial style, Thatcher's own MPs and ministers rebelled and forced her out of office in 1990.

Shaking Up the Cabinet

Politics can be brutal, particularly near the top of government. Becoming a cabinet minister can take years of hard work and political manoeuvring, but careers can be cut short on the decision of the PM or through having to resign. In addition, new politicians move into cabinet and ministers move into different jobs, all at the behest of the PM. As a result, the membership of the cabinet rarely stays the same for very long.

Some suggest these movements are disruptive to the operation of government and that we need politicians in post for a long time so that they can see government policy through properly (and some cabinet members do stay in the same job for years on end). Others suggest that disruptions reduce complacency – with no job-for-life mentality – and keep ministers on their toes.

Civil servants, rather than ministers, do the day-to-day work of government . So in some respects, which politician is actually the minister may not matter a great deal.

Falling on their sword: Ministerial resignations

Political careers that look destined for the top crash and burn in double-quick time. Even at the top of government, powerful ministers can be happily ensconced in their ministries one minute and out of office and on the back-benches in the Commons the next.

This fall from grace can be sparked by a sacking from cabinet by the PM – see 'Shifting the seats: Cabinet reshuffles' next – but it can also result from the minister resigning.

Now, unlike you and I, who probably resign to go on to a better job elsewhere, ministers who resign do so because of a political or personal issue that dictates that they simply have to go. Some ministers fall on their own sword – resign of their own accord – and others are persuaded to do so by the PM or his advisers.

Ministers take the long walk off a very short political pier for three reasons:

- **Policy differences:** Ministers are bound by collective cabinet responsibility and are supposed to go along with the decisions made by the cabinet. However, sometimes they just can't do it and as a result resign their post.

- **Mistakes:** Ministers make errors – sometimes huge ones – and in such instances opponents often call for their resignation. These days ministers are more likely to try to sit tight, but occasionally the media furore and public anger at the boob is so great that the minister in question feels that resigning for what he often says is 'the good of the party' is best.
- **Scandals:** Here's the juiciest reason of the lot (I explore a host of these tabloid fodder stories in Chapter 24). The minister becomes embroiled in a scandal involving, say, some abuse of office, deception or sexual peccadillo, and as a result he feels he'd best resign for 'the good of the party'.

Shifting the seats: Cabinet reshuffles

Once a year, generally, the PM looks to bring new people into the cabinet and get rid of those he sees as not up to the job. The PM may also promote those he sees as especially loyal, while offloading those he sees as potential future leadership challengers.

Cabinet reshuffles are big occasions in UK politics and journalists love them because they're an opportunity to gossip about which ministers are going up or down. The PM's advisers often brief prominent journalists about which minister is likely to go where, or sometimes suggest that a particular minister is close to getting the boot so as to keep that individual on his toes.

On the day of a cabinet reshuffle, the PM calls or sees in person all the ministers he wants to promote or remove. Waiting to see what the PM will do is extremely nerve-wracking for ministers and their advisers. Some political careers virtually come to an end on reshuffle day.

Not just cabinet ministers get moved on reshuffle day; junior ministers are also shunted about. These people don't hold cabinet rank but do a job within a ministry. For example, within the Department of Work and Pensions is a secretary of state for work and pensions who's of cabinet rank; below him is a minister for work, one for pensions and even one for pension reform. These junior ministers want one day to be a cabinet minister but must first prove that they make a good fist of a more lowly post and then catch the eye of the PM.

Sometimes the reshuffle is dramatic and changes the fortunes of the government for good or ill. In 1962, Conservative PM Harold Macmillan sacked seven senior cabinet ministers following the Profumo scandal (see Chapter 24 for more on this).

The move became known as the Night of the Long Knives and, although a bold step, it didn't have the desired effect. A short time afterwards Macmillan stepped down as PM on medical grounds but by then his savage cabinet reshuffle had led to him losing the confidence of many of his own MPs and cabinet.

Whispering in the PM's Ear: Special Advisers

One of the biggest changes in modern British politics is the rise of the special adviser. A *special adviser* is someone – often a journalist or expert – whose job it is to advise the minister or, in some cases, the PM. He may have particular expertise or just be a long-standing, trusted confidante of the minister in question. Regardless, special advisers have an enormous behind-the-scenes influence on government policy and, in particular, its presentation in the media and to the wider public. (Chapter 10 explores the role of the special adviser, particularly in relation to media manipulation.) During the daily cut and thrust of government a special adviser acts as gatekeeper for the minister, as well as a trusted sounding board and expert. The government of Tony Blair saw a huge explosion in special advisers in Whitehall. Blair alone had upwards of 50 special advisers, whereas the previous PM, John Major, had a mere 8.

Tony Blair's fondness for political advisers and gradual marginalisation of the full cabinet led some to suggest that he had a presidential style of government, in that he took more decision-making onto his shoulders than many previous PMs rather than relying on cabinet colleagues. In fact, Blair seemed to make many key political or policy decisions with a few close confidantes. As a result, Blair's style was termed a *sofa government*: a relaxed method of debate with a handful of people close to him, most notably his press secretary, Alastair Campbell. However, set against this theory is the fact that Blair also ceded much of his authority in domestic policy matters to his chancellor, Gordon Brown.

Turning to the Opposition: The Shadow Cabinet

Most government ministers have a shadow. A *shadow* refers to an MP from an opposition party whose job it is to put across what policies that party would do if it were in office.

So, when the secretary of state for health sets out a new policy on hospital treatment, his shadow will reveal what the opposition party would do about reforming hospital treatment if elected or simply point out what he sees as the failings in the government policy.

The *shadow cabinet* is supposed to be a government in waiting and meets regularly in the House of Commons to plan strategy. A shadow cabinet

- Sets out policies the opposition party would pursue
- Criticises the actions of ministers and exposes what it sees as failings in government
- Acts as a potential government, ready and waiting

The shadow cabinet may become the cabinet after an election. However, if the leader of the opposition later becomes PM, it's not a given that the member of the shadow cabinet responsible for education is appointed secretary of state for education. Who makes it into the new cabinet is entirely up to the new PM.

A member of the shadow cabinet is referred to as a *front bencher*. This term derives from the fact that he has the right to sit on the front bench of his party's row of benches in the House of Commons or House of Lords.

Chapter 15

Assessing Ministers and Civil Servants

In This Chapter

- Looking at government departments
- Seeing who ranks where
- Understanding the civil service
- Working up to senior civil servants
- Evaluating the pros and cons of the civil service
- Considering changes and reforms

As far as many politicians are concerned, the classic TV sitcom *Yes Minister* was more documentary than comedy because it laid bare the relationship between government ministers and their civil servants. The series showed a hapless government minister swimming against the tide of events and the machinations of his own senior civil servant, Sir Humphrey Appleby.

But despite the jaundiced eye many politicians cast towards their civil servants, one thing's for sure: how ministers and civil servants work together is key to successful governance. Civil servants are the oil in the government machine that keeps the cogs moving.

In this chapter I peer deep into the corridors of power in Whitehall and go a long way to explaining how government gets done in Britain.

Examining What Government Departments Do

Government departments, or ministries as they're called, are at the hub of UK government. Put simply, a ministry is responsible for ensuring the civil service and other state employees follow government policy. For example, if the government policy is that all seven-year-olds sit a test at school, then it's up to the education ministry to ensure this happens. In the same way, the Department of Health deals with government policies relating to the National Health Service, and the Department for Transport deals with Britain's road, rail and other transport infrastructure.

Although the prime minister (PM) and cabinet take many decisions over which policies to pursue in government, the departments are responsible for drawing up that policy, proposing new laws and ultimately implementing them. The PM and cabinet may be the showy grille on the front of the car but the government departments are supplying the administrative power beneath the bonnet.

Some departments or ministries are considered more important than others. For example, the Treasury, with the chancellor of the exchequer at the helm, is responsible for economic policy as well as tax collection and a good deal of benefit payouts. One key reason the chancellor and the Treasury are so important is that other ministers have to make their case for their departmental expenditure to them. In short, the chancellor controls the purse strings of government and that brings huge power and influence (see Chapter 14 for a fuller rundown of this role). As a result, the Treasury is seen as much more important than, say, the Department for Culture, Media and Sport.

Ranking the Departmental Hierarchy

Britain is a democracy, which means elected politicians are meant to take the decisions of government. But the government needs to make many decisions because governing over 60 million people is no small undertaking. So over time a strict hierarchy has formed within government ministries. The most senior politician is at the top – a minister – and she's served by other less senior politicians. The idea is that less senior politicians and their civil servants follow instructions from the minister at the top of the department.

From top down, the decision-making chain of command goes like this:

- **Cabinet minister:** This politician is head of the department. The minister has ultimate say over which policies she takes to the PM or cabinet and makes the really big decisions within the department. It's her job to defend the department to cabinet colleagues and to the PM, and to argue the case for more money for the department's coffers from the chancellor. Cabinet ministers are often referred to as secretaries of state.
- **Minister of state:** Below the cabinet minister are perhaps two, three or even four other ministers whose job it is to look after a particular part of the ministry's work. For example, below the cabinet minister in the Department for Work and Pensions are three ministers of state – one

for work, one for pensions and another for pension reform. Ministers of state usually have a great deal of autonomy, but on really big matters or matters that cut across the responsibilities of other ministers they refer up to their cabinet minister boss.

- **Parliamentary under-secretary:** This politician's job is to work under the ministers of state. She enjoys the trappings of a minister, in that she earns a bit more than a Member of Parliament (MP) and may have a driver, but she's still at the low end of the very greasy ministerial pole, hoping one day to climb up to minister of state, and then cabinet minister and even beyond.
- **Parliamentary private secretary:** Finally, down at the bottom of the ministerial pile, is the parliamentary private secretary (PPS). This job is filled by an MP who acts as the go-between for ministers and parliament. A PPS helps to track the opinion of backbench MPs in parliament so that the minister can get a handle on how they'll receive new policy initiatives or a particular piece of legislation. PPSs are at the bottom of the pile in status – they don't even get paid! – but they do the job because they have ambitions one day to be ministers and they have to start somewhere.

The cabinet minister and ministers of state are often referred to as the *ministerial team*, which suggests that they're supposed to work together. The PM frowns upon ministers within the same department falling out. On a more sociable note, friendships and alliances often form among members of the team, and when the cabinet minister moves on to another department – as often happens after a cabinet reshuffle, which I cover in Chapter 14 – she'll take ministers of state along for the ride.

Although, ostensibly, ministers sit at the top of the government departmental tree, they don't actually take every decision. They leave much of their daily decision-making to their civil servants, who have expertise and who, in many cases, have been doing their job for far longer than the minister.

The life of a government minister – no matter how junior – is filled with paperwork. On Thursday evening many ministers and MPs leave to go back to their constituencies. The minister's senior civil servants give her a red box containing all the paperwork she's expected to read and documents to sign in time for Monday's return to the office.

Of course nowadays, with the rise of special advisers, it's no longer just ministers and civil servants interacting; instead, cabinet ministers, even ministers of state, have their own advisers and even press officers, whom they may well listen to more than the senior civil servant.

With cabinet ministers, ministers of state, parliamentary under-secretaries and parliamentary private secretaries, you can see that lots of MPs and the odd smattering of lords are active in government. In fact, around 100 politicians – both MPs and lords – are in the government. This means that a high proportion (sometimes close to a third) of all the MPs from the biggest party in the Commons have jobs in the government, from cabinet ministers down to unpaid PPSs, which makes passing its bills through the House of Commons easier.

Until 2011, the PM would appoint the cabinet secretary, who'd appoint the permanent under-secretaries, who'd appoint other senior civil servants within the department they headed up. The cabinet secretary was in effect the head honcho of the UK civil service. Between 2011 and 2014 this important job was split up. A cabinet secretary still headed up the work of the Cabinet Office – a ministry in the government – but the old powers of appointments were hived off into a new role: the head of the home civil service. The first appointee to this big job was Bob Kerslake, who was also the permanent secretary in the Department of Communities and Local Government.

In the 2014 cabinet reshuffle these jobs were merged again. Sir Bob Kerslake resigned and Sir Jeremy Heywood took on both positions.

Although the permanent under-secretary appoints civil servants in her department, these top grade jobs aren't completely in her gift: candidates may also sit an aptitude test and attend an interview. All the interviewers have their say, but it's safe to say that the permanent under-secretary gets who she wants.

Oiling the Wheels of Government: The Civil Service

Civil servants are officials who are appointed and not elected. At last count, a staggering half a million civil servants were working across the UK for the government.

Civil servants do jobs ranging from offering employment and benefit advice at the Jobcentre Plus to serving at 10 Downing Street, the residence of the PM. Despite an often mixed press, without a civil service the government would definitely grind unceremoniously to a halt.

At first glance, working out where the civil service starts and where it ends isn't easy. By the accepted definition, the civil service doesn't include members of the armed forces, police officers, people who work for the National Health Service or local government officials. The job of anyone who works for the state is defined by the branch she works for, and she's referred to as a public sector worker. But within the public sector, you have police, hospital staff and the civil service.

When it comes to pay and conditions, the civil service is currently split into two. The Cabinet Office sets those of senior civil servants – a crucial means of controlling them. The individual department or government agency they work for set the pay and conditions for lower-level civil servants. Thus, the pay of a senior civil servant in the Department for Environment, Food and Rural Affairs (Defra) is set by the Cabinet Office, and the civil servants below make do with pay grades set out by the senior civil servants in their department. Some suggest that the two-tier approach to civil service pay is divisive, and others say that it acts as motivation on civil servants lower down the pay grades to strive to become members of the senior civil service and therefore enjoy better pay and benefits.

People often assume that all civil servants work in Whitehall or Westminster, but this simply isn't true. In fact, only one in five civil servants actually works in the capital. The others are spread around the country in different governmental departments.

Apart from the UK civil service, under the ultimate control of the Cabinet Office, two other branches of civil servants exist:

- The Northern Ireland Civil Service, which runs the government of . . . guess where? Yes, Northern Ireland!
- The Diplomatic Service deals with the implementation of foreign policy and staffs British embassies overseas.

The heads of these two separate branches of the civil service sit on a body called the permanent secretaries' management group (PSMG), along with departmental permanent secretaries.

Becoming a civil servant and doing the job

People looking to enter the UK civil service have to sit examinations testing their intelligence and problem-solving skills.

The entrance exam is just the first of many hurdles that civil servants have to jump during their career. The UK civil service is supposed to be a meritocracy and, to this end, staff looking for promotion first have to do well at their current post and then fill out an application form, and go through interviews and even an aptitude test specific to the job they're applying for. The same round of applications, interviews and tests applies for every rung of the ladder. It can be a long, hard climb to the top of the UK civil service, and few make it!

Entrance to the civil service is usually through examination but can also involve interviews and aptitude tests specific to the job you're applying for. For example, you may be tested on your writing and communication skills, numeracy or decision-making abilities.

Which jobs do civil servants do? Well, how long is a piece of string? (And there's probably a civil servant who can give you the answer to that one.) Government departments are chock-full of civil servants who have two key jobs to do:

- Advise ministers on policy matters.
- See through the implementation of government policy.

Go to your local job centre and a civil servant will be advising a job-seeker; see a hospital being built and a civil servant will be ensuring costs don't over-run; read about a new airport and a civil servant will be assessing its economic and environmental impact.

The modern civil service doesn't just recruit straight from university but looks to attract people with specialist skills mid-career.

Behaving as a civil servant

Civil servants are bound by a code of behaviour dating back to the 19th century and the so-called Northcote–Trevelyan reforms.

The Northcote–Trevelyan Report was published in 1854. It set out a blueprint for how the UK civil service should operate. Crucially, it stated that promotion within the civil service should be on the basis of merit rather than according to who your father was or whether you were the friend of another civil servant – so nepotism and favouritism were supposed to be out.

The principles of the code of behaviour include

- **Staying neutral:** Civil servants may hold particular political views but must carry out the instructions of ministers even if they disagree with them. Today, senior civil servants are barred from holding a position with a political party – such as local or even parish councillor – and can't express political views in print.
- **Staying beneath the radar:** Politicians love the limelight – just try standing between one and a TV camera crew and you'll see what I mean – but civil servants are supposed to be always in the background. Civil servants are do-ers rather than public figures.
- **Staying for the long haul:** Crucially, civil servants are supposed to stay in their jobs even when ministers and governments come and go. This principle aids continuity of government.

Leaking about the sinking

Very occasionally, civil servants see something going on in their departments that they simply can't live with and they feel compelled to reveal confidences. In 1984 Clive Ponting, a senior civil servant in the Ministry of Defence, leaked documents regarding the sinking of the Argentinian battleship the *Belgrano* during the Falklands War to an MP from the opposition Labour Party. The documents showed that the Conservative government had not revealed the whole truth about the circumstances of the sinking of the ship and the loss of over 300 Argentinian sailors' lives. Mr Ponting not only resigned his job over the leak but was also prosecuted under the Official Secrets Act; ultimately, he was acquitted by a jury.

This civil service code is intended to improve the efficiency of government action and better allow politicians to carry out the policies they were elected to pursue.

In addition, civil servants are bound by tradition and code to keep secrets. In order to work together, ministers and civil servants have to trust one another, and so discussions between ministers and their civil servants are always supposed to be confidential. A civil servant doesn't talk to the press. For one thing, this behaviour would break the Northcote–Trevelyan agreement on staying in the background. Civil servants leave it up to the minister to decide how much or how little of their confidential discussions she reveals to the public or to fellow MPs.

If civil servants were to break confidentiality, it could be embarrassing for the minister concerned. Civil service confidentiality is a reciprocal arrangement: in return, ministers take responsibility for the mistakes of their civil servants rather than hauling them over the coals publicly.

Civil servants have a very powerful trade union called the Public and Commercial Services Union to act on their behalf.

Climbing the Ranks to the Senior Civil Service

As the name suggests, senior civil servants work at the heart of government. These are the most influential civil servants in the country, often working closely with government ministers. The senior civil servants are the *crème de la crème* of UK government and are often quite highly paid and have good pensions.

Honouring civil servants

Receiving an honour is an almost automatic perk of senior civil servant status. The UK honours system is there to recognise longstanding and substantial service to the state or wider society.

Twice yearly – at New Year and on the monarch's official birthday – the monarch and the PM prepare an honours list of approximately 1,350 people who deserve recognition. Many different honours are offered, from peerages and knighthoods to OBEs (Officer of the Order of the British Empire), MBEs (Member of the Order of the British Empire) and CBEs (Commander of the Order of the British Empire).

The PM suggests honours to the monarch, and the cabinet secretary puts forward civil servants whom she believes have served sufficient time, gained enough seniority and done a good enough job to merit one. In fact, as individuals climb up the ranks of the civil service, honours become an addition to the job. For example, if the head of the home civil service isn't a knight of the realm already, he'll be made one on assuming the top job.

The most recent head count of the civil service suggests that it includes some 3,000 to 4,000 senior civil servants.

Running the day-to-day: The permanent under-secretary of state

It's time to meet Sir Humphrey of *Yes Minister* fame. Sir Humph was a permanent under-secretary of state – which is quite a mouthful – but was also the most senior civil servant in a government department. In real life, as in fiction, the permanent under-secretary oversees the day-to-day running of the department, involving jobs such as

- **Bean counting:** The permanent under-secretary is responsible for ensuring the department spends the money it has properly. As part of the job of accounting for departmental spending, the permanent under-secretary can expect to answer questions from parliamentary select committees, which I cover in Chapter 14.
- **Co-ordinating:** The permanent under-secretary chairs committees of other civil servants, helping to ensure that they're doing their job properly and carrying out government policy.

- **Advising:** The permanent under-secretary can be a key adviser for the cabinet minister on policy matters. The secretary has lots of expertise and years of experience, and also knows the fine detail of the inner working of the department. In short, a permanent under-secretary should be able to let a minister know what it's possible and practical to achieve.

The permanent under-secretary (also called permanent secretary) isn't hired by a minister, or by the PM for that matter. A person who achieves this position rises to the job through the ranks of the civil service. The head of the home civil service appoints the permanent under-secretary.

The job of permanent under-secretary is considered close to the very pinnacle of the UK civil service and with it often comes an honour – hence *Sir* Humphrey! (I talk about the honours system in the nearby 'Honouring civil servants' sidebar.) However, even permanent under-secretaries have a boss: the head of the home civil service.

The influence of the civil service over policy formation has declined over the past 30 years, mainly because ministers have been keen to employ their own advisers. These days, although still offering policy advice, many senior civil servants focus on overseeing the delivery of government policy as their prime objective.

Serving as a link: The cabinet secretary

The cabinet secretary is a very important post in government because she does the following:

- Advises the PM on non-political government matters; so, how to do things rather than how to get elected.
- Acts as a go-between for the PM and the civil service, including the head of the home civil service and permanent secretaries.
- Oversees the ministerial code that governs the conduct of ministers and sees that ministers adhere to it (if not, the secretary reports the breach to the PM and . . . bye, bye, minister!). See Chapter 14 for more on the code.
- Investigates on behalf of the PM. If, for example, maladministration occurs in a government department or perhaps a civil servant leaks sensitive information to the press, the cabinet secretary is very much the PM's enforcer in government.
- Oversees the Secret Intelligence Service (MI6).

Much of the cabinet secretary's responsibilities for the PM sound quite political in nature, but the person filling the role is bound by the civil service code (refer to the section 'Behaving as a civil servant', earlier in the chapter) and therefore is apolitical and impartial.

Evaluating the Good and Bad Points of the UK Civil Service

The UK civil service is one of the longest-standing in the world. Its professionalism has often marked the UK out as a well-governed country. Many other countries – particularly from the Commonwealth – have tried to replicate the ethos and structure of the UK civil service. And you can see why when you consider some of its key plus points:

- **Honesty:** Very few cases have come to light of British civil servants taking bribes or being corrupt. In fact, the UK civil service is noted around the globe for its honesty and incorruptibility.
- **Professionalism:** Often the civil service is a job for life; the idea is to use to the maximum the individual civil servant's skills and experience that she's built up over many years.
- **Meritocracy:** The UK civil service is a meritocracy, with competitive exams held for entry and promotion according to ability.

Nevertheless, some do have it in for the UK civil service and reckon that it's not up to scratch. I list some of their criticisms here:

- **Narrow social background:** Senior civil servants graduate almost exclusively from the UK's two great universities – Oxford and Cambridge – and tend to come from an upper-middle-class social background. Many argue, therefore, that civil servants' life experience is too narrow. (People make similar arguments about the judiciary, which I cover in Chapter 16.)
- **Self-serving:** Critics say the civil service always looks out for itself when implementing government policy. They argue that new laws and policy initiatives invariably end with the government employing more civil servants.
- **Not accountable:** Senior civil servants may have to answer to ministers and, of course, to the head of the home civil service, but mistakes rarely end with a civil servant losing her job. As a result, critics say that even poorly performing civil servants don't face sanction and that this situation doesn't help the efficiency of government.

Reforming the Civil Service

As long as the UK civil service has existed moves have been afoot to reform it. The Northcote–Trevelyan reforms of the 1850s set out the responsibilities of civil servants to their political masters, as well as a structure for recruitment and promotion. But nearly every new government says on taking office that it wants to reform the civil service and thereby end waste in government.

Ignoring the Ibbs Report

Conservative PM Margaret Thatcher went as far as setting up an efficiency unit with the objective of introducing management practices used in the private sector in an effort to reduce costs and head count. The efficiency unit produced the Ibbs Report in 1988, which concluded the following about the UK civil service:

- It's too big.
- Civil servants always play safe and don't 'think outside the box' when problem solving.
- It spends too much and offers poor value for money.

The Ibbs Report made a host of complex recommendations for reform of the civil service, including giving greater autonomy to civil servants and setting them clear goals. However, after a few years it was widely agreed that the report and its recommendations had had only a marginal effect and civil servants were largely back to their old ways.

Reducing head count: The Gershon Review

The most recent attempt to reform the civil service and public services in general was the Gershon Review in 2005. The then PM, Tony Blair, and his chancellor, Gordon Brown, asked Sir Peter Gershon to review the efficiency of the civil and public services in the UK.

Gershon recommended a host of efficiency savings, which would have seen a reduction in the civil service of around 30,000 employees. However, by 2010 the number of civil servants was actually higher than when the Gershon Report was released.

Since 2010 the number of civil servants has fallen. One estimate suggests that as many as 12 per cent of jobs have disappeared. This is partly due to the fact that the Conservative-led coalition government that was elected in 2010 under PM David Cameron promised to make cuts for ideological reasons – believing a smaller state is better for the economy and the country. But the cuts are also because the global financial crisis hit tax revenues so hard that the UK government faced a huge annual black hole in its finances. Many of the changes to the UK civil service since 2010 have been about saving money rather than following some lengthy report such as Ibbs or Gershon.

Calling the civil service to account

The civil service exists to carry out government policy, but who ensures that they're doing a good enough job? Civil servants don't go unchecked. They're monitored or their actions are held in check in the following ways:

- **Internal systems:** These days superiors target civil servants and give them feedback in much the same way as in the private sector.
- **Tradition:** The civil service has a long history and today's civil servants feel the pressure to live up to the standards of previous generations.
- **Cabinet Office:** The ultimate power in the civil service has internal disciplinary procedures for those civil servants who act in an unethical, irresponsible or even illegal way.
- **Parliament:** Permanent under-secretaries often have to appear before parliament to account for the spending and administration of their departments.
- **Civil service commissioners:** This is a board of people appointed by the monarch – not parliament or the PM – whose job is to ensure that recruitment to the civil service is purely on the basis of merit through competitive examination.

Chapter 16

Taking in the Courts and Judiciary

In This Chapter

- Delving into the UK's three legal systems
- Differentiating between civil and criminal law
- Examining the legal systems of England, Wales, Scotland and Northern Ireland
- Looking at the role of the judges and the courts in the constitution
- Judging in the European Union courts
- Protecting civil liberties through the courts

The courts and judiciary are a key part of the British state and play a huge role in determining the nation's unwritten constitution and protecting the individual from the potential abuses of the state. And increasingly, with civil liberties being squeezed, the courts are becoming a real bastion of British liberties.

In this chapter I examine the ins and outs of the UK court system from east to west, north to south, and small claims court to the UK Supreme Court. If you want to know what goes on behind the doors of the oak-panelled court rooms, this is the chapter for you.

Explaining the UK's Three Legal Systems

For many outside observers, the UK is a very confusing place. It's one relatively small but densely populated country made up of four nations: England, Scotland, Wales and Northern Ireland. Each of these separate parts of the UK has its own distinctive character, history and traditions. The UK parliament makes many of the laws. But a separate parliament for Scotland and individual assemblies for Wales and Northern Ireland all interact with the UK parliament in different ways. As I said – confusing or what? Now add that across this one country made up of four parts are three very distinctive legal systems. Perhaps you've now reached confusion overload and need a lie-down in a darkened room.

Nevertheless, the UK has three legal systems: one for England and Wales combined, one for Scotland and another for Northern Ireland. Each has its own distinctive way of doing things and different legal precedents but, in truth, what they share in common is far greater than what divides them.

Criminal laws are drawn up by the UK parliament and it's the job of the courts to see that people follow these laws. Laws made by the UK parliament are called *statute laws*. In addition, though, in civil cases judges use *legal precedent* to decide what should happen in a case; that is, they look at what previous judges have decided in similar cases.

The whole justice system – both criminal and civil law, regardless of which of the three legal systems holds sway – is based on a hierarchy, which means that the courts at the top of the pyramid hear the most serious cases and any appeals resulting from cases brought in courts at the bottom of the pyramid.

Recognising the Difference between Civil and Criminal Law

All the UK's three legal systems are divided into the same two parts:

- **Criminal law** governs offences against society and fellow citizens. The state usually brings charges in a criminal case.
- **Civil law** deals with the relationship between individuals or groups of individuals. Civil cases involve lawsuits between people and organisations on matters that don't involve the state.

Civil law is designed to help settle disputes between individuals, and criminal law is about the state taking to task individuals who've offended wider society's accepted norms of behaviour.

The structures of the criminal and civil courts are very different but at the very top – when people appeal cases – they come together.

Committing crimes against the state

Criminal law deals with stuff like burglary or violence against another person. Interestingly, when someone commits a criminal offence such as stealing a car, the crime isn't said to be against the victim but against the state – whether that be England and Wales, Scotland or Northern Ireland.

People charged with a criminal offence are tried by judges or, in the case of crown court cases, a jury, and if found guilty, they can be sent to prison or face some other punishment such as a fine or community service. The court imposes any punishment but the state executes it; thus, the court sentences the car thief to six months in prison and the state's prison service then carries out the sentence. Criminal cases often involve a jury. Trial by jury in criminal cases is seen as a key right of the British citizen.

Suing your neighbours in civil court

Civil law isn't quite as intriguing as criminal law, which is awash with human interest stories. Nevertheless, the need for a transparent and fair settling of disputes between individuals is a key component of a properly functioning society. Without the law to settle disputes, might would most likely triumph over right, with the strong riding roughshod over the weak or vulnerable.

In civil law, the state doesn't bring a case against an offender; instead, one person or group of people sues another person or group of people. For example, in a case in which heirs are arguing over who gets what under the terms of a will, no one has done anything against the criminal law but they need to settle a dispute.

The parties in dispute go to a court for judgement – which is made by a judge rather than a jury. This judgement is based on what has happened in similar cases in the past and the particular circumstances of the new case.

Examining the Basic Rights of the British Citizen

Being British brings with it certain rights and privileges, and one of the jobs of the court is to uphold these precious rights and privileges. Here's a rundown of those rights:

- **Personal data protection:** Under the terms of the 1998 Data Protection Act information about all British citizens held by government agencies and businesses has to be accurate, secure and up to date.
- **Freedom of information:** Under the 2000 Freedom of Information Act British citizens are entitled to ask for previously private information from public bodies such as local councils or the government.

- **Free health care rights:** Britain guarantees its citizens free health care through the National Health Service (NHS). Doctors' appointments, minor and major surgery as well as emergency treatment are all free.
- **Free state education:** All British children aged 5 to 16 are entitled to attend a free state school to be educated.
- **Freedom to work:** All British citizens can work without restrictions. Laws guarantee that employers can't discriminate against workers on the grounds of sex, race or religion. In addition, employers have to pay a minimum hourly wage to their employees.

Focusing on the Criminal Courts of England and Wales

England and Wales combined host most of the UK population by a long chalk so here's the logical place to start. The following sections cover criminal courts, from the lowest rung – trying the least serious criminal cases – right to the top and the appeals courts.

Starting off in a magistrates' court

Magistrates' courts try the overwhelming number of cases – around 98 per cent of all cases pass through them. They deal with crimes such as non-payment of TV licences, shoplifting and drunk and disorderly offences.

Magistrates' courts also act as a gateway to the next tier of the criminal justice system by deciding whether the evidence in the case is strong enough and the crime of sufficient gravity to be sent to crown court. In the most serious criminal cases, such as murder, the appearance of the defendant in front of the magistrates' court is little more than a formality, with committal to trial in front of the higher court a given.

One of the key distinguishing marks of the magistrates' courts is that *Justices of the Peace* (JPs) preside over them. These are ordinary members of the public from all walks of life. The only major restrictions on becoming a JP are that you don't work in the criminal justice system (as a police officer, for example) and have no criminal record. JPs are trained to hear criminal cases, adjudge guilt, pronounce correct and proportionate sentence and to know when the case should be referred on to the crown court. JPs don't do the job all on their own. They have the help of district judges and deputy district judges, who are professional, paid members of the judiciary employed by the state.

Interestingly, most people appearing before the magistrates' court plead guilty to the crime – if they don't, a greater chance exists of the magistrates referring the case to the crown court where the prison sentences handed out can be heavier. Wanting to avoid a longer sentence (and who wouldn't?), the defendant (soon to be a criminal) pleads guilty. It's then the job of the magistrate to pass the appropriate sentence.

When deciding that a crown court should hear a particular case, the magistrate may order that the defendant be held *on remand*. Being on remand means that the defendant is held in prison until the crown court can hear the case. Alternatively, the magistrate may allow the release of the defendant on *bail*, which means he's free to go about his normal life – with certain restrictions such as surrendering his passport – but must report to the crown court for trial when summoned.

Approximately 600 magistrates' courts operate across the UK. They don't sit every day, mainly because the JPs have ordinary jobs to be getting on with. Around 23,500 JPs sit in these courts.

Many politicians – particularly those not in government – like to paint a picture of the UK as an increasingly lawless society. To support this view they often point to the fact that the UK has some 85,000 people in prison. Now it's true that the UK imprisons more people per head of population than most other western European countries, but compared to the US, the UK imprisons only around one fifth of the number of people per head of population. In fact, crime rates in the UK aren't much worse than other European countries, and when compared to the Americas, Russia, Africa and large parts of Asia, they're a lot lower.

Advancing to a crown court

Crown courts hear the cases deemed potentially serious enough to merit a long custodial sentence; for example, offences such as murder, rape, manslaughter and robbery with violence.

A defendant who pleads not guilty in these cases is entitled to a trial by jury. The case is heard by a jury, normally consisting of 12 members of the public but sometimes a couple more or fewer. The jury delivers its verdict, and it's then up to the judge, who's overseen the trial and advised the jury as to the key facts of the case, to deliver the sentence or let the defendant off if he's found innocent.

A jury is made up of people selected at random from the electoral roll. They're told to turn up at a court on an appointed day and once there are assigned a trial in which they'll sit as a juror. Jury service is very solemn and those called have to give a good reason in advance for not being able to attend, or they could face being in contempt of court.

The crown court system has no room for well-meaning amateurs such as JPs. Here, the law gets very serious indeed. This court hears the worst crimes. Crown courts are usually presided over by circuit judges or recorders, who are legally trained state employees. The gravest cases are often heard by a *high court judge*, a very senior judge who has lots of experience.

The most famous crown court in England and Wales is the Central Criminal Court at the Old Bailey in London. Normally, this court hears the gravest of the grave cases and has the very best judges and court workers in place to see that justice is best served.

Making your way to the Court of Appeal

People can appeal sentences handed out by the magistrates' courts at the crown court – pretty simple, yes? People can appeal verdicts of cases adjudged in the crown court in the – you guessed it – Court of Appeal. However, when it comes to appealing decisions made by the crown courts, things get more complex.

The presumption is that appealing crown court verdicts shouldn't be too easy or lots of rightfully convicted criminals would do it. A filtering system is thus in place to prevent frivolous or just plain hopeful appeals being heard. A compelling reason must exist for the case to go to the Court of Appeal. Legitimate reasons for sending a case to the Court of Appeal include the discovery of new evidence or a flaw in the original trial.

The Criminal Cases Review Commission considers the argument for an appeal and then rules on whether the case should go to the Court of Appeal (criminal division). The Court of Appeal then decides whether a retrial is necessary, the appeal is to be turned down or a straight acquittal is in order.

One other stage of appeal is now available, the UK Supreme Court. I talk about the Supreme Court in the later section, 'Introducing the UK Supreme Court'.

It's not just the Court of Appeal that can acquit people found guilty of a crime in a crown court. The monarch – on the advice of the home secretary – can grant a pardon. If the convicted criminal has already died, it's called a *posthumous pardon*.

Hearing Civil Cases in England and Wales

A civil court's fare is wide and varied, from relatively small disputes over who gets what in a will, to wrangles between neighbours over who owns a bit of garden, right up to headline-grabbing libel actions and ultra-complex contract disputes between individuals or even big multinational organisations.

Gazing at the civil law process

Just like with criminal law (check out the 'Focusing on the Criminal Courts of England and Wales' section, earlier in this chapter), a hierarchy of courts hears civil cases in England and Wales:

- **County courts:** This lowest rung of civil court deals with the vast majority of civil disputes and generally hears matters of financial dispute. Cases that the court can hear in a single day and that relate to financial disputes of less than £10,000 go through a small-claims fast track – often called *the small claims court* by the public, although it isn't actually a separate court. Other cases progress at different speeds and are often more complex and relate to disputes over larger sums of money.

  Common cases heard by county courts include personal injury claims, lenders trying to recover unpaid debts by requesting permission to use bailiffs, and landlord – tenant disputes.
- **High Court:** As the name suggests, this court deals with cases of high value and high importance. Many libel cases end up at the High Court. In addition, through its family division, the High Court deals with high-profile divorces and disputes over medical treatment.

Appealing civil cases

Appeals against a decision made in a civil case – as in a criminal case – end up at the Court of Appeal, although in the civil division. Three judges normally hear an appeal in the Court of Appeal and reach a decision by a majority.

Having an appeal heard is far from a given. Everyone has a right to lodge an appeal but first it goes through a filtering system. In civil cases, a single judge who sits in the Court of Appeal decides whether a case is worthy of being heard at a full appeal.

Generally, the appeals process is very long and at times ruinously expensive, particularly because unsuccessful appeals can sometimes end with the losing side paying the winning side's costs, which can run into hundreds of thousands of pounds – ouch!

Taking in the Scottish Court System

Scotland united with England and Wales to form the UK in 1707 but kept its own very separate legal system. Like England and Wales, though, the Scottish system is divided into criminal and civil law. Here's the lowdown on the court system north of the border:

- **Criminal law:** Sheriff courts try minor offences, and more serious cases go to the High Court of Justiciary, which also hears all appeals.
- **Civil law:** The same sheriff courts that deal with criminal cases try most civil cases. Importantly, no financial limit is placed on disputes that a sheriff court hears, unlike the county courts in England and Wales.

  Appeals go either to the *sheriff principal* (the head sheriff in the area) or to the Court of Session. At the Court of Session a judge reviews the case alone and then a panel of judges scrutinises his decision.

No equivalent to the crown court exists in Scotland. Instead, the High Court of Justiciary performs the twin jobs of dealing with the most serious crimes and hearing appeals.

In civil cases the losers have the right of appeal to the UK Supreme Court. This isn't the case for criminal cases.

Considering the Courts in Northern Ireland

The Northern Irish legal system is almost indistinguishable from that in England and Wales. A division exists between criminal and civil law and judges' decisions can set precedents.

Magistrates and crown courts hear criminal cases (the latter for more serious offences) and county courts and a High Court hear civil cases. A separate Court of Appeal hears both criminal and civil appeals and the UK Supreme Court can review its decisions.

During the Troubles that started in the late 1960s in Northern Ireland, the British government halted trial by jury in cases where people were accused of paramilitary activities, but restored it in 2007 because the political situation had eased.

Introducing the UK Supreme Court

The legal systems of the UK aren't noted for radical reform. For instance, the framework of the English legal system has its roots way back in the 12th century and Scotland's justice system was established not long after. However, 1 October 2009 was a red-letter day for legal reform in the UK with the establishment of the UK Supreme Court.

Previously, an appeal against a verdict in either a civil or criminal law case could ultimately go all the way up to the House of Lords in Westminster. There the case would be heard by any one of a dozen appointed Lords of Appeal in Ordinary – or *Law Lords* for short – who were the nation's top judges. Such cases involved a lot of solemn language, arcane procedure and quite a bit of dressing up in robes and donning of horsehair wigs.

But from October 2009, a new body, the UK Supreme Court, took over the legal functions of the House of Lords. Initially, the Law Lords just hopped across the road from the House of Lords to the UK Supreme Court to preside over cases. However, the law setting up the Supreme Court stated that appointed judges didn't have to be members of the House of Lords.

The UK Supreme Court hears appeals on criminal and civil cases in England, Wales and Northern Ireland and civil cases from Scotland (the Scottish High Court of Justiciary still hears criminal case appeals). The court also has the power – previously held by the monarch's privy council – to decide what issues the devolved governments of Scotland, Wales and Northern Ireland can legislate upon, and what has to remain the say-so of the UK parliament in Westminster (see Chapter 17 and 18 for more on devolution).

Looking at the Role of the Judge

Whether you're considering the legal systems of England, Wales, Scotland or Northern Ireland, one thing's for sure – the judge is key. The judge serves the following functions in a courtroom:

- **Umpire:** A lawyer represents each side in a case, and it's up to the judge to make certain that these lawyers follow the rules of behaviour in court. The judge must also ensure fairness, in that both lawyers have the opportunity to have their say, submit evidence, call witnesses and ask questions of those witnesses.
- **Interpreting the law:** In a given case, oodles of previous cases could set a precedent, or parliamentary statutes (laws) could have a bearing. The judge must be aware of these precedents and statutes and correctly apply them to the case at hand.
- **Making the law:** Wow! Making the law sounds a biggie, and it is. Put simply, if a new set of circumstances has occurred in the case being heard, the decision of the judge sets a precedent for all future similar cases. This evolution of precedents is the basis of common law.
- **Handing down sentences:** In criminal cases, if the defendant is found guilty then the judge decides the sentence (working within guidelines set by the justice secretary). In civil cases, the judge decides the redress if one individual is found to have wronged another. For example, in a case of libel, a judge sets the damages.

Judges are often selected to preside over prominent public inquiries, such as the one concerning the death of black teenager Stephen Lawrence and the one examining the circumstances surrounding the death of the UK government's weapons expert David Kelly in 2004. The government prefers judges in these positions because of their experience in dealing with disputes and witnesses. However, the inquiry that reported in 2012 into the Hillsborough Stadium Disaster, in which 96 football fans were crushed to death at a football game, was overseen by the bishop of Liverpool and not by a judge. This was because a judge could be seen as too much part of the establishment and many of the families of the victims involved in the disaster felt that the establishment had not properly investigated the circumstances of the tragedy when it first occurred in 1989.

Glancing at Courts and the Constitution

Laws made by the UK parliament – called *statutes* – are the ultimate law of the land, which everyone – even judges – has to abide by. However, statutes aren't the be-all and end-all; they can't cover every individual's circumstances. So a web of hundreds of years of different judgements in cases – called *legal precedent* – sets out what's legal and what isn't. The ability of judges to set legal precedent that's then followed in future similar court cases gives them a key role in the UK's unwritten constitution.

So, campaigners for euthanasia, wanting people to be free to travel abroad to end their lives without fear that anyone travelling with them will be guilty of the crime of assisted suicide, didn't go to their Member of Parliament (MP) to get a new statute law enacted. Instead they've taken a series of cases to the UK Supreme Court in the hope of setting a legal precedent, which in effect sets new law.

The three legal systems in the UK all operate according to a hierarchical system. This means that the decision reached by the highest court in the land – now the UK Supreme Court in most cases – is binding on all lower courts and also sets a future legal precedent. But if the government enacts a new statute law that contradicts legal precedent, the statute law takes priority.

Throwing the European Union into the Mix

The UK is part of the European Union (EU) and as a result laws made by European courts apply here.

The two courts for the European Union are:

- **The European Court of Justice (ECJ):** This court is responsible for interpreting EU laws and ensuring consistent application across all 28 member states.

  If a court in an EU member state is hearing a case in which EU law comes into the equation, the judge asks the ECJ to look at the case and provide a ruling. Crucially, the court – even if it's the UK referring the case – has to follow the ECJ's decision.

- **The European Court of Human Rights:** People who feel that their rights under the European Convention of Human Rights have been violated can take their case to this court. However, the person who feels wronged must first have exhausted the legal processes in his own country, which in the UK's case usually means having gone all the way to the Supreme Court.

The European Convention on Human Rights is now part of UK law through the 1998 Human Rights Act. As a result, if someone feels that his human rights have been violated, he can go to a UK court and have it decide on the matter instead of going to the European Court of Human Rights in Strasbourg.

Fighting the Good Fight: Courts and Civil Liberties

Increasingly, in reaction to the growing powers of central government, judges see protecting the civil liberties of the British public as part of their job. Most controversially, since the terrorist attacks on the United States on 11 September 2001, the UK government has expanded its powers to detain potential terrorists. Restrictions on civil liberties in Britain over the past few years include

- **Detention without charge:** The police can hold people suspected of terrorist activities for questioning without charge for up to 28 days.
- **Asylum-seeker detention:** The Home Office often keeps people claiming asylum in the UK under lock and key while the Home Office considers their application. These people aren't guilty of a crime but the government worries that if they're allowed to roam freely, they'll simply disappear.
- **Protest restrictions:** Several instances of violence at demonstrations have led to the government imposing some restrictions on the right to protest. What's more, some sections of the press and protest groups have made accusations of heavy-handed policing at several rallies, in particular surrounding the meeting of the G20 (the world's 20 most economically advanced nations) in London in 2009.
- **Behaviour orders:** The courts may impose an order on people accused of antisocial behaviour. Anti-Social Behaviour Orders (ASBOs) place restrictions on people's movements and the courts often give them to younger people accused of vandalism, noise disturbance or petty crime. However, civil liberties groups don't like ASBOs because they feel the courts impose them willy-nilly and without due legal process, and that they stigmatise people who haven't been convicted of an actual crime. The coalition government that came to power in 2010 said it wanted to replace them with a new, more powerful and more easily enforceable Criminal Behaviour Order (CBO). But the two parties in the coalition – the Liberal Democrats and Conservatives – couldn't agree on CBOs and as a result they haven't been introduced and ASBOs still exist.

Chapter 17

Laying Bare Local Government and Devolution

In This Chapter

- Looking at local government throughout the UK
- Electing local officials
- Checking out devolution and what it means for Scotland, Wales and Northern Ireland

If you want to know how government works across the length and breadth of the UK, from the tiniest hamlet to the largest city, this is the chapter to check out. I hold up the inner complexities of local government for scrutiny from county council to town hall. I also take a brief peak into one of the big political movements of our time – devolution, with powers moving from the British government in Westminster to the powerful parliament of Scotland and the Welsh and Northern Ireland assemblies in all their Technicolor – or should that be technocratic? – glory. See Chapter 18 for even more on this.

Understanding that All Politics Is Local

Prominent American politician Thomas 'Tip' O'Neill once famously said that 'all politics is local'. He meant that what happens close to home, in the lives of electors, affects the way they view politicians and ultimately the way they vote. If an individual is made redundant or faces a hefty tax bill from her local council, it's bound to influence the way she views politicians prancing on the national stage.

Often political commentators and journalists focus on the inner workings of the corridors of power in Westminster or which cabinet minister says what, but most people really don't care that much about these goings-on. What the regular people see is how politicians and their policies influence their daily lives. It's local government by a long way that has the biggest impact rather than the MPs, ministers and party leaders.

Statute law – enacted by the UK parliament – sets out the structure of local government. For instance, through an act of parliament the UK government set up the devolved Scottish parliament and the different mayoral authorities in England and Wales.

Looking at what local government does

The Westminster parliament – or in some instances the devolved parliaments and national assemblies of Scotland, Wales and Northern Ireland (see Chapter 18 for more on these institutions) – sets the big national policies such as income tax, hospital building programmes and even whether to go to war or not. But underneath all the national action, local governments do the rest of the tasks that need doing to make society work, and what a lot of work it is! Some of the duties that local governments perform include

- Overseeing the running of state schools
- Providing social services
- Deciding upon planning issues in the locality
- Maintaining public roads and local public transport
- Arranging refuse collections and enforcing environmental health policies
- Providing local amenities such as leisure centres, libraries, museums and parks, to name just a few
- Overseeing the local police force and fire and rescue services
- Providing local social housing

No wonder that local government – along with the National Health Service (NHS) – is among the country's biggest employers.

Critics of local governments often say that they 'only empty the bins', but as you can see from the list, local governments are responsible for an awful lot of facilities and services. In fact, if no local government operated, you'd soon know about it. In the winter of 1978–79 many local government workers went on strike and chaos ensued. Rubbish wasn't collected and even the dead lay unburied in Liverpool. This period was 'the winter of discontent'. The Labour government of Prime Minister Jim Callaghan was held responsible for the strikes, and at the subsequent general election of April 1979 Labour was defeated. All politics is local!

Apart from its role in deciding planning issues, local government has no say in the running of hospitals. That job falls to the NHS. Under the current structure of the NHS the decisions over patient treatment, budgeting and even commissioning new building projects are the call of either the individual hospital or a group of hospitals called a *foundation trust.*

Funding local government

So who pays for local government in the UK? Put simply, you do. Local governments are funded in two key ways:

- A grant of money from the central UK government, raised through central taxation such as income tax or corporation tax
- Council tax levied on residents living in local homes, and business rates

About three quarters of the money spent by local authorities in the UK actually originates from the central UK government.

Why does central government give so much money to local government rather than let it raise more through local council tax? Well, the situation's a bit of a power game. If local government was able to raise as much money as it wanted locally, it could become very powerful. By keeping at least partial control of the purse strings, central government lets those in local government know who's boss.

Both local and central government are elected, and it's possible for one party to be in charge of central government while another's running a local government.

UK cities that have an elected mayor – the most prominent is London – raise money through a surcharge on the local council tax. (See 'Re-energising local government', later in this chapter, for more on the mayoral system.)

Council tax is based on property values. Each property is put into a band from A to G. Properties in band A are the smallest and cheapest, rising to band G covering the largest and most expensive homes. At the start of the financial year – in April – the local council decides how much it needs to collect from the occupiers of properties in each of the bands. People who live on their own, or are elderly or disabled can claim a discount on their annual bill of up to 25 per cent.

At times, central government is disturbed to see sharp rises in council tax and has the legal right to cap them. It tells the local council to draw up a new budget and to keep its expenditure down so that council tax bills don't rise by too much.

Taking in the structure of local government in England

Local government structure is very complex. Dividing up all the different types of local government into two is thus probably the best approach:

- **Principal authorities** deal with important local issues, such as schools, planning and environmental affairs. They have lots of civil servants and contractors working for them, and they receive money from local council tax and grants from central government.
- **Community authorities** are the most local of local government. They rely on volunteers and don't have a bureaucracy. They oversee the management of local parks and allotments and advise the local principal authority on planning issues. They're the ones who put in requests to the principal authority for it to do work on local amenities.

  Parish councils and *town councils* are the two main types of community authority in England. Prominent figures in the local community stand for election to these councils. Council members are often aligned to a particular political party but a fair number of candidates for parish or town councils stand as independents.

Most people refer to principal authorities, whether they're county or district councils or unitary authorities, simply as *councils*.

The system of principal authorities in England is a real patchwork:

- In some areas a **county council** is responsible for education, waste management and big planning issues within the county. Below the county council, **district councils** are in charge of local planning and refuse collection, as well as smaller local planning issues.
- Some parts of the country have only one tier of principal authority – catchily called **unitary authorities**. These unitary authorities in effect do the work of both a county and a district council.
- In larger cities, a combination of **elected officials** and **council members** takes charge of meeting some needs. London, with a population of 9 million, has an elected assembly and an elected mayor, as well as 32 separate boroughs responsible for delivering services to the public. Other major urban areas, such as Manchester, Liverpool and Leeds, have their own councils, with separate boroughs actually delivering the services.

Regardless of whether you live in a part of the country that's run by a county council, unitary authority or even a London borough, you get the chance to elect people as councillors. It's the job of councillors to take the big decisions in your locality and ensure that the bureaucrats running the administration do their jobs properly.

Heading north: Scottish local government

Local government structure in Scotland is much more straightforward than in England. A divide between principal authorities and community authorities (instead of parish councils the Scots have community councils) does still exist; but instead of having lots of different types of principal authority, Scotland's local government is divided into 32 unitary authorities. Some are based on county borders (and are geographically quite large) and others are based on the boundaries of the big cities – Edinburgh, Glasgow and Aberdeen.

Elections for councillors in each of Scotland's 32 unitary authorities are held every four years.

Local authorities have a statutory (legal) duty to consult community councils on planning, development and other issues directly affecting that local community. However, the community council has no direct say in the delivery of services.

The Scottish unitary authorities are funded through a combination of council tax and grants provided by the Scottish parliament. Since 2012 the Scottish parliament has had the power to vary income tax up or down by 3 pence; as yet it has never used this power, called the *Scottish Variable Rate*. Following the Scottish independence referendum in September 2014, there was a commitment by the UK government to devolve even greater powers to the Scottish government. This is very likely to include the power to set a larger range of taxes.

Heading west: Wales and Northern Ireland

Like Scotland, Welsh local government is divided into unitary authorities – 22 in total. Some are based on county borders and others take in the big cities such as Cardiff, Newport and Swansea. Below the unitary authorities are communities that act in the same way as a parish council in England and a community council in Scotland.

As for Northern Ireland, the 26 district councils don't have the same powers as principal authorities in England or unitary authorities in Scotland. Their functions include responsibility for waste and recycling services, leisure and community services, building control, and local economic and cultural development. They aren't planning authorities, but are consulted on some planning applications, and have no say over education matters, housing or road building – these are the preserve of the Northern Ireland Assembly, the ins and outs of which I discuss in Chapter 18.

Re-energising local government

It used to be the case that after a local election the newly elected councillors would meet to elect the leadership of the council, and members of the biggest party would take the senior posts such as treasurer or head of planning. In 2000 this cosy little system was shaken up when the government decided that English local authorities with populations of over 85,000 would have to choose between one of three new management structures, two of which included the introduction of an elected mayor. The three structures proposed were as follows:

- Up to ten elected councillors would form a cabinet, and one cabinet member would be designated as council leader.
- Up to ten elected councillors would form a cabinet, but instead of one of their number being leader, an elected mayor would fill that post.
- An elected mayor would get to appoint a manager, who'd then appoint a management team to oversee the daily workings of the council.

Introducing London's mayor

Most people's knowledge of the job of London mayor starts with the story of Dick Whittington, who as a boy famously walked to London with his cat, made his fortune and eventually became mayor.

But the role of mayor of London had been a ceremonial one for generations until the elections of 2000. The idea was that a major world city such as London should have a government structure that reflected its size and standing and to a degree aped those of its fellow premier cities, New York and Paris. It was decided that having a mayor of London was the only way to get some oversight of London's 32 borough councils and co-ordination of London-wide policy areas such as police and transport.

Now, London has not just one but two mayors! The main one is the mayor of London, who's directly elected by the public and has pretty substantial powers. The second mayor is called the lord mayor of the City of London. The role is largely ceremonial and the office holder isn't elected by the public. What's more, the lord mayor of the City of London doesn't represent Greater London but the much smaller – in geographic and population terms – City of London, which is the area of the capital containing many banks and financial institutions.

Ken Livingstone, who served as mayor of London from 2000 to 2008, is one of the most colourful characters in modern British politics. He shot to national prominence as head of the Greater London Council (GLC) in the 1980s. At the time he was called Red Ken as a result of his left-wing policies and criticism of the then Conservative PM Margaret Thatcher. Mr Livingstone was succeeded by the equally colourful Conservative politician Boris Johnson, who won elections in 2008 and 2012. Mr Johnson is famous for his dishevelled appearance, mop of blond hair, sharp sense of humour and unconventional utterances. He, like Red Ken before him, is a true one-off in British politics.

The mayor of London is elected by a complex voting system. In short, electors get to cast two votes – one for their first choice for mayor and one for their second choice. The first choice votes are counted and after this round all but the two candidates with the highest number of first-choice votes are eliminated. These two candidates go into a run-off. At this point, the second-choice votes are added to the first-choice and the winner is the candidate with the highest number of first- and second-choice votes. I told you this system is complex! It's called the supplementary vote system and I explore it in greater detail in Chapter 6.

Most councillors chose the first option – a cabinet and council leader – rather than an elected mayor. However, those councils deciding that they wanted an elected mayor had to have this decision ratified by a yes vote in a referendum. (In a *referendum* those people registered to vote are asked to vote on a yes-or-no question rather than for a particular candidate.) If the referendum passed, mayoral elections then took place.

Of only 17 elected mayors across England, by far the most important is the mayor of London (see the nearby sidebar, 'Introducing London's mayor'). And because so few authorities have an elected mayor, some see the revision of the system as a bit of a waste of time.

The election of Stuart Drummond as the mayor of Hartlepool in 2002 gave critics of the mayoral system ammunition. Drummond was the mascot of the local football club, Hartlepool United, and he campaigned dressed as a monkey. His one stated policy was simian in nature: he pledged to provide free bananas to schoolchildren. Drummond won by a landslide and has since won a further two terms – which shows that he must be doing something right in the job – although he did renege on his pledge to supply free bananas due to lack of funds.

Virtually all towns and cities in the UK have a mayor, only not one elected by the public. The mayor turns up at public events to represent the council and the job is largely ceremonial. The only real power a mayor has lies in chairing the meeting of the local council. Invariably, local councillors take turns to do the job of mayor.

Policing the police: The advent of police and crime commissioners

For years many had called for greater accountability for police forces in England and Wales. So, in 2012 the first elections took place across England and Wales for the brand new post of police and crime commissioner. These commissioners replaced the abolished local police authorities, and the big idea was that an individual should oversee how the police perform in a particular police authority. For example, West Midlands Police is overseen by a police and crime commissioner for the West Midlands, elected by all voters in the region.

So that they can properly bring pressure to bear on the police force in their area these commissioners have important powers:

- They decide the amount of the surcharge on council taxpayers, called the *precept*, that pays for the upkeep of the police.
- They're responsible for the appointment, suspension and dismissal of the police chief constable.

When it came to election time for the police and crime commissioners, only a very small proportion of voters turned out to decide who should have the job, and that brought the process into disrepute. In addition, people have criticised the expense of the police and crime commissioners (especially their salary), and said they impose yet another layer of bureaucracy in an already deeply bureaucratic institution – the police force.

Police and crime commissioners hold office for four years, so they next come up for re-election in 2016. Many commentators suggest that the government may abolish the post at that time.

Granting Power from the Centre – Devolution

The UK is made up of four nations or parts – England, Scotland, Wales and Northern Ireland. Each of these parts has its own unique system of local government, partly due to – drum roll, please – devolution!

Arguably the biggest constitutional change in the UK since the Second World War, *devolution* involves the UK parliament based in Westminster transferring power to the Scottish parliament based in Holyrood, Edinburgh, the Welsh Assembly in Cardiff and the Northern Ireland Assembly in Stormont, Belfast.

The UK parliament granted devolution to Scotland and Wales in the late 1990s and the Northern Ireland Assembly came into being in 1999 as a consequence of the ongoing peace process.

The new, devolved system differs from what's called a federalist system – such as operates in Germany and the United States – because the central government (the UK parliament in Westminster) can

- Take back the powers it devolved at any time by enacting a new law.
- Abolish the devolved parliaments and assemblies.

When it comes to devolution, the UK parliament in Westminster retains certain powers. *Excepted powers* stay with the UK parliament no matter what and forever. *Reserved powers* may at some later stage be transferred from the UK parliament to the devolved institution.

Although the UK central government has the right to abolish the Scottish parliament or the Welsh Assembly, it's highly unlikely ever to use this power. Such action would be considered undemocratic because it would be going against the wishes of voters in Scotland and Wales who said 'yes' in a referendum on whether to have a working parliament or assembly.

The legal right of the UK central government to take back powers has been used during the Northern Irish peace process. At times, the parties in the Northern Ireland Assembly have either boycotted the government or been unable to work together. In these circumstances, the central government of the UK has taken back the powers that it in effect loaned the assembly, but restored them when the parties settled their differences.

Scotland voted in 2014 on whether or not it wanted to go for full independence from the UK. The result was 'no', and Scotland remains part of the UK but with a devolved parliament with some tax-raising powers. I discuss the Scottish parliament and political scene in more detail in Chapter 18.

The final few days prior to the Scottish independence referendum were dominated by a commitment from the leaders of the UK parliament's three biggest parties offering to grant the Scottish parliament more powers. As a result, politician from Wales and much of England suggested that they too should have more powers.

A member of the UK parliament is called an MP, of the Scottish parliament an MSP, of the Welsh Assembly an AM and of the Northern Ireland Assembly an MLA. That's an awful lot of politicians and an awful lot of abbreviations!

Handing over power to unelected quangos

As the Welsh, Scots and Northern Irish have become empowered to have a say in their governance and make their own laws, people throughout England have come under the sway of institutions that wield a lot of power but have a name that sounds like a soft drink – quango.

Quango stands for **qua**si autonomous **n**on-**g**overnmental **o**rganisation, which in English means an organisation that does work for the government but isn't directly accountable to the public as elected officials are. The head of a quango is usually appointed by government ministers from the UK parliament or the devolved institutions.

The number of quangos shot up in the 2000s as UK government expenditure soared in a bid to deliver better public services. Prominent quangos are those in the health care field, regional development agencies and, in transport, Network Rail, which is responsible for the infrastructure of Britain's railways.

Quangos are widely criticised as being too powerful and for controlling big budgets, while subject to little accountability apart from to the minister or senior civil servants in the department they're attached to. Many Quangos bit the dust when the Coalition government came to power in 2010 in a cost cutting exercise. However, there are still plenty of them out there alive, well and costing money!

Asking the West Lothian question

Devolution is viewed in Scotland as a big success, but many people in England don't agree because of a constitutional anomaly dubbed the 'West Lothian question'. The phrase was first used by former Labour MP Tam Dalyell in 1979 when devolution was being debated in the UK parliament. The question is this: should an MP from a Scottish constituency such as West Lothian have the right to vote in the House of Commons in Westminster over laws affecting English domestic matters? This question is particularly moot because English MPs, following devolution, have no say over many aspects of Scottish domestic matters because they're in the power of the Scottish parliament and its MSPs. In fact, the Labour governments of Tony Blair and Gordon Brown were on occasion only able to gather enough MPs' votes in parliament for reforms to health and education in England – both devolved policy areas in Scotland – with the support of Labour MPs representing Scottish constituencies.

What's more, the Scottish, Welsh and Northern Irish enjoy two levels of parliamentary representation: they have their own parliament or assembly whose members they elect, and then they also get to elect an MP to the UK parliament in Westminster. The English – who are the overwhelming majority population of the UK – in comparison only have the UK parliament.

The West Lothian Question gained new relevance after the debate surrounding the Scottish Independence Referendum. Following the victory of the "No to Scottish Independence" side of the debate, the Prime Minister David Cameron said he would like to see not only further devolution for Scotland but MPs from Scottish constituencies banned from voting on laws in parliament that affected England only (in effect, looking to settle the West Lothian question).

Chapter 18

Focusing on Devolution and the Independence Debate

In This Chapter

- Constituting the UK and seeing the success of unity
- Handing power to Scotland, Wales and Northern Ireland
- Examining the great independence referendum campaign

Until relatively recently the UK was one of the most centralised countries in the Western world. Most political power rested in Westminster and Whitehall, and senior civil servants, Members of Parliament, the cabinet and of course the prime minister dictated and directed government policy. In fact, in the 1980s the UK became even more centralised when Whitehall took back much of the power held by local authorities.

Then came 1997 and the election of a Labour government, under Tony Blair, committed to the transfer of some powers from central government to the Celtic nations of Wales, Northern Ireland and Scotland. This process is called devolution. Ever since, more and more power has flowed away from Westminster and Whitehall to Holyrood in Edinburgh, Cardiff in Wales and Stormont in Northern Ireland. In 2014 Scotland even voted on whether or not to become independent (they voted no to independence but by a narrow margin), an event that would have been unheard of just 20 years before.

Say it very quietly, but the UK is well on the way to either becoming a federal state – quite like Germany – or potentially breaking apart. If you want to know more about these dramatic political cross currents, this is the chapter to check out.

Looking at the United Kingdom

The United Kingdom (UK) is made up of four very distinct parts or, for the want of a better word, nations – England, Scotland, Wales and Northern Ireland. Now how these four nations formed is a long and complex story (if you want to know it all, check out *British History For Dummies*, published by Wiley). Suffice it to say that the story involves differing geography, foreign invasions and the odd mad, bad king. This section focuses on some basics of the nations in the UK, and their union.

Considering each member of the union

Here's a little about the four nations that make up the UK:

- **England:** Nearly 50 million people live here and it's home to the UK's capital, London. England produces ninety per cent of the wealth of the UK and it also covers the largest geographic area of the island (although it's not much bigger than Scotland). It's in the main quite flat and temperate, and therefore produces the overwhelming majority of the UK's cereal crops and fruit.
- **Scotland:** Around 5 million people live in Scotland, a country nearly the size of England but a lot less densely populated. It borders England to the north, and the border area is geographically similar. However, north of the major cities of Edinburgh and Glasgow the terrain gets mountainous and people are few and far between. It's colder and wetter than England, and therefore dairy and livestock farming are key. Scotland has a legal system separate to England and politically it's the part of the UK with most devolved power. See 'Focusing on the Scottish parliament', later in the chapter, for more.
- **Wales:** Three million people live in Wales and it borders England to the west. It's quite mountainous in parts, but its geography proved less of a hindrance to invading armies from England in medieval times; therefore, it found itself subsumed with England several hundred years before Scotland. Its legal system is the same as in England, but it's economically poorer than its much bigger neighbour. Geography and climate mean that it tends to have more livestock farming than crop growth. Wales has a very distinct language, Welsh, and a much larger proportion of people in Wales speak Welsh than Scots speak the equivalent language, Gaelic, in Scotland.

- **Northern Ireland:** This part of the UK has had an unhappy and troubled recent past. It was formed as breakaway when Ireland became independent in 1922. Those people on the island of Ireland who felt themselves closer ethnically and culturally to the UK formed Northern Ireland. However, a substantial proportion of the population in Northern Ireland wanted to go into an Irish state rather than stay within the UK. Decades of violence and disagreement followed, and only recently has the tension calmed. But Northern Ireland is less a nation like Wales and Scotland and more a compromise to ease ethnic, cultural and religious tension. It has the smallest population – 1.8 million people – and is the smallest part of the UK.

Ultimately, these nations came together to form the United Kingdom (see the next section for more on the formation of the UK).

In effect, the UK is united under the rule of the monarch (the clue is in the words *United* and *Kingdom*). But as I explain in Chapter 12, the role of the monarch has changed from one of exercising direct authority – telling everyone what to do – to being a figurehead and constitutionally having to bow to the will of parliament and the prime minister. This means that for much of the UK's history the nations of Scotland, Wales and Northern Ireland have been ruled from Westminster by politicians.

The nations of Scotland, Wales and Ireland are often referred to as the *Celtic nations*. This is because they still have language and traditions dating back to when even the Romans hadn't landed on Britain's shores. England is never referred to as a Celtic nation because many of its traditions and its language came with successive invasions from north Germany (by the Anglo-Saxons, hence the word *England* as in home of the Angles, which is nothing to do with geometry!), and then in 1066 the Norman French, who were themselves descended from Scandinavian Vikings.

A right royal faux-pas

The king of rock and roll, Elvis Presley, only ever made one trip to Scotland and that was a stop-over at Prestwick Airport when he was in the first flush of fame. When interviewed by the Scottish press, Elvis committed the cardinal of saying that he was 'delighted to be here in England'. Geography was clearly not one of the king's strong suits. But at the time it was an understandable error: many foreigners would refer to Great Britain or the UK as England because it's the most populated and rich part of the country. The otherwise largely anonymous to history prime minister Campbell-Bannerman would refer to himself as the prime minister of England despite the fact that he was actually PM of the whole UK. Such slights, although rather small and in themselves unimportant, do actually emphasise something significant: for generations, many in the Celtic parts of the UK – Scotland, Wales and Northern Ireland – have felt swallowed up by England.

Forming the United Kingdom

The UK was formed at the point of a sword and the barrel of a musket. Over several hundred years, from the Middle Ages until the middle of the 18th century, a series of violent clashes and all-out wars occurred between the peoples of England, Scotland, Wales and Ireland, all of which paved the way for the formation of the UK under the dominance of the biggest kid on the block – England.

- **Wales** was the first to feel the might of England, during the reign of English King Edward I (1239–1307). English settlers conquered and colonised parts, and abolished laws and institutions, replacing them with English laws, courts and institutions.
- **Ireland** was invaded by the English and later combined English and Scottish forces over half a millennium from the 12th century onwards. The country, although never wholly cowed, was colonised in parts and laws and institutions mirrored those in England. It became an integral part of the UK, but the marriage was a difficult one. On many occasions between the 17th and early 20th centuries, the Irish mounted successive rebellions against what they saw as English rule. Eventually, Ireland gained its independence but it didn't do so as a whole entity. In the north-east of the Island – in a province called Ulster – a majority of people wanted to stay part of the UK. As a result, Ireland was portioned into the south, which is a fully independent state, and Northern Ireland, which remains part of the UK but does have some devolved powers (for details see 'Priming the peace process: The Northern Ireland Assembly', later in this chapter).
- **Scotland**, in medieval times, was recognised throughout Europe as an independent state in the same way as England was. However, the only people not to recognise this were – guess who? – the English, and more particularly successive English monarchs. For much of the 14th, 15th and 16th centuries, England and Scotland were at each other's throats. More often than not the English attempted to dominate their northern neighbour. Wars laid waste to the border areas, kings came and went, but enemies the nations remained. Then in 1603, on the death of Queen Elizabeth I of England, the Scottish King James succeeded to the English throne, and from then onwards the thrones of England and Scotland were joined. Over time, politicians in the two countries drew closer together. Fewer wars occurred and in 1707 both the Scottish and English parliaments decided that they should unite in an *Act of Union*. The Scottish parliament disappeared and from then onwards – until the return of the Scots parliament in 1999 (see 'Focusing on the Scottish parliament', later in the chapter, for more on this) – the parliament in Westminster made laws covering both Scotland and England.

For most historians, the Act of Union of 1707 marks the coming into existence of the UK. But the formation of the UK took many hundreds of years.

Understanding the success of the union

Check this out: a strong argument exists to suggest that the UK is the most politically successful nation in the history of the modern world. Yes, you read that right, old Blighty is number one!

Why is this?

- **Economics:** The two centuries following the formation of the UK saw the country move from being a relative economic backwater off the north-west coast of the European Continent to being the world's pre-eminent trading nation, producing and exporting on a scale never seen before. No nation in history has had a greater share of world trade as the UK did in the mid-19th century.
- **The empire:** With economic might came military and political power. At one stage in the reign of Queen Victoria the UK had an empire covering a third of the surface of the globe. Although by the standards of today this imperial top-dog status is morally very troubling, it wasn't to contemporaries and was a considerable 'achievement' for a small country with a small population.
- **Internal peace and stability:** France, United States, Russia, Germany, Italy, Spain and China – what do they all have in common? Well, all these countries have been beset by revolution and even civil war during the time that the UK has existed. The UK, though – other than the odd hiccup here and there – has enjoyed over three centuries of internal peace and political stability since the Act of Union.
- **Spread of cultural influence:** A Briton can go to almost all corners of the globe, open his mouth and find that someone nearby understands what he's saying. That's because English – the official language of the UK – is also a global language that billions speak or at least understand. In addition, people overseas lap up music, art and culture from the UK. This reflects the huge spread of British cultural influence, which although not strictly caused by the coming together of the UK has certainly been aided by it.

The UK's power, prestige, economic fortunes and cultural influence are all reflections of the success of the union of four nations: England, Scotland, Wales and Northern Ireland.

Breaking down of the union?

Having bigged-up the successes of the UK, know that many of them – the empire and economic growth, for instance – relate to the dim and distant past. For much of the last century, the UK's position in the world has declined and as the UK has shrunk in power, more and more people have questioned whether the union can survive much longer into the 21st century. In addition, in the smaller Celtic nations, nationalist sentiment has risen as longstanding feelings of frustration at the dominance of England within the United Kingdom come to the fore.

A key moment in the recent history of Scottish nationalism was the decision by the UK Conservative government, led by PM Margaret Thatcher in 1989, to trial a major change in taxation in Scotland a year before imposing it on the rest of the UK. The community charge, or poll tax as it was dubbed, was hugely unpopular because millions of people who hadn't had to contribute to local taxation in the past suddenly had to. The fact that the UK government – which had achieved very little electoral support in Scotland at the 1987 general election – chose to use the Scots as guinea pigs for such an unpopular policy as the poll tax led many people north of the border to call for devolution and even independence for Scotland.

Devolution Defined: Granting Power from the Centre

How did we go from Whitehall governing all the countries of the UK on all matters, to devolution of power to Wales, Scotland and Northern Ireland? This section gives you the background, and outlines the powers these parts of the union now have.

Deciding to devolve

On the election of a Labour government in 1997 the D word was on everyone's lips; no, not D for democracy, but D for devolution. A groundswell of opinion in Scotland and to a lesser degree in Wales indicated that the people of these two nations wanted to have more of a direct say in the running of their affairs. Of course they had Members of Parliament (MPs) elected to Westminster, a dedicated cabinet minister each (the Scottish and Welsh secretaries) and their own local authorities, but many talked of a 'democratic deficit' in these two nations. In particular, many people in Scotland and Wales felt aggrieved that they'd just seen 18 years of Conservative government in Westminster have a huge impact on their lives when the electorate in both countries had overwhelmingly opposed the Conservative government at the ballot box.

Looking at the pros and cons

Devolution has several advantages:

- **Greater local accountability:** More decisions are taken locally rather than in Westminster and so the public see better who's taking them. And if they prove to be unpopular decisions then punishing the offending politician at the ballot box should be easier.
- **Greater efficiency:** Local issues dealt with by local people should mean government reaching better decisions. For one thing, local lobby groups don't have to traipse down to Westminster when they want to create change.
- **Unburden the centre:** The government in Westminster no longer has to deal with the minutiae of Scottish or Welsh affairs, which should mean that it has more time and energy to focus on the 'big' national issues.

At the time and since people have posed strong arguments against devolution:

- **Cost:** Creating a whole new Scottish parliament and assemblies in Wales and Northern Ireland cost hundreds of millions of pounds.
- **Conflict with the centre:** What happens if the parliament in Westminster and the devolved parliament or assemblies don't agree? In law Westminster has priority, but disputes could damage national unity. Under the Labour government of Gordon Brown, for instance, relations with the Scottish parliament – with a Scottish Nationalist government – were notoriously bad.
- **Unfairness:** Many suggest that it's unfair to the people of England that the Scots, Welsh and Northern Irish are able to vote themselves greater state benefits. For example, people in Wales get free prescriptions and the Scots don't pay university tuition fees, which grates on many people in England who have to pay for both.

The majority of the political parties in Scotland and Wales were in favour of devolution; however, the Conservatives weren't. They said that devolution made it more likely that one day full independence would come about and the United Kingdom would break up. In effect, for the Conservatives, devolution wasn't an end point but a staging post towards independence. Although in the recent referendum on Scottish independence the Scots voted to stay in the UK, the very fact that a referendum on Scottish independence happened at all perhaps indicates that devolution can indeed be a staging post to independence.

Holding referendums

Both Scotland and Wales had referendums on whether to adopt devolution. In Scotland's case the vote was on whether to establish a Scottish parliament. In Wales the proposal was to have an assembly, which had fewer powers than a parliament (see the following sections on how the Scottish parliament and Welsh Assembly actually work). The Scots voted by a comfortable majority for a parliament. Only a tiny majority accepted the idea of a Welsh Assembly – nevertheless, it was enough.

The Scottish parliament and Welsh Assembly came into being following referendums. The Northern Irish Assembly came about as a result of the peace process negotiations; devolution was a pre-requisite of bringing the warring parties together.

Focusing on the Scottish parliament

Scotland is a nation within the UK with a long history and strong traditions. Until 1707 – and the Act of Union with England and Wales – it had its very own parliament. With devolution in 1997, it regained some autonomy.

The Scottish parliament is more than ten years old but it's already a cornerstone of the UK constitution and political state. Of all the devolved parliaments and assemblies, the Scottish parliament is the most powerful and high profile. Even those politicians who opposed its formation probably can't quite imagine the political landscape without it.

Seeing who governs and where

The Scottish parliament is based in expensive new offices in the Holyrood area of Edinburgh. In total, 129 Members of the Scottish Parliament (MSPs) represent Scotland's 5 million inhabitants.

The Scottish parliament has lots of powers and big bureaucracy. The biggest party in the parliament forms the Scottish government. At the head of this government is the *first minister* – in effect, Scotland's prime minister – and he appoints a cabinet, drawn from MSPs.

Elections to the parliament are under the catchily titled *mixed member proportional representation system*, sometimes called the *additional member voting system*. In short, 73 of the MSPs are elected under the first-past-the-post system, which means that registered electors in an individual constituency vote for the candidate they want to represent them and the candidate with the most votes wins the seat. So far, so simple! But on top of these constituency MSPs are additional MSPs who are drawn from party candidate lists. Basically, the more votes the party gathers, the more candidates from its list get a seat in the Scottish parliament.

The biggest party in the Scottish parliament is currently the Scottish National Party (SNP), which wants full independence for Scotland from the UK. However, the SNP is a minority government and as a result needs the support of other parties within the parliament to see its bills pass into law.

Those who oppose the SNP's desire for Scottish independence refer to such a change as a divorce rather than independence. The idea is that calling it divorce gives the notion of independence a very negative connotation in the minds of the electorate.

Setting policy

The policy areas devolved from the UK central government to the Scottish parliament include

- Agriculture
- Education
- Environment
- Health
- Judicial services and police
- Tourism and the arts
- Transport

In short, the Scottish parliament has the final say on most of the policy areas affecting the lives of people in Scotland. But some policy areas – called *reserved powers* – are still in the hands of the UK parliament. They include

- Defence and national security
- Taxation
- The power of the Bank of England to set interest rates
- The power to negotiate foreign treaties and declare war

Although central government sets tax policies, the Scottish parliament can change tax rates. The Scottish parliament has the right to vary income tax in Scotland by up to 3 pence in the pound. It's then free to spend the money raised as it sees fit.

Laying down the law in Scotland

Like the Westminster parliament, ministers and individual MSPs propose legislation – in bill form – that other MSPs then debate and vote upon. The process is roughly based on the Westminster parliament: MSPs propose bills on the floor of the parliament and then the bills move through a committee stage.

Here's how bills in Scotland become law:

1. **Introductory stage:** The minister or individual MSP proposing the law formally introduces the bill to the parliament, outlining the general principles behind it, and provides supporting documents that indicate how much the new law will cost. MSPs then debate the bill, and if a majority of MSPs agree, it moves on to the next stage of the legislative process.
2. **Committee stage:** The details of the bill are examined by a committee of MSPs whose job it is to consider amendments to it. This process can be exhaustive and time-consuming.
3. **Final vote stage:** A meeting of the full Scottish parliament debates and votes upon the amendments to the bill made at committee stage. After this, they vote on the bill as a whole. If a majority agrees, the bill needs only royal assent from the UK monarch – a constitutional formality – to become law.

Like the UK parliament in Westminster, a bill has a much better chance of becoming law if it's proposed by a government minister rather than an individual member.

Parliament typically sits on Tuesdays, Wednesdays and Thursdays, from early January to late June and from early September to mid-December, with two-week recesses in April and October.

Like in Westminster, it's a job of the parliament to scrutinise the actions of the executive – the Scottish government. To this end, the first minister and other ministers in the Scottish government regularly attend sessions of the parliament. MSPs are free to ask them questions about what they and their departments are doing. The most prominent question time takes place each Thursday between 12 and 12:30 p.m. when the parliament is sitting. Here, MSPs get to grill the first minister on the performance of the government.

Welcoming in the Welsh Assembly

The Welsh Assembly, or National Assembly for Wales as it's more formally known, was introduced at around the same time as the Scottish parliament. However, the Welsh Assembly doesn't have quite the same powers as the Scottish parliament. The assembly can make laws – called *assembly measures* – but these laws can be vetoed by the secretary of state for Wales, who's a minister in the UK government based in Westminster.

The Welsh Assembly is allowed to legislate on pretty similar policy areas to those of the Scottish parliament, including

- Agriculture
- Education
- Environment
- Health
- Transport
- Tourism and the arts

Wales shares its legal system with England, so the assembly doesn't need power related to the judiciary or courts; this is left up to the UK parliament in Westminster.

The Welsh Assembly doesn't have powers to raise taxes or even to vary income tax rates.

A total of 60 elected members sit on the Welsh Assembly. As in the Scottish parliament, members are elected by a combination of the first-past-the-post and additional member systems.

Currently, a coalition of the Labour Party and the nationalist Plaid Cymru holds a majority in the Welsh Assembly. Somewhat controversially, the assembly has used money from the UK government in Westminster to provide Welsh residents with free NHS prescriptions, charge students less for university tuition and offer discounted local authority care home fees. The controversy arises because these are all things that people in England have to pay more for, which has prompted critics to suggest that devolution favours Wales at the expense of the English majority.

Although Plaid Cymru is a nationalist party – like the Scottish National Party – it doesn't, as yet, have a policy of full independence, unlike the SNP. Instead, it wants to see greater devolution from Westminster, with the Welsh Assembly getting the same legal powers as the Scottish parliament.

Priming the peace process: The Northern Ireland Assembly

The Northern Ireland Assembly is no ordinary legislative body; it's the embodiment of a long-cherished desire for peace, an end to conflict and a new age of co-operation. It was born as a result of the Good Friday Agreement in 1998, which finally brought some peace to Northern Ireland and ultimately an end to armed conflict between the warring paramilitary groups: the republicans, who wanted Northern Ireland to join with the Republic, and the loyalists, who wanted to keep Northern Ireland within the United Kingdom.

The Northern Ireland Assembly has law-making powers but with a twist – the assembly's constitution is designed to breed co-operation between the political parties rather than conflict, as is so often the case in the Westminster system. For example, its executive – in effect, the cabinet – isn't made up of members of the biggest party in the assembly (as it would be in Westminster). Instead, seats on the executive are distributed according to the number of seats a party has in the assembly. So, for example, the Democratic Unionist Party currently has 36 of 108 seats in the assembly, which is equivalent to just over a third of all the seats, and as a result it also holds just over a third of the ministerial posts in the executive.

Although the Northern Ireland Assembly is as much about breeding co-operation and peace as devolved government, at times the parties in it simply haven't been able to get along and work together in government. As a result, the assembly has been suspended four times since its inception – the longest period was between 14 October 2002 and 7 May 2007. When this happens, the Northern Ireland secretary, a government minister in Westminster, assumes the powers of the assembly.

The Northern Ireland Assembly can make laws in the following policy areas:

- Agriculture
- Culture, arts, leisure and tourism
- Education
- Employment
- Environment
- Health
- Trade and investment

Two of the most important jobs in the executive of the Northern Ireland Assembly are the first minister and deputy first minister. The leaders of the two biggest parties in the assembly (by number of seats) fill these two positions.

As in Scotland and Wales, the Northern Ireland Assembly has no right to legislate in certain areas, such as on foreign and defence policy. In addition, the Northern Ireland Assembly can't legislate on criminal law or the police service, as well as – more bizarrely – consumer protection matters or telecommunications.

Paying for it all: The Barnett Formula

The Barnett Formula may sound like the title of the worst thriller novel you could ever read (apart from perhaps *The Cricklewood Ultimatum* or *Casino Dagenham*) but it actually refers to the official mechanism that the UK Treasury uses to adjust the amount of money it distributes from UK taxes to Scotland, Wales and Northern Ireland. As with many things in politics, the Barnett Formula is a temporary fix that's become much more permanent. It was devised by a civil servant, Joel Barnett, in the 1970s to ease disputes in the cabinet between the Welsh and Scottish secretaries over cash. The formula itself has no legal backing by an act of parliament and the Treasury could change or dispense with it at any time. However, to scrap it now would be highly controversial because the likes of Scotland do very well out of it.

At first glance the Barnett Formula seems straightforward: money flows from the UK Treasury to Scotland, Wales and Northern Ireland according to their relative populations. However, the Barnett Formula only applies to expenditure in areas that are devolved – for example, in Scotland and Wales, health and education are two devolved areas. All other money flowing from the UK treasury to Wales, Scotland and Northern Ireland is on an ad hoc basis, so not subject to the Barnett Formula.

Wales and Northern Ireland have to rely on direct grants from the UK Treasury, the size of some of which are dictated by the Barnett Formula. In Scotland, though, the position is complicated further because the Scottish parliament also has the right to raise or cut income tax rates by 3 pence in the pound, giving it an extra source of potential revenue.

Many in England argue that the Barnett formula is unfair. For example, reassessments of the Barnett Formula are infrequent, and as a result quite a time lag can occur before the amount of money distributed under Barnett reflects population changes. In the past three decades the population of England has been growing far faster than Scotland, but this is barely reflected in the cash distributed under Barnett. The result? Public spending in Scotland per capita is around 10 per cent higher than in England at present.

But for every commentator in England saying that the Barnett Formula is flawed, just as many in Scotland are bemoaning the fact that the billions of pounds of tax revenues that flow from North Sea oil and gas each year go directly to the UK Treasury. In fact, many of those who are in favour of Scottish independence say that Scotland would be a very rich country if only it could hold on to North Sea oil and gas revenue, most of which comes from waters off the coast of Scotland. The counter-argument is that the government uses the money for expenditure on areas of key national interest, such as defence spending and paying interest on the national debt, all of which benefit Scotland as well. See the next section for more on the great Scottish independence debate and the role that finance plays in it.

Treading the Path to Scottish Independence

Scotland was an independent state right up until the early eighteenth century and it has retained many of the trappings of independent statehood even within the UK. For example, Scotland's legal system is different to that of the rest of the UK and it even prints its own money – the Scottish Pound – unlike, say, Wales, which circulates the British Pound.

Nevertheless, for the best part of three centuries Scotland has been happily ensconced in the UK, but in recent decades there has been a move towards greater autonomy and growing calls for independence. Increasing numbers of politicians, academics and ordinary members of the public have started to question whether or not Scotland would be better off governing itself again – as it used too – and leaving the UK. Powers have flowed back to Scotland from Westminster – through devolution – but still many remain dissatisfied, suggesting that this process is nothing but a staging post to a fully independent Scotland.

Scotland may be looking for independence but it doesn't mean that Wales and even Northern Ireland are treading the same path. In fact, according to opinion polls in Wales, next to no support exists for full independence. As for Northern Ireland, because of the historic dispute between the protestants, who feel closer to the UK, and Catholics, who feel closer to the Republic of Ireland, little chance exists of a drive for an independent Northern Ireland.

Deciding to hold a referendum

Many observers of how devolution has worked in Scotland suggested that it would be merely a first step towards full independence. Their theory was that after the Scottish people and their politicians got used to governing themselves in areas such as education and health, and the other devolved policy areas, they'd want to go the whole hog and gain control over taxation and foreign policy and become an independent state with membership of the European Union (EU) and the United Nations (UN).

Independence was the avowed aim of the Scottish National Party and its leader and the country's first minister, Alex Salmond. The other main political parties in Scotland – Labour, Conservative and Lib Dem – were opposed to independence.

Those in favour of independence argued:

- The UK government acts for the whole of the UK and this can sometimes be detrimental to the interests of the people of Scotland.
- Scotland loses out because it's unable to run its own foreign missions and embassies and has to rely on the UK Foreign Office to represent its interests overseas.
- Scotland has very distinctive traditions and tends to adopt more socialist policies than those in England. Independence would mean the Scots being free of interference from England.

The SNP often cited the decline of the Scottish fishing fleet as an example of the UK government choosing UK-wide interests over Scottish ones. Over the past two decades the Scottish fishing fleet has been systematically reduced due to negotiations on fishing quotas carried out by the UK government with other members of the EU. The argument goes that the UK government, by trying to get a good deal for the whole of the UK, hung the Scottish fishing fleet out to dry.

The main argument against full independence was that it's better to be part of a powerful country like the UK, with a seat on the UN Security Council and major voting rights in the EU, than to be a relatively small independent country.

But the SNP was the party for independence, and it was the party in power. And so in 2010 it called for a referendum in Scotland on full independence, as well as on whether or not the UK parliament should devolve some more of its powers to the Scottish parliament in Holyrood.

Braving the arts: Cultural shifts to Scottish independence

Anyone looking down the list of shows at the Edinburgh cultural festival in 2013 and 2014 will be able to testify that the independence debate is widely reflected in the arts – many stand-up comedy, plays and even contemporary dance shows were themed around independence. This is no new thing, though: over the past two decades the debate over an independent Scotland has raged in the arts north of the border.

Many famous actors and artists have come out in favour of independence. The biggest name in the Yes camp has been Sean Connery, a.k.a. James Bond, who issued his rallying cry from his home in Marbella. More recently some supporters of Scottish independence have even revisited the works of the most famous poet Robert Burns (1759–96) to suggest that he was a very early proponent of Scottish independence.

And what of William Wallace, the Scottish freedom fighter from the Middle Ages? He was far from a household name even in Scotland until the Mel Gibson Hollywood blockbuster *Braveheart* hit the big screen. The big-budget cinema epic played fast and loose with history, but its portrayal of a Scottish leader standing up to the (very) nasty English characters in the film hit a real sweet spot for the Scottish public. The story of William Wallace and his struggle against English oppression has in no small way added some romance to the calls for Scotland to be independent once again – as Mel (sorry William) says in the film, 'You can take our lives, but you will never take our freedom.' Stirring stuff!

Many within the arts community argue that an independent Scotland will be better placed to nurture new and exciting arts, while being more sensitive to cultural traditions. Of course, in reality much of the public spending on arts is local, with local councils in the main, but the impression still remains that it isn't right that Scottish culture could be dependent on a bureaucrat in Westminster for grants and aid.

Holding a referendum on independence wasn't in the power of the Scottish parliament: only the UK parliament in Westminster could authorise such a referendum. However, seeing the groundswell of opinion in Scotland for a referendum on independence, the UK government decided to give the Scottish parliament the right to call such a referendum, provided it could agree over what to put on the ballot paper. Ultimately, the Scottish parliament decided that instead of offering three options – the status quo, greater devolution or full independence – the ballot paper would simply ask: Should Scotland be an independent nation?

Many politicians in Scotland had wanted a further option called devolution max to be included in the referendum ballot paper. In effect devolution max or devo max for short is the proposal for the Scottish parliament to have far greater powers than at the moment but stops short of full independence. The

UK government rejected this proposal but during the run up to the independence referendum the odds on a 'yes' vote shortened and in a bid to keep the union together the party leaders of the three main UK parties gave a vow that they would grant devo max following a no vote.

Voting for 'Better Together' rather than 'Yes'

The referendum night of 18 September 2014 was dramatic. Although the polls indicated that Scotland would narrowly vote to remain part of the UK, no one could be sure until the votes were counted. Over three centuries of history lay at a crossroads. Eventually, the polls were proved right and those campaigning for a No vote – as in No to independence – won the day. However, the debate in the year before had been a heated one and the eventual result was close, with 45 per cent of those people who cast their ballot voting for independence.

The following sections outline some of the main reasons and debates that led to a small majority of Scots to vote to stay in the UK.

Putting a spanner in the works: Scotland and EU membership

Opinion polls suggest that Scotland is the part of the UK that's most pro-EU. The SNP leader and first minister Alex Salmond has talked glowingly about how an independent Scotland could play a major role in the EU. However, as the debate over independence heated up many top lawyers said that if Scotland were to become independent, it would no longer have membership of the EU. The UK is a member of the EU, not Scotland, and by leaving the UK Scotland would therefore also be leaving the EU. Then Scottish goods imported to the EU (including what remains of the UK) could be subject to the same tariffs as goods from anywhere outside the EU. The SNP has said this is nonsense and that Scotland would remain in the EU even if it was no longer part of the UK, but several EU countries, in particular Spain – which has its own independence movements to deal with – have said that as far as they're concerned Scotland wouldn't be a member of the EU if it became independent.

It wasn't just EU membership – or lack of it – that would be a barrier to an independent Scotland. It turned out that it would have to apply for membership to all manner of global institutions, such as the United Nations and the World Bank. That's a lot of application forms to fill out!

Keeping or losing the pound?

For a state to be truly independent it needs its own currency. This allows politicians and domestic bankers the chance to set interest rates and to print or not to print more money – both key tools in controlling inflation and boosting economic growth. However, during the great independence debate the independent governor of the Bank of England, Mark Carney, said that Scotland as an independent country would probably not be allowed to keep using the UK pound.

For Scotland, losing the pound could mean:

- **Higher interest rates:** An independent Scottish currency wouldn't be as widely sought after by international currency traders as the UK pound, so to attract people to buy into a new currency interest rates would likely have to go up.
- **A new Scottish central bank:** All currencies need a separate central bank to administer them. This would be expensive and disruptive to set up. In addition, because of Scotland's relatively small population, a Scottish central bank would probably not be able to call on as much reserves as, say, the Bank of England (which is currently the UK central bank). This would matter if a financial crisis occurred such as the one in 2008. How would an independent Scottish central bank have the resources to bail out the banks, as the Bank of England did in 2008?
- **Higher currency conversion costs:** The overwhelming amount of 'international' trade that an independent Scotland would undertake would be with . . . guess which country? Yes, the UK. And each of these trades in both directions would mean converting the new Scots currency into UK pounds and vice versa. So every trade would entail currency traders taking commissions, a massive expense to business and individuals on both sides of the border.

Roughly 11 per cent of world trade is transacted using UK pounds. This makes it the fourth most widely used currency in the world. A new Scots currency would be much smaller and less in demand.

Adding up the cost: Independence could prove expensive

The sheer cost of setting up an independent state played a major role in the eventual defeat of the independence lobby. Here are some of the extra costs an independent Scotland would incur:

- **Defence:** Scotland would need to equip and pay for its own military rather than contribute to the UK defence budget. This would cost billions, according to most estimates. In addition, Scotland would probably have to apply for membership of the North Atlantic Treaty Organisation (NATO) because at present membership belongs to the UK.

- **Administration:** The Scottish parliament would have to set up whole new government departments and employ thousands of civil servants to take on the work that the UK government in Westminster had previously done.
- **Embassies and foreign relations:** The UK has some of the swankiest high-profile embassies in the world and spends hundreds of millions on foreign relations and intelligence gathering. Independent Scotland would have to go it alone.

The preceding list offers just a sample of what independence would mean to both the UK and Scotland. From competing in international sporting events to issuing passports, a break-up of the UK would mean whole new layers of bureaucracy and cultural separation. Nevertheless, those calling for a Yes vote in the independence referendum nearly won, showing the strong pull of their arguments.

Boiling it right down: It's the economy!

Probably the biggest area of debate in the prelude to the independence referendum vote was the economic effects of Scotland going it alone. Apart from arguments over the effects of losing EU membership and the pound (see the preceding sections), those against independence made the following points:

- **Flight of financial services:** Banks and insurers are two of the biggest parts of Scotland's economy. Many feared that these firms would up sticks and move to the UK post-independence because of concerns over tariffs and the need for a robust, strong central bank.
- **Lack of investment:** Those against independence said that Scotland would be a lot less attractive to foreign investment, which is crucial to jobs and bringing foreign exchange into the country.
- **Over-reliance on oil and gas:** Scotland has lots of oil and gas, but does it have enough? Some suggest that the well, so to speak, is already running dry and that the contribution to the economy of oil and gas over time will diminish sharply. In turn this will mean it's harder to provide an independent government with the funds it needs to pay for public services.

Although a majority of Scots who voted wanted to stay in the UK, the margin was quite narrow. If in the future Scots held another referendum on independence, the result could be quite different.

Who ran the better campaign?

Although the Scots voted to remain within the EU, many commentators thought that the Yes to Independence campaign was better run than the Better Together one. Generally, the Yes campaign could call upon many younger supporters and their canvassing activities were on a bigger scale. In addition, opponents accused the Better Together campaign of just focusing on the negatives – what Scotland would lose by becoming independent rather than emphasising the positives: longstanding bonds of family and shared institutions between Scotland and the rest of the UK. In fact, most observers reckon that the Yes campaign was more effective, apart from the measure that ultimately really counted: the ballot box!

Part IV
Politics Worldwide

Five of the biggest UN agencies

The following list contains some of the big UN agencies, many or all of which you may have already heard of in the media:

- **United Nations Scientific and Cultural Organisation (UNESCO):** UNESCO is meant to contribute to peace and security by promoting international collaboration through education, science and culture in order to further universal respect for justice, the rule of law, human rights and fundamental freedoms. To bring extra publicity to its work, UNESCO employs a series of celebrity ambassadors, including actress Angelina Jolie and tennis ace Roger Federer.
- **World Food Programme (WFP):** As the name suggests, the WFP is about feeding people who are starving. It's the biggest of the UN's humanitarian organisations. The WFP is based in Rome and has offices in more than 80 countries. The main job of the WFP is distributing food to people who are suffering from drought or famine. It saves the lives of hundreds of thousands of people each year, and in some years, millions.
- **World Health Organisation (WHO):** The WHO's objective is to combat disease, especially infectious disease – new threats such as Ebola, as well as established ones such as malaria – and to promote the general health of the people of the world. As part of its work, WHO organises mass vaccination programmes.
- **World Bank (WB):** This body acts like, well, a bank, making loans to countries for development programmes whose stated goal is to reduce poverty.
- **International Monetary Fund (IMF):** The IMF oversees the global financial system and the economic policies pursued by individual countries. It tries to ensure that governments follow sensible policies – not borrowing money that they can't afford to pay back, for example – and looks to create a global financial system whereby all countries can enjoy growth.

Find out more about British Politics at www.dummies.com/extras/britishpolitics.

In this part . . .

- Understand Britain's place in the world.
- Find out more about the UN, the G8, the G20 and NATO.
- Take a closer look at the European Union and how it works.
- Discover more about how democracy works in the United States.

Chapter 19

Understanding Britain's Place in the World

In This Chapter

- Moving from empire to somewhere in the middle
- Getting into bed with the European Union
- Maintaining a special relationship with the United States
- Reckoning with China
- Heading up the Commonwealth of Nations
- Policing the world

Britain may be an island but it has always engaged with the rest of the world, from the days of exploration and empire through to the export of British music and culture.

In this chapter I take an honest look at Britain's relationship with its close neighbours in Europe and further afield to the former colonies, the rising powerhouse China and, of course, the United States.

Declining Fortunes: From Empire to the Middle Ranks

If you find yourself an old atlas – and I'm talking early 20th century, here – and turn to a map of the world, you see an awful lot of countries coloured in pink – India, the West Indies, large tracts of Africa and even Canada and Australia. Are they pink because they're hot countries and therefore suffer a bit of sunburn? No, map-makers used pink to indicate which countries belonged to the British Empire.

At its height, the British Empire spanned around a quarter of the globe and held sway over the lives of hundreds of millions of people. As Cecil Rhodes, the Victorian imperialist, once said, 'To be born British is to win first prize in the lottery of life', and indeed, for those Brits who got to travel the world and govern other people as imperial civil servants, this may have seemed the case. It was also said at around the same time that the sun never set on the British Empire – an expression of both its geographic spread and what seemed its eternal nature.

However, within a century the British Empire had considerably diminished and Britain's role in the world also shrank. What happened? Well, Britain got involved in the two world wars, which virtually bankrupted the country and drained its natural and manpower resources. Meanwhile, many of the countries in the empire developed their own independence movements, perhaps buoyed by Britain's sudden fragility.

When the end of the empire came, it did so relatively quickly. Encouraged by the US government – which wanted to expand its own influence and to which the British government owed huge debts – the empire rolled up. First India became independent, followed by colonies in the West Indies and finally those in Africa. In fact, within 25 years of the end of the Second World War, Britain's once massive empire consisted of a handful of islands and far-flung outposts.

Britain's empire lasted for a few hundred years and once even contained territories that became part of the United States. It was a deeply racist institution and white people from the empire were granted self-government early on while countries in Africa and the West Indies had to wait a long time for self-government or independence. Put simply, not many British politicians of the 19th and early 20th centuries believed that non-whites could be trusted to run their own affairs – I told you it was racist!

Probably the most famous figure who protested against British rule was the Indian Mahatma Gandhi. He was an inspiration to tens of millions of ordinary Indians and he believed passionately that the country should rule itself rather than be ruled by Britain. He led a boycott of British goods and embarked on hunger strikes and peaceful protests. He gathered much support in Britain for his aims and eventually, shortly after the end of the Second World War, India was granted its independence. However, Gandhi didn't live to see his newly free country blossom, because he was assassinated in January 1948.

Forging a New Role in Europe

With Britain's empire gone and the economy struggling under the debts and other burdens of the Second World War, Britain started to view its role not as a superpower, like America and Russia, but as a leading nation within Europe, on a par with France and Germany.

To this end, throughout the 1960s and 1970s the British tried to join the newly formed European Economic Community (EEC), now called the European Union (EU), in the hope of improving trade with the continent. Initially, the French objected to the UK's entry, with President Charles de Gaulle famously vetoing it. But the EU finally allowed the UK to join in 1973.

Conservative Prime Minister (PM) Edward Heath negotiated Britain's entry into the EEC. It was the culmination of years of diplomacy – particularly when it came to easing the fears of the French – and a triumph for Heath. He often said that he saw Britain's place as a part of Europe rather than as a go-it-alone power. He recognised that Britain had declined as a military, financial and economic power and saw that it could only retain influence on the world stage by working with other nations of similar populations, such as France and Germany.

UK and Europe: Growing together or growing apart?

In many respects the UK hasn't been as close to the continent politically and economically as it is today since the Reformation in the mid-16th century. The UK is part of the *single European market*, which means that goods and people can move freely across the whole of the EU – 28 countries and 500 million people. In addition, many of the laws affecting the daily lives of Britons are initiated in the institutions of the European Union.

English is very much the language of business on the continent and millions of Britons travel there for work or pleasure each year. In many respects you could say that Britain has become part of a European super-state. Whereas 20 years ago it was a given that the EU was moving towards being a super-state and that Britain had a choice of joining in or going it alone, the nature of what was once called the 'European project' has changed.

The expansion of the EU into the former Warsaw Pact countries in 2004 has been key in diluting the idea of an EU super-state. The nations of the east (Warsaw Pact) survived under Soviet tyranny for four decades after the end of the Second World War and, having newly gained their independence, many are now loath to sign over more powers to a centralised EU state. So the reluctance to join the European project felt by a majority of Britons – according to opinion polls – which angered many of the EU's partners such as France, Belgium and Germany, is now echoed in other parts of Europe. In addition, the recession that gripped the globe and Europe from 2008 onwards has damaged relations between many EU countries. For instance, the Greeks resent many of the austerity cuts they had to impose as a pre-condition of getting aid from Germany to help bail out their government finances.

The EU's march to super-state status isn't so self-assured, and although membership of it has changed Britain, ultimately Britain's membership has also changed the EU; it was the UK that was instrumental in bringing the former Warsaw Pact countries of Eastern Europe into the EU.

And not only in terms of trade and the EU did the UK start to look to the continent of Europe rather than to the wider world. The Cold War and the threat to Western Europe from the Soviet Union led to the formation of the *North Atlantic Treaty Organisation (NATO)*, a military body meant to ensure collective security. The UK, with a strong military, was a leading member of NATO, often working closely with the US.

By the 21st century the majority of Britain's trade was with its EU partners (before the Second World War less than a quarter of the nation's trade was with Europe) and much of its diplomacy was carried out jointly with the other members of the EU, particularly France and Germany.

Not all British politicians are enthusiastic towards the EU. Many argue that the EU is trying to become a super-state and reduce the power of the nation state. Critics suggest that the EU's institutions, such as the commission and parliament, are corrupt and that the famous Common Agricultural Policy (CAP) – see Chapter 21 for more on this – is a massive waste of resources. People critical of the EU who think that Britain would be better off out of it are called *Eurosceptics* and they often join the Conservative and UK Independence parties (UKIP).

Assessing the Special Relationship with the United States

Watch any of the 24-hour news channels for long enough and you're bound to hear the phrase *special relationship* in reference to Britain's close ties with the United States. In this case, a special relationship doesn't mean that Britain and the US are going to move in together, pick furnishings and share a toothbrush holder. Instead, it harks back to the Second World War when the UK and US were allies and fought and beat Nazi Germany and Japan. The two countries worked incredibly closely together and this relationship carried on into the post-war period when Western Europe was threatened by the Soviet Union. The countries share the same language and both are democracies. In addition, a long history exists of Americans working and living in Britain and vice versa. The bonds between the two countries are indeed strong and are historical, economic and cultural in nature.

However, it's often said that the UK lays too much store by the special relationship and, according to some critics, that the UK follows US foreign policy too slavishly. For example, during the run-up to the war in Iraq in 2003 the British PM Tony Blair was caricatured as a poodle of the US president George W. Bush because not only did he support the US-led invasion but he also sent thousands of UK military personnel into the conflict.

The phrase *special relationship* was first coined by British PM Winston Churchill in the aftermath of the Second World War. Churchill felt the closeness of Britain's relationship with the US not only because of the co-operation between the two nations during the war but also because his mother was American. (Winston Churchill was one of Britain's great PMs and is covered in more detail in Chapter 23.)

We may not be in the throes of a world war, yet the US and UK military and intelligence services still co-operate and share an awful lot of information. Often the two nations find themselves together on peace-keeping duty around the globe and with the same diplomatic goals. Why is this? Well, both countries are democracies and have strong cultural and economic ties, so it's understandable that their national interests often coincide.

Looking Further Afield to the Rise of China

If you want to see proof of the dramatic rise of China, look no further than your own sitting room. The TV you watch, the sofa you sit on, the coffee table you place your mug on – chances are they're all manufactured in China or by Chinese-owned firms. Even in international banking, once seen as an Anglo-American domain, five of the world's top ten banks – measured by the value of the assets they hold – are from China, with just one from Britain.

China is very much becoming the centre of the world economy. Its growth is awe-inspiring and at this point looks almost limitless. It's estimated that within ten years the Chinese economy will be bigger than that of the US. Some commentators suggest that what's happening is a form of reverse imperialism: the countries of the West – such as Britain, the US, Germany and France – are now finding the businesses, land and natural resources they once owned around the globe being rapidly supplanted and taken over by Chinese firms, all backed by what's still ostensibly a communist Chinese government.

Britain exports very little to China; in fact, Scotch whisky is probably the biggest export. In contrast, China exports large quantities of manufactured goods to the UK. But with China racing to superpower status, much of Britain's future fortunes will be tied to how well it can forge trading and other links with it. Developing this relationship is one of the major challenges of the rest of the 21st century and with it rests the UK's future prosperity – or lack of it!

It's not just the Chinese who are playing rapid catch with the West; India, a country with over a billion people, is growing at a lightning-fast pace. For instance, India produces more engineering graduates each year than the estimated number of engineers in the whole of the UK.

Leading the Commonwealth of Nations

Britain may have lost an empire but it's gained what's called the *Commonwealth of Nations*. The Commonwealth is an international organisation made up almost entirely of former member states of the old British Empire including Australia, India and South Africa as well as lesser-known countries such as St Kitts, Lesotho and Malta. The aim of the Commonwealth is to promote peace, economic growth and cultural co-operation. Fifty-three states are members (plus the UK) – around a quarter of all the countries in the world.

When the Commonwealth was formed it was called the British Commonwealth, which was a nod to the UK's top dog status as the former imperial power. However, this name was changed to the Commonwealth of Nations, reflecting perhaps the decline of Britain's power around the globe and the desire of the member nations to appear to be a collection of equal nations rather than being under the banner of a former imperial power.

The head of the Commonwealth is the British monarch. This role is largely ceremonial, with the monarch making speeches and turning up for the opening session of the biennial Commonwealth conferences. Interestingly, the British monarch is the actual head of state of 16 of the 53 member states of the Commonwealth. Although the title is largely symbolic, the current British monarch takes her role as head of the Commonwealth very seriously indeed.

Members of the Commonwealth are supposed to adhere to the 1971 Singapore Declaration. This states that members should try to promote peace, human rights, individual liberty, equality and free trade. However, members have often broken with the ideals of the declaration, with some having very dodgy human rights records.

Member states that move too far away from the ideals of the Commonwealth can be suspended from the organisation. Nigeria, Pakistan and, more recently, Zimbabwe have all been suspended over concerns related to human rights or election fraud. Even the idyllic island of Fiji was suspended between 1987 and 1997 after the democratic government was ousted by a military takeover.

Every two years the heads of government of all the Commonwealth nations meet for a big conference. Prime ministers and presidents from all around the globe jet in to discuss all manner of stuff, from improving global trade to issues of security and international development. These heads of government meetings last several days and are usually held in a nice sunny location.

The Commonwealth has its very own civil service – the Commonwealth Secretariat. Based in London, the Secretariat's wide-ranging jobs include:

- Organising the heads of government meeting and drawing up agendas for this important biennial shindig

- Providing economic and social development help to poor member states – in effect, providing them with a professional civil service
- Working to encourage member states to talk to one another so as to increase co-operation and ensure peace

The Commonwealth Secretariat has a politician sitting at the top making the big calls: the Commonwealth secretary-general, who is elected by a vote at the heads of government meeting every four years. The Commonwealth secretary-general's job is to be a mouthpiece for the Commonwealth, embodying the organisation's shared aims, such as preserving human rights and supporting free trade. The present secretary-general is Kamalesh Sharma, an Indian politician.

One of the fun things about the Commonwealth – apart from the sunny locations that host the heads of government meetings – is that membership brings with it the right to field a team at the Commonwealth Games. The *Commonwealth Games* resemble a mini-Olympics and are held every four years. Top athletes represent their nations by competing in all manner of sporting and athletic events. The most recent Commonwealth Games were held in Glasgow in 2014.

Many of the Commonwealth nations share traditions relating to the old British Empire; for example, playing cricket and rugby, driving on the left-hand side of the road and enjoying Westminster-style parliamentary democracy. And above and beyond all this, of course, is the English language, which people speak as a first or second language in many parts of the world.

Ruling the Waves: British Overseas Territories

You may not realise it but the British Empire actually still exists in the 21st century. It may not cover huge tracts of the globe and hold hundreds of millions of people in its sway, but some states, called *British Overseas Territories*, are, in essence, still run by the UK.

Fourteen British Overseas Territories exist in total, many of which you may not have heard of: Anguilla, Bermuda (very nice and sunny), British Antarctic Territory (very chilly), British Virgin Islands (no comment), Cayman Islands, the Falkland Islands (their flag has a sheep on it!), Gibraltar (rocky, warm and famous for its monkeys), Montserrat, Pitcairn Islands, Saint Helena, Ascension and Tristan de Cunha, South Georgia and the South Sandwich Islands (tasty place, I hear), the sovereign base areas of Akrotiri and Dhekelia in Cyprus, and, finally, the Turks and Caicos Islands.

In population terms, the British Overseas Territories are tiny. The most populous by far is Bermuda, with around 67,000 people; the smallest is the British Antarctic Territory, which has a dozen scientists and a few million penguins. In fact, if you were to add up the population of all 14 British Overseas Territories, it would come to fewer than 300,000 – around the same size population as Northampton or Stoke!

Why does Britain still retain these territories and furthermore why do the local people still want the Brits hanging around? The simple answer is that Britain wants to retain rights to have military bases in these countries, but also stays out of a sense of responsibility. Many of these countries are so small that they'd find it very hard to survive without the government services and investment that being a part of Britain brings. Many of the people have strong historic ties with Britain. The Falkland Islands, for instance, has fewer than 3,000 people but most of them are descendants of British whalers and emigrant farmers in the 19th century. Plus, people from the Overseas Territories are entitled to full British citizenship, which means that they're allowed to work anywhere in the European Union.

Playing the Role of World Police Officer

Britain may no longer be a world superpower but it's no slouch in the military stakes. It's famous for having well-trained, completely voluntary armed services (many European nations rely on conscription) that can be deployed in trouble spots around the globe in double-quick time. Britain's a key member of NATO and a permanent member of the UN Security Council,

Deterring the unthinkable: Britain and the bomb

One of the reasons the UK is still ranked as a bit of a military powerhouse is that it retains a nuclear deterrent. Through missiles carried on its fleet of nuclear submarines, the UK still has a nuclear strike capability. The full horrors of this power are probably not worth thinking about but the retention of the *nuclear deterrent* was a powerful symbol of Britain's and the West's ability to face potential Soviet aggression in Europe. Britain's nuclear power status was hugely controversial in the 1980s, with peace activists calling for the country to disarm.

Nowadays the Soviet threat no longer exists, yet Britain retains its nuclear weapons capability along with the US, Russia, China, France, Israel, India and, most recently, Pakistan. Why does Britain keep its weapons now that the Soviet Union is no more? Well, the politicians (and most politicians from most parties support Britain keeping its nuclear bombs) say that it's essential for Britain to keep its nuclear weapons in a world where the likes of the tyrannical North Korean regime are making efforts to become fully fledged members of the nuclear club.

which I talk about in the next section. In fact, over the past 20 years the UK has acted as peacekeeper in places as diverse as Bosnia in the Balkans and Sierra Leone in sub-Saharan Africa. The UK has also become embroiled in two bloody wars in Iraq and Afghanistan in support of the US's action in what's been dubbed the 'war on terror' following the 11 September 2001 attacks on the United States.

Under PMs Tony Blair and Gordon Brown, Britain became a leading proponent of helping out poorer nations in the developing world. Both Blair and Brown cajoled other leaders into writing off some African countries' debts, as well as committing more cash in the form of aid and grants to help the poorest nations in the world improve their infrastructure.

Sitting at the Top Table: The UN Security Council

Due to its status as one of the five victorious powers at the end of the Second World War, the UK has a place on the United Nations (UN) Security Council. The Security Council is the muscle behind the UN (an organisation I talk about in detail in Chapter 20). It can deploy peacekeepers and impose sanctions.

Each of the five 'permanent' members – the US, the UK, Russia, China and France – has the power of veto; as a result, the Security Council can only decide on action if the five members are in agreement. Membership of the UN Security Council gives the UK a lot of power in international diplomatic circles.

The power of veto is useful, if rarely used by the UK. Since the UN started in 1947 up until 2007, the UK has vetoed some 32 resolutions out of a total of nearly 2,000. The US, on the other hand, has vetoed 82 and the Soviet Union/Russia 123.

Fifteen members make up the Security Council: the five permanent member countries and ten other nations elected by the full membership of the UN (around 200 countries), each of which remains on the council for two years. These non-permanent members can vote on UN resolutions but have no power of veto.

The UN produces resolutions – about 40 to 50 per year, on average – telling members how they should behave, which can be backed up by military force if the Security Council agrees.

Some suggest reforming the UN Security Council, as its five permanent members reflect the international power politics of the mid-20th century rather than the 21st. To this end, according to some, both the UK and France should lose their permanent status and be replaced by a representative from the European Union. However, unsurprisingly both Britain and France are opposed to this idea and suggest instead that other major powers, such as Brazil and India, should become permanent members of the Security Council – although without the power of veto.

Chapter 20

Taking In the International Stage

In This Chapter

- Establishing the United Nations
- Monitoring financial groups – the G8 and G20
- Forming trading blocs
- Partnering with the World Trade Organisation
- Noting the rise of China
- Joining NATO for military support

You live in a rapidly changing, globalising world. What goes on in neighbouring nations and faraway countries has an impact, both big and small, on your life and the prospects for the UK as a whole. In this chapter, I cast the net far and wide to outline the big international organisations whose actions are helping to shape the world in the 21st century. If you want to know more about the wider world, this is the chapter for you!

Starting at the Top: The United Nations

The United Nations, or UN, as it's most commonly known, is the closest thing the planet has ever had to a world government. No fewer than 193 nations are members of the UN, accounting for some 99 per cent of the population of the globe. Each member state sends its own ambassador and team of diplomats to the UN so that they can meet other diplomats, talk about the shared problems of humankind, and resolve and prevent conflicts – or that's the theory. The great British prime minister Winston Churchill once said that 'to jaw-jaw is better than to war-war' and the UN is the ultimate exercise in 'jaw-jaw'.

The UN was formed at the end of the Second World War – a war that claimed the lives of more than 50 million people. Leaders of the countries involved in the conflict decided that, after such a cataclysm, having an international body where nations could air and debate their views was necessary, and to this end established the United Nations in 1945.

In essence, the UN is supposed to be a force for good in the world, doing its best to prevent war and aid those who are economically disadvantaged, starving or at risk of catching infectious disease.

The UN is an immensely powerful organisation because it expresses the collective will of 193 nations. The moral weight the UN carries gives it a lot of legitimacy. Governments that ignore it or act against its wishes may not survive for long. A government that flies in the face of UN resolutions can find that other nations refuse to trade with it – a process called *sanctions* – or be subject to military action from an international force under the banner of the UN (I talk more about the UN and its military muscle in the upcoming 'The Security Council').

The UN has six official languages: Arabic, Chinese, English, French, Russian and Spanish. All documents are printed in each of these languages. However, ambassadors from member states can use their own language to make speeches because literally hundreds of interpreters work at the UN, translating what each member says.

Among diplomats and politicians you often hear the phrase 'the will of the international community'. More often than not, this phrase refers to the opinions of the UN as expressed through its resolutions. It's a bad idea for governments to go against 'the will of the international community' as this could lead to trade sanctions and even in extreme cases military action.

The UN's headquarters are in New York City, in the United States. Since the end of the Second World War the US has been widely recognised as the most powerful nation in the world, so it's probably appropriate for this international organisation to be based there.

The small plot of land around the HQ of the UN, although located in New York, is actually *international territory*, which means that the US government and local police force have no rights there. The UN headquarters is, in effect, its own state.

Delving into how the UN works

The UN isn't just a talking shop. It has its own civil service, called the UN Secretariat, and a host of satellite organisations through which it works to achieve its aim of facilitating peace and development around the globe. The UN even has its own court – the International Court of Justice – which oversees the trials of people who've committed war crimes or crimes against humanity. The next sections cover the five principal parts of the UN and the role of each in how the organisation works.

The UN has its own constitution called the *UN Charter*, which sets out the jobs of each of the five parts, as well as the role of the UN secretary-general. In addition, the charter sets out certain rights that individuals can expect in relation to how their government treats them, such as the fairly fundamental 'right to life'.

The General Assembly

The *General Assembly* is where all 193 member states meet to discuss world affairs, such as admission or suspension of new member states, whether or not UN members should send food or economic aid to a state, or where one country's border should stop and another one start. Basically, the UN General Assembly can discuss anything that occurs in international politics.

The General Assembly may make recommendations for a course of action after taking a vote and member states are expected to abide by these recommendations. In effect, the General Assembly can tell countries what to do.

Each member state has one vote in the General Assembly, so voting rights aren't weighted in terms of population or economic power. China, with over a billion people and a massive economy, has one vote, and the Cook Islands, with a tiny population and an even smaller economy, has the same.

Usually, the General Assembly needs a two-thirds majority to pass a recommendation, but on some minor matters, a majority of nations voting in favour is enough.

However, the General Assembly doesn't have the right to make recommendations relating to peace and security – when countries are at war or close to war. This is the preserve of the UN Security Council, which I cover in the next section.

The Security Council

The *Security Council* is the body providing the UN's muscle. It's made up of the biggest military and economic powers – as they were in around 1945 – as well as a host of nations voted into their seats by all General Assembly members for a two-year term. The Security Council is important for two reasons:

- It deals with matters of international security and peace. Resolving and preventing conflict was, after all, the main reason for setting up the UN in the first place.
- Whereas the General Assembly can recommend that nations follow a course of action, the Security Council can resolve that they do. The difference lies in the fact that member states can follow a resolution from the Security Council with action. Ignoring a resolution can lead to sanctions and even military action from other member states. In addition, only the Security Council can authorise the deployment of peacekeepers to the world's trouble spots.

Saddam, the UN and WMDs

Back in 2002 the United States and allies such as the UK and Australia got very hot under the collar about Iraqi leader Saddam Hussein. The US said that Hussein was arming his nation with so-called weapons of mass destruction (WMDs).

The UN Security Council had passed a resolution calling on Hussein to allow UN weapons inspectors to check out whether he had any WMDs. After years of fleeting co-operation, UN inspectors concluded that Hussein had questions to answer over WMDs. This conclusion was seized upon by the United States, which used Hussein's widely perceived non-co-operation with a UN resolution as the legal justification for launching a war on Iraq.

Eventually, Hussein was deposed (and subsequently tried and hung for war crimes) but inspectors found no WMDs in Iraq.

Meanwhile, a bloody civil war started in Iraq and many nations not allied to the US argued that what it had done – under the guise of a UN resolution – was illegal. The controversy continues, and more than a decade on Iraq is still riven by internal conflict between different sectarian groups. In 2014, for instance, a huge swathe of northern Iraq fell into the hands of an Islamic militant guerrilla group called IS (Islamic State).

The UK is one of the five permanent members of the UN Security Council – along with France, the US, China and Russia. This gives the UK extra-special powers (no, not the ability to scale tall buildings in one bound or see through walls), including the permanent right to sit on the UN Security Council and to veto resolutions. Only the five permanent members of the UN Security Council have the right of veto, which means they can stop any resolution under discussion.

The power of some of the permanent members – such as France, the UK and, to a lesser extent, Russia – has dwindled since 1945. Some argue that new powerhouse nations, such as India, Brazil, Japan or Germany, should replace the less powerful permanent members. However, none of the 'big five' wants to make way just yet!

A UN resolution is a very big deal. Since 1945, fewer than 2,000 resolutions have been passed and countries are expected to follow them.

The United Nations Charter gives it the power to keep international peace through military intervention if necessary. Now the UN doesn't deploy peacekeepers to every conflict zone; the Security Council normally requires some sort of ceasefire or peace process to already be in place. The role of the troops on the ground is to try to stop war breaking out again and to create the right atmosphere for a lasting peace.

Member states of the UN don't just support it with money and the provision of ambassadors and diplomats; they also supply troops for UN peacekeeping duty when asked. For peacekeeping duties, troops are usually drawn from a host of nations – sometimes as many as two dozen – and the troops obey the orders of a single force commander appointed from the senior military of one of the nations supplying troops. Meanwhile, a representative of the secretary-general, normally a senior world statesperson, takes care of the diplomatic side of the peacekeeping operation.

People often refer to UN peacekeepers as *blue helmets* or *blue berets* after their distinctive headwear.

The UN can't be everywhere and sometimes it asks a regional military organisation such as NATO (see the section 'Providing the Military Might: NATO', later in this chapter) to do the peacekeeping for it. Although UN peacekeepers generally aren't expected to fight, NATO has traditionally taken a more robust role. In the war in Kosovo in the late 1990s, NATO actually went on the offensive against Serbia and its allies in order to ensure eventual peace.

The UN Secretariat

The *UN Secretariat* is effectively the UN's civil service. Its jobs include carrying out studies, providing information and executing administrative tasks for the Security Council and other UN bodies. The Secretariat is expressly charged with meeting the needs of UN bodies and not UN member states. So, for example, a British person working for the UN Secretariat takes his or her instructions from the appropriate UN body rather than the British government.

The UN secretary-general heads up the Secretariat. This post is usually held by an eminent politician from one of the General Assembly's member states. The secretary-general picks Secretariat staff; generally, they're noted civil servants from member governments around the globe.

The UN secretary-general is one of the most important roles in world politics. Not only is the secretary-general in charge of the UN Secretariat and the figurehead of the UN, speaking for the collective will of the General Assembly and Security Council, but he or she's allowed, under the UN charter, to bring matters to the attention of the Security Council for its consideration. The current holder of the post is the former South Korean prime minister Ban Ki-moon.

The Economic and Social Council (ESC)

The *Economic and Social Council* is a group of member states charged with promoting economic and social co-operation and development around the globe. In particular, the ESC's main objectives are as follows:

- Promoting higher standards of living, full employment, and conditions of economic and social progress and development
- Helping to solve international economic, social and global health-care problems
- Encouraging international cultural and educational co-operation as well as respect for human rights

Yes, I know, even just one of the objectives of the ESC is massive. So how does it try to achieve what looks almost impossible? The ESC looks to co-ordinate the work of the main UN agencies (more about these in the upcoming section 'Taking in UN agencies'), governments and even non-governmental organisations (NGOs), such as big international charities, around the globe. The theory is that solutions to really huge problems – such as the spread of HIV/AIDS in the developing world – can only come from nations, charities and UN agencies all working together in a co-ordinated fashion so as to target aid and education. The ESC provides a forum for all these governments, different NGOs and the UN's own agencies to gather and formulate action plans.

The ESC has 54 member states. All the large, powerful nations, such as the US, China, India and Japan, are represented, as are France and the UK. The ESC holds several meetings throughout the year, preparing for a four-week session in July each year. The really big discussions about and decisions on the problems of the world occur at this session.

The International Court of Justice (ICJ)

As the name suggests, the *International Court of Justice* is the legal arm of the United Nations. It's where politicians and military leaders who commit war crimes or crimes against humanity stand trial. The ICJ is located in The Hague in the Netherlands, rather than in New York (where the rest of the UN is headquartered).

The ICJ (or *international criminal court* as it's also known) doesn't sit that often but exists for when wrongdoers are arrested. In part, it's supposed to act as a deterrent, to stop government leaders committing barbarous acts. The most prominent ex-leader recently tried at the ICJ is the Bosnian Serb Radovan Karadžić, accused of committing war crimes in the former Yugoslavia at the end of the 20th century. The case, which began in 2008, is now finally reaching the end, with the defence resting in March 2014.

The ICJ exists to try leaders who've committed terrible acts against their own people or those of other nations. The idea is that any leader thinking of perpetrating such crimes can expect to be brought to justice eventually – if not by his or her own people then by the UN through its court of justice.

Taking in UN agencies

Much of the work of the UN isn't done in New York at the General Assembly or by the Secretariat, but instead by UN agencies. The 17 UN agencies range from low-profile ones dealing with global postal services; to those bringing aid to the world's starving, and promoting better health and education in the developing world; then through to the very big and important World Bank.

Some countries really rely on these UN agencies; in fact, without them it's fair to say that some already troubled nations would slip into absolute chaos. Hunger, illness and acute poverty would present even greater problems than they do already.

The following list contains some of the big UN agencies, many or all of which you may have already heard of in the media:

- **United Nations Scientific and Cultural Organisation (UNESCO):** UNESCO is meant to contribute to peace and security by promoting international collaboration through education, science and culture in order to further universal respect for justice, the rule of law, human rights and fundamental freedoms. To bring extra publicity to its work, UNESCO employs a series of celebrity ambassadors, including actress Angelina Jolie and tennis ace Roger Federer.
- **World Food Programme (WFP):** As the name suggests, the WFP is about feeding people who are starving. It's the biggest of the UN's humanitarian organisations. The WFP is based in Rome and has offices in more than 80 countries. The main job of the WFP is distributing food to people who are suffering from drought or famine. It saves the lives of hundreds of thousands of people each year, and in some years, millions.
- **World Health Organisation (WHO):** The WHO's objective is to combat disease, especially infectious disease – new threats such as H1N1 (swine flu) and SARS, as well as established ones such as malaria – and to promote the general health of the people of the world. As part of its work, WHO organises mass vaccination programmes.
- **World Bank (WB):** This body acts like, well, a bank, making loans to countries for development programmes whose stated goal is to reduce poverty.
- **International Monetary Fund (IMF):** The IMF oversees the global financial system and the economic policies pursued by individual countries. It tries to ensure that governments follow sensible policies – not borrowing money that they can't afford to pay back, for example – and looks to create a global financial system whereby all countries can enjoy growth.

Saving the planet (hopefully): The UN and climate change

One of the most pressing issues facing the world and therefore the UN is climate change and how to confront it. Every reputable scientist agrees that the earth is warming at an alarming rate and that something has to be done to avoid an ecological catastrophe.

Through the Earth Summit in Rio de Janeiro in 1992, the Kyoto Protocol in 1997, the Copenhagen UN Climate Change Summit in 2009 and then another Earth Summit back in Rio in 2012, the leaders of the world's nations have been trying to find a way to reduce carbon emissions and at least halt climate change, if not ultimately reverse it.

In the run-up to such a major international conference, the diplomats from the member nations discuss their relative positions with the objective of reaching final agreement at the conference table.

Many argue that the United States is too powerful within the IMF and World Bank as a result of its government providing much of the finance for the loans and aid distributed by the two organisations.

Bringing Out the Big Guns: The Role of the G8 and the G20

The UN isn't the only big international organisation. Consider also the *G8*, or *Group of Eight*, which started as the Group of Six in 1975 and expanded to its current size in 1997. The G8 encompasses the seven largest world economies of the time, plus Russia.

But times have changed, and in 1999 the *G20*, or *Group of Twenty*, was formed. Composed of finance ministers from the 19 countries with the largest economies, plus the European Union, the G20 seeks to find ways to stabilise the world economy.

The G8 and G20 are, of course, really big deals, but they aren't the only game in town. The World Economic Forum, held in Davos, Switzerland each winter, brings together the shining lights of world business – tycoons, lobbyists, intellectuals, big-name politicians and the small matter of a few thousand journalists. They talk about trends in the world economy, technological development and the environment.

Starting small with the G8

The G8 is made up of seven of the world's biggest economies: Canada, France, Germany, Italy, Japan, the UK and the US. The eighth member (by invitation rather than size of economy) is Russia, but at the time of writing this county is suspended following its annexation of the Crimea in 2014.

The G8 was originally formed to increase economic co-operation and promote growth among member economies, but its role has expanded to include international development (in particular among the world's poorest countries), environmental concerns, international law enforcement and even world health issues.

Unlike the UN, the G8 itself isn't a powerful body – for example, it can't deploy peacekeepers. Instead, it gains its clout from the fact that the member states are the most economically powerful in the world, and the G8 countries agreeing to do something and carrying it through can have a huge influence on global events.

The leaders of the G8 nations – the presidents and prime ministers – take it in turn to be the president of the organisation and to host the annual summer summit. At the summit they discuss a wide variety of topics and formulate common policies that members should pursue, such as cutting global carbon dioxide emissions or forgiving the debts of poorer countries. These summits are a very big deal, with literally thousands of diplomats gathering as well as representatives from other nations, the European Union, and the United Nations and its agencies, such as the World Bank.

In recent years, the three days of the G8 summit have drawn protests from anarchists and anti-capitalist and environmental groups. Sometimes these protests have become violent; at other times, such as the 2005 summit in Gleneagles in the UK, not so much. Gleneagles saw 225,000 people taking to the streets of the nearby city of Edinburgh to urge the G8 leaders to do more to alleviate poverty in Africa.

The G8 isn't just about presidents and prime ministers getting together and having a chinwag every year. Throughout the year the finance and environment ministers of the G8 meet to maintain co-operation between summits.

The G8 is a wealthy club. The eight member states represent some 14 per cent of the world's population but nearly 60 per cent of its wealth. In addition, the G8 nations have military might; £7 out of every £10 spent globally on defence comes from the G8 countries. The G8 is also exclusive. Many commentators question the relevance of the G8, because the giant populations and economies of China, India and Brazil aren't in the club, having to make do with membership of the G20 instead.

Changing times: G8 morphing into G20

The world's altering fast, particularly with the rise of China and India, and all major international organisations are racing to catch up. The G8 may have seven of the largest economies in the world as members but it doesn't have *the* seven largest economies in the world. China, by some measures, has a bigger economy than Japan, and India is racing into the list of the top ten largest economies. Meanwhile, some of the established G8 nations are slipping down the pecking order, with Mexico recently overtaking Italy in terms of economic size.

To deal with these economic shifts, in 1999 the G8 group of nations decided that, instead of the finance ministers of the G8 meeting regularly to decide world economic policy, the finance ministers of the 20 biggest economies in the world should meet. Thus, the G20 was born. Suddenly, countries like Argentina, Indonesia, Saudi Arabia and, of course, India, Brazil and China got a seat at the top table and a say on some of the big issues affecting the world economy. The world financial crisis of late 2008 emphasised the shift of economic power away from the West to the East and the developing world.

The G20 nations account for a staggering two-thirds of the world's population (thanks in no small part to China's inclusion), as well as 85 per cent of the world's wealth.

The G20 concerns itself primarily with economic co-operation and ensuring stability and growth in the world economy; its brief is therefore a lot less wide-ranging than that of the G8.

Looking at the Regional Trading Blocs

Nations that are near each other geographically often do most of their trading with each other. For example, the UK's biggest trading partner isn't the United States or China: it's Germany, which is only a short flight away.

As a result of shared trading interests, the world is divided into trading organisations that look to promote co-operation and free trade in their own parts of the globe. These organisations don't stop at just negotiating trade deals between member states and outside countries; they also often delve into other areas of politics such as shared diplomatic objectives or addressing environmental concerns. In many respects these trading blocs have developed into power blocs; although short of being federal states, they still look to carry members in a similar direction.

The idea's a simple one, if you think about it: in a globalising world, relatively small nations, like the UK, have a better chance of exerting influence on world events through membership of a bloc of countries. Some of the major trading or power blocs are:

- **European Union (EU):** This is the bloc the UK belongs to. Its 28 member states account for 500 million people, with a combined wealth even greater than that of the United States. (See Chapter 21 for the full low-down on the EU.)
- **North American Free Trade Agreement (NAFTA):** This contains Canada, Mexico and the US, and looks to encourage the free movement of goods and people within the three member states.
- **Asia-Pacific Economic Co-operation forum (APEC):** This is the bloc for countries fronting the Pacific Ocean, as the name suggests. A total of 21 member states comprise APEC, including China, Russia and the United States.
- **Cairns Group:** This bloc contains some of the world's leading food producers and exporters rather than nations sharing borders or even an ocean. Argentina, Australia, Brazil and Canada are leading members.

The Chinese government recently stated that it wants to establish a new trade bloc with its relatively near neighbours in Asia, such as Korea and Indonesia.

Factoring in the World Trade Organisation

The World Trade Organisation (WTO) promotes the free movement of goods and services around the globe. It encourages member states (all 151 of them) to abolish or reduce tariffs placed on imports and to stop paying subsidies to their own industries. Negotiations are often mired in controversy, however, and can take a long time; the present round of world trade talks, called the Doha round, for example, has been going on since 2001!

The WTO is the only international agency overseeing world trade and ensuring that every nation sticks to the agreements it's signed up to. When nations are involved in trade disputes – for example, the US is always trying to get the EU to let in more of its beef exports – the WTO judges who's in the right and who's in the wrong. However, the WTO prefers to let nations discuss compromise solutions, which can take years to agree upon.

The WTO can impose trade sanctions on countries that it thinks are breaking the rules and imposing unfair tariffs on imports or subsidising their own industries to give them an unfair advantage. However, sanctions are rare as they tend to damage everyone concerned.

Playing the Power Game: China Taking Over from the United States

According to political scientists, the 20th century was the American century but the 21st century will belong to the Chinese – and it's certainly looking that way!

In the last two decades, the Chinese economy has gone from being mostly agriculturally based to being technologically advanced and producing stunning growth. Some of the statistics emerging from China are amazing: a new power station is built each week; nine cities in the country are more populated than London; 260 million people are under the age of 14 (that's four times the entire population of the UK); and more people now use the Internet there than in the US. China isn't just an arriving world power; it's arrived. It used to be said that 'all roads lead to Rome'; a truer phrase nowadays would be 'all roads lead to China'.

Yet China still has a long way to go to catch up with the old 20th-century superpower, the United States, in terms of wealth and military might. The US spends roughly ten times as much as the Chinese on its military, and car ownership in the US is seven times greater than in China. What's more, the average American enjoys wealth and a standard of living that the average Chinese person can barely dream of. Life expectancy in China is still five years less than in the US. China, though, is undoubtedly flexing its political as well as its economic muscles – and, many believe, at the expense of the West and the US.

Some of the key ways China is trumping the US in the global power politics game include

- Looking to form trading and political blocs with near neighbours and other emerging economies.
- Securing natural resources from African and Arab nations through bilateral trade and aid agreements, sometimes negotiating with regimes that many in the West view as having poor human rights records.
- Stockpiling large amounts of money made through having a substantial trade surplus and using it to buy US government debt. This situation is worrying for some because if China was to sell this debt in a hurry, US government finances could collapse.

Comparing the rise of communist China with that of the world's largest democracy

Many in the West are frankly frightened by the onward march of China, partly because it's not a democratic country. In fact, China is a communist regime (check out Chapter 4 for the full ins and outs of communism), which many in the West abhor. What's more, the Chinese government routinely suppresses civil liberties and is alleged to have carried out atrocities in Tibet. The Chinese state also executes thousands of its own citizens each year for crimes that in some cases would merit only a short prison sentence in the UK.

Against this backdrop, many in the West are looking at the equally stellar growth of the Indian economy for a ray of hope. India – unlike China – is a democracy; in fact, many of its institutions are based on the British model, because it used to be a British colony. Yet, like China, India has a huge population (in excess of one billion) and its economy is growing at a furious rate, particularly in providing services and new technology.

Political scientists may have got things wrong and the 21st century may be the Indian century rather than the Chinese one. If that's the case, many in the West will be mightily relieved.

China is the world's biggest exporter, particularly of manufactured goods, whereas the US is the world's biggest importer. In fact, China enjoys a massive trade surplus with the US – which means that it sells many more goods to the US than it imports from the US.

Providing the Military Might: NATO

The West still has a few cards up its sleeve regardless of the seemingly unstoppable march of China (refer to the preceding section). Led by the United States, the West has by far the strongest and best-equipped military machine in the world, embodied in NATO. The 28 member states in NATO include Canada, France, Germany, Poland, Spain, Turkey, the UK and the US.

Simply put, *NATO (North Atlantic Treaty Organisation)* is a military alliance set up after the Second World War in response to a widely perceived threat from the Soviet Union. This alliance is based on the simple statement that an attack on one NATO state is an attack on all. Three of the member states – France, the UK and the US – can back up this statement with nuclear weapons.

The immediate reason for NATO's existence – the threat from the Soviet Union – disappeared along with the Berlin Wall after 1989 and many questioned whether or not the organisation still had a purpose. However, civil wars in the Balkans in the 1990s highlighted the need for its existence, because it was NATO that eventually imposed peace on the troubled region.

Rather than reducing its membership since the end of the Soviet threat, NATO has in fact increased in size. Many nations that were previously members of the Warsaw Pact – and thus allied to the Soviet Union – are now members of NATO.

More recently, NATO got involved in conflicts outside of Europe and the North Atlantic, most notably in Afghanistan against the Taliban, a group closely allied to the extremists who carried out the 11 September terrorist attacks on the US in 2001.

The UK has been one of the two leading countries in NATO – in terms of military spending – since its inception, but it's the US that supplies most of the troops and money underpinning it.

France has had a difficult relationship with NATO. Former French president Charles de Gaulle actually withdrew the nation's troops from NATO command in 1959, arguing that the US and UK were too powerful. Gradually, though, after de Gaulle's death, the French re-integrated into NATO and their troops now take part in exercises and combat operations when required.

Chapter 21

Expanding Horizons: Europe and the EU

In This Chapter

- Recognising the European Union's importance and its goals
- Building relationships inside and outside the EU
- Agreeing to major EU treaties
- Examining EU budgets

In this chapter, I take you on a tour of the UK's nearest neighbours and look into the inner workings of an institution – the European Union – that has a massive influence on everyday life in the UK. Many say that the UK's future is as part of what amounts to a united states of Europe; others disagree and want the UK to skedaddle out of the EU and go it alone. Read this chapter to get a better idea of what they're going on about.

Understanding the EU and How It Works

The European Union – or EU, as it's known – is an extraordinary institution. It can trace its roots back a couple of centuries to when Tsar Nicholas of Russia talked about a union of European states. More recently, in the 1940s, British wartime prime minister Winston Churchill envisaged a United States of Europe. But these two great leaders could have no idea just how powerful an institution would emerge in the late 20th century when the Europeans – who'd been fighting each other from year dot – finally decided to pull together.

To appreciate why the EU came about you have to understand that its formation came a little over a decade after the end of the Second World War, in 1957. For its originators, the EU was seen as a way of reducing national competition and antagonisms that had so disastrously plunged the continent into war. I talk more about the history of the EU in the nearby sidebar 'Expanding the EU: Six become 28'.

Expanding the EU: Six become 28

The EU has undergone a tremendous transformation in the more than 50 years of its existence, no less than in the number of countries that belong. Originally, six countries signed the Treaty of Rome (1957) that set up the EU – Belgium, France, Germany, Italy, Luxembourg and the Netherlands. But back then the founders scrupulously avoided the U word – union; instead, they called the new organisation the very exciting-sounding European Economic Community (the forerunner, formed in 1951, was called the European Coal and Steel Community – most riveting!). However, the diplomats at the signing said that the Treaty of Rome was 'the first stage in the federation of Europe'. In other words, economic co-operation today, constructing a new state called Europe sometime tomorrow!

The European Economic Community was a roaring success, with member states' economies booming. Soon other states – including the UK – wanted to join. However, the six original members knew they were onto a good thing and took some persuading to let other countries join their now-wealthy club. First up, they allowed Denmark, Ireland and the UK to join in 1973, followed by Greece in 1981, and Spain and Portugal in 1986. In 1995 Austria, Sweden and Finland came in.

But by far the biggest expansion of the EU took place in 2004 when the Czech Republic, Estonia, Hungary, Latvia, Lithuania, Poland, Slovakia and Slovenia came into the EU, as well as the small Mediterranean island states of Cyprus and Malta.

EU expansion hasn't stopped there. Bulgaria and Romania became members in 2007 and Croatia in 2013, and even more countries are trying to join, including Albania, Bosnia and Herzegovina (worth lots of points in a game of Scrabble if you could use proper nouns), Iceland, Macedonia, Serbia and Turkey.

The key facts in the following list highlight just how big a deal the EU is to the UK – which is part of it – and in the wider world:

- The EU encompasses 28 countries from the Russian Steppe in the east, the Arctic Circle in the north, the shores of Africa in the south and the coast of Portugal in the west.
- Up to 500 million people live in the EU member states (compared to the just over 300 million people who live in the United States).
- The economies of the EU combined comprise the biggest economy in the world, bigger even than that of the US.
- The EU may be made up of separate states but citizens across all countries are allowed to work in any state.
- The EU is a huge free trade area, called the *single European market*, with all member states able to sell goods and services to each other free of tariffs or quotas.

- The EU has its own currency, the euro, which most member states trade in. The euro is one of the world's great currencies, rivalling the dollar for the number of transactions carried out using it.

To be able to join the EU, a state must meet the Copenhagen Criteria, named because the European Council agreed upon them in the Danish capital. The criteria say that member states have to respect human rights and the rule of EU law (which I talk about in the upcoming 'Looking at law-making and the legal system'), as well as open their borders to trade and workers. Generally, a country has to be in Europe to be a member of the EU. However, the bulk of Turkey's land mass is in Asia and yet the EU is considering it for membership.

The UK refused to join the EEC (forerunner of the EU) at its inception in 1958 – we really didn't want much to do with those foreigners, don't you know, old chap! – and instead went about forming its own economic club, the European Free Trade Association (EFTA) with nations such as Denmark (5 million people) and Switzerland (7 million people). But some UK politicians realised that EFTA wasn't quite as good as belonging to the EU, which had France and Germany in its ranks, and began negotiations for the UK to join it.

Checking the goals of the EU

European politicians often disagree about the EU's purpose. Some see it as merely a free trade area; others view it as much more a precursor to a United States of Europe. But everyone can agree that the EU looks to achieve some fundamental goals that include:

- Promoting free trade between all member states and the free movement of people to live and work wherever they wish. That freedom of movement is quite a big deal for many people.
- Preventing any member state gaining an unfair trading advantage through its government subsidising domestic industries.
- Ensuring greater harmonisation of national laws relating to business and the consumer.
- Protecting EU businesses from unfair competition from countries outside of the EU.

Jacques Delors, the French politician and former president of the European Commission (see 'The European Commission' a bit later on for more), is widely seen as the spiritual father of *European federalism*: the belief that a United States of Europe should exist. Delors campaigned for closer integration of member states and the establishment of the *euro*, the single European currency. For a while in the early 1990s Delors became a hated figure for some in the British press because he was seen as trying to strong-arm Britain into joining a United States of Europe. Famously, one *Sun* newspaper headline of the time read 'Up Yours Delors', accompanied by a picture of a hand holding up two fingers – most rude!

Examining EU institutions

The EU breaks down into four parts, each with its own role and powers. The following sections cover these parts.

The Council of Europe isn't an EU organisation at all, but a group of 47 European states whose collective objective is to encourage peace, understanding and democracy in Europe.

The European Commission

The European Commission is the executive body of the European Union. This body makes major decisions and draws up laws for consideration by the European parliament and Council of Ministers.

The Commission has 28 members – one for each member state – appointed by their respective governments. Each commissioner fills a specific role and is meant to act in the interests of all member states rather than the nation she hails from. As far as the UK is concerned, commissioners are often senior politicians in the twilight of their political careers. They may have been prominent government ministers in the past but the prime minister has now appointed them to the role of commissioner.

The president's role resembles that of the UK prime minister – orchestrating meetings of the Commission, which in turn works a bit like the UK cabinet. Currently heading the Commission is the former Luxembourg prime minister Jean-Claude Juncker. The election of Juncker in 2014 was highly controversial in the UK. Mr Juncker was seen by prime minister David Cameron as a politician who believed that the EU should move towards closer integration – a United States of Europe. Mr Cameron and most within the Conservative party he leads oppose greater integration and therefore Cameron didn't want Juncker. However, he was in a minority of just two in Europe – with Hungary the only other EU state to side with Britain and oppose Juncker's election – and as a result Mr Juncker got the top job after all.

Here are some of the Commission's major powers:

- Draft EU law.
- Represent the EU at trade negotiations such as those of the World Trade Organisation (refer to Chapter 20 for more on the WTO).
- Develop trade and political strategies for the EU as a whole.

The Commission shares out jobs between the 28 commissioners and their countries. As a rule, the most important jobs go to the commissioners from the biggest countries in the EU – France, Germany, Italy, Spain and the UK. Often countries try to secure the right to appoint a commissioner to a role that suits their national interests. So, for example, the French president may be chosen to decide who's agriculture commissioner, and the British PM may be chosen to appoint the competition commissioner.

The Council of the European Union

Laws and directives drawn up by the European Commission have to go through the Council of the European Union before they actually become law. The Council is made up of representatives from the individual states but they're not meant to remain neutral as commissioners are (see the preceding section); ministers are specifically in place to represent the interests of their member states.

What's more, unlike the egalitarian make-up of the Commission, where each state gets a commission appointee, in the Council of Ministers each country is allocated a block of votes relative to its size. So, for example, the countries with the biggest populations – France, Germany, Italy and the UK – get 29 votes each (which is a little unfair on the Germans because they have by far the highest population) and other countries get fewer votes. For example, Poland gets 27 votes, the Netherlands 13, and tiny Malta (with only 421,000 people) gets 3. Bear in mind, though, that the number of votes isn't completely relative to the population size; it's only a broad approximation, and some of the smaller countries are over-represented and the bigger ones under-represented.

The purpose of assigning these voting blocks is so that the Council can reach a majority and therefore decide to pass or reject laws drawn up by the Commission. But actually the Council doesn't need a majority – nothing's so simple in the convoluted world of the EU. Instead, from 1 November 2014, 55 per cent of the states representing at least 65 per cent of the EU's population have to be in favour for a law to pass. This outcome is catchily called a *qualified majority*. Under this system of voting, no single member state can effectively stop laws on which the others agree.

The representatives of the Council are often senior politicians from the member states, and each country has a representative for each of the big policy areas. For example, the UK has a representative whose speciality is the environment and another who's an expert on trade, and so on. These specialist representatives often meet to thrash out agreements in their individual policy area. Meanwhile, behind the scenes civil servants from the member states carry out much of the negotiating.

The European Council

The European Council is made up from the heads of government from all the member states. It meets at least twice every six months to discuss the major issues affecting the EU, such as its international relations and what future EU treaties will cover.

The European Commission drafts the laws for the EU and the European Council sets the broad framework of policy direction. So, for example, if the European Council says it would like to see closer harmonisation of rules governing trade among EU member states then it's up to the Commission to draft specific laws to see that happens.

In terms of actual powers, the European Council doesn't have many apart from the right to appoint the president of the Commission, which itself is quite significant because it's often the president who sets the agenda for law-making in the EU and acts as its figurehead. But despite having only limited powers, the Council is incredibly important within the structure of the EU because of the authority of the people who attend. They are, after all, the leaders of governments, so what they say – if they agree – usually goes in the EU.

Meetings of the European Council are often dominated by arguments over how the EU is spending its money and whether or not the powers of the EU should expand – inevitably at the expense of the powers of the nation states.

In 2009, under the terms of the Treaty of Lisbon, a new post was created in the EU: the president of the European Union. This is largely a figurehead role. The president is supposed to co-ordinate the work of the European Council and represent the EU at world summits.

The European parliament

Finally, we get to a body that you may be aware of because, lo and behold, you actually get to vote on its membership. Every five years voters from all 28 member states get to choose their Member of the European Parliament (MEP) (refer to Chapter 6 for the lowdown on how this election works).

But what powers does the European parliament actually have, considering that the Commission draws up the laws and the Council of the European Union approves them? Well, the main task of the European parliament is to debate and suggest amendments to the laws that the Commission draws up. The parliament is full of elected representatives – unlike the Commission or Council of the European Union – and when they vote to amend a law or to say that a law shouldn't go ahead, what they say has considerable sway on the debate. After all, to completely ignore the parliament and what it says would be undemocratic.

The powers of the European parliament have grown in recent years. Under the terms of the 1997 Amsterdam Treaty – yes, the EU loves its treaties – the parliament was given 'co-decision' status with the Council of the European

Union. Under the procedure set up in the treaty, the Commission presents a proposal to parliament and the Council that can only become law if both reach agreement. If the two bodies disagree, a conciliation committee – made up of MEPs and councillors – meets to thrash out a compromise. If either body rejects the draft law, it's then up to the Commission to either amend the law and reintroduce it to the Council of the European Union and the European parliament or withdraw it altogether.

Some suggest that the EU is more autocratic than democratic because so much of the law-making power is in the hands of the European commissioners, who are appointed by the governments of the member states rather than directly elected by the people.

Looking at law-making and the legal system

The EU is now much more than a club with members striving for free trade and to promote economic growth. It actually has many of the hallmarks of a state. It has its own parliament, president, courts and even, crucially, laws. (The preceding section, 'Examining EU institutions', covers the various arms of the EU.)

In member states – including the UK – EU law has the same weight (and sometimes more) as laws made by the domestic parliament. In 1986 the UK parliament passed the Single European Act, which in effect provided the green light for EU law to be binding in the UK. At one stroke, laws made by the EU had precedence over laws made by the UK parliament. This was a big day in the history of Britain's unwritten constitution, which I talk about in Chapter 12.

In areas concerning competition and the operation of what's called the *single European market* (in essence, the free movement of goods and people), EU law actually has precedence over domestic laws. So, for example, a law made by the UK parliament that limits the number of cars imported from Germany would be superseded by the EU law that forbids quotas on any goods coming from a fellow member state.

Two main types of EU law exist:

- **Direct effect law:** This comes about when member states sign up to an EU-wide agreement. The terms of the EU agreement supersede any national laws.
- **Directive law:** Under this type of law, basically the EU directs the member states to do something and they then have to alter their own domestic laws in order to conform to the EU directive.

Nearly all EU laws originate with the European Commission, which is made up of representatives from member states.

The EU has an ambassador to the United Nations, and the president of the European Commission attends meetings of the G8 group of nations (discussed in Chapter 20). In addition, the EU has its own flag and, that crucial trapping of nationhood, a national anthem: Beethoven's 'Ode to Joy'.

Getting litigious: The European Court of Justice

Just like a nation state, the EU has its own court system. However, this court system is designed to augment the courts of member states rather than supplant or rival them.

The European Court of Justice (ECJ) is responsible for interpreting EU laws and ensuring consistent application across all 28 member states. If a court in an EU member state is hearing a case that involves EU law, the domestic court asks the ECJ to look at the case and then give a ruling. The domestic court is then bound by the decision of the ECJ.

Protecting human rights in the European Court of Human Rights

The Council of Europe set up the European Court of Human Rights to uphold the European Convention on Human Rights, which sets out basic freedoms that all people in the EU can expect, such as the right to life, liberty and freedom from torture; and the right to a fair trial, privacy and to marry whomever they please.

If an individual feels these freedoms have been contravened, she can take the case to the European Court of Human Rights. However, the person who feels wronged must first have exhausted the legal processes in her own country. The European Court of Human Rights is only ever a last resort and the process of getting a case heard there can be painfully slow.

Forming Relationships Within and Outside the EU

The EU is more than an economic club but slightly less than a fully fledged state. Over time its influence over member states and on the international stage has grown, and whenever major decisions in world politics are being taken a representative of the EU is normally involved. But as well as playing a role at the top table of international politics, the EU is concerned with issues such as expanding its membership, securing natural resources – most particularly oil and gas for its massive industries – and helping ensure peace and security within Europe itself.

Arguing against EU expansion

Some politicians within the EU – particularly in France and Germany – have been less than pleased about its huge expansion in the early years of the 21st century. They have several problems with this expansion, such as

- The new members have voting rights in EU institutions that have diluted the power of the bigger countries, in particular France and Germany, who've been used to getting their own way on some of the big key issues.
- Many of the newer member states are poor and thus a drain on the EU's development and the Common Agricultural Policy budget.
- The migration of people from the poorer new member states to the richer western European states in search of jobs and a better standard of living is worrisome.

Former French president Jacques Chirac, although ultimately accepting expansion of the EU, wasn't particularly happy about it. He famously told the leaders of the new members in 2004 that they needed to get 'better manners' and was furious when they sided with Britain – and against France – over a series of key decisions.

All EU member states have to agree to the entry of a new member state before it can happen. In effect, any member can veto a country trying to enter the EU.

Representatives of the EU – whether they be civil servants or the president of the Commission – are in attendance at the meetings of all the world's main international bodies (such as the UN, G8, World Bank or World Trade Organisation) and major conferences such as those held to discuss climate change.

Looming giant: Russia on the doorstep

The EU's relationship with Russia is a knotty one. Russia was once one of two world superpowers but has now lost this status. However, this giant country, with a population greater than Germany, the UK and the Netherlands combined, is still formidable. Russia has a massive army, limitless natural resources and a difficult history with western Europe, having been invaded by the Germans, the British, the Turks, the Swedes and the French over the past couple of centuries. In the aftermath of the Second World War Russia controlled eastern Europe through installing a series of brutal puppet regimes, and for 40-odd years squared up to the North Atlantic Treaty Organisation (NATO) in what's known as the Cold War. In short, plenty of history exists between Russia and the countries of the EU.

But the simple truth is that the EU needs good relations with modern Russia because it happens to be one of the most oil- and gas-rich countries on earth. Russia has massive pipelines carrying gas from east to west, and if it cut off energy supplies, most of western Europe would be plunged into darkness. But Russia needs the EU too, because the money it earns from the economies of western Europe is of huge importance to its economy and government.

Many fear, though, that Russia will use the fact that the EU is so dependent on the energy it supplies as a means to exert political pressure – and, frankly, Russia would be a mug if it didn't, at least in some ways. As a result, some members of the EU – most notably Germany – have tried to forge good relations with the Russian government. Meanwhile, the UK, which is seen as close to the US diplomatically and is less reliant on Russian energy, has what people widely deem to be poor relations with the government of Russia.

Testing question: Is Turkey really part of Europe?

The question of Turkey is perplexing many leading EU politicians. Put simply, Turkey would love to join the EU, and some countries, such as the UK, are quite happy for it to do so. However, other countries – most notably France – are worried that Turkish entry into the EU would change the EU for the worse. These are some of the reasons given for not allowing Turkey entry into the EU:

- Turkey is poor compared to most of the EU nations; it also has a massive population in excess of any member of the EU.
- Turkish agriculture isn't very advanced compared to the EU; as a result, the country may be a major drain on the resources of the Common Agricultural Policy budget.
- Turkey is a Muslim country and the EU is made up of ostensibly Christian states; some suggest this would alter the character of the EU.
- Turkey is actually geographically in Asia rather than Europe.
- For many years Turkey has had a poor human rights record and its government stands accused of mistreating its Kurdish minority.
- Turkey is in disagreement with Cyprus over the existence of a separate Turkish-backed state in the north of the island.

The anti-Turkey lobby raises quite a few issues, but some very good reasons also exist for allowing Turkish entry; some of these simply involve seeing the negatives (as perceived by entry opponents) as opportunities:

- Turkey is huge and presents a great development opportunity and export market for EU goods and services.

- Accepting a predominantly Muslim country as a member of the EU will help build bridges with the Islamic world and promote peace.
- Although part of Asia, Turkey has always played an important role in European affairs and many of its institutions are more European than Asiatic.
- Turkey's human rights record has improved, as have recognition of individual liberties and freedom of the press, and many suggest the improvement is because the Turkish government seeks EU entry.

Bringing peace to the Balkans

Fighting in the Balkans region of Europe ended late in the 1990s, but the images of ethnic cleansing and bombing of civilians scars Europe's collective consciousness well into the 21st century.

The peace process in the Balkans has seen the gradual break-up of the old Yugoslav state and greater autonomy for the Croats and Bosnian Muslims from the majority Serbs. These changes are due in no small part to the diplomatic efforts of the EU – backed up with the military stick of NATO.

The EU exerted pressure not just through its economic might and the fact that its members – most notably Britain and France – are strong military powers, but also by offering the long-term carrot of eventual membership in the EU to those countries that follow the path to peace.

In the 1990s Serbia, for example, was effectively at war with NATO and the militias it supported had perpetrated the worst war crimes seen in the European continent since the end of the Second World War. Nowadays, the Serb government no longer backs these militias, has handed over war criminals responsible for brutality and wants eventually to become a member of the EU.

The EU doesn't have a standing army but many of its states are also members of NATO, which is the most powerful military machine in the world.

Pigging out: Financial crisis causes fault lines in EU

For much of its existence, the EU has been widely seen as helping the poorer nations of southern and eastern Europe develop. Grants of money and the economic and political stability that EU membership brings have helped countries like Spain, Italy, Portugal and Greece improve their infrastructure and economic performance.

But then came the great financial crash of 2008, and the likes of Portugal, Italy, Greece and Spain got into such huge economic trouble that they were unflatteringly dubbed the *PIGS* by some wealthier northern European countries within the EU.

Unemployment shot up in all the PIGS to levels not seen since the Great Depression of the 1930s. The German government, which has the biggest purse in the EU, insisted on massive cuts to government spending in the PIGS before they received any financial help. The governments imposed austerity measures and put the economies of the PIGS on the straight and narrow. But people in all the PIGS were angered – Greeks, for instance, burned effigies of the German chancellor (the equivalent of the UK prime minister) Angela Merkel in the street – and the resentment bred by this clash between north and south in the EU may take a generation to get over!

All the PIGS were member of the euro currency, which meant that much of the financial aid they received in the years following 2008 came from the European Central Bank (ECB). But in reality the ECB itself is effectively supported by the German government.

Understanding Britain's thorny relationship with the EU

The UK may have been a member of the EU for over 40 years (it joined in 1973) but its relationship with other members has at times been strained. In fact, things got so bad in the early 1990s that some politicians from other EU states suggested that the UK should leave. However, doing so was never a serious possibility.

At the heart of the UK's problems with the EU has been a difference in vision of what the EU should be about. Put simply, most British politicians and political parties would like to see the EU remain purely concerned with promoting free trade and movement of people. Yet some EU states – most notably Germany, the Netherlands, Belgium and Luxembourg – have a drive to change the EU from an economic union of states into an actual political union of states – a United States of Europe. These politicians, called *federalists*, would like to see member state governments become subservient to an overarching pan-European government. For these people, the EU isn't an end in itself but a means to an end – a staging post along the way to a European super-state.

In the UK many people are opposed to the EU gaining more powers and having further influence over British life. These people are generally referred to as *Eurosceptics*.

The two major UK political parties – Labour and Conservative – may both have had their spats with other EU members, but ultimately they believe that the UK is better off within the EU. From a purely financial viewpoint, the vast majority of UK exports are bought by other EU members.

But the word *Brexit* has entered the UK vocabulary. It doesn't refer to a new type of breakfast cereal, but is a merging of the words *Britain* and *exit*, and describes the growing possibility that in the near future Britain will exit the European Union.

The rise in popularity of the UK Independence Party (UKIP) – which wants Britain to withdraw from the EU – has led to a sea change in British politics over future relations with the EU. Many in the UK don't like the idea of a United States of Europe and would like to see powers that the UK has surrendered to the EU repatriated to the UK. Some, such as UK prime minister David Cameron, believe in negotiation to recover powers; others, such as UKIP leader Nigel Farage, believe that only by Brexit will the UK be truly free to decide on its own affairs once again.

Table 21-1 shows that strong arguments exist on both sides of the Brexit debate.

Table 21-1 Brexit Pros and Cons

Reasons for Brexit	*Reasons for Remaining in the EU*
UK parliament is top dog once again and laws made by EU institutions are irrelevant.	The EU is the UK's biggest export market so laws that apply in the EU still affect it, but Brexit means the UK has no say in those laws.
The UK no longer has to contribute to EU budgets, a saving of billions of pounds per year.	The UK may no longer have to pay towards the running costs of the EU but it also no longer benefits from development grants.
The UK will be free to negotiate its own trade deals, rather than being bound by EU-wide trade agreements that in some cases harm British business.	The UK is relatively small (accounting for roughly 4 per cent of the global economy) and may find it tough to negotiate advantageous trade agreements on its own.

The Conservative party, under the leadership of David Cameron, has promised a referendum in 2017 on whether the UK should withdraw from the EU. This referendum is now enshrined in UK law so it has to take place, unless of course parliament repeals the law.

Putting Pen to Paper: Major European Treaties

The EU should have a 'work in progress' sign above its door because although it's more than 50 years old it seems to be forever changing. The biggest changes have been brought about by an expansion of membership – from 6 to 28 members in less than 60 years. Meanwhile, the wider world hasn't stood still, with trading blocs rising across the globe (check out Chapter 20 for more on these) and, of course, the massive economic and political progress of China and India. Against such a backdrop and adding in new global challenges, such as tackling climate change and poverty among the nations of the developing world, it's understandable that the EU seems to be forever examining itself, its institutions, how it does business and its relationships with member states.

This self-examination has led to the creation of a series of key treaties that have resulted in profound changes to the EU and, indirectly, Britain's relationship with it.

A rundown of the big European treaties and what they've meant in practice follows:

- **Maastricht (1992):** This treaty paved the way for the creation of a single European currency called the euro (see the nearby sidebar 'One currency to fit all'). In addition, the treaty increased judicial co-operation between states, set out some key social rights for citizens of member states (such as not being forced to work long hours) and got member states to work towards forming a single EU foreign policy rather than each state pursuing its own agenda on the world stage. The Maastricht Treaty was seen as a victory for those who supported the idea of a federal European super-state.

  The negotiations before the signing of the Maastricht Treaty were highly controversial in the UK. The UK government at the time – led by the Conservative prime minister John Major – demanded and won opt-outs from the social rights part of the treaty and the move towards a single European currency. When Tony Blair's Labour Party swept to power in 1997, it dropped the opt-out on social rights but chose to remain out of the single currency; the UK thus still has its own currency – the pound – whereas most countries in the EU use the euro.

- **Amsterdam (1999):** This treaty looked to inject a little more democracy into the EU law-making process. The European parliament, with its elected members, gained more rights to approve or block laws drawn up by the European Commission. The terms of this key treaty also guaranteed the free movement of people within the EU.

- **Nice (2004):** This treaty was all about reforming the institutions of the EU to cope with the ultimate expansion of membership to 27 states. Seats on the Council of Ministers and in the European parliament were redistributed.
- **Lisbon (2007):** More powers for the European parliament and a tweaking of how voting in the Council of the European Union would work were two of the administration highlights of this treaty. In addition, a charter of fundamental rights – a bit like the Human Rights Act – was made binding on all member states. The treaty also set up the post of a new European Union president, which was first taken up in 2009. This treaty was ratified by all member states in late 2009.

Just because a government signs an EU treaty doesn't make it law. In most member states the domestic parliament has to *ratify* – debate and vote upon – the treaty before it's actually made into law. An EU treaty only comes into law across the EU if every member state ratifies it.

Holding the Purse Strings: EU Budgets

Just as in many a marriage, some of the biggest tear-ups in EU history have boiled down to one subject – money. Under EU rules, each member pays a levy roughly proportionate to the size of its economy and this money is then collected together to pay for the following:

- Bureaucracy – the EU civil service
- MEPs' pay and expenses
- The Common Agricultural Policy
- Grants to member states to help fund infrastructure projects
- Grants to help areas of member states suffering severe economic deprivation

Arguments arise when member states meet to discuss who should be paying what into the EU. The German government, for example, gets back only half of what it contributes in terms of grants and payments under the Common Agricultural Policy. On the other hand, Poland gets around four euros for each one it contributes to the EU budget. Little Luxembourg does best, though, getting around five times as much as it pays in, and that's one of the richest countries – measured in euros per head of population – in Europe. Go figure!

The Council of the European Union and the European parliament set the EU's budget each year. The Council gets to set the budget for the Common Agricultural Policy (explained in the next section). The parliament decides other expenditures, such as grants to member states to improve infrastructure or for job creation schemes in deprived areas. The Council and parliament draw up their budget estimates and the Commission consolidates them into a draft EU budget. Both the Council of the European Union and the parliament can amend it and then both bodies have to approve this final budget.

Accounting for the Common Agricultural Policy

Nearly half of all the money the EU spends goes towards carrying out the *Common Agricultural Policy (CAP)*. To understand why agricultural policy is so important, you have to go back to the aftermath of the Second World War when much of Europe was starving. Many leading politicians in France and Germany decided that making sure that Europe could feed itself in future should be a key objective of the EU. They didn't care whether the EU achieved this goal through direct aid from the EU or by raising tariffs on imported food. As a result, the CAP was born. This policy guarantees EU farmers a minimum price for their crops, while preserving the rural heritage of the EU.

With the promise of the EU buying their products even if the consumer didn't want them, EU farmers just produced more and more. In the 1980s the CAP was brought into disrepute when the EU purchased and stockpiled unused foodstuffs – dubbed 'the butter mountain' and 'the wine lake' by the British press. At the same time, an offshoot of the CAP, called the *Common Fisheries Policy*, was causing controversy because it was leading to the large-scale decommissioning of fleets in Scotland.

In recent years, though, the CAP has started to change, with farmers in the nations that joined the EU in 2004 benefiting from subsidies and investment to modernise their agriculture. However, among many British politicians CAP is still a byword for waste and protectionism.

Getting a rebate

Compared to the amount of money that member state governments spend each year, the EU is quite frugal. In 2013, for instance, it spent less than 10 per cent of what the UK government spent that year.

Each year the UK gets a rebate on its contributions to the EU because it has a small agricultural sector that receives limited sums from the EU. Yet, as one of the biggest economies in the EU, the UK has to stump up billions of pounds in contributions. The UK's rebate is a way of trying to redress the balance. Basically, the UK makes its contributions to the EU and then receives money back in the form of aid. At the end of the year the EU works out how much the UK has given and how much the EU has spent on the UK. The UK then receives a rebate based on this difference. The rebate is calculated as approximately two thirds of the amount by which UK payments into the EU exceed EU expenditure returning to the UK. The retention of the rebate has caused several arguments at meetings of heads of state in the past, particularly with the French!

One currency to fit all

No world economic power would be complete without its own currency. And guess what? The EU has its own currency – the euro – which you've probably used if you've holidayed on the continent in the past few years.

The euro is currency across 18 of the EU's 28 member states and all the big nations in the EU (excluding Britain) use it. In fact, a grand total of 350 million out of the EU's 500 million inhabitants use the euro.

Internationally, the euro has proved a big hit in a relatively short period of time; only the US dollar is used in more transactions across the globe. However, the new super-currency soon ran into difficulties. The 2008 global financial crisis left many countries in the Eurozone and four in particular – Portugal, Italy, Greece and Spain (unflatteringly called the PIGS) – in an economic mess. Millions of people lost their jobs and the PIGS plus the likes of Ireland had to ask the European Central Bank (which sets interest rates for the Eurozone) for cash. Many economists argued that if these countries still had their own currencies and were able to set their own interest rates they'd have avoided much of the pain of the financial crash. Some even speculated that the euro currency could collapse, but this never came to pass – no bad thing because the consequences of a currency crash can be devastating on an economy. Nevertheless, the shiny promise of the euro currency seems a little tarnished.

Chapter 22

Leading the Free World: US Politics

In This Chapter

- Charting the US's influence in the UK and around the world
- Focusing on how the US government works
- Getting laws passed in the US
- Judging disputes: the work of the Supreme Court
- Looking at political parties and influences

The United States is the only superpower in the world at the moment. Although some argue that the US is in decline, it's still at the heart of international politics. Ask any British politician which relationship is most important to the UK and he'll answer 'the United States'. No understanding of the wider world, and for that matter Britain's place within it, is possible without knowledge of the inner workings of the US political system, from the role of Congress and the Supreme Court to that of the president, unarguably the planet's number-one politico.

If you want to know more about the premier nation in the world and why so often what the president says goes, this is the chapter for you.

Understanding US Influence in the Wider World and in the UK

Whatever the critics of America say – and plenty of those exist, even in a friendly country like the UK – it's still the number-one democratic nation in the world. Despite the rise of China, the US is also the number-one economy, with the most widely used currency – the dollar – in the world. In fact, the scale of America's wealth and influence around the globe is difficult to overestimate.

Here are some of the keys to America's dominance on the world stage:

- **Military might:** The US has the most expensively equipped and best-trained military in the world. In brutal terms it's top dog at making war and this fact guarantees huge influence.

  For example, if the US threatens military intervention in one of the world's trouble spots, generally the warring parties sit up and take notice. The US armed forces are probably the only military capable of placing huge numbers of troops on the ground virtually anywhere around the globe in a matter of weeks. In essence, the US carries an awfully big military stick around with it and that spells power.
- **Cultural output:** Been to the cinema lately or turned on a music radio station? Well, if you did, you probably had a taste of American culture. US culture dominates the planet, with teenagers and adults around the globe – from China to Chile – wanting a little slice of the American way of life. Their news channels and television programmes inform debate around the world. American actors, artists and even politicians are widely known, demonstrating that the US is still the pre-eminent cultural influence on the planet.
- **Economic powerhouse:** The military and cultural might of the US is probably nothing compared to its economic influence. US businesses employ millions all over the world and are involved in securing natural resources and marketing their wares on a global scale. What's more, the American consumer is responsible for huge wealth generation. Without the seemingly insatiable desire among Americans for cheap manufactured goods, no Chinese economic miracle would be underway.
- **Technological leadership:** The US undoubtedly has a disproportionate number of great academic institutions that have helped produce some of the key advances in technology over the past few decades. From the Internet to successful pharmaceuticals to the iPod, the US is the world's biggest technological power. In fact, its military and private-sector research and development are several years ahead of even those of western Europe and China. This situation gives the US a lead when designing new products to sell globally. People often say that what's happening in the US this year will happen in the UK the next, highlighting just how advanced the good old US of A actually is!

The US has a population of around 300 million, making it the third most populous nation in the world behind India and China. It's also the fourth largest by size behind Russia, Canada and (only just) China.

People often refer to the president of the United States as the most important person in the world, and the long, drawn-out US election process often attracts huge global media coverage. For example, the election of the US's first black president, Barack Obama, in 2008 sparked intense interest around the world. On a visit to Germany, Obama spoke to a crowd of over 100,000 people in Berlin. This phenomenon was dubbed Obama-mania and he was portrayed by some commentators – particularly in western Europe – as the saviour of America's reputation in the wider world.

Being buddies: The US–UK special relationship

The phrase *special relationship* was coined by the British wartime PM Winston Churchill in 1946. Churchill, who I cover in detail in Chapter 23, was himself half-American and had just spent four years working closely with two US presidents helping beat Nazi Germany, so he had personal reasons to big-up the US–UK relationship.

But the special relationship phrase struck at a truth. The two countries share a common language, a lot of history and a very similar culture. In fact, the British often refer to the Americans as 'cousins', emphasising this closeness.

But the special relationship isn't all about being misty-eyed and chummy; the two nations' governments have, since the end of the Second World War, often held similar foreign policy objectives and their intelligence and armed services work very closely together.

Some of the key reasons the special relationship between the UK and the US is still alive and kicking more than half a century after it was recognised include

- **Military alliances:** And I'm not just talking Second World War here; in fact, US and UK troops have fought side by side in lots of major conflicts in the past 60 years, including the Korean War in the 1950s, two wars in Iraq and, most recently, in Afghanistan.

  The US and UK are both members of the North Atlantic Treaty Organisation (NATO), which was set up in 1949 to defend Europe from Soviet invasion, and of the United Nations Security Council. (Chapter 20 has more on these important international bodies.)

- **Cultural links:** I could write a whole book on the cultural links between the two countries. In music, literature, advertising, television and even blogging, the common language and shared cultural experience mean that American and British citizens often see the world through the same prism.

- **Common values:** Both the US and UK are democracies. In fact, they're two of the oldest democratic nations in the world. In addition, both have a long history of respecting individual liberty and free speech. These values may seem the norm to you, but for most people around the world free speech and democracy are either alien or relatively new concepts. These common values between the US and UK deepen and widen the specialness of their relationship.

Growing apart? Recent problems with the special relationship

Not everything's rosy in the US–UK garden. In recent years the political and even cultural links between the two countries seem to be getting less pronounced. Some say that the special relationship isn't so, well, special any more.

Some reasons the special relationship between the UK and US may be in trouble are

- **War in Iraq:** The US-led invasion of Iraq in 2003 was hugely controversial around the globe. Many saw it as an illegal and aggressive war waged on the admittedly despotic regime of Saddam Hussein. The decision by UK prime minister Tony Blair to follow the US into Iraq was very unpopular among the British people. Overall, the Iraq war and the subsequent retaliation by Islamic militants led many in the UK to question the special relationship and the motives of the US.
- **Population change in the US:** Much of the special relationship is based on use of a common language, yet the US population is changing and a large proportion of people in America now speak Spanish as a first language. In fact, some suggest that within 50 years more people will speak Spanish than English. This situation is bound to weaken one of the key bonds between the two countries.
- **Growing bonds between the UK and Europe:** The UK is very much a key player in the European Union (EU) these days (refer to Chapter 21 for more). This means that much of the UK's trade and diplomacy is with near neighbours like France and Germany rather than with the US. As a result, although still hugely important, the strong ties with the US are no longer as crucial to the UK economy as they once were.
- **Rise of China:** On the flip side, the UK is no longer as important a trading and economic partner to the US either. In fact, the US takes most of its imports from China, the rising superpower in the East. The government in Washington sees its relationship with Beijing as far more important than the one with London or, for that matter, western Europe.

- **Trade disputes:** The UK and US are now in opposing economic blocs, which I talk more about in Chapter 20. The UK is a part of the EU and the US signed the North American Free Trade Agreement. These blocs are in constant dispute over the imposition of import tariffs and paying of subsidies, which is bound to loosen the bonds between the US and UK.

Such was the level of support shown by Tony Blair for America's policies in Iraq and Afghanistan in the early 2000s that he was referred to by political opponents in the UK and even internationally as America's poodle – hardly a flattering image for a British prime minister. That fact has affected relations ever since: British prime ministers no longer see it as electorally beneficial to be the bosom buddy of the US president.

Looking at the US System of Government

The US national anthem, 'The Star-Spangled Banner', refers to America as the 'land of the free' and this is how millions around the globe see the place. Much of the positive press the US receives has its roots in what's widely seen as the nation's strong democracy. But backing up this democracy is one of the most famous documents in the world – the US Constitution.

The American War of Independence eventually gave birth to the world's first written constitution – oddly enough called the US Constitution – which was adopted in 1787. The Constitution lays out what all the branches of American government do and lists their individual powers, as well as setting out the relationship between the government and the citizens it serves.

The US Constitution is alterable, and in fact has been amended 27 times. The first ten amendments were added when the ink on the Constitution was barely dry. Those first ten amendments are called the Bill of Rights and they set forth civil liberties such as freedom of speech, association and the press. The amendment process isn't one to be undertaken lightly or quickly. Two thirds of the members of both houses of Congress may propose an amendment, and then three quarters of state legislatures must ratify it. Alternatively, two thirds of state legislatures can call for a constitutional convention to consider an amendment, which three quarters of the state legislatures must then ratify. So far, all amendments have been passed using the first method.

The US Constitution is a very valuable and precious document and is kept under lock and key. The next sections offer a basic rundown of what's in it and the institutions of governance it establishes.

Starting off by breaking with the British

It's a little hard to believe that the most powerful nation in the world was once a colony of farmers, fur traders and merchants ruled by the British Empire. However, a little over two and a quarter centuries ago that's exactly what the United States was.

Several countries had a go at colonising the North American continent – the French, the Spanish and even the Russians – but it was the settlers from the UK that made the biggest impact. From a few boats full of settlers in the early 17th century, the American colony grew until it rivalled the UK in terms of population and wealth.

At that point, the relationship changed. Unhappy with the way they were governed – and taxed – from London, the American colonists revolted, and after a long, bloody and humiliating war (from Britain's perspective), the American colonists gained their independence from the UK and the United States of America was born.

George Washington isn't just a great figure, he's probably *the* greatest figure in American history. He was the general who led the American forces in their victory over the British (after escaping death and defeat several times). He was also America's first president, and you find a picture of him in nearly all American schools, as well as on the one-dollar note. George Washington's a massive figure state-side; his face is even carved into the rock of Mount Rushmore.

British – American relations took a long time to improve after the War of Independence. In fact, the two countries were at war again in 1812, during which British troops burned down the White House. Later down the line, during the American Civil War, the British supported the Confederate states in the south, who were eventually defeated by the Unionist northern states. And in the last century, 1931 to be precise, US President Hoover drew up plans for a naval war with Britain following trade disputes between the two nations.

Building the houses of Congress

The US Congress is made up of two elected chambers: the House of Representatives and the Senate.

The 435 members of the House of Representatives each represent a district in an individual state – like a constituency in the UK – and serve a two-year term. The House is meant to be directly responsive to the people.

Each of the 50 states elects two senators. The Senate is supposed to be a more deliberative body than the House, and senators serve six-year terms, with the idea that they'll be less influenced by the whims of popular opinion and more forward-looking.

Elections to the US Senate are staggered so that one third of the membership stands for election every two years. So, for example, in 2016 a third of all senators will stand for election and in 2018 another third and in 2020 another third. In 2022 the senators who were elected in 2016 will have to stand for re-election and in 2024 the ones who were elected in 2018 will face the voters again, and so on.

Congress has the power to

- Levy taxes and authorise the government's budget
- Make laws
- Declare war
- Issue patents and copyright and set weights and measures (it may not sound as big as the other three but this power has a huge impact on everyday life!)

Members of Congress introduce new bills – which are in effect proposed changes to the law. Often laws are proposed at the behest of America's powerful lobbying groups (I discuss how pressure groups work in the UK in Chapter 9). A staggering 40,000 lobbyists are active in Washington alone, which works out to around 75 lobbyists for every member of Congress.

Because of its power to veto presidential appointments and treaties, the Senate is considered the more powerful of the two houses of Congress.

Establishing the presidency

The head honcho, the main man, the *numero uno*, the big cheese; however you want to describe the president of the United States, one thing's for sure: no job in the world is bigger.

Under the US Constitution, the president has the power to

- Appoint a cabinet to head up US government ministries (called agencies or departments in the US).
- Appoint justices to the Supreme Court (see the upcoming 'Judging disputes: The US Supreme Court' for more on this body).
- Enter into international treaties, with Senate approval.
- Act as commander-in-chief of the armed forces. In wartime the president has final say over strategy.

- Veto laws passed by Congress.
- Grant pardons or reprieves to people who've been convicted of crimes or those facing trial for an offence.

Congress, not the president, has the power to declare war, but as commander-in-chief of the armed services, the president has the power to send troops into military conflict for up to 60 days before having to get Congress's permission. So, in effect, the president has the power to make war.

Only the president gets to nominate cabinet members and top judges, but all appointments have to be 'with the advice and consent' of the US Senate. The president says who he'd like for a particular job and then the Senate discusses and ratifies that appointment, normally with senior senators sitting as a committee to interview the president's candidate.

Treaties negotiated by the president must be ratified by a two-thirds majority vote in the Senate to take effect.

Since the US Constitution was amended in 1951 (after Franklin D. Roosevelt was elected president four times), the president can only be elected to two, four-year terms of office.

Exploring the mystique and power of the presidency

The president may have plenty of powers under the US Constitution, but it's more than that which gives the person who works from the Oval Office of the White House in Washington a mystique and aura quite unlike that surrounding any other high office in world politics.

The US president has such a hold on international attention because

- The president is the head of state – in effect, the embodiment of America internationally.
- The president's role of commander-in-chief puts him in charge of the most powerful military in the world.

It may be helpful to think of the president as a combination of the UK prime minister and the UK monarch – a head of state and the pre-eminent politician rolled into one.

The president may only have the power to veto bills from Congress but in reality he'll often get a friend or party ally in Congress to introduce a bill he'd like to see become law. In effect, the president has the right to introduce bills to Congress but they have to go through the same consideration process as any other bill.

Electing a president

The election of a president of the United States every four years is always a big deal and an exhaustive process. Long before election day, leading politicians from each of the two main political parties – Republican and Democratic – compete in a series of state elections called *primaries*, in which mostly party members vote. Candidates win a certain number of votes from each primary, which convert to votes for that candidate at the party's convention, held in late summer. The votes of each candidate are totted up and whoever has the most is declared winner. That individual then becomes the party's presidential candidate at the subsequent nationwide election in November.

On election day itself, voters in each state have a choice between the two party candidates, and sometimes a third-party candidate if he can qualify to get on the ballot. Unlike in the primaries, the candidate who receives the most votes in a state wins all that state's electoral college votes. (This is a process established by the Founding Fathers whereby representatives of each state are given a vote as to who should be President.) So, for example, whoever polls the most votes in Florida wins that state and gets to take all the votes for that state in the electoral college, regardless of the size of the actual victory margin. Electoral college votes are awarded according to a state's population, so the more populous states come with more electoral college votes.

At the end of the night, all the electoral college votes collected by the candidate are totted up, and whoever has the greatest number is declared the winner and will be the next president of the United States.

Exploring presidential perks and perils

The president has his own private jet aircraft called Air Force One, which is no small two-seater, but a jumbo jet the size of a commercial airliner. Why so big? Well, this plane is supposed to be a working office for the president that can house dozens of staff members and, of course, provide a safe haven in case of war. The idea is that in times of crisis the president can be safe from harm on Air Force One so that the government still has a leader.

The goodies don't stop with a plane. The president has access to a huge nuclear bunker and a country retreat called Camp David. Camp David doesn't involve tents and queuing at the shower block but is a luxurious property where the president can entertain world leaders and get away from it all. The prime minister in the UK has something similar – although a lot smaller – called Chequers.

The job of president of the United States isn't a particularly safe one, and I don't just mean there's a danger of getting thrown out of office. In total, the US has had 44 presidents since the first, George Washington. Of these, four – Abraham Lincoln, James A. Garfield, William McKinley and John F. Kennedy –

have been assassinated while in office. President Ronald Reagan managed to survive being shot in an assassination attempt in the early 1980s. Perhaps one of the first things a newly elected president should do is call a life insurance broker!

The president has a vice – no, not drinking too much or being over-friendly with the opposite sex (although quite a few past presidents have done both!) – but a vice president; in effect, a deputy. The vice president advises and campaigns at election time with the president, and should the president no longer be able to serve, the vice president steps into the breach and becomes president until the end of the four-year term of office.

Looking at great US presidents

The United States has had good, bad, mediocre and even great presidents. Here's a look at some of the real stars of the Oval Office:

- **Thomas Jefferson (1801–09):** The third president of the United States and principal author of the Declaration of Independence wasn't just a president but also a great political thinker, horticulturist, architect, archaeologist and even palaeontologist. He was very much in favour of allowing individual states to get on with their own affairs without too much interference from the federal government in Washington. He also cut taxes, added the state of Louisiana to the US and made importing slaves into the US illegal.
- **Abraham Lincoln (1861–65):** The giant 16th president of the US led the victory of the northern states (called the Union) over the Confederate southern states in the bloody American Civil War. He reformed taxes and the army, made some incredible political speeches and, crucially, declared the abolition of slavery. He was assassinated by John Wilkes Booth on a night out at the theatre in 1865.
- **Franklin D. Roosevelt (1933–45):** Another wartime president, this time the Second World War, this polio-struck president was elected in the midst of the Great Depression and his economic 'New Deal' programme is often seen as crucial in helping to alleviate terrible poverty and unemployment in the 1930s. In wartime he led the US very ably against Nazi Germany and Imperial Japan until his death in 1945.
- **John F. Kennedy (1961–63):** Often simply JFK, Kennedy was one of the most iconic of presidents. Youthful, good-looking and charming, he seemed to have everything. He was elected in a narrow victory in 1960 but proceeded to inspire the nation with great speech-making and by facing down the Russians over the Cuban missile crisis. He set the country on course for its successful moon landings. His assassination in 1963 shocked the world and gave him an added aura of potential cruelly denied. In public opinion polls Kennedy consistently emerges as one of the great presidents.

Impeaching the president

The president may be the most powerful politician in the world but that doesn't mean that he can do anything he wants. The US Constitution was designed specifically to prevent the rise of a tyrannical figure – like Stalin in Russia or Hitler in Germany – as president. The system has inbuilt checks on the power of the president, such as only the houses of Congress being able to make laws and wars requiring their approval. And then, of course, a series of individual citizen rights is set out in the Constitution.

Congress's ultimate check on the president is the power of impeachment. *Impeachment* is the removal from public office of the president or other official on the grounds that he's acted unlawfully in some way.

In an impeachment proceeding, a committee of the House of Representatives passes, by majority vote, articles of impeachment. In effect, articles are just like charges of a crime. The full House of Representatives then holds hearings to investigate the claims of the articles of impeachment. If a simple majority of House members votes for impeachment, the trial moves to the Senate. To convict, the Senate requires a two-thirds majority. If impeached, the president is, well, no longer the president. The job then falls to the vice president, who serves the remainder of the four-year term of office.

Impeachment is a very serious undertaking and has happened very rarely in US history. Two presidents have undergone impeachment proceedings:

- Andrew Johnson was narrowly acquitted by a vote in the Senate in 1868.
- More recently, President Bill Clinton was accused of lying to a grand jury over his actions regarding an affair with White House intern Monica Lewinsky in 1998. (Chapter 24 has more on this scandal.) The House of Representatives approved the impeachment articles but the majority of Senators voted against impeachment, which meant Clinton was acquitted and remained in office.

However, even the threat of impeachment can have a big effect on the actions of the president. In 1974 Richard Nixon became the first president to resign from office following widespread calls for his impeachment over the Watergate scandal.

Impeachment isn't reserved for the president. Other senior office holders in US federal and state government can also be impeached if they're believed to have committed crimes. In fact, since the US Constitution set down the process of impeachment in 1789, the House of Representatives has initiated such proceedings against 63 individuals.

Judging disputes: The US Supreme Court

Apart from the president and the houses of Congress, the other major cog of US government is the Supreme Court, whose job it is to act as the protector of the Constitution. The Supreme Court is the highest court in the country and hears cases in which constitutional questions are at stake.

The head of the court is the chief justice of the United States. Working alongside him are eight other Supreme Court judges, making a grand total of nine justices. The fact the number is odd is significant, because it ensures that a tie never occurs in votes taken by the justices. The court requires only a majority to deliver a verdict; even five votes to four carries the day.

The president appoints new Supreme Court justices, when a vacancy arises, and generally looks to install people who share his political and social viewpoints. For example, a Republican president may look to appoint a justice who has quite conservative views on political and social issues. However, the Senate has to approve the appointment of a Supreme Court justice, and senators hold hearings in which they interview the candidate to ensure that he's experienced and capable of doing the job.

The Supreme Court decides whether the circumstances of the case in front of them are constitutional or unconstitutional. The court also acts as a final court of appeal for the country's lower courts.

The Supreme Court employs a filtering system for cases it should or shouldn't hear. The Court hears a case only if it must

- Resolve a conflict in the interpretation of a federal law or a provision of the Constitution.
- Correct a major departure from the accepted and usual course of judicial proceedings.
- Resolve an important question of federal law, or expressly review a decision of a lower court that conflicts directly with a previous decision of the Court.

Once appointed, Supreme Court justices have *life tenure*, which means that usually only the grim reaper can remove them from office! Of course, they can choose to retire from the job.

Probably the most controversial case heard by the Supreme Court in modern times is Roe versus Wade. This case dates back to 1973 and concerned abortion. A pregnant woman named Roe (an alias) wanted the legal right to have an abortion in the state of Texas, which outlawed it. She took her case to the state court, where the district attorney, Henry Wade (hence Roe versus Wade), argued against the right to have an abortion. Eventually, the case found its way to the Supreme Court because it was considered potentially unconstitutional to make a woman have a baby she didn't want. The Supreme Court decided that Roe could have the abortion and this decision set a precedent across the country. Many Christian groups and Republican Party members argue that the Supreme Court decision was wrong and would like to see the decision reversed.

Considering the not-so-great US presidents

A total of 44 presidents is bound to produce a few duffers. Here are some of the men (no woman has yet scooped the top job) who really didn't make a good fist of things in the Oval Office:

- **Warren Harding (1921–23):** In polls of political scientists, Harding constantly comes out at the bottom of the pile. Why? Well, he appointed his cronies to the top jobs in government and they were, to put it bluntly, corrupt. Dogged by scandal, he dropped dead from a heart attack (mid-conversation with his wife) after only two years as president.
- **Herbert Hoover (1929–33):** He was president at the onset of the Great Depression in the 1930s that saw millions of people worldwide thrown out of work. His economic policies were widely seen as having made the disastrous economic situation even worse, so much so that the shanty towns that sprang up to house the homeless around some of America's big cities were called Hoovervilles. He even wanted to ban beer – not a vote winner!
- **Richard Nixon (1969–74):** Old Tricky Dick, as he was nicknamed, was a consummate politician who opened up a political dialogue with China, entered into nuclear disarmament talks with the Soviet Union and even started to scale back the unsuccessful war in Vietnam. All these are good things, so why the bad reputation? Well, Nixon had to resign from office after the Watergate scandal, in which he and his advisers were revealed to have broken the law. See Chapter 24 for the lowdown on Watergate.
- **George W. Bush (2001–09):** Initially seen as a hero after the terrorist attacks on the US by Islamic extremists in 2001, George W. proceeded to embroil the country in an expensive, bloody and ultimately highly unpopular war in Iraq. What's more, during his presidency the world came to the brink of economic collapse due to a banking crisis. He was often derided by critics as inarticulate and simply not up to the job.

Passing a Bill into Law

Individual members of either the House of Representatives or Senate, or sometimes members from both houses, introduce bills. The relevant standing committee then considers them. For example, a bill relating to agriculture will be considered by the agriculture standing committee of the body it was introduced in.

Committees usually hold open meetings in which they invite interested parties to testify about the bill or the issue it addresses. At the end of the hearing committee members vote on whether to recommend the bill to the full body. If the vote is no, the bill is effectively dead, but if the committee recommends the bill, the relevant house of Congress consider it. The house debates and may amend the bill, followed by a vote.

A bill approved by one house is considered, often concurrently, by the other, which may pass, reject or amend it. In order for the bill to become law, both houses must agree to identical versions of it. If the second house amends the bill, a conference committee, made up of members from both houses, considers the differences between the two versions. The committee produces a final draft of the bill, and the two houses of Congress vote on it. If the bill gets the green light, all well and good, but it's not law yet – it needs the approval of the president first.

Bills that propose levying a new tax have to originate in the House of Representatives rather than the Senate, according to the US Constitution.

The US is a federal state, which means it's made up of lots of largely autonomous individual states. Laws passed by Congress apply to the whole country, but in many areas, such as criminal justice, the states are left to decide their own policies without interference from Congress.

Often Congress is referred to as *Capitol Hill* because of the area of Washington where it's located. In the same way, the British refer to their own parliament as Westminster after the area of London that the Houses of Parliament stand in.

Throwing Political Parties into the Mix

The US political system, like the UK's, has political parties right at its heart. The two main parties are the Democratic and Republican parties, both of which are chock-full of history. If a politician wants to get anywhere at election time, he has to represent one of these two parties.

Not only leading national and state politicians represent political parties. People stand for election as representing a political party in all manner of local elected offices. For example, the person standing for election to be in charge of refuse collection in a town or city signs on as a Republican or Democrat on the ballot paper, as do people standing in local mayoral elections.

Some people have tried to break the stranglehold of the two main parties on American political life by launching a third party. The most recent – and certainly best-funded – example was when the billionaire businessman Ross Perot formed the Reform Party and ran for president in 1992 and 1996. His platform promised to fight drugs, control the sale of guns and tax foreign imports. His policies were very popular with the American public but Perot, personally, was less so. However, in the 1992 presidential election he scooped 19 per cent of all votes cast. At the 1996 election he was less successful, attracting just 8 per cent of all votes cast.

Each main party has its own symbol. The Democrats are represented by a donkey, which you may feel isn't particularly flattering (donkeys are hardly noted for their skills in government) but actually refers to a former Democratic leader depicted in a cartoon riding a jackass (again, not flattering). The Republicans are represented by an elephant, which again harks back to the days of political cartoons. Symbols do have a practical purpose, though, because they often appear alongside the names of candidates on the ballot paper. A voter seeing a donkey next to a candidate's name automatically knows that person represents the Democratic Party.

After the 2008 elections, the Democrats were in the ascendancy. President Barack Obama won the White House and Democrats held a majority of seats in both houses of Congress. However, within a couple of years President Obama faced hostile Republican majorities in both houses of Congress. Like in the UK, the fortunes of the political parties tend to ebb and flow. In the 1950s, 1980s and early 2000s the Republicans were in the pole position, but in the 1960s, 1970s and 1990s the Democrats often had control of Congress and the presidency.

Voting with the Democrats

The older of the two parties, the Democratic Party traces its roots back to the elections of 1800. It tends to gain most of its support along the eastern and western seaboards, among ethnic minorities and in the big cities. Some of the great Democratic presidents include Franklin D. Roosevelt and John F. Kennedy.

The Democratic Party tends to pursue more liberal, left-wing policies, believing in a degree of state intervention to help the poor and neediest in society. Democrats favour a minimum wage and government action to protect the environment.

Siding with the Republicans

The more socially and politically conservative of the two parties, Republicans stand for minimal government interference in people's lives and in the affairs of individual states by the federal government. Republicans tend to believe in letting business get on with what it's good at – making money – and support low taxes but strong national defence.

Republicans have had their fair share of admired presidents, such as Abraham Lincoln (the first Republican president), Dwight D. Eisenhower and Ronald Reagan.

Rallying the religious right

One of the most significant developments in modern American politics has been the growth in power and influence of what's been called the *religious right*. The US is a deeply religious country, with the majority of citizens regularly attending a place of worship.

Many Christian groups have taken their observance a stage further, looking to see their religious faith expressed through politics. More often than not, these people – and we're talking tens of millions of people across the country – have gravitated towards the Republican Party. At election time, for the Republican Party this situation has proved both

- A blessing because the religious right supporters are very keen on turning up to vote, which in a society with very low voter turnout – often fewer than 60 per cent of eligible voters actually do so in Congressional and presidential elections – can be quite a boost to the Republican Party.
- A curse because the views of the religious right can be quite unpopular among many Americans (for example, they're staunchly anti-abortion), which turns off many moderate voters whom the Republican Party needs to attract to win elections.

Partying with the tea party

One of the phenomenons of recent years has been the rise of what has been called the Tea Party, encompassing many pressure groups on the right of the political spectrum – from pro-life anti-abortion groups through to anti-gun-control groups. Why the silly name? Well, it relates to the Boston tea party, a key event in the American revolution when Boston residents rebelled against the hated tea tax of the British. Tea Party activists, though, do take this a little literally, with some insisting on turning up to public meeting in full American revolutionary regalia with tea bags hanging from their hats! But the Tea Party is no laughing matter – despite wearing tea bags, they represent millions of American voters who are very politically motivated.

The Tea Party isn't actually a political party, but instead a political movement that looks to draw on the ideals of the *founding fathers*, those men who drew up America's Constitution. One thing that unites them is a dislike of big-spending, interfering government in Washington.

Some of the key policies that the religious right would like to see pursued include

- Criminalising abortion
- Retaining the death penalty
- Doing away with welfare benefits
- Saying Christian prayers in schools across the country every day
- Teaching the creationist interpretation of human history alongside the scientifically accepted doctrine of evolution

During the 2008 and 2012 presidential elections, the Democrats undertook a massive Internet campaign to encourage more people to vote. They reckoned that only through increasing voter turnout could they overcome the effects of the religious right turning out and voting Republican. This tactic obviously worked a treat, because their candidate, Barack Obama, beat the Republican candidates, John McCain in 2008 and Mitt Romney in 2012, in the elections.

Republican Party candidates have actually adopted many of the policies that the religious right would like to see pursued.

Linking up: UK and US political parties

The special relationship between the UK and US also applies to the two nation's political parties. The Democratic and Republican parties in the US and the Labour and Conservative parties in the UK have close ties, and share ideas, information and even personnel.

Naturally, the Conservative Party has closer ties with the Republican Party than it does with the Democrats, mainly because they're both on the right of politics and share similar ideals such as a smaller role for central government and low taxes. On the flip side, the Labour and Democratic parties are close because they share ideals such as the state providing better welfare for the less fortunate.

Part V
The Part of Tens

Enjoy an additional Part of Tens chapter online at www.dummies.com/extras/britishpolitics.

In this part . . .

- Find out more about the ten greatest Prime Ministers.
- Discover the ten most significant (and at times sordid!) political scandals of all time.
- Investigate the major political events that formed the modern political world.
- Look at future political and economic trends.

Chapter 23

Ten Great Prime Ministers

In This Chapter

- Leading with aplomb
- Reforming and improving
- Taking care of the people

The role of prime minister (PM) is the top job in British politics. Although technically just a Member of Parliament (MP) and a servant of the monarch, the reality is that the PM has huge powers, from appointing the heads of government ministries to negotiating treaties with foreign powers. Of the 51 people who've been British PM, plenty of them have been mediocre performers, and some have made a downright bad fist of the job. Yet a select band of men and one woman have been, well, rather special, making an extraordinary contribution to shaping Britain and the wider world.

In this chapter I look at the brightest stars in the prime ministerial sky. If you want to know who's made the biggest splash while occupying 10 Downing Street, this is the chapter for you.

Our Finest Hour: Winston Churchill (1940–45 and 1951–55)

Although this chapter is about the greatest prime ministers, one stands head and shoulders above the rest. In the BBC's poll of the Greatest Ever Britons, conducted at the end of the last millennium, Winston Churchill came top.

As prime minister during the Second World War, Churchill proved the truth of the maxim 'cometh the hour, cometh the man'. An avowed hater of the tyrannical Nazi regime (which had overrun neighbouring France in May 1940), Churchill, through his force of character and will, galvanised the British people into believing that they could win the war and that what seemed like the darkest hour of the Blitz bombing of London in 1940–41 was actually the nation's finest hour.

When the Allies won the war in 1945, Churchill was recognised as a truly great world leader, yet the electorate still voted him out of office in favour of a Labour Party that promised to construct a welfare state. Churchill wasn't finished, though: he won the 1951 election and, although past his best as a politician, he bestrode the international stage as a colossus, forging stronger relations between the UK and the United States.

Even with politics out of the equation, Churchill was still a great person; a journalist, wit, brave soldier and winner of the Nobel Prize for Literature – his was a life less ordinary. It's easy to see why the word 'Churchillian' means strong, committed leadership.

The Welsh Wizard: David Lloyd George (1916–22)

War is a crucible of politics that exposes leaders prone to dithering and incompetence and brings to the fore those who are highly capable and charismatic. In 1916, with the First World War going badly for Britain, the nation needed new leadership. Herbert Asquith, the prime minister at the time, was largely seen as indecisive and not up to the task. In his cabinet, the munitions minister David Lloyd George had dramatically overhauled the production of artillery shells and he seemed like the only man with a plan.

Lloyd George deposed Asquith as prime minister and set about reforming government with the sole objective of winning the war. Britain won in 1918 and Lloyd George was instrumental in constructing the peace at the Versailles Conference that followed in 1919. Lloyd George served as PM until 1922 and granted votes for certain women in 1918 (full female suffrage was granted in 1928).

For much of his political life Lloyd George was an outsider. For starters, he was the only PM whose first language wasn't English – it was Welsh. He also didn't come from an aristocratic background. Lloyd George was seen by many colleagues as deceitful in his dealings and as PM he was embroiled in a scandal over the sale of honours. He was also the last leader of the Liberal Party to make it to the post of prime minister.

The Iron Lady: Margaret Thatcher (1979–90)

Britain's one and only female PM makes it into the list not because of her gender but because she's widely recognised as the single most important driving force in British politics since Churchill. Margaret Thatcher, the daughter of a grocer from Grantham in Lincolnshire, went on to study chemistry at Oxford University. In a sexist environment, in the most old-fashioned of political parties – the Conservatives – Thatcher managed to get herself selected as a parliamentary candidate, elected as an MP and into the cabinet. She became leader of the party in 1975 following the Conservatives' two election defeats the previous year.

In the 1979 general election many of the senior men in her party were expecting Thatcher to fail in the heat of battle, but she managed to win a majority in parliament. She stayed in the role for 11 years, fighting a successful war in the Falkland Islands against Argentina, reforming public services, passing anti-union laws, lowering taxes and overseeing a rebirth of British business. By any estimate, she was a great PM.

However, Thatcher was a deeply divisive figure; she didn't like criticism from colleagues, could be domineering of her cabinet and was intolerant. Many people in the industrialised north of England see her as responsible for the destruction of their jobs and communities. The miners' strike in 1984 (about the planned closure of pits) that led to the defeat of the strikers and a victory for Thatcher embodied a bitter, divided Britain overseen by the PM dubbed the 'Iron Lady'.

The Trailblazer: Robert Walpole (1721–42)

Robert Walpole was the first politician to be recognised by historians as prime minister – although the phrase 'prime minister' wasn't used at the time. He inherited a difficult economic situation, with thousands of Britons having lost their life savings in the speculative 'South Sea Bubble' in 1720 (when people invested in the South Sea Company, only for the bubble to burst). His policies successfully dealt with these economic problems and the country enjoyed huge wealth. Walpole was a major figure on the international stage, negotiating favourable treaties for Britain and keeping the country out of a bloody continental war over succession to the throne of Poland.

The Walpole era is seen as a crucial one in the development of Britain as a world power, with the country consolidating its empire – including in North America – and major cultural figures, such as Jonathan Swift and Samuel Johnson, doing their thing. Despite all this, probably Walpole's biggest legacy was the establishment of the job of prime minister itself.

Robert Walpole was the first PM to occupy 10 Downing Street in London, the official residence of British prime ministers ever since. The house was originally three houses, but was knocked into one under King George II.

The Great Reformer: Clement Attlee (1945–51)

To look at, Attlee had a bald domed head and a trimmed moustache and seemed every inch the chartered accountant. But still waters run deep. Attlee – a capable deputy prime minister in the wartime coalition government run by Winston Churchill – had risen seamlessly in the ranks of the Labour Party to become leader at the election in 1945. The party's pledge to create a welfare state helped win it a landslide against Winston Churchill's Conservatives, and Attlee, the small man from working-class roots in Putney, was PM.

The next six years saw nothing less than the creation of what many people would consider modern Britain. The National Health Service was founded and large tracts of industry were taken into public ownership. Britain's poor could suddenly expect financial help from the state instead of a cold shoulder. Attlee oversaw a reduction in inequality and an overhaul of the education system. Internationally, Attlee took the first steps in dismantling the British Empire, with India finally granted its independence in 1948. In six years, Attlee's government changed Britain forever. The reward was to be defeated by a resurgent Conservative Party under Winston Churchill in 1951.

The First Spin Doctor: Benjamin Disraeli (1868 and 1874–80)

Britain's one and only PM of Jewish heritage (pretty extraordinary in what at the time was a deeply Christian country), Disraeli was the master of the art of public relations when PR was unknown. He was the first major British politician to sell to the public the idea of Britain as a major world empire. He made Queen Victoria – with whom he shared a warm friendship – empress of India and worked to extend the British Empire into the Middle East and Asia upon which 'the sun would never set'. He was noted for getting Britain involved again in continental European politics. Since the end of the Napoleonic Wars in 1815 Britain had deliberately stayed out of European affairs, adopting a policy dubbed 'splendid isolation'. Disraeli, though, became actively involved in major treaties and negotiations with continental powers, particularly at the Congress of Berlin in 1878 when, through skilful negotiations, he limited the growing influence of Russia in the Balkans. Some of Disraeli's other foreign adventures were less successful; the British invasions of Afghanistan and the land of the Zulu in South Africa resulted in some military defeats. One of Disraeli's domestic policy achievements was the Reform Act 1867, which increased the number of people (all men back then, of course) who were allowed to vote.

Outside Number 10, Disraeli was no slouch with the pen, writing bestselling romantic novels: from PM to Mills and Boon!

The Grand Old Man: William Gladstone (1868–74, 1880–85, 1886 and 1892–94)

Disraeli's arch-rival was the great Liberal politician and four-time prime minister William Gladstone. The Grand Old Man (GOM), as he was nicknamed, was noted for his very, very long speeches, and apparently Queen Victoria once criticised him by saying, 'He talks to me as if I were a public meeting.' His bitter rival Disraeli twisted the GOM nickname, saying it actually stood for God's Only Mistake.

Gladstone was a giant of late Victorian politics. He was a major proponent of free trade and the removal of tariffs on imported goods, and he supported electoral reform, allowing more men to vote. To his credit, Gladstone was opposed to the expansion of the British Empire into the heart of Africa in search of natural resources, although ultimately he could do little about it. Closer to home, he wanted the Irish to have home rule (in effect, self-governance), and if he'd had his way, the troubled history between Britain and Ireland of the last century may have been very different. However, Gladstone couldn't get his way because his Liberal Party enjoyed only a slim majority in parliament and considerable opposition to home rule existed.

Gladstone had a high moral code that was adopted by many Victorian men of means. Even as prime minister he used to walk the streets at night trying to persuade prostitutes to give up their way of life and go to church. He eventually gave up being PM aged 84, drawing to a close probably the most eventful and long-lasting political career of 19th-century British politics.

Shaking Things Up: Robert Peel (1834–35 and 1841–46)

Robert Peel was one of British history's great doers. Prime minister twice, he was also responsible for setting up the British police force – the police nickname Bobby is short for Robert, and they were originally called Peelers!

Peel was alarmed at the increase in crime and, in the face of fierce opposition from those who feared that the police could be used by a tyrannical government to crush any opposition, he went about replacing the old method of policing by city watches and sheriffs with a uniformed and professional police force. So next time you get stopped for speeding, you know who you have to thank!

Another crucial contribution by Peel was repealing the Corn Laws. Imported corn was taxed, which although it protected the livelihoods of many British farmers, meant that many poverty-stricken industrial workers had to pay way over the odds for that most basic of foodstuffs, bread. Scrapping the Corn Laws opened Britain up to the mass importation of foodstuffs from the prairies of North America and sent bread prices tumbling. British workers could afford bread, but many farmers in the UK went to the wall in the last three decades of the 19th century in what historians dub the Victorian agricultural depression.

Peel's reforming zeal didn't stop at the Corn Laws; he also introduced the Factory Act 1844, restricting the number of hours that women and children could work. Less happily, he re-imposed income tax, which had been suspended in 1815.

But it was the Corn Laws repeal that split the Tory party of the day down the middle and left Peel out of office. His own party, the Tories, had failed to support the repeal and Peel had had to rely on votes from the rival Whig party.

The Second Master of Spin: Tony Blair (1997–2007)

The fresh-faced and affable Tony Blair promised, in the words of his Labour Party election song of 1997, that 'things can only get better' for Britain under him as prime minister. It seemed for a few years that he was right. The country boomed economically and culturally, with the advent of Brit Pop and Cool Britannia. Britain seemed to be going through a giant make-over and would come out the other side more attractive and vibrant.

Working alongside his chancellor and successor, Gordon Brown, Blair introduced the minimum wage and tax credits for families, and made the Bank of England independent from government interference. He also helped bring peace to Northern Ireland after a quarter of a century. Britain's relations with the European Union improved, with Blair instrumental in the expansion of the EU from 15 to 27 member states. In Africa, too, Blair made significant strides in persuading other world leaders to forgive the debts of the poorest countries and up their aid commitments. So far, so good. Then came Iraq.

On the premise that the Iraqi dictator Saddam Hussein had weapons of mass destruction, Blair took Britain into an invasion of Iraq alongside the United States. Many British and international politicians suggested that the war was illegal and unnecessary, and the case against Blair deepened when, after Hussein's defeat, inspectors found no actual weapons of mass destruction. A bloody civil war in Iraq followed and Blair was portrayed in some media as 'Bliar' and even a war criminal for his actions. What's more, many of the media manipulation techniques that had been deployed by Blair's powerful press secretary Alastair Campbell (check out Chapter 10 for more on him) started to backfire, and opponents and the media accused the Blair government of being more about political spin than substance.

Dogged by criticism, Blair retired as PM in 2007 to make way for Gordon Brown. His timing couldn't have been better – he narrowly avoided the world economic crisis that started in the summer of 2008 and Labour's election defeat in 2010. No wonder he was nicknamed 'Teflon Tony' for the way scandal never stuck to him.

Wiser than His Years: William Pitt the Younger (1783–1801 and 1804–06)

Just 24 when he became prime minister, William Pitt the Younger was the son of a previous PM, the aptly named William Pitt the Elder. Although barely out of his school uniform, William Pitt the Younger is one of the greats. In a time when PMs were lucky to last a few months in the role (the three previous PMs had managed just 18 months between them), he was a real survivor and was in place for a whopping 18 years, winning three general elections. Even after his resignation in 1801, he was back again three years later for another two-year term before dying in office at the age of 46.

The not-quite-so-great prime ministers

For every great prime minister there've been at least a couple of total duffers. Here's my list of the worst PMs in British history:

- **Lord North (1770–82):** Through incompetent diplomacy and military tactics, North managed to lose the United States colony to the American revolutionaries.
- **The Duke of Portland (1807–09):** Only in office for two and a half years, the duke spent most of that time infirm, despite the fact that the country was at war with France during his prime ministership and needed strong leadership. He left the cabinet to its own devices to such an extent that two members of it, George Canning and Lord Castlereagh, even fought a duel to settle a dispute over whether British troops should be sent to Portugal or the Netherlands. The result of the duel? Canning missed by a mile and Castlereagh shot him in the thigh, with non-fatal consequences.
- **The Duke of Wellington (1828–30 and 1834):** The duke was an awful politician, and about as far from a conciliator as you could begin to imagine, alienating friends and opponents alike and becoming massively unpopular in the country. In his second stint as PM in 1834 most senior politicians refused to work with Wellington, so for a few months he was PM, chancellor of the exchequer, foreign secretary and home secretary, and was lousy at all of them!
- **Neville Chamberlain (1937–40):** Chamberlain was no doubt a very capable politician but his greatest folly was his belief that he could appease Nazi Germany. He couldn't. After shamefully allowing Germany to grab large parts of its neighbours, Britain was forced into declaring war anyway after the invasion of Poland in September 1939.
- **Sir Anthony Eden (1955–57):** Debonair and brave, Eden seemed every bit the politico, but in 1956 he got Britain involved in a disastrous scheme to snatch the Suez Canal from the Egyptians (whose country it happened to be in) and was forced to back down by the threat of American economic sanctions. Eden resigned soon after what became known as the 'Suez Crisis'.

But it's not just political – if not actual – longevity that marks Pitt out. He was ultra-effective in the top job. He set about reducing the national debt, called for reform of the *rotten boroughs* (parliamentary seats with only a few electors – in effect the property of local landowners so they could get whomever they wanted elected), was a staunch opponent of the slave trade and, from 1793, was a wartime leader against France. His second period as PM saw Britain win the crucial battle of Trafalgar as well as form key alliances against France with Russia and Sweden. Pitt even introduced income tax, but the less said about that, the better!

All in all, not bad for a man given the top job at just 24 years old.

Chapter 24

Ten Major Political Scandals

In This Chapter

- Call girls, spies and sex
- MPs' expenses and government at war
- Politicians falling foul of the law
- Scandals across the pond

In this chapter I look at some of the major scandals to rock the political scene in Britain over the past century, and three from over the pond in America. Some scandals have led to the downfall of presidents and party political leaders, others to imprisonment and disgrace . . . all have provided fine fare for the press.

A Very British Sex Scandal: John Profumo

The news of an affair between the dashing (married) Conservative minister John Profumo and call girl Christine Keeler exploded over the British political scene like an atom bomb. The two had met at a party hosted by a member of the aristocracy and had embarked on a short affair in 1961. The story had the added spice that Keeler had also been having an affair with a Soviet spy: you just couldn't make it up! The James Bond style espionage overtones gave the press a field day.

Facing difficult questions, Profumo lied about the affair to the House of Commons and from that moment his fate was sealed. Profumo resigned in June 1963 but the story was far from over. Leading judge Lord Denning conducted an investigation to see whether the affair had led to any UK state secrets finding their way to the Soviets. The Denning Report was published in September 1963 and within weeks the Conservative prime minister

Harold Macmillan had resigned after being diagnosed (wrongly, it turned out) with cancer. Macmillan was replaced by the affable old Etonian Sir Alec Douglas-Home.

The Profumo affair had a tragic postscript: the socialite Stephen Ward, who'd introduced Profumo to Keeler, killed himself after being found guilty in a court of law for living off immoral earnings (legal-ese for being a pimp).

The effect of the Profumo affair was to blow away the veil of privacy surrounding the private lives of British politicians once and for all. Whether or not MPs and ministers were having affairs was now fair game for newspaper coverage. Head to Chapter 10 for more on politicians and the media.

From Moats to Maltesers: The MPs' Expenses Scandal

In 2009, the highly secretive expenses system of MPs was exposed to public scrutiny and scorn when the *Daily Telegraph* published details bought from a source working within the Houses of Parliament. MPs had been due to release limited details of their expenses but the *Telegraph* story trumped this. The editor of the newspaper had a team of over 20 journalists trawl through the expenses data and expose what amounted to sheer extravagance and in some cases even potential criminal activity.

The *Telegraph* found that MPs had claimed for items such as cleaning their moats, building duck houses for their private lakes and repairing swimming pools. At the other end of the scale were claims for trivial items such as sweets, chocolate biscuits and toilet brushes for their fully furnished second homes. It seemed to many people that MPs were trying to milk the system for all that it was worth. The worst examples of alleged expenses fiddling related to second-home allowances – MPs can claim mortgage payments and other expenses on a second property that they're meant to live in when parliament is sitting.

The story ran throughout the early summer of 2009 and public anger grew, with headlines screaming that MPs simply 'Don't get it' and that they were taking advantage of ill-defined rules to do what looked to many like fiddling expenses.

Eventually, MPs agreed to reform their expenses. Michael Martin became the first speaker in four centuries to resign his post, several dozen MPs stepped down at the 2010 general election, and a handful were convicted of fraud and went to prison.

Running Out of Control: The Westland Affair

Whether or not struggling UK helicopter firm Westland should merge with a European or American rival is the sort of decision that comes across the desk of cabinet ministers every day of the week. But somehow this routine event nearly led to the collapse of the Conservative government of Margaret Thatcher in 1986.

The secretary of state for defence, Michael Heseltine, wanted Westland to merge with European rivals, while the trade and industry secretary, Leon Brittan, preferred it to go with an American firm. At a heated cabinet meeting, Brittan carried the argument and Heseltine stormed out, saying that he hadn't had a proper hearing, and announced his resignation. This was pure political theatre and turned a disagreement between ministers into a full-blown political crisis.

Worse was to follow for the Thatcher government, as Heseltine claimed publicly that the prime minister had been stubborn (not an unknown trait of Margaret Thatcher; see Chapter 23 for more on her). Earlier, a letter criticising Heseltine's conduct, written by a senior civil servant, had been passed to the press in what was widely seen as an attempt to smear the former defence minister. It turned out that the letter had been released at the behest of Heseltine's bitter rival, Brittan. The result of this political bun fight was that Brittan resigned and the competence of the Thatcher government was called into question.

During a parliamentary debate to discuss the scandal, Thatcher reportedly had a draft resignation note in her handbag. However, she never delivered it, and instead gave a sterling defence of the government's policies.

Nevertheless, the Westland affair damaged the government, and four years later Heseltine ran against Thatcher in an election for the leader of the Conservative Party. Thatcher won the first ballot but was fatally weakened by the lack of support she'd been shown by Conservative MPs and resigned. The complex Westland affair can be seen as the root of the downfall of Thatcher, one of the 20th century's most controversial but also highly capable prime ministers.

Scandal of Mass Destruction: The David Kelly Affair

Britain's involvement in the war in Iraq in 2003 was heavily based on the premise that the Iraqi dictator, Saddam Hussein, had been stockpiling weapons of mass destruction (WMDs). But Iraq didn't have any WMDs (more than likely, Hussein had destroyed them a few years prior to the war), and many politicians and commentators questioned whether the government had lied to the British public over the reason for going to war with Iraq.

Journalists and politicians started to investigate the run-up to the war and the official documents that the government released to support the claims of Prime Minister Tony Blair that Iraq had WMDs. They paid particular attention to a dossier that the government released outlining what the UK intelligence services knew about Iraqi WMDs. The 'dodgy dossier', as it came to be known, claimed that Iraq could make a military strike with chemical weapons within 45 minutes.

BBC journalist Andrew Gilligan interviewed the government scientist David Kelly over the claims. Gilligan said that Kelly had told him that the claims made in the dossier had been 'sexed up' by Blair's press secretary, Alastair Campbell. This was sensational stuff and parliament started to investigate the claims.

Under huge pressure, David Kelly tragically took his life, and the government launched a special investigation under the judge Lord Hutton to explore the circumstances surrounding his death. The investigation found that the BBC report had been poorly put together and that the evidence didn't support the claim that the WMD dossier had been 'sexed up'. Within hours the BBC's top management resigned and Campbell said that he'd been vindicated. Longer term, though, the government's victory seems to have been tarnished. The claim of the existence of WMDs in Iraq became discredited and many members of the public sided with the BBC, suggesting that the Hutton Report was a whitewash. Campbell left his post soon afterwards and so did Blair in 2007, with his poll rating plummeting and some suggesting that he'd tricked the country into going to war in Iraq.

Roll Up, Roll Up: How Much for This Knighthood?

The UK honours system (awards given by the state to notable individuals) is meant to recognise outstanding contributions to society, culture and government. The prime minister recommends who should receive an honour and the monarch bestows it. The highest bidder shouldn't be able to simply buy an honour! But from 1920, Prime Minister David Lloyd George allowed the government to basically sell honours bestowed by the monarch for cash donations. A few tens of thousands of pounds could buy a knighthood; more and you could buy a peerage. Lloyd George seems to have wanted the money not for personal gain but to help fund a new political party with, of course, him at the helm. But many members of the aristocracy who'd held their titles for hundreds of years were furious that Lloyd George was devaluing the honours system. However, Lloyd George wasn't acting against the law – although selling honours did later become illegal. Lloyd George failed in his mission to form a new party and after 1922 was never prime minister again.

An act of parliament in 1925 outlawed the practice of selling honours.

The scandal echoed in events of 2007, when senior fundraisers of Blair's Labour Party were accused of giving out honours to party donors. The 'cash for honours' affair involved a police investigation and Tony Blair was interviewed. However, no charges were brought and the case was dropped.

How the Mighty Fall: Jonathan Aitken and Jeffrey Archer

Lying in court is a serious offence – just ask two former Conservative MPs, Jonathan Aitken and Jeffrey Archer. Both men were involved in separate high-profile libel actions.

Aitken defended himself against allegations that a Saudi prince had paid for his stay at a Paris hotel (embarrassing, but not illegal). He lied under oath and tried to get his family to cover up the lie. When it became clear that Aitken had committed perjury, he admitted what he'd done. He resigned and spent 7 months in jail (he was sentenced to 18). He spent his time inside writing about his experiences and became a campaigner for prison reform. The costs of the libel action he'd taken against the *Guardian*, which had exposed his links to the Saudis, left Aitken bankrupt.

The fall of novelist and politician Jeffrey Archer was even more dramatic than Aitken's. The flamboyant Archer won a libel action in 1987 against a tabloid newspaper that alleged he'd slept with a prostitute. He won record damages and his political career rocketed – so much so that he was nominated as the Conservative candidate for mayor of London in 2000. But Ted Francis, a friend of his (and with friends like this, who needs enemies?), said Archer owed him money and revealed that the alibi that had helped convince the court that Archer was telling the truth in his libel action 13 years before had been fabricated. And thus the whole sorry saga unfolded. Archer resigned his candidacy and was put on trial for perverting the course of justice – an even more serious offence than perjury – and was sent to jail for four years. While inside Archer penned a three-volume book outlining his experiences, called simply *Prison Diary*.

Murder Plot? The Jeremy Thorpe Affair

Jeremy Thorpe was leader of the Liberal Party in the 1960s and 1970s. He was a brilliant orator with a shrewd mind, but he seemed to have skeletons galore in his cupboard. A married man, Thorpe was alleged to have embarked on an affair with male model Norman Scott in the 1960s (when homosexuality was still illegal). Scott made several allegations to senior Liberals and to members of the British establishment about the affair he said he'd had with Thorpe. In 1975 a former airline pilot, Andrew Newton, confronted Scott with a gun and shot the dog Scott was walking – the poor beast's name was Rinka and in the press the story became known as Rinkagate. Newton claimed that Thorpe had hired him as a hitman. Thorpe was arrested and tried at the Old Bailey in London in 1979. By this time Thorpe's once great career was in tatters, although he was found innocent at his trial.

The Fall of a President: Watergate

Political scandals don't come any bigger than Watergate; there's even an Oscar-winning movie called *All the President's Men* about it! In the run-up to the 1972 presidential election a break-in occurred at the Democratic campaign headquarters at the Watergate complex in Washington. The burglars had links with members of successful Republican candidate Richard Nixon's administration. This was bad enough, but investigative reporters working for the Washington Post discovered that Nixon's aides had attempted to cover up the links between the burglars and people in the Nixon administration later emerged – Nixon had withheld sound recordings made in the president's office.

Following a series of newspaper stories by *Washington Post* reporters Bob Woodward and Carl Bernstein, a Senate investigation was launched. Members of the Nixon administration started to testify against one another. The scandal acted as a cancer on the presidency over a period of months, with member after member of the administration coming forward to testify. No one's sure how much Nixon knew about the break-in or the attempts at a cover-up, but ultimately he lost the confidence of the American people and the Senate. Facing the possibility of *impeachment* – a trial that can lead to the removal of office – in 1974 Nixon became the first president in US history to resign his office. Several of his close aides and allies in the White House subsequently served jail sentences for their role in the cover-up.

The effects of the Watergate scandal were so great – after all, it brought down the most powerful politician in the world – that other scandals are often given the moniker 'Gate'.

More Sordid Scandal Stateside: The Monica Lewinsky Affair

President Bill Clinton was always known as a bit of a ladies' man but few realised just how much until he was elected president of the United States. His brief affair with intern Monica Lewinsky nearly cost him the presidency when, while giving testimony in a sexual harassment case, he swore that he didn't have sex with her. Unluckily for him, and hygienically minded people everywhere, Lewinsky still had the stained dress to prove it.

Clinton had to retract his statement and apologise for his lewd activities to his wife and country on live television.

Despite attempts to have him impeached, Clinton, the family man, remained popular and is considered by many to have been a highly effective president. He served two terms before retiring in 2000. Lewinsky went on to sell a book about the affair. And hopefully visited a dry cleaner.

Murder in the Orient: The Neil Heywood Affair

If any scandal encapsulates the shifting sands of the world economy and the emergence of China as a world superpower, it's the murder of British businessman Neil Heywood. In November 2011, what seemed like a routine business trip to China ended in tragedy when Mr Heywood was found dead in his hotel room. The first reports from police suggested Mr Heywood had died of alcohol poisoning. However, the local police chief, a Mr Wang Lijun, then fled to the American Consulate and told a very different story: that Mr Heywood had been poisoned and that people close to Bo Xilai, a very important figure in the Chinese communist party and tipped as a future leader of China, had been involved in the murder. A full investigation followed, and within a fortnight Mr Xilai had been sacked from his job and his wife, Gu Kailai, charged with murder.

The story became a sensation across the world because it encompassed big business and shone a light on the secretive world of Chinese politics. At the trial Gu Kailai admitted to the poisoning – tests showed that Mr Heywood had been a victim of cyanide – and was sentenced to a minimum term of 14 years in prison along with her bodyguard, who was convicted of complicity. Although Bo Xilai wasn't involved in the killing, his career was in tatters and some officials close to Mr Bo Xilai also lost their positions as a result. What had been a dastardly crime morphed into a power struggle at the top of Chinese politics.

Chapter 25

Ten Political Events That Shaped the Modern World

In This Chapter

- Beating down the Berlin Wall
- Coming together for peace and prosperity: The European Union
- Bringing a new age of terror: 9/11
- Emerging into freedom: Nelson Mandela and South Africa
- Gazing over the brink: The financial crisis

When asked by a journalist what was likely to blow his government off course, former British prime minister Harold Macmillan quipped, 'Events, dear boy, events.' And it's true that events, however minor they seem at the time, change the political landscape forever.

In this chapter I choose ten events that fundamentally altered the political world we live in during the second decade of the 21st century.

Hell on Earth: The Second World War

What to say about a conflict that saw the deaths of over 50 million people, the mass extermination of minorities such as the Jews and other atrocious war crimes – apart from acknowledging that between 1939 (the outbreak of war) and the final defeat of Nazi Germany in 1945, many parts of the European continent and the Soviet Union were transformed into hell on earth. Eventually, though, the allied nations – Britain, the US, France, the Soviet Union and China – defeated the axis powers of Nazi Germany, Japan, Italy and several assorted puppet regimes.

The world was changed forever. The old empires of France and Britain were disbanded, Germany was divided for over 40 years, Japan moved from a country governed by a god-like monarch to a flourishing democracy and China became a communist state. These are just some of the political implications of the terrible war.

Following the end of the Second World War, Europe was divided into two major military power blocs. The western European nations and America formed NATO (North Atlantic Treaty Organisation) and the eastern European nations and the Soviet Union formed the Warsaw Pact. Both of these military power blocs kept large numbers of troops in Europe in preparedness for war with one another. Historians refer to this sometimes very tense stand-off as the *Cold War* and it lasted from the late 1940s until the fall of the Berlin Wall in 1989.

Breaking Down the Barriers: Nixon and China

US President Richard Nixon is famous for being the first holder of the office to resign his post, following the Watergate scandal (see Chapter 24 for more on this almighty political tear-up). But one of Nixon's enduring legacies is that he was the first US president to actively seek to improve relations with the Chinese government.

Prior to Nixon's visit to China in 1972, American–Chinese relations had been poor. Put simply, the richest nation in the world, America, didn't get along with the most populous nation. This discord was primarily the result of China being a communist state and America a capitalist one. The two countries had actually fought a war in Korea in the 1950s and the Chinese disliked the fact that the Americans supported Taiwan, which was basically governed by anti-communist Chinese.

But Nixon's decision to visit broke the ice between the two nations and, although not exactly ushering in an immediate period of co-operation and friendship, it opened up genuine channels of communication that could help forge peace. Nowadays, the Chinese and American governments communicate on a very regular basis, and the two nations sometimes co-operate on the world stage. Nixon's visit also heralded China's opening up to Western ideas such as freeing up markets and promoting individual enterprise. Chinese communism is now mixed with a healthy dose of Western capitalism, which has provided a huge impetus to the stellar growth of the Chinese economy since the 1990s. Nixon's visit paved the way for China's assent to world superpower status.

Ending Communism in Europe: The Fall of the Berlin Wall

Many Germans who lived through the events of November 1989 still have to pinch themselves to check that they really did all happen. The tyrannical East German regime, which for four decades had been backed by the communist Soviet Union, literally fell apart in a matter of days, mostly through people power.

The Berlin Wall, which was built in 1961 and divided the German capital between east and west, had been a potent symbol of the Cold War that had been going on since soon after the end of the Second World War between the capitalist West, led by the US and the UK, and the communist Soviet Union. The wall had been constructed to stop East Germans fleeing to the more prosperous and democratic West Germany. Undeterred, hundreds of East Germans had tried to get over or under the wall; many were captured, imprisoned and even shot.

It seemed that the wall would last forever, but in 1989 the East German regime started to crumble. The Soviet Union was changing its approach to the world under the leadership of Mikhail Gorbachev. The Soviets were trying to improve relations with the West, and Gorbachev saw the Berlin Wall and the repressive East German regime as, quite literally, a major barrier to good relations with the West. Gradually, opponents of the East German government started to detect that the Soviets wouldn't intervene in any uprising.

Slowly but surely, East Germans started to take to the streets in protest and the East German government leaders realised that the game was up and that they couldn't rely on Soviet military intervention to quell the protests.

The East German government resigned and within a couple of days the guards on the Berlin Wall had opened its gates to allow anyone to enter free West Berlin. For many East Berliners this was their first chance to see the West, and they liked what they saw. Within a few weeks, Germany was on the way to re-unification; no longer split between East and West Germany but unified as a democratic powerhouse of over 80 million people in the middle of Europe.

Other east European states soon followed East Germany's lead and threw off their old communist regimes. Now these former Soviet bloc countries are part of the European Union and all are democracies. The fall of the Berlin Wall is probably the single most important event in European politics in the past 50 or so years.

Choosing peace over war: The Gorbachev experiment

Much of the credit for the peaceful transference of former eastern European communist regimes to democracies belongs to the Soviet leader of the late 1980s and early 1990s, Mikhail Gorbachev. Although a communist, he saw that the Cold War between the West and East was impoverishing his own and other eastern European people. He wanted to reduce repression and encourage free enterprise – a sort of communism-lite. However, within a few years, the communists were out of power in the Soviet Union and the power and influence of the old world superpower diminished. However, the policies of openness and free enterprise resounded around eastern Europe, and when the crunch came and the people rose up to overthrow their communist regimes, Gorbachev, against the advice of his military, chose to let the eastern European nations go their own way. He chose peace over war and was awarded the Nobel Peace Prize in 1990.

Coming Together: The March of the European Union

When the Treaty of Rome formed the European Economic Community in 1957, people didn't see it as a particularly big deal. In essence, six countries (France, Germany, the Netherlands, Belgium, Luxembourg and Italy) were simply signing an agreement to help boost economic co-operation. But what they were doing was laying the groundwork for what has become, as the modern European Union, one of the world's great trading blocs (with an economy bigger than the United States) and a super-state in its own right, with its very own flag, currency and parliament (refer to Chapter 21 for more on how the EU institutions work).

The European Economic Community (the EU today) expanded to include the UK, Denmark and Ireland in 1973, Greece in 1981, and Spain and Portugal in 1986. The biggest influx of new members was in 2004, when many of the former communist eastern European states, such as Poland and the Czech Republic, joined. Today the EU encompasses 28 members and now even has a president.

Over its history the EU has helped to create a massive free trade area and managed to ease many of the ancient rivalries between European states that lay behind the two disastrous world wars of the 20th century. Peace in Europe is in no small part due to the advent of the EU.

Pulling Aside the Bamboo Curtain: China's March to Superpower Status

China is a superpower – potentially as powerful as the United States. More than a billion people live in China, which is more than twice the population of the entire 28-country European Union. The economy is growing at a rate that the likes of America and Europe can only dream of and a new power station opens on average once a fortnight. It seems that after generations of underdevelopment, civil war, political turmoil and, in much of the countryside, intense poverty, China is taking its place at the top table of both the world economy and international politics.

What's more, China has become the workshop of the world and the money it earns from all its exports has allowed it to build a huge national cash pile. China is using the money to make major overseas investments, particularly in mineral-rich parts of the globe such as Africa and South America. Many political observers and economists have said that the 20th century was America's century; the 21st is shaping up to be China's.

Long Wait for Freedom: The Release of Nelson Mandela

The apartheid regime of South Africa is recognised as one of the most despicable of modern history. The state was run on the premise that white South Africans were intrinsically superior to the black majority, who were deemed only good for performing menial tasks. That such an evil doctrine could survive into the 1990s is difficult to believe, but it did.

Successive apartheid governments in South Africa kept the black majority poor, ill-educated and in a position of subjugation to the wealthy whites. They forced blacks to live in poverty-stricken townships and attend poorly financed black-only schools, while the whites owned the farmland and had the best schools and all the professional jobs.

Anti-apartheid groups such as the African National Congress (ANC) clashed violently with the police. ANC leading light Nelson Mandela was imprisoned off the coast of Cape Town in Robben Island jail for 27 years, charged with treason. During his long incarceration, Mandela became a symbol of hope for millions around the world that one day the evil doctrines of apartheid would be defeated and all South Africans treated equally regardless of the colour of their skin.

Slowly but surely, international pressure took a toll on the South African regime; sanctions hurt the white ruling classes and they started to see that at some stage, in order to be accepted in the wider international community, they must dismantle apartheid.

Like the fall of Soviet Union-backed governments in eastern Europe at around the same time, the end of apartheid was quick and surprisingly bloodless. Mandela was released from prison in February 1990 and in a press conference broadcast worldwide he called for an end to apartheid but also for peace and reconciliation between black and white. The once political prisoner Mandela was elected president of the new Republic of South Africa in 1994.

Mandela's message of peace and reconciliation undoubtedly helped heal some of the wounds of South African society and his time as president saw the country take its place again in the international community. Mandela was awarded the Nobel Peace Prize in 1993 and lived until 2013.

Terror from the Skies: 9/11

Few who lived through 11 September 2001 will forget it. Planes hijacked by Al-Qaeda terrorists struck the twin towers of the World Trade Center in New York and the Pentagon building in Washington. Thousands of innocent people died and a terrorist group only a few people had heard of became worldwide news. Al Qaeda wanted to force the US to stop supporting Israel and to remove troops based in the Middle East.

The implications of 9/11, as it became known, were far wider and deeper than the atrocities of the day. The US government under President George W. Bush started to detain people around the globe who it suspected of being linked to Al-Qaeda. The US, aided by Britain, invaded Afghanistan, the base of operations for Al-Qaeda, and removed the governing Taliban regime. In Iraq, the US used a rather tenuous link between the country's dictator Saddam Hussein and Al-Qaeda as one of the justifications for an invasion.

On the other side of the coin, other Islamic extremist groups used 9/11 as a rallying call; they detonated bombs in Bali, Madrid and London. The US 'war on terror' has dominated international events ever since the moment the first of the twin towers was struck by the hijacked planes.

Bringing Down a Dictator: War in Iraq

The regime of Saddam Hussein had long been in the sights of the Americans. Hussein's invasion of neighbouring Kuwait in 1990 had sparked a massive counter-strike by an international force led by the US. At the time, Hussein had come within an ace of being deposed as dictator, yet he clung on to power.

Twelve years later the US decided that the Iraqi dictator's continued flirtation with weapons of mass destruction and alleged involvement with international terrorism was justification to go to war again. This time around the US was supported by a limited group of countries, including most notably the UK and Australia.

The invasion of Iraq was over in double-quick time, and Hussein was captured and later put on trial and executed by his own people. However, the presence of so many US troops attracted insurgents from neighbouring countries Iran and Syria, who started a guerrilla war against the US and its allies.

The violent conflict continued for several years and more than a thousand American and several hundred British soldiers lost their lives. Much of Iraq descended into bloody civil war and the Iraqi government, backed by the US, struggled to survive. In 2014 much of the north of Iraq was under the control of Islamic militants from the IS group (Islamic State), and the Iraqi government – still backed by America but no longer militarily – seemed to be powerless to do anything about this state of affairs.

Gazing Over the Brink: The Great Credit Crunch

In 2008 a host of American, British and European banks came to the brink of bankruptcy due to the poor investments they'd made. If the major banks had gone under, the world could have fallen into an economic depression at least as great as that of the 1930s, with tens if not hundreds of millions of people losing their jobs and life savings.

Facing a financial Armageddon, the US, UK and European governments bailed out the banks by effectively transferring the bad debts onto their own books. Suddenly, the taxpayer was in hock for hundreds of billions of pounds, having taken on what are called *toxic debts*. Governments will be paying the bill for the crash for a generation to come.

But longer term, one thing's for sure: the financial crash of 2008 struck at one of the major props of American power. The American government owes huge sums to the Chinese and much of the wealth of the West now flows to the East. When historians write the history of the world in the 21st century, they may see the financial crash of 2008 as a key staging post in the transfer of world power from West to East.

Crazy for You: Obama-Mania

The election of the first black president of the US, Barack Obama, is one of those 'Pinch me; am I dreaming?' moments. Obama, a lawyer by profession, was a rank outsider for the Democratic nomination to run as president. Not only had no black politician made any real headway in a presidential election before, but Obama was seen as inexperienced and an unknown quantity. But Obama has charisma and star quality in bucket loads. He fought and won a tight contest with political heavyweight Hillary Clinton (wife of former president Bill Clinton) for the Democratic position and then beat the Republican candidate John McCain hands down in the final presidential ballot.

But Obama's election success isn't just about one notable politician pulling off a major coup; it's fundamentally about a country with a huge black and Hispanic minority – many of whom have felt disenfranchised by the white population – becoming, well, much more equal. One of his first acts was to abandon the unpopular foreign policies of his predecessor George W. Bush. Many in western Europe breathed a sigh of relief when Obama was elected because they felt that a calming influence had emerged on the world stage to take on the most difficult but most powerful job in the world. But over the course of his presidency people have seen Obama as often taking too long to make decisions and unwilling to take a strong stance against the proliferation of nuclear weapons in Iran and North Korea. Many see the Obama presidency as a missed opportunity to halt America's relative decline in the world, against the likes of China.

Chapter 26

Ten Political Trends for the Future

In This Chapter

- Voting online
- Modernising India and China
- Replacing the dollar
- Living with global change

Former British prime minister Harold Wilson once said that 'a week is a long time in politics'. But what about one, five, ten or even twenty years?

In today's fast-paced, interconnected, rapidly globalising world, political careers can end in a jiffy, international alliances form and then fragment in double-quick time, and the fortunes of great nations can rise and fall overnight. Plotting these changes is the work of journalists, historians and that wacky group of funsters, the political scientists, but here's my attempt to gaze into the crystal ball and predict the future of politics.

In this chapter, and in no particular order, I look at some of the political trends that may well play a big role in future politics in Britain and around the world. Some are educated guesses, others seem nailed-on certainties; only time will tell!

Broadening Democracy: Internet Voting

Great democracies like the UK and US are suffering from low voter turnout; anything up to a half of electors are failing to cast their ballots (check out Chapter 6 for more on this). Some commentators put this down to a widespread disillusionment with politicians and political parties in general – you know, the man or woman down the pub saying 'politicians are all the same'. But another reason for low voter turnout is that many people are too busy to make their way to a polling station, queue up and cast their ballot.

The logic is that if voting were made easier, more people would vote, which means turnout would be higher, helping to really validate the election process. People could vote online, simply logging into the election website, keying in a personal identification number and ticking the box by their chosen candidate. Internet voting would be cheaper to boot, with fewer staffed polling stations open on election day. Internet voting would also make it possible for voters to express their views on individual topics such as whether or not a particular piece of legislation should be passed. In effect the Internet opens up the possibility of easy-to-organise referendums.

Some people are worried that Internet voting could lead to fraud, and wonder who'll monitor the machines that tally up all the votes. In addition, some fear that whoever operates the Internet voting system could tell who voted for which candidate, which destroys the secret element of the ballot. Nevertheless, in both the US and UK, a growing groundswell of opinion is in favour of Internet voting.

Rising Power: Indian Modernisation

India is the world's biggest democracy, encompassing more than a billion people. The economy is rapidly expanding, literacy rates are rising and the country also has millions of English speakers able to deal with companies and individuals in the US and UK. India also has a three-hundred-million-strong 'middle class' with generous disposable incomes. India is one of the growing forces in the world economy and may even eventually replace the US as the world's most prosperous democracy.

In the not too distant future, India is likely to take its place at the top table of international politics. It will soon have a large enough economy to enter into the G8 group of nations and there's talk of it having a permanent seat on the United Nations Security Council (refer to Chapter 20 for more on the UN).

Loosening the Shackles: Chinese Democracy

When the pro-democracy protestors pitched up in Tiananmen Square in Beijing in 1989, the end of the Chinese communist regime seemed at hand. Even when the communists brutally crushed the protest and imposed martial law, it still only seemed a matter of time before democracy would come to China. Since then, though, the communist leadership has been remarkably adaptable. They've overseen a massive liberalisation of the economy, allowing some people to own their own property and businesses and accumulate wealth. In effect, communism has survived by ditching much of what communism actually stands for (refer to Chapter 4 for more on this ideology). But survive it has. The Chinese Communist Party's position seems unassailable. It even controls people's access to media, and curtails the use of the Internet, not allowing access to websites deemed anti-Chinese.

Many commentators argue that, as the Chinese economy continues to expand, the Chinese will ultimately want more freedom to express themselves and elect a different government. In short, as China becomes more Western in terms of wealth, it will eventually become more Western in terms of its politics. The progress – or otherwise – of democracy in China is a key trend to watch for in the 21st century.

China has the second largest economy in the world and is growing annually at around 8 to10 per cent. Compare this to the US or Europe, where economies are growing by 2 to 3 per cent at best. You can see why China is rapidly catching up with the Western countries in terms of the size of their economy and living standards.

Securing Natural Resources: Chinese Control of Africa

For hundreds of years, Western nations strived to secure the abundant natural resources of Africa, such as minerals and precious metals. But in the first decade of the 21st century the Chinese have looked to conclude trade agreements and buy up large tracts of land and industries within Africa.

China says that it's simply securing resources for its industries, which in turn supply the West with goods. However, some observers suggest that what's happening is no different from previous 'scrambles' for Africa: paying local corrupt governments in order to get natural resources on the cheap, ultimately providing little or no benefit to the ordinary people of Africa.

China's presence in Africa is an emotive subject but one that's bound to see the country even more powerful globally and even, who knows, replace the US as the world's biggest economy.

Out with the Old: Replacing the Dollar

Ever since the end of the Second World War the major currency around the globe has been the US dollar. In fact, nearly seven out of ten international trading transactions are done in dollars. Barrels of oil and ounces of gold are priced in dollars, not pounds, euros or Japanese yen. The dollar is called the world's *reserve currency*, which means many countries hold a large amount of dollars that will always be acceptable to international markets if another currency becomes untradeable because of an economic crisis.

But the mighty dollar isn't as mighty as it once was, particularly after the financial crisis affecting Western banks in 2008 (refer to Chapter 25 for more on this momentous event). The crisis resulted in a massive expansion of US government debt and weakened the dollar's hold on being the world's reserve currency. Some experts suggest that oil or gold should be traded in euros or Chinese yuan.

No longer using the dollar as a trading currency would make it harder for the US government to persuade other countries – China in particular – to buy its debt (the fact that most world trade is carried out in dollars makes it more attractive for investors to buy bonds issued by the US Treasury). The decline of the dollar would be a key sign that the balance of the world economy was shifting from the US to China and India.

Constructing a Super-State: Expanding the European Union

The European Union (EU) is a major trading bloc; a super-state in the making. The EU currency, the euro, is used widely around the globe and with a population of 500 million people in 28 member states and an economy bigger than that of the US, the EU is increasingly invited to the top table of international events; for example, the president of the European Commission – a part of the EU 'government' – attends meetings of the G8 group of most powerful nations. Talks are under way to bring Iceland and the Balkan countries into the EU, and also Turkey, which has a massive population.

However, not all within the EU are happy with the idea of an EU super-state. Some powerful politicians in the UK, Ireland and east European nations are reluctant to surrender national sovereignty to EU institutions such as the Commission and the parliament. In fact, some suggest that the drift of law-making powers from parliaments of member states to the EU has dwindled and that the EU will stop short of becoming the super-state envisaged by many.

World Going Dry: Shortages of Water

Sat in the seemingly permanently raining UK, believing that the world could be running short of drinking water is a bit difficult. However, a massively expanding population combined with climate change and mass deforestation is turning once-fertile wetlands into desert. Some parts of the world, particularly the Middle East, are already relying on technology to make seawater drinkable.

Some political scientists suggest that, in future, wars will be fought over securing vital water supplies rather than over territory or oil.

The United Nations estimates that up to 880 million people around the globe – that's roughly one in eight of the global population – have access to a barely adequate or inadequate water supply. This doesn't just mean that people go thirsty; dirty water also leads to disease. The World Bank says 88 per cent of all deaths from disease are related to inadequate water supply.

Black Gold: Scrambling for Oil

Oil companies have drained many of the world's big oil fields and are now trying to drill in areas of outstanding natural beauty such as Alaska and possibly one day even Antarctica.

Experts reckon that the peak of oil production was struck some ten years ago and now the world is on a downward path to running out of the most precious of fossil fuels. But just as the world's stock of oil is dwindling, demand is rising, thanks to the massive industrial growth of China and, to a lesser extent, India and Brazil. No wonder the price of oil has shot up five-fold since its lows at the start of the millennium. Many said that the US-led invasion of Iraq in 2003 was motivated by the need to secure oil supplies.

A world without oil is looking like a distinct possibility by the middle of the century. The doomsayers suggest this will lead to a massive fall in industrial production, people will have to give up their cars and power supplies will be under threat. But others say that oil is a dirty, polluting fuel and we'd be better off without it; technologies are available to help the world cope without oil, to enable people to drive their cars, and for industrial production to continue.

How the world learns to live without oil will be one of the great political, economic and social stories of the 21st century.

Risking Our Future: Climate Change

The world has heated up more in the past century than in the previous three thousand years. Most scientists blame human activity, saying climate change has coincided with global industrialisation and that pollution means the planet is retaining more heat from the sun. A smaller group of scientists suggest that the temperature of the planet varies over time and that increasing *greenhouse gases* (gases that purportedly heat up the atmosphere) are due to the natural release of carbon into the atmosphere rather than human activity.

The effects of climate change could be catastrophic for humanity as sea levels rise, countries disappear, deserts expand and millions are made homeless.

If human activity is to blame, then climate change can only be slowed by getting governments, individuals and industry to curtail the release of greenhouse gases into the atmosphere. Many of the world's leading industrial nations have agreed to reduce greenhouse gas emissions by 2020 to help slow climate change but the economic expansion of China and other developing countries means putting these changes in jeopardy. Some measures that may help are the development of cleaner fuels and helping developing nations adopt greener technology to reduce their dependency on fossil fuels.

Upping Sticks: Global Population Moves

Some of the problems facing governments around the globe, such as climate change and water shortages, are going to have a huge impact on the lives of ordinary people. Some scientists suggest mass population moves in Africa and Asia will occur due to parts of the globe becoming difficult to farm and live in. The majority of the world's population lives in the countryside, working on farms and looking after livestock. If climate change makes these places uninhabitable, the people are going to have to move to neighbouring countries in richer parts of the world such as Europe or parts of Asia.

Immigration is going to be a big issue, as the 21st century progresses, for most nations around the globe.

Index

• A •

• B •

• C •

• E •

• G •

• H •

• J •

• K •

• L •

• M •

• N •

• O •

• Q •

• R •

• S •

• U •

• W •

About the Author

Julian Knight was born in 1972 in Chester. He was educated at the Chester Catholic High School and later Hull University, where he obtained a degree in History.

Julian has been a journalist since 1998 and has written for the *Guardian*, Financial Times Group and many other publications.

From 2002 to 2007 he was the personal finance and consumer affairs reporter for BBC News. Since 2007 he has been the Money and Property editor of the *Independent on Sunday* and has won many industry awards for his journalism. Julian is the author of *The British Citizenship Test For Dummies*, *Wills, Probate & Inheritance Tax For Dummies*, *Retiring Wealthy For Dummies* and *Cricket For Dummies*.

He currently lives in Solihull where he is standing as a candidate for Parliment.

Dedication

To my wife Philippa for everything.

Publisher's Acknowledgements

We're proud of this book; please send us your comments at http://dummies.custhelp.com. For other comments, please contact our Customer Care Department within the U.S. at 877-762-2974, outside the U.S. at (001) 317-572-3993, or fax 317-572-4002.

Some of the people who helped bring this book to market include the following:

Acquisitions, Editorial and Vertical Websites

Project Editor: Iona Everson

Commissioning Editor: Mike Baker

Proofreaders: Andy Finch and Charlie Wilson

Publisher: Miles Kendall

Consultant Editor: Michael Pattison

Composition Services

Project Coordinator: Melissa Cossell

FOR DUMMIES®

A Wiley Brand

SELF-HELP

978-0-470-66541-1

Creative Visualization For Dummies

978-1-119-99264-6

978-0-470-66086-7

LANGUAGES

978-0-470-68815-1

978-1-119-97959-3

978-0-470-69477-0

HISTORY

978-0-470-68792-5

978-0-470-74783-4

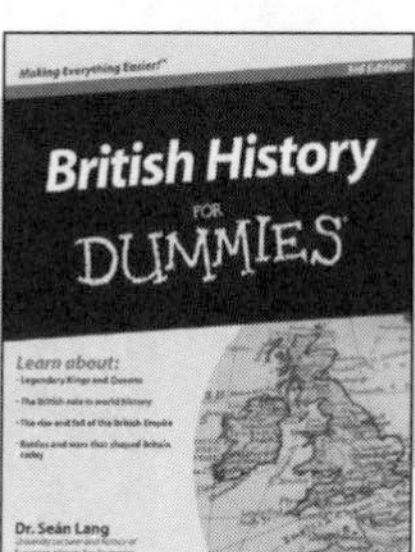

978-0-470-97819-1

Laptops For Dummies 5th Edition
978-1-118-11533-6

Management For Dummies, 2nd Edition
978-0-470-97769-9

Nutrition For Dummies, 2nd Edition
978-0-470-97276-2

Office 2013 For Dummies
978-1-118-49715-9

Organic Gardening For Dummies
978-1-119-97706-3

Origami Kit For Dummies
978-0-470-75857-1

Overcoming Depression For Dummies
978-0-470-69430-5

Physics I For Dummies
978-0-470-90324-7

Project Management For Dummies
978-0-470-71119-4

Psychology Statistics For Dummies
978-1-119-95287-9

Renting Out Your Property For Dummies, 3rd Edition
978-1-119-97640-0

Rugby Union For Dummies, 3rd Edition
978-1-119-99092-5

Stargazing For Dummies
978-1-118-41156-8

Teaching English as a Foreign Language For Dummies
978-0-470-74576-2

Time Management For Dummies
978-0-470-77765-7

Training Your Brain For Dummies
978-0-470-97449-0

Voice and Speaking Skills For Dummies
978-1-119-94512-3

Wedding Planning For Dummies
978-1-118-69951-5

WordPress For Dummies, 5th Edition
978-1-118-38318-6

Think you can't learn it in a day? Think again!

The *In a Day* e-book series from *For Dummies* gives you quick and easy access to learn a new skill, brush up on a hobby, or enhance your personal or professional life — all in a day. Easy!